IRVINE VALLEY COLLEGE LIBRARY

DISCARD

Becoming a Critical Thinker

A User-Friendly Manual

Sherry Diestler
Contra Costa College

Prentice Hall, Upper Saddle River, New Jersey 07458

Library of Congress Cataloging-in-Publication Data

Diestler, Sherry.
  Becoming a critical thinker : a user-friendly manual / Sherry Diestler.
    p.   cm.
  Includes index.
  ISBN 0-13-744335-8 (pbk.)
  1. Critical thinking—Study and teaching (Higher)   2. Critical
thinking—Problems, exercises, etc.   I. Title.
LB2395.35.D54   1998
370.15'2—dc21   97-45965
                                                               CIP

*In memory of Anne Goldstein,
and for Al, John, Zachary, Jenna, Laura, and Amy.
May they continue her legacy of
discernment and compassion.*

Editor-in-Chief: Charlyce Jones Owen
Acquisition Editor: Karita France
Production Liaison: Fran Russello
Project Manager: Jill Schoenhaut/
  ComCom

Prepress and Manufacturing Buyer:
  Tricia Kenny
Cover Design: Rosemarie Votta

This book was set in 11/13 Aster by ComCom
and was printed and bound by RR Donnelley & Sons Company.
The cover was printed by Phoenix Color Corp.

© 1998 by Prentice-Hall, Inc.
Simon & Schuster/ A Viacom Company
Upper Saddle River, New Jersey 07458

Earlier edition copyright © 1994 by Macmillan Publishing Company

All rights reserved. No part of this book may be
reproduced, in any form or by any means,
without permission in writing from the publisher.

Printed in the United States of America

10 9 8 7 6 5 4 3 2 1

ISBN 0-13-744335-8

Prentice-Hall International (UK) Limited, *London*
Prentice-Hall of Australia Pty. Limited, *Sydney*
Prentice-Hall Canada, Inc., *Toronto*
Prentice-Hall Hispanoamericana, S.A., *Mexico*
Prentice-Hall of India Private Limited, *New Delhi*
Prentice-Hall of Japan, Inc., *Tokyo*
Simon & Schuster Asia Pte. Ltd., *Singapore*
Editora Prentice-Hall do Brasil, Ltda., *Rio de Janeiro*

Contents

Foreword

This book is fresh air. Consider the title. Consider the word "Becoming." The word is a reminder. It is a reminder that the tasks, skills, mind sets, ways of life, involved in thinking critically are ongoing. Someone with whom I spent a quarter century inclined to end a conversation, "And you call yourself a critical thinker!" Half the time she was right. Everyone can get better. The state indeed is one of "becoming."

What is this "it," this state? It is the art of asking right questions, including right questions about one's own thoughts. It's the art of mustering reasons. Accordingly, it's the art of obtaining the right facts—knowing where to look for them and of measuring to what degrees they count. It's the art of pinpointing the real issue and of noticing when an arguer evades it.

The "it" is not just an art, it's a disposition and a commitment. In their place tantrums may be fine, but not usually. Judiciously employed logic, cool thinking, gentle persuasion, are normally superior by far.

What passes for this book's field—what is variously called argumentation, informal logic, critical thinking, argument rhetoric—has until recently to an extent been clogged—with legalese and Latin, with philosophical and sciences theory. Of it could be said what one Victorian said of the Common Room at Balliol College, Oxford, that it "stank of logic."

Not anymore. This book is nearly devoid of clogs. It's indeed, as its title proclaims, "user friendly."

Perry Weddle
Center for Reasoning Arts
Editor, CT News
CSU-Sacramento

Preface

Everyone thinks. If you ask people where they stand on a particular issue, they will usually tell you what they believe and give reasons to support their beliefs. Many people, however, find it difficult to evaluate a written or spoken commentary on a controversial issue because both sides of the controversy seem to have good arguments.

The *critical* thinker is able to distinguish high-quality, well-supported arguments from arguments with little or no evidence to back them. This text is meant to train students to evaluate the many claims facing them as citizens, learners, consumers, and human beings; it is also designed to help students become more effective advocates for their beliefs.

Becoming a Critical Thinker is designed to be interdisciplinary and to be useful in courses in critical thinking, informal logic, rhetoric, English, speech, journalism, humanities, and the social sciences. It has also been used as either a required text or a supplement in nursing programs and in workshops in staff development and business management. The skills that distinguish critical thinkers across various disciplines are presented in a clear and comprehensible manner.

Unique Features

The process of becoming a critical thinker takes place when ideas are both clearly understood and put into practice. For this reasons, many elements of the text have been chosen because of their practical application for the student:

1. Each concept is explained with examples, and the examples often proceed from the personal to the social or political. In this way, students can see that the same skills used in understanding arguments in daily life are used in analyzing political and commercial rhetoric.
2. Graphic illustrations help students visualize important concepts.
3. Exercises of varying levels of difficulty are given throughout the chapters to help students practice critical thinking skills.
4. Emphasis is placed on understanding and analyzing the impact of print and electronic media on arguments.
5. Students are taught to construct and present arguments so that they can gain skill and confidence as advocates.

6. There is an early and primary emphasis on understanding conflicting value systems and on ethics in argumentation and decision-making.

7. The articles and essays selected for use in the text are contemporary and express a variety of political viewpoints and ethical concerns.

8. Multicultural perspectives are presented throughout, in examples and articles. Many exercises and assignments encourage students to understand the perspectives of others and to broaden their own perspectives.

9. There is a variety of writing and speaking assignments at the end of each chapter.

10. The text is supplemented with an instructor manual and a floppy disk which contains examples of critical thinking principles which can be used for classroom discussion.

Specific Changes in the Second Edition

This second edition of *Becoming a Critical Thinker* has been created with two priorities in mind: to retain the user-friendly format of the first edition and to update readings and concepts so that readers will enjoy the application of critical thinking principles to current issues.

New features in the second edition include:

1. Expanded supplementary resources for instructors. These include an instructor manual with tests for each chapter, discussions of chapter exercises, and suggestions for teaching critical thinking concepts. In addition, a floppy disk has been created to enhance lecture material with interactive applications of many topics covered and to provide additional student practice.

2. New articles and essays. These writings include such current topics as: The relationship between the Pentagon and the film industry, the implications of the demand for a "mixed race" category on census forms, the impact of legislation limiting affirmative action, the impact of Wal-Mart's decision to carry only "family friendly" CDs in their stores, Asian political assumptions that affect the world marketplace, research on the effects of educational television on children's test scores, a debate on the salaries of professional athletes, and the differences in communication styles of men and women (from respected researcher Deborah Tannen).

3. New user-friendly elements. Some of the more complicated figures illustrating concepts have been replaced with clearer ones. The dis-

cussion of causation and generalizing from analogies have been placed in an expanded section of inductive reasoning, and Chapter 6 is now fully devoted to fallacies. New games, exercises, and writing assignments have been added. Chapter 10 on the influence and power of media in shaping information has been expanded and moved to Chapter 7, since most instructors we interviewed said that they preferred covering media literacy earlier. We have used the opportunity of the second edition to clarify all of the basic concepts covered in the first edition.

Acknowledgements

My husband, John Diestler, has been an invaluable help in many ways. He provided expertise on the "user-friendly" format; he worked out preliminary designs for the logos and figures in the text; and he made useful suggestions on the manuscript throughout its production.

I thank my editors Angela Stone and Karita France for their expertise and collaboration in bringing this edition to completion, and my former editor Maggie Barbieri for her great work on the first edition.

I especially want to thank Jill Schoenhaut for her guidance, patience, and professionalism in supervising the text's production.

I am grateful to the following instructors who used the text in their critical thinking classes, helped create exercise and writing assignments and made useful suggestions for the second edtion: Candy Rose, William Dorman, Bruce Reeves, Linda Berry, Lee Loots, Steve Storer, Connie Missimer, Marlys Mayfield, Betty Duffy, and John Splaine.

In addition, I wish to thank the following reviewers for their invaluable advice and encouragement: Mark Weinstein, Montclair State; David Seiple, Columbia University; Jarrett Leplin, University of North Carolina; Janet Maddeu, El Camino College; Sahotra Sarkar, Boston University; Lynn Phelps, Ohio University; Connie Anderson, Diablo Valley College; Donna Bestock, Skyline College; and Perry Weddle, CSU-Sacramento.

I am grateful to Rob Akiyama, Jenipher Goldstein, and Peter Burch for reviewing the manuscript and making helpful suggestions. I also want to thank Peter Chignell, Linda Ellman, and Elisabeth and Arthur Worthington for suggesting interesting and relevant articles for the text.

For their practical help that allowed me the time and energy to write the text, I have many friends to thank, but in the interest of space will limit these to my father, Al Goldstein, Kathleen and Hugo Santucci, Mary Kinaga, Vona Lorenzana, Peter Burch, Edda Moore, and John, Zachary, Jenna, Laura, and Amy Diestler.

Above all, I am grateful to the Creator of the human mind.

CHAPTER ONE

Foundations of Arguments

What Is a Critical Thinker and When Do You Need to Be One?

A critical thinker understands the structure of an argument, whether that argument is presented by a politician, a salesperson, a talk-show host, a friend, or a child.

This chapter will cover:

◆ The structure of an argument
◆ The three parts of an argument: issues, reasons, and conclusions

We live in what has been called the Information Age because of the many messages that we receive daily from newspapers, magazines, radio, television, books, and the Internet.

Sometimes we turn to this information for its entertainment value, such as when we watch a situation comedy, listen to music, read the sports page, or participate on-line in a chat room. But in a democratic society, in which the people are asked to vote on candidates and political propositions, we also need to use print and electronic sources to help us make decisions about the direction our community, state, and nation will take.

We need to know how to understand and evaluate the information that comes our way. This book will give you tools for coming to rational conclusions and making responsible choices.

A critical thinker is someone who uses specific criteria to evaluate reasoning and make decisions.

When you learn to communicate well in a formal situation, your skill usually transfers to informal situations as well. For example, if you learn to make an effective informative speech in the classroom, you will also feel better about introducing yourself at parties or making a spontaneous toast at your brother's wedding. The same principle applies to critical thinking skills.

When you can listen to a presidential debate and make good judgments about what each candidate has to offer, you may also be more thoughtful about less formal arguments that are presented, such as which breakfast cereal is best for you or which car you should buy. You will be better prepared to deal with sales pitches, whether written, televised, or personal.

The methods of discernment and decision making that you will learn apply to choosing a viewpoint on a political issue or to choosing a career, a place to live, or a mate.

In short, critical thinkers do not just drift through life subject to every message that they hear; they think through their choices and make conscious decisions. They also understand the basics of both creating and presenting credible arguments.

The Structure of Argument

"The aim of argument, or of discussion, should not be victory, but progress."

Joseph Joubert, *Pensees* (1842)

When most people hear the word *argument,* they think of a disagreement between two or more people that may escalate into name-calling, angry words, or even physical violence.

Our definition of argument is different. When critical thinkers speak about arguments, we are referring to a **conclusion** that someone has (often called a claim or position) about a particular **issue.** This conclusion is supported with **reasons** (often called premises). If an individual has a conclusion but offers no reasons why he has come to that conclusion, then he has only made a statement, not an argument.

Political slogans, often found on billboards or in television advertisements, are good examples of conclusions that should not be relied upon because supporting reasons are not offered. If you see a billboard that proclaims, " A vote for Johnson is a vote for the right choice," you are encountering a conclusion with no evidence, which does not constitute an argument.

Critical thinkers withhold judgment on such a claim until they have looked at evidence both for and against Johnson as a candidate.

An argument has three parts: the *issue,* the *conclusion,* and the *reasons.*

The Issue

The issue is the question that is being addressed. It is easiest to put the issue in question form so that you know what is being discussed. When you listen to a discussion of a political or social issue, think of the question being addressed.

Examples of Issues:

- Should North, Central, and South Americans work together to combat acid rain?

- Should air traffic controllers be given periodic drug tests?

- Should we have a flat tax rate?

- Are the salaries paid to professional athletes too high?

The same method of "issue detection" will be useful in understanding commercial appeals (ads) and personal requests.

More Examples of Issues:

- Is Alpo the best food for your dog?

- Should you marry Leslie?

- Should you subscribe to the *Wall Street Journal?*

Another way to isolate the issue is to state, "The issue is whether _____".

- The issue is whether aspirin can prevent heart disease.

Issues can be about facts, values, or policies. Factual issues concern whether something is true or false, as in the following examples:

- Does aspirin prevent heart disease?

- Are smog-control devices effective in preventing pollution?

- Do we have enough money to buy a new car?

Issues about values deal with what is considered good or bad or right or wrong, as, for example:

- Is there too much violence on television?

- Is marriage better than living together?

- Are salaries of executives of major corporations too high?

Policy issues involve taking action; often, these issues emerge from discussions of facts and values. If we find that, in fact, smog-control devices are effective in preventing pollution and if we value clean air, then we should support policies that enforce the use of these devices. If aspirin prevents heart disease and we value a longer life, then we should ask a doctor whether we should take aspirin. If we do have enough money for a new car and we value a car more than other items at this time, then we should buy the new car.

Every decision that we need to make, whether it involves public or private matters, will be made easier if we can define exactly what it is that we are being asked to believe or do. Discourse often breaks down when two or more parties get into a heated discussion over different issues. This phenomenon occurs regularly on talk shows.

For example, a recent television talk show featured the general topic of spousal support, and the issue was "Should the salary of a second wife be used in figuring alimony for the first wife?" The lawyer who was being interviewed kept reminding the guests of this issue as they proceeded to argue instead about whether child support should be figured from the second wife's salary, whether the first wife should hold a job, and even whether one of the first wives was a good person.

A general rule is that the more emotional the reactions to the issue, the more likely the issue will become lost. The real problem here is that the basic issue can become fragmented into different sub-issues so that people are no longer discussing the same question.

SKILL

Understand the issue, make sure that everyone is discussing the same issue, and bring the discussion back on target when necessary.

When you listen to televised debates or interviews, note how often a good speaker or interviewer reminds the audience of the issue. Also notice how experienced spokespersons or politicians will often respond to a direct, clearly defined issue with a pre-programmed answer that addresses a *different* issue, one they can discuss more easily.

If a presidential candidate is asked how he is going to balance our federal budget, he might declare passionately that he will never raise taxes. He has thus skillfully accomplished two things: he has avoided the difficult issue and he has taken a popular, vote-enhancing stand on a separate issue.

 EXERCISE

Purpose: To be able to identify issues.

1. Read an essay or an editorial, study an advertisement, listen to a radio talk show, or watch a television program about a controversial issue. Decide whether the issue is primarily one of fact, value, or policy. Define the issue and see if the speakers or writers stay with the issue.

    In particular, try to find an example of a person who is asked to respond to one issue and instead gives an answer to a different issue. Check to see whether the interviewer reminds the speaker that he or she has not answered the question.

2. By yourself, or as a class, come up with as many current issues as you can. Think of both light and serious issues; consider campus, community, social, national, and international concerns. Now, look at your list of issues and choose three that really concern you. Then, try to choose three about which you are neutral. Finally, answer these questions:

    a. What is it about the first three issues that makes you concerned?

    b. Why are you neutral about some issues?

    c. Do you believe there are issues on the list that should be more important to you? Why or why not?

REMINDER

Whenever you are confronted with an argument, try to define the issue and put the issue in question form.

The Conclusion

Once an issue has been defined, we can state our conclusion about the issue. Using some examples previously mentioned, **we can say yes or no to the issues presented:** yes, I believe air traffic controllers should be tested for drug use; yes, I want to subscribe to the *Wall Street Journal;* no, I will not marry Leslie at this time, and so on. We take a stand on the issues given.

The conclusion can also be defined as the position taken about an issue. It is a claim supported by evidence statements. These evidence statements are called reasons or premises.

We often hear the cliché, "Everyone has a right to his or her opinion." This is true, in the legal sense—North Americans do not have "thought police" who decide what can and cannot be discussed. When you are a critically thinking person, however, your opinion has *substance*. That substance consists of the reasons you give to support your opinion. Conclusions with substance are more valuable and credible than conclusions offering no supporting evidence.

The term *conclusion* is used differently in different fields of study. The definition given here applies most correctly to the study of argumentation. In an argumentative essay, the thesis statement will express the conclusion of the writer. In Chapter 3, you will note a related definition of conclusion used by philosophers in the study of deductive and inductive reasoning. In addition, the term *conclusion* is used to describe the final part of an essay or speech.

REMINDER

Conclusions are the positions people take on issues. Other words used to mean conclusions are claims, viewpoints, opinions, and stands. We use the term conclusion because most people who teach argumentation use the term. The other words listed can mean the same thing.

How can we locate the conclusion of an argument? Try the following methods when you are having trouble finding the conclusion:

1. Find the issue and ask yourself what position the writer or speaker is taking on the issue.
2. Look at the beginning or end of a paragraph or an essay; the conclusion is often found in one of these places.
3. Look for conclusion indicator words: *therefore, so, thus, hence.* Also, look for indicator phrases: *"My point is," "What I am saying is," "What I believe is."* Some indicator words and phrases are selected to imply that the conclusion drawn is the right one. These include: *obviously, it is evident that, there is no doubt (or question) that, certainly,* and *of course.*
4. Ask yourself, "What is being claimed by this writer or speaker?"
5. Look at the title of an essay; sometimes the conclusion is contained within the title. For example, an essay might be called "Why I believe vitamins are essential to health."

 SKILL

Find the conclusion or conclusions to an argument. Ask yourself what position the writer or speaker is taking on the issue.

You may hear people discussing an issue, and someone says, "I don't know anything about this, but . . ." and proceeds to state an opinion about the issue. This comment is sometimes made as a means of continuing a conversation. Critical thinkers take a stand only when they know something about the issue; they give reasons why they have come to a certain conclusion. Of course, a critical thinker is open to hearing new evidence and may change his or her opinion on issues as new information becomes available.

EXERCISE

Purpose: To be able to isolate conclusions.

Take your list of issues from Question 2 in the previous exercise. Choose four issues and, in a simple declarative sentence, write your conclusion for each one.

Example:
Issue: Should air traffic controllers be given periodic drug tests?
Conclusion: Yes, air traffic controllers should be given periodic drug tests.

The Reasons

> *"Everything reasonable may be supported."*
>
> Epictetus, *Discourses* (2nd century)

Reasons are the statements that provide support for conclusions. Without reasons, you have no argument; you simply have a statement of someone's opinion, as evidenced in the following limerick:

> I do not like thee, Doctor Fell
> The reason why I cannot tell
> But this I know, I know full well
> I do not like thee, Doctor Fell.

Reasons are also called *evidence, premises, support,* or *justification.* You will spend most of your time and energy as a critical thinker and responsible writer and speaker looking at the quality of the reasons used to support a conclusion.

Here are some ways to locate the reasons in an argument:

1. Find the conclusion and then apply the "because trick." The writer or speaker believes _____ (conclusion) because _____. The reasons will naturally follow the word *because.*
2. Look for other indicator words that are similar to *because: since, for, first, second, third, as evidenced by, also, furthermore, in addition.*
3. Look for evidence supporting the conclusion. This support can be in the form of examples, statistics, analogies, reports of studies, and expert testimony.

THE BORN LOSER reprinted by permission of Newspaper Enterprise Association, Inc.

There is a world of difference between supporting a political candidate because his policies make sense to you and supporting the same candidate because he or she looks like a good person. Information in the following chapters of this book will give you skills to help you decide how a reason supports a conclusion.

Critical thinkers focus their attention first on the issue being discussed, second, on the conclusions taken, and third, on the reasons given to support or justify the conclusions.

SKILL

Find the reasons that support the conclusion.

REMINDER

Since the reasons answer the question "Why do you believe what you believe?" a good trick in isolating the reasons is to write the conclusion and then add the word because.

Example:
I believe student athletes should be paid (conclusion) **because:**

- they are committed to certain hours and demands on their time

- they are making money for their schools

EXERCISE

Purposes: To be able to use reasons to support a conclusion. To use knowledge gained in this chapter to both analyze and construct basic arguments.

1. Write a short rebuttal to the above example, using reasons to support your conclusion.
2. Take your conclusions from the exercise on conclusions and support each conclusion with at least three reasons. This exercise can be done alone or in classroom groups, in writing or as a short speech. You might also have one group present the "pro" side of an issue and another group the "con."

3. Get the editorial page of your favorite newspaper (including your campus paper) and list the issue, conclusion, and reasons given for each editorial. Use this format:

    The issue (question) is:

    The conclusion of this writer is:

    The reasons he/she gives are:

    Then evaluate the editorial by answering the following questions:

    a. Was the writer clear about the reasons given for the conclusion?

    b. Were there other reasons that could have been included in the argument?

    c. Did the writer express any understanding for an opposing viewpoint? If so, how? If not, can you articulate an opposing viewpoint for the editorial?

    d. Were you convinced by the editorial? Why or why not?

4. Read the following editorials, essays, letters, and writings. Then, isolate the issues discussed, the conclusions of the writers, and the reasons given for the conclusions. Answer the following questions:

    a. Are the reasons given adequate to support the conclusions? If not, what other reasons could have been given?

    b. Do you agree or disagree with the conclusions? If you disagree, what are your reasons for disagreeing?

War on Drugs Fails; We Need New Approach

by Daryl A. Bergman

The war on drugs is an abysmal failure. A fresh and bold approach is needed—beginning with the legalization of marijuana and the registration of drug addicts. It's also necessary to look to other countries such as Holland, that have been successful curbing drug associated crime through the legalization of marijuana. The legalization of pot would:

- Eliminate the stepping stone to harder drugs.

- Eliminate the crime associated with large dollar street transactions.

- Provide taxes to step up law enforcement efforts (meth labs, heroin smuggling) and rehab programs.

- Free space in jails housing non-violent criminals, saving incarceration costs.

The registration of addicts would:

- Eliminate the use of dirty needles, decreasing victims of AIDS, Hepatitis B and C and associated health care costs.

Let's move forward to save our children.

Cause, Not the Effect

by Patrick Burns

The real problem we face is that society never directly addresses the problems, only the symptoms.

Gun control opponents and gun control advocates have spent millions discussing the effects of the availability of guns. That's not the concern; the concern is what is done with the guns. Switzerland has issued a machine gun to every male of military age. Most of the homes in that country are fully armed, yet no one reads of their terrible gun connected crimes.

Nearly ninety percent of all crimes in the U.S. are connected in some fashion to drugs or alcohol. If substance abuse were solved, isn't it logical that the crimes connected to it would decrease? And would there still be this battle about gun control?

As long as our society continues to placate and enable by providing access to harmful substances, then we will also reap violence and murder.

Let us focus on the source of our problems, not on the specific symptoms.

Is it because as a society, we are so selfish as to be unwilling to eradicate such harmful substances and thereby give up our momentary fixes? Such short-term thinking leads to the long-term problems we face today.

Drug use is increasing at an alarming rate. How is that going to improve our society? Think about it.

Nothing Positive in Airbag News

by Jack Hagerty

While it is always gratifying to be able to say "I told you so," there can be nothing positive about the current revelations of the tragedy concerning airbags.

I have been an opponent of airbags (which are not technically *air* bags but sodium azide bags, that being the chemical which explodes to fill the bag with gas) since the beginning. Most people don't realize how old the concept is, having been developed in automotive research laboratories of several universities in the 1960s. The government tried to mandate airbags in the early 1970s, but the industry successfully resisted for more than 10 years before succumbing and introducing them on the driver's side in the late 1980s.

Why should I object to a device that has proven life-saving potential? Well, outside of the current headlines about children and small adults being killed, the answers are many. First is the psychological aspect. I've dealt with explosive devices long enough both professionally and as a hobby (I am president of the largest hobby rocketry club in Northern California) to feel uncomfortable driving around with an armed pyrotechnic device aimed at my face! Beyond that, though, are the many technical shortcomings of airbags:

- Airbags are designed for a single type of crash: the single-impact, straight frontal collision. They provide no protection from multiple-impact, side-impact, corner-impact, rear-impact or roll-over collisions.

- Airbags have a limited range of operation. Despite the way they look in commercials, airbags are not big satiny pillows that balloon up gently to catch you; they explode with tremendous violence and then deflate—all in less than $\frac{1}{10}$ of a second. This means that they are ineffective at speeds below 35 MPH (because the bag deflates before you reach it) and over 65 MPH (because you hit the steering wheel or dashboard before the bag inflates).

- Airbags do not work well unless you are right in front of them, so all manufacturers require that you wear a seat belt to hold you in position—and refer to the bag as a "supplemental" restraint system.

- Airbags are designed to work with the "average" adult which, of course, is the problem associated with the current headlines.

- Even with people satisfying all of the above criteria, there have been many documented classes of injury associated with airbags: abrasive burns of the face and hands due to the friction from the bag hitting the skin, bronchitis caused by the release powder (which coats the bag to keep it from sticking to itself) being rammed down the throat, and eyeball trauma.

To be fair, seat belts can also cause damage ranging from minor bruising to torn chest muscles and dislocated shoulders, but I know of no case where someone was killed by a belt in an accident that they would have otherwise survived had they not been wearing the belt.

Properly fastened 3-point seat belts of the type found in every car prior to the introduction of airbags provide protection superior to airbags in all types of crash situations and speeds, except single frontal impact within the speed range of the airbag, where they are roughly equal. Seat belts can be adjusted to properly fit anyone from a small child (one old enough to be out of the child safety seat) to the largest adult.

- Finally, there is the issue of disposal. Only a tiny fraction of all bags installed are ever deployed, and since we are pumping them into the automotive population at the rate of some tens of millions per year, how do we get rid of them? Ever see the "care" with which your average wrecking yard disassembles a car, usually with a torch? Add to that the fact that sodium azide is incredibly toxic and a known carcinogen and it makes me not want to visit auto salvage yards anymore.

When the flaws in the system began to appear (e.g. no protection in side and corner impacts) the response was typical bureaucratic defensiveness. Rather than admit that the program doesn't work, they are mandating more of what doesn't work in the form of side airbags, which are beginning to appear in the doors of higher-end cars. In addition, they want to require warning labels on the dashboards of new cars, and automakers are having to send letters to the tens of millions of owners of airbag-equipped cars warning them that the device installed to protect them may actually kill them. It seems sometimes that the madness never ends.

In summary, then, we have a government-mandated system that is both flawed and of limited effectiveness. It replaced an existing belt system that was superior in every way, being cheaper, simpler, and more effective. The problem is that seat belts require active involvement on the part of the occupant to actually put them on.

Air bags were designed to protect those too lazy or ignorant to protect themselves. The irony is that it turns out that manually fastened seat belts are required anyway for the airbags to have even their minimal effectiveness, so what's the point?

For my personal cars I have a 1974 Alfa Romeo and a 1984 Saab, both bought new and kept in perfect running condition. Until airbags disappear from the U.S. automotive scene, I have bought my last new car.

Chapter Highlights

1. Critical thinking about information is necessary in order for us to make clear decisions as citizens, consumers, and human beings.
2. An argument consists of issues, conclusions, and reasons.
3. The issue is the question that is raised; our decisions are made easier if we can define the issues on which we are asked to comment or act.
4. The conclusion is the position a person takes on an issue.
5. Reasons, often called premises, provide support for conclusions; reasons are acceptable or unacceptable on the basis of their relevance and quality.

Articles for Discussion

These two articles give differing viewpoints on the same issue. Read both and then consider the questions that follow.

Talk-show Host Angers Disabled Community

Hand Deformity Inherited from Mom
Sparks L.A. Dispute

by Michael Fleeman
Associated Press, September 2, 1991

LOS ANGELES—Aaron James Lampley, all 7 pounds, 14 ½ ounces of him, was only a few hours old when a local radio station dedicated a show for the second time to the circumstances and controversy surrounding his birth.

In addressing the matter again, KFI-AM last week refueled a dispute that pitted the station against activists for the disabled and raised questions about freedom of speech and society's treatment of the disabled.

Aaron Lampley was born Wednesday morning, with ectodactyly, which leaves the bones in the feet and hands fused. His mother, local TV anchorwoman Bree Walker Lampley, also has the condition and knew the child had a 50 percent chance of inheriting it.

Her other child, a daughter, has the condition as well.

Before the boy's birth, KFI outraged the KCBS-TV anchorwoman and advocates for people with disabilities with a July 22 call-in show in which host Jane Norris asked whether it was fair for Walker Lampley to give birth when the child had a "very good chance of having a disfiguring disease."

Critics of the show said it smacked of bigotry and illustrated societal prejudice and lack of understanding toward the disabled. KFI said the matter was handled properly and that radio talk shows are appropriate forums for controversial issues.

In KFI's second visit to the subject, this time with Norris acting as guest on Tom Leykis' afternoon show, Norris accused Walker Lampley of orchestrating a campaign to discredit her and contended she had a First Amendment right to discuss the matter.

"I was supportive of Bree's decision," Norris said on the show. "All I did, and have done, is voice my opinion of what would be right for me. I thought I handled the topic sensitively, but all [Walker Lampley has] seen fit to do is slander me."

Norris' statements did nothing to cool the situation.

"They came on the air supposedly to set the record straight. In our view, she set the record even more crooked," said Lillabeth Navarro of American Disabled for Access Power Today.

"This is like a bunch of thugs ganging up on the disability community. It just rained forth what caused us to be outraged to begin with."

Navarro said activists planned a protest at KFI studios.

The demonstration is part of a grass-roots campaign organized in part by a media consulting firm hired by Walker Lampley and her husband, KCBS anchorman Jim Lampley.

The company, EIN SOF Communications, gives the disability rights community a public voice. The firm has sent tapes of the Norris show to disability rights groups and is helping to file a complaint with the Federal Communications Commission.

In the original show, Norris said she wasn't intending to dictate what Walker Lampley should have done. But she said she couldn't have made the same decision if she were in Walker Lampley's position.

Norris said there were "so many other options available," including adoption and surrogate parenting, and "it would be difficult to bring myself to morally cast my child forever to disfigured hands."

Throughout the show, Norris seemed to take issue with people who disagreed with her.

After a caller named Jennifer from Los Angeles said, "I don't really see why it's your business," Norris responded, "Well, I think it's everybody's business. This is life. These things happen in life. What's your problem? Do you have a problem talking about deformities?"

Norris also repeatedly referred to Walker Lampley's condition, ectodactyly, as a disease, even though it is a genetically caused disability.

Walker Lampley and her husband, in interviews before their child was born, said Norris' first program was an attack on the handicapped and Walker Lampley personally, and was full of errors and poorly chosen remarks.

"I felt assaulted and terrorized," Walker Lampley said. "I felt like my pregnancy had been robbed of some of its joy."

She added, "I felt disappointed that someone would be so insensitive."

Radio Show on Rights of Disabled Defended

Crippled Woman's Pregnancy Debated

Associated Press

LOS ANGELES—The chairman of the Equal Employment Opportunity Commission said a local radio station shouldn't be disciplined for a talk show that debated whether a disabled TV anchorwoman should give birth.

Chairman Evan J. Kemp, who is disabled and confined to a wheelchair, said he was "appalled and sickened" by the majority of callers to the KFI program who said KCBS anchor Bree Walker Lampley had no right to become pregnant and should abort if she did.

However, Kemp said the right of free speech should protect KFI from any Federal Communications Commission action.

Kemp's statements were published in the Los Angeles *Times.*

Lampley, who was pregnant at the time of the July 1991 broadcast, lodged a complaint to the FCC and asked for an investigation. The newswoman, her husband, co-anchor Jim Lampley, and more than 20 organizations for the disabled asked the agency to examine whether the station and its owner, Cox Broadcasting Corp., should lose their license, be fined or reprimanded.

The couple charged the broadcast was not a thorough discussion, but rather an attack on Lampley's integrity without inviting them to appear and harassed callers who attempted to express contrary views.

Lampley gave birth five weeks after the broadcast to a boy who had the same genetic condition as his mother—ectodactylism, in which the bones of the hands and feet are fused. There was a 50 percent chance that the baby would have the condition.

Kemp said he was not speaking out as chairman of the Washington, D.C.-based EEOC, but as a "severely disabled person" with a rare polio-like disease—Kugelberg-Welander—that may be inherited.

He said he plans to write to the FCC to defend grass-roots discussions and radio talk shows such as the KFI program as necessary forums.

Questions for Discussion

1. The author of the first article states that this controversy "raised questions about freedom of speech and society's treatment of the disabled." What were the questions—that is, issues—that were raised?
2. Take one of the issues raised by the talk show controversy and discuss how well it was defended by those mentioned in the articles.
3. Comment on the following excerpt from the first article. What is your opinion of the host's response to the caller?

   After a caller named Jennifer from Los Angeles said, "I don't really see why it's your business," Norris responded, "Well, I think it's everybody's business. This is life. These things happen in life. What's your problem? Do you have a problem talking about deformities?"

4. Are there any issues discussed by radio and television talk shows that you consider inappropriate? Are certain

groups targeted for criticism and others left alone, or is every topic fair game? Give examples to support your answer.

5. Each article used a different subheading to explain the controversy. The first article's subheading reads: "Hand Deformity Inherited from Mom Sparks L.A. Dispute." The second article's subheading reads: "Crippled Woman's Pregnancy Debated." How do these different subheadings frame the issue? To what extent do you think they are fair and accurate statements about the controversy?

 ## Ideas for Writing or Speaking

1. Consider the following quote from the first article: "Critics of the show said it smacked of bigotry and illustrated societal prejudice and lack of understanding toward the disabled. KFI said the matter was handled properly and that radio talk shows are appropriate forums for controversial issues." The framers of our Bill of Rights did not anticipate the phenomenon of broadcast media. Based on your understanding of the freedom of speech, are there any issues that should not be discussed in a public forum? Does sensitivity to the feelings of a particular group make some topics less desirable for public discussion? State your conclusion and support it with reasons.

2. Take a stand on one of the issues involved in these articles. Write an essay or give a short speech, expressing your viewpoint and supporting it with reasons.

3. Imagine that you are a program director for a radio talk show. What guidelines would you give your talk-show hosts? Give reasons for each guideline. Share your guidelines in a group or write them in essay form.

4. Write or speak on the following: Given the power of talk-show hosts to influence large numbers of people, do you believe there should be stricter licensing requirements for this pro-

fession, as there are for doctors, lawyers, and accountants, in order to ensure a uniform code of journalistic conduct? If so, why? If not, why not?

More Ideas for Writing or Speaking

1. Think about an issue that really interests you; it might be an issue currently being debated on your campus, or a community or national problem. The editorial pages of campus, community, or national newspapers may give you more ideas to help you choose your issue.

   In the form of an essay or a brief speech, state the issue and your conclusion and give at least three reasons to support your conclusion.

   In the classroom, take a few minutes for each person to share his or her speech or essay and see if the rest of the class understands the issue, conclusion, and reasons of the speaker. Don't use this exercise to debate issues (that will come later). At this point, strive only to make yourself clear and to understand the basic arguments of others.

2. Letter or speech of complaint: Practice using your knowledge about the structure of argument by writing a letter of complaint or doing a classroom "complaint speech."

   Constructive complaining is an important life skill. Use this letter or speech to express your dissatisfaction. Choose the most relevant aspects of the problem to discuss. A clear statement of the issue, your conclusion, and reasons distinguishes "whining" from complaining. Whereas "whining" could be characterized as a long string of feelings expressed vehemently about random aspects of a problem, a true complaint describes the nature of the problem in an organized fashion. Sincerely expressed feelings then add richness to the clear and organized content.

   To make the complaint clear, be sure to support your ideas with examples, illustrations, instances, statistics, testimony, or visual aids. To make your feelings clear, you can use vivid language, humor, sarcasm, understatement, exaggeration, irony, and dramatic emphasis.

Examples of topics for the complaint speech/essay: a letter or speech to a city planning commission about excessive airport noise, a letter to a supervisor about a change in salary or working conditions, a complaint to neighbors about reckless driving in the neighborhood, a complaint to housemates about sharing the workload, a letter or speech to insurance agents about rates for college students.

CHAPTER TWO

Values and Ethics

What Price Ethics and Can You Afford Not to Pay?

A critical thinker understands the value assumptions underlying many arguments and recognizes that conflicts are often based on differing values.

This chapter will cover:

◆ Value assumptions
◆ Conflict between value assumptions
◆ Ethics in argumentation
◆ Ethical decision making

In the first chapter, we discussed the structure of argument, including issues, conclusions about issues, and reasons used to support conclusions. Chapters 4, 5, and 6 will examine the quality of evidence given to support conclusions. This chapter and Chapter 3 will cover the assumptions underlying arguments that influence all of us as we consider claims and take positions on issues.

Assumptions are ideas we take for granted; as such, they are often left out of a written or spoken argument. Just as we can look at the structure of a house without seeing the foundation, we can look at the structure of an argument without examining the foundational elements. To truly understand the quality of a house or an argument, we need to understand the foundation upon which it is built.

Assumptions made by speakers and writers come in two forms: value assumptions and reality assumptions. *Value assumptions* are beliefs about how the world should be and *reality assumptions* are beliefs about how the world is. We will look at reality assumptions in Chapter 3. In this chapter, we will focus on value assumptions that form the foundations of arguments; we will also examine ethical considerations in argumentation and decision making.

Consider the values expressed in the following newspaper column. Compare the answers given to the question "What fictional character do you admire most?" What are the different values represented by the choices? Do you think the careers chosen by the respondents reflect their values?

Question Man: Fictional Character You Admire Most?

by Kris Conti
San Francisco Chronicle, January 28, 1990

Female, 23, curatorial assistant:

Howard Roark of *The Fountainhead,* for never compromising his standards. His self-centeredness and arrogance was a problem, but I admired the fact that he had standards and lived by them. It seems that standards are fairly loose, sort of ad hoc. People go by the situation they're in rather than a set of standards that they follow. I admire someone who has ideals.

Female, 31, bank teller:
Scrooge. He was a cad but when he had a chance to turn his life around he did. I admire his ability to turn his life around, because it's hard to change. He finally found that being rich is not what makes you happy. That being a true giver and a caring person are very rich qualities, and you can be happy in spite of poverty and adversity.

Male, 28, office manager:
Bugs Bunny. I admire the way he outsmarts his rivals and talks his way out of adverse situations. He always gets the best of any situation. Of course, in the cartoon universe, it doesn't matter how, so it's not applicable in the nonanimated universe. Who's going to discuss morals once you throw the law of physics and gravity out the window?

Male, 38, nuclear industry engineer:
Mr. Spock. He always has the answer. Whatever the problem is, he's always got the solution. He's witty. He's got a great sense of humor. It's just a subtle-type humor. I love that his character is very intelligent. Everything to him has a logic. It has to be logical. It has to click for him in a logical, rational way or it isn't happening.

Female, 25, Salvation Army program assistant:
Cinderella. She overcame through all the hardships she had to face and kept that spirit of endurance and forgiveness. She just kept plugging away and was humble. She served her stepsisters and stepmother and didn't gripe. We could all be a little more serving. Not to the point of being oppressed, but be more serving like she was.

© *San Francisco Chronicle.* Reprinted by permission.

STOP AND THINK
What fictional character do you admire most? What does your answer reveal about your values?

Value Assumptions and Conflicts

Have you ever noticed how some issues are really interesting to you while others are not? Your interest in a particular question and your opinion about the question are often influenced by your **values,** those ideals, people, or things you believe are important and that you hold dear.

Value assumptions are beliefs about what is good and important, that form the basis of opinions on issues.

These assumptions are important for the critical thinker because:

1. Many arguments between individuals and groups are primarily based on strongly held values that need to be understood, and, if possible, respected.
2. An issue that continues to be unresolved or bitterly contested often involves cherished values on both sides. These conflicting value assumptions can be *between* groups or individuals or *within* an individual.

Almost everyone in a civilized society believes that its members, especially young and defenseless members, should be protected. That's why we never hear a debate on the pros and cons of child abuse—most of us agree that there are no 'pros' to this issue. Similarly, we don't hear people arguing about the virtues of mass murder, rape, or burglary.

Our values, however, do come into the discussion when we are asked to decide how to treat the people who do engage in these acts. Some issues having a value component would be:

Should we have and enforce the death penalty?
Should rapists receive the same penalties as murderers?
Should we allow lighter sentences for plea bargaining?

Although most of us value order and justice, we often disagree on how justice is best administered, on what should be done to those who break the law.

REMINDER

When you read or hear the words should or ought to, you are
probably being addressed on a question of value.

You can see that the question of the death penalty centers on
a conflict about the priorities of justice and mercy, two values
cherished by many. Of course, a good debate on this issue will
address such factual (not value-based) issues as whether the
death penalty is a deterrent to crime and whether the penalty is
fairly administered throughout the country.

Keep in mind, however, that most people who argue passionately about this issue are motivated by their values and beliefs concerning justice and mercy. Often these values are shaped
by significant personal experiences. In fact, we generally hear arguments involving values by persons who are deeply concerned
about an issue. Both sides of arguments involving values are
likely to be persuasive because of the conviction of their advocates.

In coming to thoughtful conclusions on value-based arguments, the critical thinker needs to decide which of two or more
values is best. In other words, the thinker must give one value or
set of values a higher priority than the other.

Examples

We often hear arguments about the legalization of drugs,
gambling, or prostitution. People may claim that legalizing
these activities would lessen crime, improve public health, and
direct large sums of money to the government and out of the
hands of dealers, bookies, and pimps. Those who oppose legalization of these activities may have equally impressive arguments about the problems the community would face if these
activities were legalized. We need to understand the root of
this argument as a disagreement about which is more important:

1. Cleaning up the crime problems caused by underground activities linked to illegal vices, that is, the value of taking care of the immediate problem, or
2. Maintaining our standards of healthy living by discouraging and making it a crime to engage in activities that we as a culture deem inappropriate and harmful, that is, the value of honoring cultural standards and long-term societal goals.

If most people in our society believe that taking drugs, gambling, and prostitution are morally wrong, then no list of advantages of legalizing them would be persuasive. Thus, the argument starts with understanding whether the conclusion is based upon values; relative societal benefits have a much lower priority for those who believe we cannot condone harmful activities.

SKILL

Understand that different values form the basis of many arguments and that conflicts are often based on differing values.

Think of a decision you might be facing now or in the future, such as whether you should work (or continue working) while attending school, which career you should choose, or which person you should marry. An internal conflict about a decision often involves an impasse (being stuck) between two or more values.

Let's say you are undecided about continuing to work. You want to devote yourself to school because in the long run you can get a better job (long-term goal). On the other hand, you'd really like the money for an upgraded lifestyle—a car or better car, money to eat out, and nicer clothes.

Your career decision may involve a conflict between the value of serving others in a field such as nursing or teaching and the value of a secure and substantial salary (such as you might find in a business career) that would help you to provide better for your future family.

You might think of getting serious with one person because he or she has good prospects for the future and is ambitious, but another person is more honest and has cared for you in both good and bad times. In this case, the conflict is between security (or materialism) and loyalty.

EXERCISE

Purpose: To isolate value conflicts and to understand how different conclusions can be based on conflicting values.

Try to isolate the various value conflicts in these personal and social problems. You can do this on your own, with others, or as a classroom exercise. Some of the issues may involve more than one set of conflicting values.

Note especially how sometimes both values are important and we as persons or as citizens need to make tough decisions for which there are no easy answers. Creating policies for difficult problems means giving one value a higher priority than another.

The first one is done for you as an example.

1. Should teenagers be required to obtain the approval of their parents before they receive birth control pills or other forms of contraception?

    The conflict in this issue is between the value of individual freedom and privacy on one side and parental responsibility and guidance on the other.

2. Should birth parents be allowed to take their child back from adoptive parents after they have signed a paper relinquishing rights?

3. Should you give your last $40.00 of the month to a charity that feeds famine-stricken families or use it for some new jeans you've needed?

4. Should air traffic controllers be given tests for drug use?

5. Should persons be hired for jobs without regard to maintaining an ethnic mix?

6. Should prisoners on death row be allowed conjugal visits?
7. Should superior athletes receive admission to colleges regardless of their grades or SAT scores?
8. Should criminals be allowed to accept royalties on books they've written about the crimes they committed?

An important issue involving conflicting value priorities is that of equal opportunity in educational and employment opportunities. In the 1970s, affirmative action policies were initiated in universities in an attempt to create a more level playing field for those who had been disadvantaged and discriminated against. Affirmative action has been a controversial topic in the 1990s; some people believe that it has achieved its original purpose and others believe that efforts to dismantle equal opportunity policies will take us back to segregationist conditions of the past. There are even those who contend that affirmative action is discriminatory to some minorities; Joan Beck, writing in the *Chicago Tribune*, made these observations before mandated affirmative action was removed from the University of California:

Do Colleges Treat Asian-American Applicants Fairly?

by Joan Beck
Chicago Tribune, August 24, 1989

It almost sounds like a replay of 1970s affirmative action battles. But it has an Oriental twist.

This time, it's Asian-Americans complaining that they aren't getting a fair deal in admissions to top-level colleges, even though their share of student slots far exceeds their percentage in the population.

The case they make is opening up old conflicts about quotas and goals, about affirmative action and excellence, about whites versus minorities, and about racism and equal opportunity in America.

The uneasy accommodations of the '80s in college admissions may be coming apart at the top, for the curious reason that too many Asian-Americans are—or are perceived to be—too smart. . . .

. . . Berkeley, which has been extremely aggressive—and successful—in recruiting minority students, has been under fire for several years for discriminating against Asian-Americans in its admissions choices. The university has used slightly higher standards for them than for other applicants and turned down some who would have gotten in had they been white or members of another minority.

What few people are saying out loud is that increasing the number of Asian-Americans in the most selective schools will necessarily come at the expense of white students. Berkeley's student body is now 48.5 percent white—giving whites less representation on campus than in the population of the state as a whole.

The real problem is not racism, but the convoluted, complex policies most colleges have adopted to avoid it. They're trying to remedy centuries-old problems with preferential treatment for some minorities that, in effect, penalizes whites and now Asian-Americans.

Colleges are essentially attempting to reconcile competing values: Academic excellence, affirmative action and a diverse student body. The results, inevitably, are controversial admissions decisions.

Neither grades nor test scores are completely reliable measures of academic ability, for example. "Diversity" is difficult to define, requires flexible admissions standards and hurts the well-qualified students who are left out in the process.

(Colleges traditionally have bent admission standards for promising athletes, children of alumni and well-connected families, perhaps even a trombone player needed by the marching band, and for other reasons.)

If racial and ethnic "diversity" in the student body of a prestigious college is an acceptable goal, then Asian-Americans don't have a legitimate complaint; they are very well represented, indeed.

But by traditional standards of academic merit, they do have a justifiable case—even if the criteria are expanded to include such qualities as leadership, extracurricular activities and volunteer work. So does every applicant who loses out to a candidate who brings nontraditional qualifications such as the ability to overcome racial, cultural, physical or economic disadvantage and whose admission to college can be seen as furthering vital national goals.

There is no easy resolution to these issues. And there won't be until race and ethnicity are no longer so divisive.

© Copyrighted Chicago Tribune Company. All rights reserved. Used with permission.

Decisions made about which values take priority in college admissions have a real and lasting impact on people's lives.

Consider the following two articles, which show contrasting effects of affirmative action. What do you believe is the most equitable way to resolve the competing values represented by this issue?

Affirmative Action Triumphs:

The Untold Stories

by Paul Rockwell
Oakland, California

Eva Jefferson Paterson is Executive Director of the Lawyers Committee for Civil Rights, one of California's most brilliant attorneys. She is an African-American and a beneficiary of affirmative action.

She recently told a personal, uplifting story to a crowd of 3,000 cheering University of California, Berkeley, students.

"I got into Boalt Law School (U.C. Berkeley) through an affirmative action program, a program that gave me the opportunity to study law. (She was a classmate of Lance Ito.) Affirmative action gave me an opportunity, but I cracked the books, did the work, and passed the tests."

Ms. Eva Paterson passed the bar exam on the first round. On her indefatigable speaking tours, she often gets applause and laughter when she mentions that Pete Wilson failed the bar exam twice. (He finally passed.)

"Never apologize for affirmative action," she tells the crowd, "I am proud of affirmative action because I am qualified."

Stories of hope abound. The Eva Paterson story is not unique. California is full of thousands of affirmative action triumphs—stories of opportunity, realized potential, and achievement rarely told on the public airwaves.

When Pete Wilson launched his anti-immigrant, anti-affirmative action campaign, no doubt he expected affirmative action beneficiaries would be cowed into hiding and silence.

How wrong Wilson was!

Not only are women and communities of color coming together, affirmative action beneficiaries and participants are speaking out in public. At long last we can listen to real people whose opportunities were expanded, whose own lives were enhanced, and whose humble communities were served, by affirmative action.

Antonia Hernandez, well-known defender of Latino rights, is president of the Mexican-American Legal Defense and Education Fund. Class-action suits, redistricting cases are some of her legal triumphs.

It was affirmative action that helped change the course of her life. Her family lived in La Cruces and worked in the cotton fields, until her uncle brought the entire family to Los Angeles, "all crunched up" in an old Chevrolet.

"I was," she writes, "an immigrant kid out of East Los Angeles. Without affirmative action I would not have had an opportunity to go to U.C.L.A. and explore horizons that were never opened to my parents. Huppies—upwardly mobile Hispanics—do not acknowledge sometimes that affirmative action has opened doors for them. They feel uncomfortable with what they perceive as a negative tag. We need to openly say we are examples of the success of affirmative action.

"I am a kid out of Garfield High School in East Los Angeles. I am a pretty bright individual and I had decent grades. I was just dirt-poor. My parents lived in the projects and I dreamed of going to Cal State L.A. because it was just across the street. That is as far as my dreams would take me. I am sure that I was judged by standards other than just grades or test scores. They saw in me a burning determination, the drive, the willingness to work. They gave me a break, but I am not the only one. It happened to thousands of Latinos who went to medical school, to architectural school."

Were public standards lowered to make room for Antonia Hernandez? Or was the public, which pays for the University system, better served by giving her an opportunity?

Standards were not lowered, Ms. Hernandez says. "That is the beauty of affirmative action. It gives the flexibility to find new standards that are more relevant, more current, taking into account our past and present history of exclusion." Universities enable individuals to build personal careers. But public universities also serve a larger public purpose. Improving legal services in the Hispanic communities is a noble goal.

Ronald W. Johnson is director of financial aid at U.C.L.A. He worked 15 years at U.C. Davis. As a young African-American he came to California from Brooklyn, New York, and he has dedicated the last 21 years of his life to higher education.

"I know for certain," he writes, "that were it not for affirmative action, many doors would have been closed. My accomplishments weren't given to me because of who I knew or who my father knew. They weren't handed to me because of how well I played sports. I earned my accomplishments through hard work, integrity and intelligence. But I knew I had a lot to be thankful for, most of which were the many doors of opportunity that opened for me to show my attributes. . . .

"I know that all of my qualifications have nothing to do with my race, but rather with who I am as a person. But what if I had never had the opportunity to show others my skills to manage? What if I had never had the opportunity to show others my ability to lead? My future, and the future of those lives I have touched, would never be realized. Whether it's due to racism, closed doors, or perhaps the non-existence of affirmative action, the results would have been the same—lack of opportunity."

Affirmative action programs are not unique to women and people of color. White males are beneficiaries of many types of special programs, including programs that make exceptions to strict meritocracy. Albert Vetere Lannon lives in San Francisco. He writes: "The fact is that we older white men are beneficiaries of affirmative action. I'm a tenured teacher now, but seven years ago, I was a high school dropout. I entered San Francisco State University at age 50 through the re-entry program, a form of affirmative action. I graduated with honors and am working on a master's degree in history."

"Affirmative action benefited me directly, and I am now able to give something back to the society that gave me a hand."

Stories of hope, of opportunities that serve a higher public purpose, are rare in our cynical media. But the stories of Eva Paterson, Antonia Hernandez, Ronald Johnson, and Albert Lannon manifest the real significance of affirmative action. Affirmative action is one way to discover and realize human potential, and affirmative action is good for America.

Paul Rockwell, formerly assistant professor of philosophy at Midwestern University, is a writer and children's librarian in the San Francisco Bay Area. He is chair of "Angry White Guys for Affirmative Action."

The Backlash of Affirmative Action

by Martin Geraghty

Chicago Tribune, October 21, 1996

Martin Geraghty is Senior Vice-President of Collins Tuttle & Co., Inc.

It's in her eyes, mainly. That's where you see Debbie's 11 years of pent-up bitterness at the injustice of affirmative action. She's listened for years to the lie that mandatory racial and gender discrimination benefits women. She knows the names and faces of the feminist elites whom TV adores. They've been babbling for years at her about how it's really good for her and for all other women to deprive Gerry, her husband, of the promotion he earned in 1985. And she turns away.

Gerry, my brother-in-law, has always wanted to be a cop. He earned a bachelor's degree in criminology 20 years ago. He finally got his sergeant's badge and his white shirt in March. But for 11 years, Debbie watched him seethe at the cruelty of a system that tested first his skills and then his great heart. When Harold Washington was mayor, Gerry took a sergeant's exam that was indisputably non-biased, fair to all, racially (and every other way) neutral. Out of nearly 4,000 officers who took it, he scored in the top 15 percent.

Soon he would be promoted. Soon the extra $700 per month would take some of the strain off his family's finances. Soon the decision Gerry and Debbie made when they adopted the first of their two sons would be justified. Yeah, they could have used the extra money from Debbie's excellent job with the insurance company, but little Brian (and a couple of years later, his baby brother David) deserved a mom at home. So that's where Debbie stayed.

Now most folks agree that babies, and bigger kids, are better off in the presence of a mom who'll talk to them and play with them and read to them and drop whatever she's doing to find a toy or wipe a nose or kiss a bump. But to do that all day, every day, a mom usually has to hook on with a male. If that male is white (which happens in quite a few cases) the notion of affirmative action as "good for women" gets turned on its head.

At its most basic level, affirmative action says to women: "If you have babies and turn over their daily care to someone else so you can work, we'll penalize others (white males and all who depend on them) in your favor. But if you marry a white male, we'll victimize you by depriving him of simple justice."

It's easy today to find overwrought racial and feminist activists who'll slander America as "most racist . . . most bigoted . . . most sexist . . . worse than ever before . . . etc." But this great land, its values twisted by a misguided need to balance every conceivable scale, is the only nation in history where active discrimination against its majority population is not only permitted—it's required.

Racial discrimination has always been ugly. It's bad when it arises out of personal human meanness or ignorance. But Jim Crow laws earlier in this century, and affirmative action today, have been even more pernicious because of the official sanction they've enjoyed. The victim must not only endure; he must know that his own government, with society's assent, is the agent of his suffering.

And make no mistake. Every affirmative action decision is a cruel zero-sum game with a victor and a victim. Luckily for the elites who so casually espouse affirmative action, it falls most heavily on the white, working-class male who works where racial and gender nose-counting is easier to do.

The elites who prattle on about "redressing wrongs" and "200 years of injustice" find it very easy to ignore the folks who will bear the cost of that redress. But until they have looked Gerry, and especially Debbie, in the eye and tasted the pain of affirmative action, they are hollow saints, casually, painlessly bestowing on one group of victims what rightfully belongs to a new set of victims.

© Copyrighted Chicago Tribune Company. All rights reserved. Used with permission.

Questions for Discussion

1. What are the competing values that businesses, government agencies, and colleges are attempting to reconcile with their employment and admissions policies? In what ways can these values be reconciled?
2. What values are most important, in your mind, when considering college admissions and job advancement policies? Should these values be the same for private universities and corporations as for state-supported universities and government agencies?
3. Do you believe that there comes a time when inequities in a society have been addressed or do you believe that we will always need to have policies in place that assure diversity in admissions and hiring?

Ideas for Writing or Speaking

Part A: List some values you hold. These can be character traits, such as honesty, fairness, and compassion. You can also list such concerns as peace, freedom of speech, family ties, ethnic identity, health, wealth, competition, or cooperation.

To isolate some of your values, consider the professions that interest you. If you want to be a high school coach, you may value sports, young people, and/or education. If you want to be an artist, you may value beauty and creativity.

Also, consider how you spend your free time. Different values may be expressed by those who spend time reading science fiction, shopping, volunteering at a nursing home, socializing, or working on a political campaign.

Try to list at least three values reflected in your life.

Part B: Choose a controversial issue and take a position on this issue; your position should reflect a value you hold. Examples of controversial topics with a value dimension include capital punishment, surrogate parenting, homelessness, nuclear power, active and passive euthanasia, socialized medicine, welfare, immigration, and environmental policies. You might look up issues that are currently being considered by the Supreme Court; many of the court's rulings establish the precedence of one value over another.

After you have chosen an issue and taken a position reflecting your values, arrange your ideas in the following manner:

1. Give several reasons to support your position. Give both moral and fact-based reasons. Use examples and evidence to strengthen your reasons.
2. State some good reasons why you think a person might believe the opposite of what you believe. For example, if you are against compulsory drug testing for athletes, state why someone might argue in favor of it.
3. Conclude by indicating if and how your initial belief was changed by considering the opposite viewpoint. Or, conclude by stating why your initial belief was not changed, despite your fair consideration of the arguments against your belief.

Ethics—An Important Dimension of Values

"Without civic morality, communities perish; without personal morality, their survival has no value."

Bertrand Russell, "Individual and Social Ethics," *Authority and the Individual* (1949)

For our purposes, we will examine ethics as one dimension of values. **Ethics,** sometimes called morals, are standards of conduct that reflect what we consider to be right or wrong behavior. Many conflicts about values involve an ethical dimension, that is, we are asked to choose whether one action or policy is more ethical than another.

Look at the difference in the following value conflicts:

Should you take a job that pays more but has evening hours you value for studying or should you take a job that pays less but gives you the hours that you want?

If you arrive home and notice that a cashier at a store gave you too much change, should you go back to the store and return the money?

Note that in the first example you need to decide what you value more—the extra money or the working hours you want. There is no ethical (good–bad) dimension to this decision; you can still study even if you take the job with the less desirable hours.

The second dilemma is about your personal standards of right and wrong, or good and evil. Do you inconvenience yourself by making a trip to the store or sending the money back because you believe it is wrong to take what does not belong to you? Or do you believe that if you didn't intend to take the money, you are not responsible? What are your standards of right and wrong, especially regarding relationships with others?

Philosophers and theologians have grappled with theories of ethical behavior for centuries. Several schools of thought about ethics have emerged. Some of the more common are listed below. Note the substantial similarity among the principles listed.

LIBERTARIANISM

Value Assumption:
The highest value is to promote the liberty of all.

Principles:
Behavior is considered ethical when it both allows for one's individual freedom and does not restrict the freedom of others.

Examples:
Honesty is important because dishonesty restricts the freedom of others. Education is good because it increases personal freedom.

Violence, oppression, and poverty are bad because they restrict freedom.

Freedom of speech and assembly are important; restrictions on the right of any group to speak and assemble threaten the rights of other groups.

Reporters should not have to reveal sources of information because that would restrict the freedom of the press.

UTILITARIANISM

Value Assumption:
The highest value is that which promotes the greatest general happiness and minimizes unhappiness.

Principles:
Behavior is judged according to its utility (usefulness) in creating the greatest human well-being. Actions are considered in terms of "happiness" consequences.

Examples:
Giving to others is good when it makes people, including the giver, happy. Giving would be discouraged if it caused greater unhappiness in the long run, as in the case of giving treats to children who throw tantrums.

National policies should consider the happiness consequences for the majority of the people affected by the policy. Taxing the rich might be better than taxing the middle-class, since more people are middle-class and would feel the pinch of taxes to a greater degree.

Societal rules that maximize the possibilities of individuals flourishing and prospering involve all of our "enlightened self-interest." Selfishness and greed are bad when they don't make it probable for most people to be happy.

Freedom of assembly for "hate groups" might be restricted because of the strife and unhappiness they would cause to a larger number of citizens.

Hardship and difficulty may be necessary in order to achieve desired results in the long run; people may derive happiness from intensive labor, as when a sports team trains and works for an ultimate victory or when a student works hard for a good grade.

EGALITARIANISM

Value Assumption:
The highest value is equality. Justice and fairness are synonymous with equality.

Principles:
Behavior is ethical when the same opportunities and consequences apply to all people. We should treat others as we wish to be treated.

Examples:
Since people are equal, discrimination of any kind is unethical. People should not take more than their fair share; they should give to those who have not received their fair share.

Punishment for crimes should be exacted in a fair manner; the poor and unknown should not be given harsher sentencing than the rich and famous.

If the justice system allows for unequal or unfair treatment of certain individuals or groups, then the system needs to be changed to ensure fairness for all citizens.

JUDEO-CHRISTIAN PRINCIPLES

Value Assumption:
The highest values are to love God and to love one's neighbor.

Principles:
Ethical behavior is based on biblical principles found in the Ten Commandments and other prescriptions, and on the desire to please and honor God.

Examples:
Since all people are created by God, all should be treated with love and respect.

People should not steal, cheat, lie, or envy because these acts are contrary to biblical principles; they are not loving to others and they dishonor God.

When values conflict, resolution comes by doing the most loving, God-honoring act. For example, some Christians lied to SS officers about hiding Jewish people during the Nazi occupation; had they turned them over to the officers, the Jewish people would have been sent to concentration camps and/or killed.

Universal Ethical Norms or Universal Action-Guiding Principles

Value Assumption:
Universal ethical principles exist and are self-evident (prima facie) and obvious to rational individuals of every culture.

Principles:
Individuals should act in accordance with these principles for the betterment of the individual and the society.

Examples:
A modern system of prima facie principles has been developed by Michael Josephson, of the Josephson Institute. His list includes honesty, integrity, fidelity, fairness, caring and respect for others, accountability, and responsible citizenship. Implications of these values are that individuals should not steal, should be responsible enough to avoid drinking when working or driving, and should be informed voters and contributors to the larger society.

Values cited above are to be honored and values such as materialism and self-centeredness are to be discouraged.

SKILL

A critical thinker is aware of his or her standards and knows the reason a value-based decision has been made.

One Bandit's Ethic

Harper's Magazine, January 1992

We all have personal standards. Consider this list of personal rules that Dennis Lee Curtis, an armed robber in Rapid City, South Dakota, was carrying in his wallet when he was arrested in June of 1991.

1. I will not kill anyone unless I have to.
2. I will take cash and food stamps—no checks.
3. I will rob only at night.
4. I will not wear a mask.
5. I will not rob minimarts or 7-Eleven stores.
6. If chased by cops on foot I will get away. If chased by a vehicle I will not put the lives of innocent citizens on the line.
7. I will rob only seven months out of the year.
8. I will enjoy robbing from the poor to give to the poor.

© 1992 by *Harper's Magazine.* All rights reserved.
Reprinted from the January 1992 issue by special permission.

STOP AND THINK

Look at the standards given by Dennis Lee Curtis; what general principles are revealed by this list? Do these principles fit into any of the schools of thought covered in the previous section?

EXERCISES

Purposes: To discover how policy debates are influenced by ethical standards, and to discover personal standards and principles that determine how ethical dilemmas are resolved.

1. Review the systems of ethics just discussed. Individually, or in groups, come up with examples of situations where the principles of one of these systems clashes with the principles of another. You may want to bring in recent local or campus controversies, such as the one detailed in the following excerpt from a college newspaper.

   Discuss the conflicting value principles represented by your examples.

Example:

In the following case, a murder was committed on campus and a newspaper photographer took pictures of the scene. The police wanted these pictures to help them identify the suspects; the photographer did not want to turn his work over to the police because he felt that would compromise the freedom of the press. Can you see that this issue involves a conflict between libertarianism (freedom of the press) versus utilitarianism (the police concern about promoting the general welfare by identifying and prosecuting criminals)?

Staffer Gets Subpoenaed

by Steve Logan,
Advocate, October 11, 1996

Police services Lt. Paul Lee delivered a subpoena to *Advocate* photographer Soren Hemmila Thursday morning to appear in Superior Court in Martinez at 1:30 p.m. Tuesday.

Lee delivered the subpoena through District Attorney William Clark and the San Pablo Police Department in connection with photographs taken of the scene after Christopher Robinson's murder on campus September 25.

Hemmila and the *Advocate* have refused to turn over unpublished photos, taken shortly after the murder, to the San Pablo Police Department.

California's shield law is designed to help news organizations protect sources and information from outside forces, including law enforcement agencies. The law also states a journalist cannot be held in contempt of court for refusing to turn over unpublished work.

Hemmila believes the photographs are protected by the shield law.

The *West County Times* reported Thursday that San Pablo police believe the photos could give them important information in prosecuting the case of the three suspects who have already been taken into custody and charged with Robinson's murder.

Hemmila said he arrived on the crime scene just as the police were putting up yellow tape. Among the photographs taken, but not published, included shots of the crowd in the background.

Hemmila said San Pablo Det. Mark Harrison first came to ask for the negatives "nicely," on Monday.

"I don't like being part of the investigation in this case," Hemmila said Thursday after receiving the subpoena. "I'm willing to do what it takes to protect our rights."

The subpoena said the photographs will be helpful to the police in three ways. Section one said the credibility of an eyewitness who commented in last Friday's story which ran in the Advocate needs to be evaluated.

Section two said the photographs will show the crime scene closer to the time of the shooting, which will allow the prosecution to evaluate the weight of the physical evidence which included expended casings at the scene.

Section three said the photographs may show whether the attack was "planned, a surprise attack, or a chance encounter that turned violent."

Hemmila said it would set a bad precedent if the Advocate turned over the photos.

"If we make it a [practice] to turn over the negatives to police agencies, they'll expect it in the future and they'll expect it from other publications.

"I don't want the public to think that journalists are part of law enforcement or acting in their behalf."

2. Consider your own definition of ethical behavior; it may fit into one of the schools of thought outlined in this chapter or it may be a combination of several approaches. Then, using your own principles, try to be completely "ethical" for one

week. As often as possible, ask yourself "What is the best way to respond to this situation?" Keep a daily record of your ethical challenges. Then, report your successes and failures in dealing with these situations.

Here are some examples of common ethical dilemmas: should you defend a friend who is being criticized by another friend? Should you give to a homeless person who approaches you? Should you tell the truth to someone even if it hurts their feelings? Should you tell your instructor that several students cheated when she answered a knock at the classroom door? Should you tell callers your roommate isn't home if she asks you to? Should you complain about rude treatment in a store? Should you copy a friend's tape of your favorite music rather than buying your own copy?

Your own situations will be unique. If time permits, share some ethical dilemmas that you encountered with the rest of the class.

3. Consider the following situations alone or with a group:
   a. You and your friend are taking the same required history class; you are taking it on Mondays and Wednesdays and your friend is taking it Tuesday evening. You have given up much of your social life to study for this class because the tests are hard. One Monday after the midterm, your friend calls you and wants to know what was on the test since he partied too hard over the weekend and didn't study. You have a good memory and could tell him many of the questions. Do you tell him what was on the test?
   b. You go to a garage sale and notice a diamond ring that is being sold for $10.00. You know that the ring is worth far more than that. What do you do?
   c. The manager of the fast-food restaurant where you work is selling food that is not fresh or prepared according to the standards of the company. You have complained to him, but he has done nothing despite your complaints. You need this job, and the location, hours, and pay are perfect for you; in fact, this boss has tailored your working hours to your class schedule. Nevertheless, you are concerned about public safety. What do you do?

   d. You are a member of a city council and you have a seri-
      ous problem of homelessness in your city. A businessman
      offers you $100,000 in aid for the homeless if you will let
      him build an office building over a popular park. How do
      you vote?

Ideal Values versus Real Values

If you completed the last exercises, you may have realized that
ethical behavior is easier to discuss than it is to carry out. We have
complex needs and emotions, and situations are also complicated. Even with good intentions, we sometimes find it difficult
to choose ethical behavior.

   Because of the difficulty of living up to our standards, most
of us can make a distinction between our ideal values and our
real values. An **ideal value** can be considered a value that you
believe to be right and good, but have not put into practice
in your life. A **real value** is a value that you consider to be
right and good and actually act upon in your life. As critical
thinkers, it is important for us to understand and be honest
about our own behavior and to distinguish our words from our
actions.

   People may say they value good citizenship; they believe people should be informed about candidates and issues and express
their viewpoints by voting, but they may continue to vote without studying issues and candidates. In some cases, the value of
citizenship is only an ideal. For the value to be real, it must be
carried out in the life of the individual claiming that value. Consider the following dialogue from Dr. Laura Schlessinger's book
How Could You Do That?:

   Stephanie, twenty-one, is a virgin and had planned to stay
   that way until she's married. But now she finds herself
   very attracted to somebody . . . did I say "very"? She'd
   hoped that her values, the rules, would protect her from
   temptation. Now she is set adrift without a paddle be-

cause she discovered that values don't function like an automatic, invisible protective shield.

"Just in case I start dating him, do you have any advice on how to stay a virgin?"

"You mean you have values until temptations ride into town, then the values sneak out during the night? The town ain't big enough for both values and temptations. Values keep us steady through times of deep temptation. They are our road map through the minefields of challenge. It is easy to say you have values, and easier still to live up to them when you're by yourself in the middle of the ocean."

"That's true."

"Values are truly only shown to exist when they are tested. If it is meaningful for you to reserve sexual intimacy for marital vows, if you feel that doing so elevates sex and you, that is admirable."

"Yeah, but how do you make the values do their thing to keep you from doing something else?"

"Values only have the power you infuse into them with your respect for them and yourself, and your will. Values without temptations are merely lofty ideas. Expediting them is what makes you, and them, special. That requires grit, will, sacrifice, courage, and discomfort. But it is in the difficulty that both the values and you gain importance. The measure of you as a human being is how you honor the values.

"When you begin dating him, clarify your position of intercourse only within marriage. If he tries to push you away from that position, you know he values you only as a means of sexual gratification. If he gets seductive and you're lubricating from your eyeballs to your ankles, this is the moment when you choose between momentary pleasure and long-term self-respect."

"That is the real choice I'm making at that point, isn't it?"

There is no fast lane to self-esteem. It's won on these battlegrounds where immediate gratification goes up against character. When character triumphs, self-esteem heightens.

One caller asked, "What if I'm too weak?" I answered that the road to unhappiness and low self-esteem is paved with the victories of immediate gratification.[1]

Copyright © 1996 by Dr. Laura C. Schlessinger. Reprinted by permission of HarperCollins Publishers, Inc.

 EXERCISE

Purpose: To understand the difference between real and ideal values.

List five of your real values and five of your ideal values.

1. Describe what it would take for these ideal values to become real values for you. Think about why you have not made these ideal values real in your life.
2. Then explain what changes in your habits and your priorities would be involved in order for these values to be real for you.

Example:
"One of my ideal values is physical fitness. I believe it is important for everyone to keep their bodies strong through exercise and good eating habits.
"As a student, I don't take the time to exercise every day or even every other day. Since I quit the swim team, I hardly exercise at all. When I do have spare time, I sleep or go out with my girlfriend. Also, I eat a lot of fast foods or canned foods because I don't cook.
"For this ideal value to become real for me, I would have to graduate and have more time. Or, I would have to make the time to exercise. The best way would be to combine going out with my girlfriend with exercising. She likes to skate and play basketball, so we could do that together. Getting more exercise is a real possibility.

---

[1]   Dr. Laura Schlessinger, *How Could You Do That?:* (New York: HarperCollins Publishers, Inc., 1996) pp. 151–152.

"Eating right is probably not going to happen soon. I would have to learn to cook or to marry someone who would cook for me. At this point in my life, I can't see how I could have a healthier diet, even though it is an ideal for me. But it's just not important enough for me to learn at this time."

Ethics in Argumentation

"It is terrible to speak well and be wrong."
Sophocles, *Electra* (c. 418–14 B.C.)

Ethical concerns are central to any message. Those who seek to influence votes, sales, or the personal decisions of others need to:

- be honest about their conclusions and reasons

- not leave out or distort important information

- have thoroughly researched any claims they make

- listen with respect, if not agreement, to opposing viewpoints

- be willing to revise a position when better information becomes available

- give credit to secondary sources of information

EXERCISE

Purpose: To examine the ethical dimensions of an argument.

Listen to a political speech or a sales pitch or read an editorial essay. Then evaluate the message, stating whether the writer or speaker met the criteria given for ethical argumentation.

You might also use one of your own essays or speeches; analyze it to see whether you were as honest as you could have been and whether you credited secondary sources of information.

Ethical Decision Making

"Every man takes care that his neighbor shall not cheat him. But a day comes when he begins to care that he does not cheat his neighbor. Then all goes well."

Ralph Waldo Emerson, "Worship," *The Conduct of Life* (1860)

The first step in clear-headed decision making is knowing your principles and standards. In considering difficult decisions, there are several "tests" that can be useful to apply to your known principles. These tests can help you to assess how well your decision adheres to your standards.

1. The Role Exchange Test. This test asks you to empathize with the people who will be affected by the action you take. You try to see the situation from their point of view. You ask yourself how the others affected by your decision would feel and what consequences they would face.

You also ask whether it would be right for the other person to take the action if you were going to be the one experiencing the consequences of the decision. Using your imagination, you change places with the person or persons who would receive the effects of your decision. In short, you decide to treat the other person as you would want to be treated in his or her place.

For example, you see your brother's girlfriend out with other men. You hesitate to tell him because of the hurt it would cause and because you feel it's not really your business to interfere. However, when you do the role exchange test, you decide to tell him because you realize you would want to know if you were in his situation.

2. The Universal Consequences Test. This test focuses on the general results (consequences) of an action you might take. You imagine what would happen if everyone in a situation similar to yours took this action—would the results be acceptable?

Under the universal consequences test, if you would find it unacceptable for everyone in a similar situation to take this action, then you would reject the action.

For example, imagine that you are asked to join a community program for recycling cans, bottles, and paper. You enjoy the freedom of just throwing everything together in the trash, but you stop and assess the consequences of everyone refusing to recycle. Your assessment causes you to join the program.

3. The New Cases Test. This test asks you to consider whether your action is consistent with other actions that are in the same category. You choose the hardest case you can and see if you would act the same way in that case as you plan to act in this case. If you would, then your decision is consistent with your principles.

For example, you are deciding whether to vote to continue experiments that may be successful in finding a cure for AIDS but involve injecting animals with the HIV virus. Your principle is that cruelty to animals is not justified in any circumstance. To formulate a new, harder case you might ask yourself if you would allow the research to be conducted if it would save your life or the life of your child. If you would, then you might reconsider your voting decision and reassess your principles.

Another example involves our previous article on whether a photographer should turn over negatives to the police if it would help detectives identify and prosecute murder suspects. You may believe that freedom of the press cannot be compromised and, therefore, the photographer should be able to keep the negatives out of the investigation. Using the new cases test, imagine that someone you love dearly was the murder victim and that these photographs are the link to catching the person who killed him or her. Would that knowledge change your value priorities in this case?

4. The Higher Principles Test. This test asks you to determine whether the principle on which you are basing your action is consistent with a higher or more general principle you accept.

For example, let's say your roommates are not doing their share of the housework so you are considering not doing your own share. However, because you value promise-keeping and integrity, you realize that it is important to keep your part of the bargain regardless of what they are doing with their part. You decide to keep doing your share and to talk with them about keeping their part of the agreement.

 EXERCISE

Purpose: To be able to utilize tests for ethical decision making.

Option one: Think about an ethical dilemma you are facing or have faced in the past. If you did the exercise on being ethical for a week, you may have a recent example. You may also use the examples listed in that exercise. In addition, you might consider a difficult ethical dilemma from your past. Then, follow the directions given below.

Option two: Think about an ethical dilemma your community or nation is facing; you might also consider an international ethical dilemma. Some examples include the use of scientific information gained by Nazi experimentation on holocaust victims, the apportionment of funds to poverty-stricken nations, the exporting of cigarettes to other nations, and the rationing of health care. Then, follow the directions.

Directions:
1. On your own or in class groups, take the dilemma through each of the four tests. Write about what each test tells you about the course your decision should take.
2. Come to a conclusion about the decision. Justify your conclusion by referring to the cumulative results of the tests.

Example:
"My friend helped me to get a job at his company and, after only a few months, I was told that he and I were both being considered for a promotion to management. He worked at the job for a year and he's getting married soon, so he really needs this job. I wouldn't even have known about the possibility of working there if he hadn't told me about it and arranged an interview for me. The dilemma is, should I take the promotion if it's offered to me or refuse it, knowing that it will then go to him?"

The role exchange test asks me to look at the situation from his point of view. It would hurt him in two ways if I took this promotion: mainly, he would lose the income and the chances for advancement that go with this position. Also, he would be hurt because he helped me to get this job and then I took a promotion he might have had. There's nothing wrong with my looking out for my own future, but in this case, it would be at his expense.

The universal consequences test asks me to look at general consequences of my decision and determine if it would be acceptable for everyone in this situation to take a similar action. A positive general consequence might be that all of the best people would be given promotions regardless of who needs the promotion most. The negative general consequence would be that people would routinely put their own desires ahead of what might be more fair and what might be best for other people, a "me-first" mentality.

The new cases test asks me to pick the hardest case I can and see if I would act the same way in that case, to determine whether I am consistent. To me, the hardest case would be if my parent would be given the promotion if I didn't take it. I don't live with my parents anymore, but I would step down if it meant that either of them could have the promotion.

The higher principles test asks me to look at my own ethical standards to see if my actions fit into these standards. This test is hard to use, because I value both my own advancement and my friend's welfare. But I can find the higher principle of fairness; I don't feel that it would be fair for me to take a job that he would have had since he is the person responsible for my being in the position to take it.

In conclusion, I won't take this job if it is offered to me. It would be hurtful to my friend, who cared enough about me to help me get a job. Also, I wouldn't want to live in a world where people always climbed over one another to achieve success. If it were my parents, I wouldn't take a job that they wanted, even if it would benefit me personally. Finally, I believe in the principle of fairness, and I don't think it would be fair to take a promotion from a friend who gave me the opportunity to work for his company.

When we make ethical decisions, it is important that the actions taken are congruent with our values. When our actions go against what we believe is right, we are prone to rationalize our behavior, rather than to admit we are not always ethical. Consider this list of common rationalizations used to justify unethical conduct.

Common Rationalizations

Ethics in Action, January–February, 1991

I. "If It's Necessary, It's Ethical."
Based on the false assumption that necessity breeds propriety. Necessity is an interpretation, not a fact. But even actual necessity does not justify unethical conduct. Leads to ends-justify-the-means reasoning and treating assigned tasks or desired goals as moral imperatives.

II. "If It's Legal and Permissible, It's Proper."
Substitutes legal requirements (which establish minimal standards of behavior) for personal moral judgment. Does not embrace full range of ethical obligations, especially for those involved in upholding the public trust. Ethical people often choose to do less than they are allowed to do and more than they are required to do.

III. "I Was Just Doing It for You."
Primary justification of "white lies" or withholding important information in personal or professional relationships, especially performance reviews. Dilemma: honesty and respect vs. caring. Dangers: violates principle of respect for others (implies a moral right to make decisions about one's own life based on true information), ignores underlying self-interest of liar, and underestimates uncertainty about other person's desires to be "protected" (most people would rather have unpleasant information than be deluded into believing something that isn't so). Consider perspective of persons lied to: if they discovered the lie, would they thank you for being considerate or feel betrayed, patronized, or manipulated?

IV. "I'm Just Fighting Fire with Fire."
Based on false assumption that deceit, lying, promise-breaking, etc. are justified if they are the same sort engaged in by those you are dealing with.

V. "It Doesn't Hurt Anyone."
Rationalization used to excuse misconduct based on the false assumption that one can violate ethical principles so long as there is no clear and immediate harm to others. It treats ethical obligations simply as factors to be considered in decision making rather than ground rules. Problem areas: asking for or giving special favors to family, friends, or politicians, disclosing nonpublic information to benefit others, using one's position for personal advantages (e.g., use of official title/letterhead to get special treatment).

VI. "It Can't Be Wrong, Everyone's Doing It."
A false "safety in numbers" rationale fed by the tendency to uncritically adopt cultural, organizational, or occupational behavior systems as if they were ethical.

VII. "It's OK If I Don't Gain Personally."
Justifies improper conduct done for others or for institutional purposes on the false assumption that personal gain is the only test of impropriety. A related more narrow excuse is that only behavior resulting in improper *financial gain* warrants ethical criticism.

VIII. "I've Got It Coming."
Persons who feel they are overworked or underpaid rationalize that minor "perks" or acceptance of favors, discounts, or gratuities are noth-

© 1985 Universal Press Syndicate

"Wait a minute, Stan. ... These are good hubcaps. If we don't take 'em, it's a cinch some other bears will."

The Far Side by Gary Larson
THE FAR SIDE © FARWORKS, INC. Used by permission of UNIVERSAL PRESS SYNDICATE. All rights reserved.

ing more than fair compensation for services rendered. Also used to excuse all manner of personnel policy abuses (sick days, insurance claims, overtime, personal phone calls or photocopying, theft of supplies, etc.)

IX. "I Can Still Be Objective."

Ignores the fact that a loss of objectivity always prevents perception of the loss of objectivity. Also underestimates the subtle ways in which gratitude, friendship, anticipation of future favors, and the like affect judgment. Does the person providing you with the benefit believe that it will in no way affect your judgment? Would the benefit still be provided if you were in no position to help the provider in any way?

Reprinted by permission of the Joseph and Edna Josephson Institute of Ethics.

 EXERCISE

Purpose: To understand common rationalizations used to excuse unethical behavior and to see how these apply to specific cases.

Give examples for each of the above rationalizations. For example, under **I. "If It's Necessary, It's Ethical,"** you might cite unethical behavior on the part of campaign representatives carried out to ensure the election of their candidate. Or, consider the following case:

Ohio Reverend, Feeding Poor with Illegal Stamps, Faces Jail

by Mitch Weiss,
Associated Press, *Contra Costa Times*, November 17, 1996

TOLEDO, OHIO. The Rev. Slim Lake sees nothing wrong with buying food stamps illegally and using them to feed the homeless, recovering alcoholics, and drug addicts—he's an urban Robin Hood to some.

Authorities, however, say the "Rev. Slim" is breaking the law and have charged him with food stamp trafficking.

The ex-con and founder of God's Church of the Streets faces 15 to 40 years in jail. He seems undaunted.

"You know, I've been buying food stamps to feed my congregation since I started my ministry," Lake said. "How can you put somebody in jail for feeding the hungry? If that's a crime, then put me in jail."

Lake has served barbecued ribs, chicken and ham sandwiches to as many as 300 people at an inner city park every Sunday for seven years.

He buys the food with the stamps and some of the $1,600 in disability pay he receives each month since he hurt his back in 1980 while working as a city street cleaner.

Not everyone loves Lake, a former drug dealer, crack addict and street hustler who has been arrested more than 30 times. Some residents of a housing project near the park say the man born Charles Lake is bad news.

"I just don't trust him," said Charles Robinson, 52. "I don't know what it is. He brings in a bad group of people. Bad group."

Lake has been in and out of jail since 1978, when he accidentally shot a friend in the head.

The friend survived, but Lake served six months in jail and once he got out, he sold drugs and stolen goods.

He says God told him to establish his church, and to some residents Lake is a godsend.

They say he helps when they are in trouble, takes them to supermarkets to buy groceries and is around just to talk.

"He's just like a brother and good friend," said Willie Valliant, a 37-year-old recovering alcoholic and drug addict.

Lake admits he buys the food stamps at discount rates on the street and exchanges them for food, but said he was set up.

His arrest came after an undercover police officer offered him $500 worth of food stamps for $300, he said.

Try to come up with a variety of situations—personal, social, and political—in which these rationalizations are used. If the class is doing this exercise in groups, the examples can be shared with the entire class.

Consider whether you rationalize any of your behavior in the ways mentioned on the list of common nationalizations.

Chapter Highlights

1. Value assumptions are beliefs about what is good and important or bad and unimportant; because these beliefs are taken for granted, they are part of the foundation of a person's argument.

2. Conflicts between value assumptions need to be addressed before fruitful discussion over value-saturated conclusions can take place.
3. Ethics are standards of conduct that reflect values.
4. There are several schools of thought about ethics, including libertarianism, utilitarianism, egalitarianism, Judeo-Christian principles, and universal ethical norms.
5. Ideal values are held by an individual in a theoretical sense; real values are held theoretically and also practiced.
6. Ethics are evident in our behavior as we advocate for ideas and make decisions.
7. Several "tests" have been developed to help people make ethical decisions: these include the role exchange test, the universal consequences test, the new cases test, and the higher principles test.
8. Ethical decision making is undermined when common rationalizations are used to support unethical practices.

Articles for Discussion and Composition

It May Not Be Plagiarism, But It's a Rip-Off

by Howard Rosenberg
Los Angeles Times, July 11, 1990

TV news fibs in so many ways.

If it's not the playacting of ratings sweeps series, it's the false promise made to hold viewers through a commercial, that titillating stories are "coming up next." If it's not on-camera reporters taking bows for the work of off-camera field producers, it's newscasts blending electronic press kits in with staff-gathered news.

These are relatively small deceptions.

As the following episode shows, the more you perpetuate the small lie, the easier it is to step up to the big one.

It was last Thursday and featured on KCAL Channel 9's "Prime 9 News" at 10 p.m. was a breezy story lamenting the decline of that great

American institution, the drive-in movie. The tape package was introduced live from the studio and given a voice-over narration by KCAL's hammy entertainment reporter, John Corcoran.

Afterward, anchors Larry Carroll and Kate Sullivan seemed pleased with Corcoran's story.

One problem. A small one, really . . .

It *wasn't* Corcoran's story. It was Gloria Hillard's story.

"I was angry," said Hillard, a CNN reporter covering entertainment from the network's Los Angeles bureau. "One of the most sacred tenets of journalism is that you don't take someone else's words and pass them on as your own."

Not sacred to everyone, obviously.

Hillard's story aired July 4 on CNN, a witty, charming enterprise piece that was shaped in such a personal way that it bore her signature as a reporter. "I guess Corcoran saw my piece, liked it and decided to make it his own," Hillard said.

The story is small, but the principle big, with the terrible P-word looming. "I would be highly offended to be called a plagiarist," Corcoran said later.

Like slapping your own dust jacket on someone else's book, Corcoran gave the drive-in story a brief live intro and close from the anchor desk. Otherwise, the story presented as his on KCAL was virtually a twin of Hillard's—but about a minute shorter.

Gone were a few fleeting sound bites, including Hillard's stand-up in the parking lot of a Culver City drive-in—couldn't have that if it was Corcoran's piece. Gone also was Hillard's voice. But her written words remained with only slight changes, spoken instead by Corcoran as if they were his.

How is it that Hillard's two-minute 40-second story—not only her footage and interviews but also her 226-word script—were at Corcoran's disposal?

Along with KTLA Channel 5 and KTTV Channel 11 in Los Angeles and many other independent stations throughout the nation, KCAL has a reciprocal agreement with CNN for mutual use of stories. Wire services such as the Associated Press have similar agreements with their clients.

In another way that deceit is built into the system, stations don't even have to credit CNN, who thus becomes a party to the deception.

"They are free to use our material in any way they want," said CNN's Los Angeles bureau chief, David Farmer. He said that he'd heard of nothing akin to the Hillard-Corcoran matter previously happening in Los Angeles. "But I feel it must happen quite a bit around the country," he added. "We facilitate it by sending out scripts."

There surely are newspapers, too, that attach their own reporters' bylines to wire stories—but no newspapers with integrity.

Hillard said she knew CNN had agreements with stations for exchanging footage, but didn't know that these agreements provided for verbatim use of scripts without attribution.

Legal it may be.

Ethical it isn't.

Corcoran sounded almost shocked that anyone would think that his usurping Hillard's words without giving credit was either misleading or unethical. "I don't have any problem with it ethics-wise," Corcoran said. "Ninety-nine percent of my stuff I write. I didn't rewrite that one, and part of the reason is that I'm moving my family into a new house." Well, as long as there's a valid reason.

Corcoran noted that using words written by others without attribution "is standard procedure throughout television. When anchors read copy written for them by others," he added, "they don't say, 'written by so-and-so.'"

Because CNN allows its scripts to be used "word-for-word," Corcoran insisted, his voice-over with Hillard's words was not plagiarism. Besides, he added, "I put my own inflections on a story."

Words by Hillard, inflections by Corcoran.

"I'm not the kind of guy who's gonna go out and steal anybody's work," Corcoran said. "Trust me."

Yet the narrations on the CNN and KCAL stories track almost identically, as the following excerpts show.

Hillard: And remember that pizza? It's still here, and of course kids even work up a real good appetite at the drive-in's playground. And the drive-ins are a pretty good bargain at $4.50 for adults, and kids under 12 are free.

Corcoran: And remember that pizza? It's still here, and of course kids even work up a real good appetite at the drive-in's playground. And the drive-ins are pretty good bargains. That's $4.50 for adults. Kids under 12 are free.

Hillard: And how about a kid's point of view on drive-ins over walk-ins?

Corcoran: What about drive-ins over walk-ins?

Hillard: But they're disappearing. The Studio Drive-In is one of only a couple dozen left in Southern California. And it's scheduled for the bulldozer. The high cost of land outbid the box office, and soon the condos will be here.

Corcoran: But drive-ins are disappearing. The Studio Drive-In is one of only a couple of dozen left here. And it's scheduled for the bulldozer. The high cost of land outbid the box office, and soon the condos will be here.

And so on and so on the two stories went . . .

KCAL news director Bob Henry saw nothing improper in what Corcoran did and, incredibly, refused to discount the possibility that the same thing could happen again with his blessing.

He called this "a non-issue." Making Hillard's work sound almost too trivial to matter, he said that "a feature on drive-ins is sort of a discretionary story."

Yet it was significant enough for KCAL to use in an evening newscast and then repeat the next day in its noon newscast. KCAL, Henry snapped, can "use news from CNN any way we want."

While ethics, like drive-in movies, fade into the sunset.

© 1990, *Los Angeles Times.* Reprinted by permission.

Questions for Discussion

1. What is the ethical problem discussed by the author of this article?
2. Do you agree with the author's conclusions?
3. Are there situations you can think of in which something may be legal but is not ethical? What about situations in which something is not legal but is ethical?

Music, to Wal-Mart's Ears, Should be "Clean"

by Steve Morse
Boston Globe, Dec. 9, 1996

Today's pop music stars are more and more running up against the Wal-Mart—meaning the 2,300 stores across the nation that won't carry record albums with "parental advisory" stickers and will even ask artists to change objectionable lyrics and CD covers.

These "clean versions" are then stocked on the shelves of the retail giant, which last year accounted for nearly 10 percent of the 615 million compact discs sold domestically in what has become an annual $12 billion dollar recording industry.

Wal-Mart is the country's leading pop music retailer, but there are growing fears among musicians, record executives and media watchdogs that Wal-Mart's role of "Morality Police," to quote one record executive, may change the way that music is made.

"Wal-Mart is a great place to buy shirts, but I wouldn't buy my music there," cautions Chuck D of the rap group Public Enemy, who admits to cleaning up select versions of the group's last record to appease Wal-Mart.

It's a bible-belt mentality, but as an artist, you have to decide whether you're going to put up or shut up," Chuck D added during a recent stop in Boston.

An extensive letter-writing campaign, fueled by anti-censorship groups like the Massachusetts Music Industry Coalition, the California-based Parents for Rock and Rap and Ohio-based Rock Out Censorship, is now taking complaints to Wal-Mart directly.

More Support than Complaints

Yet Wal-Mart spokesman Dale Ingram, reached at the company's headquarters in Bentonville, Arkansas, says that letters of support for Wal-Mart's policies far outnumber the complaints. "Many of our customers understand what we're attempting to do here." he says, "We don't have a bank of censors. We're really just like all retailers. We want to know what our products are."

Wal-Mart has asked artists and their labels to clean up records for years, but the issue crystallized with a recent *New York Times* article and the banning of Sheryl Crow's new album because of the lyric: "Watch our children as they kill each other with a gun they bought at Wal-Mart discount stores." Crow refused to change the verse.

(Not all Wal-Marts sell guns and company spokesman Ingram says that stores comply with local laws regarding firearms. However, Wal-Mart has been sued twice by relatives of people killed with guns bought at its stores.)

The number of albums affected is small—about 10 to 15 out of the several hundred albums released each month—it's the principle of censorship that has rankled many musicians.

However, as singer Adam Duritz of the Counting Crows notes, "It's a legal form of censorship. It's a shame, but I don't see how you can possibly legislate against it."

Even other retailers are upset. "I'm disgusted, but not with Wal-Mart," says Russ Solomon, owner of Tower Records. "They have a right to sell anything they want, as we all do. I'm disgusted by the record companies that pander to them by changing the albums."

The profit motive is the culprit here. "We would change an album if an artist went along with it," says Andre Harrell, president and CEO of

Motown Records. "We've changed records by (rapper) Da Brat. We found out that a lot of little kids buy her records, even 9-year-old kids. So we felt this was one way to reach them." "The key informing principle is that everybody is apprised of it and everybody agrees to it," says Timothy White, editor of Billboard.

Covering the Covers

Many artists have made adjustments. Alternative pop singer Beck agreed to delete an obscenity for a cleaned-up version of his first album. "Mellow Gold," sent to Wal-Mart and K-Mart stores. Rappers Busta Rhymes and Junior M.A.F.I.A. have done clean versions of albums (which have the words "clean version") written on them.

The Butthole Surfers agreed to change their name to B.H. Surfers on CD jackets. John Mellencamp recently agreed to airbrush out images of Jesus Christ and the devil on his latest CD, "Mr. Happy Go Lucky."

Mellencamp spokeswoman Dawn Bridges says, "John didn't design the cover or conceive it, so he doesn't feel terribly personal about it. He said. 'It's OK, fine.' It's not like he was asked to change his music."

Meanwhile, Wal-Mart is adamant about doing nothing wrong. "When you serve 70 million customers a week, you're going to have some people who disagree with you sometimes," says Ingram.

Reprinted courtesy of *The Boston Globe.*

Questions for Discussion

1. What is the conflict of values between stores like Wal-Mart and musicians? What priority do you put on these values?
2. To what extent do you think the "profit motive" is involved on both sides of this controversy?
3. Have big retailers gained too much control over consumer choices or are there other ways to have convenient access to CDs?
4. How do you define broad terms like *censorship* and *obscenity?* Is it censorship for a retailer to refuse to sell music when it believes the majority of its customers would find the music offensive? What kinds of lyrics, if any, would you call ob-

scene? Would a lyric suggesting that people of one group kill people of another group be protected as free speech? Why or why not?

Student Markets Primer on the Art of Cheating

Rutgers Senior Finds His $7 How-To Is in Demand Among College Students

by Anthony Flint
Boston Globe, February 3, 1992

One of the hottest books on college campuses isn't the latest collection of Calvin and Hobbes—it's a book about cheating.

"Cheating 101" is a how-to guide on shortcuts to a degree—effective places to hide crib sheets, systems of foot signals for sharing multiple-choice answers, places to buy term papers, and dozens of other tips.

Michael Moore, 24, a Rutgers University senior and author of the book, has sold 5,000 copies, mostly at Rutgers, Ohio State and the University of Maryland. He recently returned from a marketing road trip to Penn State. And he plans to go to Boston, home to 11 colleges and universities, to hawk the $7 book around spring break.

"We're going to hit Boston right after we hit Daytona Beach in March."

Moore, a journalism major, contracts with a printer to produce the 86-page book and sells it mostly out of his home in Hopewell, N.J. But because of the book's popularity, he takes sales operations on the road from time to time. Sometimes aided by a pre-visit article in a student newspaper, he sets up a table in a fraternity house or a room on campus and watches the money roll in.

"Students love it," said Moore, who described his weekend selling session at Penn State University and St. Francis College as "a mob scene." The trip was good for 1,150 copies.

Moore said that in addition to students snapping up the guide, several college administrators, lawyers and clinical psychologists have ordered it too—presumably as a form of counterintelligence.

Moore makes no excuses about the profits he reaps from the book, and acknowledges that he set out to make money. But he also considers "Cheating 101" to be a commentary on the shortcomings of higher education: ill-prepared professors more concerned with research, dreary required courses and the lack of training for real-world applications.

"I thought it would be a good opportunity to point out what I believe are the permanent problems in education," said Moore, who said his experience in college has been sour. "It's an indictment of the system. Maybe somebody will make some changes, to curb cheating and make college a better place."

Cheating, Moore said, is a response to the shortcomings that students see. It flourishes because often professors are not interested or look the other way, he said.

"Students just don't cheat because they're lazy or hung over," he said. "They see a professor who's not interested in what they're doing, so students aren't going to be interested in learning. That's a natural defense mechanism."

Rutgers officials, while praising Moore's entrepreneurial skills, have sharply criticized "Cheating 101" as a blatant violation of academic ethics. Some have drawn parallels to Michael Milken and Ivan Boesky, describing the book as the scholar's quick—and dishonest—route to success.

The penalties for cheating vary from school to school, but frequently include suspension or expulsion. Most colleges spell out the rules against cheating or plagiarizing in student codes provided to all freshmen.

Some educators are using the book as an opportunity to teach about ethics. Carol Oppenheim, a communications professor at Boston's Emerson College, recently led a discussion with students on whether a student newspaper should run an advertisement for the book.

"It's an interesting teaching opportunity about a real ethical dilemma," Oppenheim said.

Moore said the wrath of college administrators is to be expected. "It's a manual about their mistakes, their shortcomings and failures. It's like a bad audit."

But he denies that he is engaging in anything dishonest or unethical.

"I don't think people that are buying the book have never cheated before. They already know a lot of the methods. I'm not making a cheater out of anybody," he said.

"There's 'Final Exit,' a book on how to get out of drunk driving, a book on how to get out of speeding tickets," Moore said. "I'm making an honest living. I'm not dealing drugs. I'm just exercising my First Amendment rights."

Reprinted courtesy of *The Boston Globe.*

Questions for Discussion

1. Comment on Moore's statements: "They see a professor who's not interested in what they're doing, so students aren't going to be interested in learning. That's a natural defense mechanism."

   "It's an indictment of the system. Maybe somebody will make some changes, to curb cheating and make college a better place."

   "I don't think people that are buying the book have never cheated before. They already know a lot of the methods. I'm not making a cheater out of anybody."

   "I'm making an honest living. I'm not dealing drugs. I'm just exercising my First Amendment rights."

2. If your professor for a particular course looked the other way when students cheated, would you feel justified in cheating? Why or why not?

3. Do you find that the discussion of this book by the *Boston Globe* and advertisements for the book in student newspapers gives the book a legitimacy that it might not otherwise have? Would it make students feel more or less inclined to read it? On what do you base your answer?

4. Should Moore be allowed to advertise in student newspapers and to sell his book on campus? Why or why not?

5. What is the "real ethical dilemma" concerning this book that is mentioned by Professor Oppenheim? Do you believe there are other ethical dilemmas involved?

6. Is it OK to cheat if you feel that the system is cheating you?

Ideas for Writing or Speaking

1. Take a position on Moore's criticisms of "ill-prepared professors more concerned with research, dreary required courses, and the lack of training for real-world applications." To what

extent, if any, is Moore's perception valid? If not, why not? If so, what should be done about these problems? Give reasons for your conclusion.

2. Consider Moore's comment that the book "Cheating 101" is an effective "commentary on the shortcomings of higher education." Write on either the shortcomings or benefits of higher education as if you were trying to convince someone who was considering going to college. Use your own experience as support, but include objective sources of evidence as well.

3. See if your college has a code of ethics about cheating and plagiarizing. If so, write about this code; take a position on the principles given (agree or disagree with them) and give support for your conclusions. If your college does not have a code of ethics, write one and justify (give reasons for) each of the principles you include.

4. "The Legacy I'd Like to Leave"

Imagine that you are eighty years old. Your son, daughter, niece, nephew, husband, wife, friend, or co-worker is making a speech about you at a party held in your honor. In this speech, he or she mentions your fine qualities and the things you have accomplished in your life. He or she talks about the special traits you have that are treasured by those who know and love you. Write the speech, using this format:

   a. List personal qualities and how they have been specifically evidenced in your life.

   b. List the accomplishments you will have achieved. Again, be specific in your descriptions.

   c. Then, analyze what you would need to do (either internally or externally, or both) to merit that kind of tribute in your senior years. What ideal values would have to become real for you? What choices would you have to make about your career, your personal life, and your priorities?

5. Write an essay in which you take a position (agree or disagree) on one of the following quotes. Support your conclusion about the quote with specific reasons.

   a. "Uncle Sam has no conscience. They don't know what morals are. They don't try to eliminate an evil because it's evil, or because it's illegal, or because it's immoral; they eliminate it only when it threatens their existence."
       Malcolm X, *Malcolm X Speaks* (1965), p.3

    b.   "The difference between a moral man and a man of honor is that the latter regrets a discreditable act, even when it has worked and he has not been caught."
        H.L. Mencken, *Prejudices: Fourth Series* (1924), p.11

    c.   "The great secret of morals is love."
        Percy Bysshe Shelley, *A Defence of Poetry* (1821)

    d.   "We must never delude ourselves into thinking that physical power is a substitute for moral power, which is the true sign of national greatness."
        Adlai Stevenson, speech, Hartford, Connecticut, September 18, 1952

  e. 1. Judgments are absolutely necessary. Without them, the issue of choice has no meaning because everything is equal.

      2. I believe we are the sum total of all that we do, i.e. what we "do" is who we "are." This is true because as adults we make deliberate choices in our actions. Therefore, our actions describe our inner selves, what sacrifices we're willing to make, what evil we're willing to perpetrate. It is with awareness that we persist in negative, ugly, and destructive deeds in one or more areas. Our actions are the blueprint of our character.

  3. Values give meaning to live, and all its otherwise mundane aspects.

Dr. Laura Schlessinger, *How Could You Do That?* HarperCollins (1996), p.189

CHAPTER THREE

Reality Assumptions

It's Eleven O'Clock: Do You Know Where Your Assumptions Are?

A critical thinker understands that people have different assumptions about the world that form the basis for their opinions; he or she also examines these assumptions.

A critical thinker understands basic patterns of deductive and inductive reasoning.

This chapter will cover:

◆ Reality assumptions
◆ Patterns of deductive reasoning
◆ Introduction to inductive reasoning

We learned in the last chapter that when an issue involves a conflict of values, we need to examine those values foundational to the argument under consideration; in other words, there is no point in bringing in evidence to support a point of view until we address the issue of clashing values.

For example, if someone believes that legalizing drugs is morally wrong, he or she will probably not be moved by a lot of statistics that show that we could save money and cut down on crime by legalizing drugs. An individual with a strong value assumption on an issue is not usually swayed by a discussion of practical benefits of a policy or an action that contradicts his or her values. When a discussion neglects to consider conflicting value assumptions on both sides of an issue, stalemates occur, and new and improved evidence does little to help these stalemates.

The critical thinker who wants to argue on a value-saturated issue needs to clearly and directly address the conflict in values and try to persuade the other side to rethink their value assumptions on that issue.

Reality Assumptions

Another foundational aspect to any argument is the underlying assumptions about reality that the various advocates for an issue hold. Reality assumptions are beliefs about what is true and factual about the world. They are based on the unique experience and education of each individual. Reality assumptions are sometimes directly stated by a writer or speaker and they are sometimes implied.

REMINDER

While conflicts in value assumptions address the question "What is right?" or "What should we do or be?", conflicts in reality assumptions address the questions "What is true and factual?" and "What do we take for granted or as a given fact?" Critical thinkers need to be aware of the assumptions that are basic to arguments they are hearing or making.

The fascinating element of assumptions is that they are often hidden to the people arguing for different conclusions. Finding hidden assumptions in arguments is like reading or watching mysteries; you accumulate clues from what people say and then make guesses about what important things they *believe* but aren't directly *stating*.

One person may assume that the only way to deal with terrorists is through a show of strength, whereas another person assumes that the only effective approach is negotiation. Notice that these two individuals probably hold the same values; both believe terrorism is wrong and is a global problem.

They also may share the value of the importance of world peace. Their conflict is about effective methodology; that is, they have different ideas (assumptions) about what terrorists are like and what works best in dealing with them. They have different views of reality.

REMINDER

An assumption can be defined as a belief, usually taken for granted, that is based on the experience, observations, or desires of an individual or group.

When two people or two groups hold different assumptions, they need to stop and examine the underlying assumptions that frame their arguments rather than building arguments on those assumptions. As hidden assumptions are brought to the surface, light is shed on the different positions taken on an issue. Then "all the cards are on the table" and people have the opportunity to modify assumptions or to see more clearly why they have a strong conviction about an assumption.

SKILL

A critical thinker examines the reality assumptions of self and others that form the foundations of arguments.

DETECTING REALITY ASSUMPTIONS

One reason that some assumptions are hidden from us is that they are so deeply ingrained; they may only surface when we come across a person or a group who holds different assumptions. We may be confronted with a set of assumptions different than our own when we are involved in a classroom debate. Or, this process of confronting the "facts" that we take for granted may occur when we are in an unfamiliar situation, like when we travel to a new place and are exposed to a different culture.

Most North Americans assume if an interview or meeting is set for 1:00, then the arrival time should be slightly before 1:00, but people from other cultures may view time more loosely. The expected arrival time could be anywhere between 1:00 and 3:00 for members of some cultures. Because of the differing assumptions across cultures, North Americans who are sent abroad by their organizations are often given training about the assumptions commonly made in the country they will be visiting.

When traveling to another country, we can be sensitive to what is expected of us as visitors. In defending our conclusions on an issue, however, we need to bring the differing assumptions to light so that the discussion is clear and rational.

Examples of Differing Reality Assumptions

- Some people assume that anyone can change and, therefore, that any prisoner can be rehabilitated. Other people assume there are individuals who are "career criminals" with no hope of being rehabilitated.

- Some people assume that the way to increase employment is to lower taxes. Other people assume that the way to increase employment is to establish more federal programs that would provide jobs for the unemployed.

- Some people assume that homosexuality is a condition established in the genetic code before birth. Other people assume that homosexuality is a result of a set of environmental circumstances.

Other assumptions involve differing definitions of words:

- One person assumes that "love" is an emotion that may or may not be permanent. Another person assumes that "love" is a commitment that is not based on emotional changes.

In an article on the dispute among obesity experts over the definition of fat, Steve Rubenstein writes:

> The United States defines a fat person as anyone with a "body mass index," or BMI, of 27.6 or higher. The World Health Organization defines a fat person as anyone with a BMI of 25 or higher." As a result of these different definitional assumptions, "Americans don't actually weigh any more, according to the latest numbers. But, in keeping with the leaner international threshold for fatness, more of them are fat.[2]

The key here is to realize that individuals make assumptions about reality, whether we realize it or not. We need to examine the assumptions we make and try to detect the assumptions that others make. When we have a foundational disagreement about reality assumptions, we should discuss those assumptions before we discuss any arguments built upon them. For example, if we believe that people can be rehabilitated, we must understand why we believe that and be able to defend our basic belief. We also need to understand why someone else would believe that people cannot be rehabilitated.

Often, individuals presenting arguments will comment: "you are assuming that . . ." or "this argument is based on the assumption that . . . ." These phrases help us identify the foundational, but unstated, elements of an argument.

For example, in a *New York Times* report on the efforts of both Democratic and Republican candidates to present themselves as

[2]　Steve Rubenstein, "Millions Suddenly Became Fat Without Gaining Any Weight," *San Francisco Chronicle*, October 11, 1996, page A6.

champions of the fight against breast cancer, cancer researchers questioned the politicians' assumptions about the disease. One politician from New York claimed that he would shut down an incinerator plant that is throwing carcinogens into the air and water. A New Jersey politician, running for the senate, stated, "The breast cancer rates in New Jersey remain the highest in the nation. There must be a reason, an environmental cause."

The article continues with the scientists' responses to these claims:

> Scientists are disturbed by the misleading information in some campaigns. Dr. Sheila Zahm, deputy chief of the occupational epidemiology branch at the National Cancer Institute, said: "There's not a lot of information linking environmental exposures to breast cancer," even though researchers have looked. What's more, she said that the statement that New Jersey has the nation's highest cancer rate is wrong. The District of Columbia has that distinction, with Delaware second. New Jersey is tied for third with Rhode Island.
>
> . . . Other scientists are repelled by what they see as the condescending assumption in these campaigns: that mentioning breast cancer is a sure way to win the female vote.
>
> Dr. Barbara Weber, a breast cancer researcher at the University of Pennsylvania calls the breast cancer strategy "pretty demeaning." The assumption, she said, is that "women don't care about the deficit or education or Medicare." It suggests, she said, that "what we care about is whether we ourselves will get breast cancer."[3]

THE NEED TO EXAMINE ASSUMPTIONS

In our age of accelerated research in many fields, ideas that were once readily accepted have come into question. Researchers discover that what was assumed to be factual may not be true; it may have been true at one time or it may never have been true at all.

---

[3] Gina Kolata, "Vying for the Breast Vote," *New York Times*, November 3, 1996.

When we build an argument on assumptions that are not grounded in fact, our arguments are faulty and the actions we recommend will not achieve our desired ends. We may sound logical and reasonable, but we are leading ourselves and others astray.

Consider, for example, the following excerpt from an article on suicides in the state of Washington:

Contrary to perceptions, far more people in King County die by their own hand each year than are murdered.

In 1994, 207 people in King County killed themselves, while 109 people were victims of homicide, according to a report on suicide being released by the Seattle-King County Department of Public Health.

"Suicide is one of the major public-health problems in our community," the report begins.

It is the second most common cause of death in the county among adults ages 20 to 24. White and Native American men have the highest suicide rates of all race and gender groups.

. . . The study also debunks a stubborn myth: that the area's often gloomy weather contributes to high suicide rates. The study shows no significant seasonal trend in the rate of deaths. In fact, the number of suicides in King County in 1994 was highest for the month of July.

Other findings: terminal or chronic illness is the top probable cause for suicide.

Other factors: a decline in the quality of life, unemployment, marital and financial problems, relationship problems.

. . . People may think suicides are rarer than they are because the media seldom report them. The media's attention to homicides might lead people to think someone is murdered on every street corner, says Bill McClure, a medical investigator in the King County medical examiner's office. "You're much more likely to pick up your own gun," he said. "The media is very skewed in what they report. Unless you're Kurt Cobain, it doesn't get covered."

. . . Most media don't report suicides, but make exceptions when they are committed in a public place and attract a great deal of attention, or when the person is very prominent in the community.[4]

Good researchers and investigative reporters often uncover questionable assumptions like the ones noted in this article. When we examine assumptions with the goal of discovering what is true, we can take more useful action. Some of the reality assumptions that were discovered to be false about King County include:

1. Homicide is more common than suicide.
2. Gloomy weather is a major factor in the area's high suicide rates.

Considering the new research from the county's Department of Public Health, supervisors in the Seattle-King County may want to put more funding into preventing suicides instead of concentrating their efforts mainly on homicides. In so doing, they can focus on fighting the most common causes of suicide. Rather than looking for antidotes to gloomy weather, they can support efforts to control pain for those who suffer from terminal or chronic illness; also, county officials can offer more services to people who are unemployed or struggling with financial and relationship problems.

Assumptions should be examined in the light of the best available research; then decisions can be optimally helpful and productive.

Another example of the need to examine assumptions relates to the use of prescription medicine. Because of the availability of a variety of new medications and treatments, doctors and pharmacists have to consider more factors in treating patients than they may have in the past. Since harmful, and even fatal, side effects can occur when two different drugs are prescribed to the same patient, pharmacists have to make judgment calls about whether to assume that doctors understand about the drug in-

---

[4]   Jennifer Bjorhus and Peyton Whitely, "New Report Debunks Myths on Suicide," *Seattle Times*, February 15, 1996.

teractions they have prescribed. An investigation by *U.S. News and World Report* states:

> The most crucial link is the doctor. Thus, many pharmacists told *U.S. News* that when the same doctor prescribes two interacting drugs, they are less likely to question his judgment. "If the prescriptions came from two different doctors, that would warrant a call," says pharmacist Gordon Tom of San Francisco. "But if it's the same doctor, we assume he's aware of the interaction." Recent studies show that such trust is often misplaced. The Seldane-erythromycin interaction (which can cause irregular heartbeat, cardiac arrest, and sudden death) is a case in point: despite widely disseminated warnings by the drugs' manufacturers and the federal Food and Drug Administration, 3 to 10 percent of doctors last April still were prescribing the two drugs together.[5]

This investigative report also warns consumers not to assume that pharmacy computer systems that check for drug interactions are always accurate. Dr. David Kessler, past commissioner of the federal Food and Drug Administration, is quoted as saying, "It is simply untenable in 1996 to walk into a pharmacy and receive a bottle of pills and no other information. It is not good patient care."[6]

To prevent patients from making harmful assumptions, pharmacists now ask patients to wait for consultations about the medications they are receiving.

As critical thinkers, we need to actively discover and then question the assumptions underlying arguments so we are not building on a foundation of falsehood. Conversely, when we critically examine what it is we take for granted, we have the advantage of gaining a strong and solid conviction for those ideas and principles we believe to be true. Knowing *why* we believe *what* we believe helps us to be more credible and effective when we present an argument. Examining the reality assumptions of

---

[5] Susan Headden, *U.S. News & World Report,* August 26, 1996, p. 53.

[6] Ibid.

others helps us to understand and assess their arguments more fully.

EXERCISE

What are the assumptions?
Purpose: To detect unstated reality assumptions.

One way to detect reality assumptions is to create a brief outline of an argument you hear. Consider the following examples:

Trials and executions should be televised—the public has the right to know what's going on in our courts. Information about the judicial system needs to be more widely disseminated.

Analyzing this brief argument with the skills we've discussed so far, we could outline the argument as follows:
   Conclusion: Trials and executions should be televised.
   Reason: The public has the right to have more information about the courts and the judicial system.
   Value assumption: Freedom of information is an important value.
   Reality assumption: Televising trials and executions would inform the public about our judicial system.
   Let's look at another brief argument, outlining the conclusion, reasons, value assumptions, and reality assumptions.

All teenagers should have the Hepatitus B vaccination starting at twelve years old. Hepatitus B is a sexually transmitted disease that can be fatal. It can also be transmitted through I.V. drug use.

   Conclusion: All teenagers should have the Hepatitus B vaccination.
   Reasons: Hepatitus B is a sexually transmitted disease.
   Hepatitus B can be fatal.
   It can be transmitted through I.V. drug use.
   Value Assumption: Health and prolonged life are important.

Reality Assumptions: Teenagers are all at risk of being sexually active or using drugs. Children are at risk for these activities starting at age twelve. A vaccination will protect teenagers from the effects of this disease.

Taking these examples, can you create different arguments based on different assumptions about reality?

Now, look at the statements below and find possible assumptions that are being made by the speaker. Often, more than one possible assumption can be found.

After you have completed this exercise, discuss whether you agree with the assumptions you discovered.

1. This is a receptionist position, so we need a mature woman for the job. It's important that our clients feel comfortable as soon as they walk in here.
2. You can't go to the party in that outfit. Everyone will think you're completely clueless about how to dress, and no one will want to be seen with you.
3. The death penalty is proof that we value revenge more than we value people. We should save and rehabilitate people rather than giving up on them.
4. Charlene is really successful—she's only 28 and she's making $70,000 a year!
5. There is good news in that rape is on the decline in this county—there are 20 percent fewer police reports this year than last year at this time.
6. Bolger's coffee is the best—it's mountain grown. That gives it great taste.
7. The people in that town don't care about the homeless—their city council voted against contributing $2000 to a county fund to help the homeless.
8. They won't trade their lunches if you give them Twinkle cupcakes, and Twinkle will give them the energy they need to do well in school.
9. You're going to love this blind date—I've known him since fourth grade and he's a great friend of mine.
10. Let's put the county dump in Smallville—they haven't had a turn as a dump site yet.
11. Let's just live together—why do we need a piece of paper to prove our love?

12. I believe in legalizing marijuana for medicinal purposes. Marijuana should not be legalized for recreational use because it is a mind-altering and habit-forming drug; marijuana is also a gateway to harder drugs like cocaine.

Read the following article about a jury trial, keeping in mind the various assumptions that contribute to the outcome of the trial.

Acquittal Outrages Women

Jury Blames Provocative Miniskirt for Assault

by Brian Murphy
Associated Press

FORT LAUDERDALE, FLA.—Sexual assault counselors and women's groups reacted with anger and disbelief Thursday to a jury's acquittal of a rape suspect on the grounds that the woman wore a lace miniskirt without underwear.

"It's a fairly horrendous verdict," said Ellen Vargyas at the National Women's Law Center in Washington, D.C. "No one, regardless of how they are dressed, should be allowed to be raped under a knife."

The three male and three female Broward Circuit Court jurors publicly justified their verdict Wednesday to acquit a 26-year-old drifter, who then was ordered returned to Georgia to face several other rape and assault charges.

"We felt she asked for it for the way she was dressed," said jury foreman Roy Diamond. "The way she was dressed with that skirt, you could see everything she had. She was advertising for sex."

"She was obviously dressed for a good time, but we felt she may have bit off more than she could chew," said juror Mary Bradshaw.

The 22-year-old woman testified that Steven Lord abducted her at knife-point from a Fort Lauderdale restaurant parking lot in November 1988 and raped her repeatedly during a trip north on Interstate 95. She said she escaped five hours later.

Defense attorney Tim Day told jurors the woman agreed to have sex with Lord in exchange for $100 and cocaine, but later changed her mind.

Jurors said they also were swayed by the woman's calm demeanor in court, compared to the emotional testimony of a 24-year-old Georgia woman who claims Lord raped her at knife-point last year.

"When the Georgia woman testified, my heart sank," said juror Dean Medeiros. "But when the other one testified, she didn't appear to be shaken up. Basically, we didn't believe her story."

"I thought this was 1989," said Alexander Siegel, attorney for the woman, who was jailed six days in June after failing to answer subpoenas for court appearances. "I guess this means every pervert and nut out there has a license to rape any person who dresses in a manner they think is provocative."

"The whole idea that a woman is asking for it is horrendous," said Dorothea Gallagher of the National Organization for Women's Broward County chapter.

Questions for Discussion

1. What are the underlying assumptions made by the prosecution, the jurors, and the defense in this case?
2. If the plaintiff (the raped woman) had agreed to sex in exchange for $100 and cocaine, but later changed her mind, as stated by the defense, could the defendant have justified or defended his actions? What assumption guides your answer?
3. What assumption underlies the juror's comment, "She didn't appear to be shaken up . . . we didn't believe her story"?

EXERCISE

Purpose: To find assumptions made by professionals in various fields.

Consider your major area of study. What are some assumptions made by people in that field? For example, if you study dance therapy, then you must assume that dance can be psychologically helpful to people. If you study ecology, then you must believe that the environment is a system that needs to be balanced.

Example:

"I am studying Early Childhood Education. It's because I assume children need some structured experiences before they get to kindergarten. I also assume they learn best if they have lots of time to be creative and explore. And I assume they need lots of interaction with other kids to learn to share and relate.

"I have argued with some of my teachers who assume children should learn to read before kindergarten. We know that children can learn to read early and they can learn some math, but my assumption is they'll burn out if they have to study so young. And I also assume they'll catch up and be happier than kids who had to read so soon."

Deductive Reasoning

Up to this point, we have defined the basic elements that make up arguments: issues, conclusions, reasons, value assumptions, and reality assumptions. Now we want to look at the structures of argument, the patterns of reasoning we use in coming to conclusions about information. Knowing common patterns of reasoning will help you:

1. to understand the reasoning process
2. to evaluate the reliability of arguments you hear
3. to discover and examine assumptions underlying reasons and conclusions

Behind even our simplest thoughts and decisions, we can find a pattern of reasoning that led to the thought or decision. Let's take a fictional example of a student with a heavy class schedule. Tom is awakened in the morning by a clock radio; to get a little more sleep, he turns on the snooze alarm. After the third press of the snooze alarm, he gets serious, jumps out of bed, and gets ready for his eight o'clock class. He puts a frozen break-fast in the microwave oven and carefully removes it a few min-utes later. Tom then turns on the T.V., hears an ad for affordable life insurance, and quickly changes the channel. He listens to an ad for a psychic hotline, featuring a famous actress who claims that her psychic told her things that only her closest associates would know. He changes to the weather channel and notes that rain is expected in the afternoon. Tom then looks at the clock, re-alizes that he is leaving later than usual for his class, grabs his hooded raincoat, and rushes out the door. He waits until he is close to the freeway before putting his seat belt on. As he drives onto the on ramp of the freeway, Tom notices two men hitch-hiking in his direction, but he ignores them.

In each phase of Tom's first morning hour, he made deci-sions. If we break these decisions down, we can find a pattern of reasoning for each one. As discussed in the first section of this chapter, we are constantly acting on the basis of reality assump-tions, and we don't usually need to question them. For example, Tom knows that the food cooked in microwave ovens is hot, so he was careful in removing his breakfast. He has found the local weather report to usually be accurate, so he takes his raincoat with him. He knows from experience that his teacher for the eight o'clock class often gives a quiz at the beginning of the hour, so he hurried in order to be in class on time. Consider the rea-soning Tom used for some of his other actions; what might he have reasoned about the alarm clock and the seat belt?

Some of Tom's reasoning is more complicated. He is not in-terested in life insurance, even though he is engaged to be mar-ried in two months, because he reasons that he is too young to die anytime soon. He doesn't pick up the hitchhikers because he reasons that, even though they look like nice guys, there are two of them and they might be criminals; why take any chances?

The psychic information sounds interesting, but he just doesn't believe it. After all, the psychic hotline makes plenty of money from their 900 number. Also, he reasons, if psychics are so knowledgeable, why don't they solve more crimes?

In many of our daily decisions, we don't spend a lot of time questioning our thinking. However, in the important decisions of our life as people in relationships, as citizens, and as consumers, we do need to question why we believe what we believe.

How can we examine how we think when we need to question our own reasoning or the reasoning of others? What tools are available to help us look critically at information and make reasonable decisions? How can we know that we are being "logical" in our thinking?

Those who study reasoning have come up with two general frameworks for understanding how we think: **deductive** and **inductive reasoning.** By understanding these structures, we can examine our own beliefs and evaluate the arguments presented to us. This information empowers our thinking and decision making.

Deductive arguments follow formal patterns of reasoning and are aimed at establishing the certainty of a conclusion. The conclusion's certainty is established when deductive arguments contain true premises (reasons) that are stated in the correct form.

Validity in Deductive Arguments

Fallacious and misleading arguments are most easily detected if set out in correct syllogistic form.

Immanuel Kant

In conversation, we often hear the phrases "That makes sense" or, conversely, "That's not logical." Patterns of deductive reasoning, which are discussed in this section, help us to test whether our thinking is logical.

In a deductive argument, formal patterns are used to test the logic of our reasoning. These patterns give us a tool for "quality control"; when the correct deductive form is followed, we call the argument valid. When the form of a deductive argument is incorrect, the argument is considered invalid; even if the conclusion is true, an invalid form means the conclusion cannot be inferred from the given premises.

Deductive patterns are judged by both form and content. Correct form is the essential ingredient of a valid argument. When correct form is established, we then consider the content of the argument; that is, we examine the truth of the reasons given to support the conclusion.

STOP AND THINK

Form and content are two parts of many disciplines. When someone learns to play an instrument, she first learns how to hold the instrument and how to shape her hands or lips in order to produce the correct sound. When the form is correct, then focus goes to content; the correct notes and expressions are learned and developed. When learning a sport, instructors will first tell students how to hold the ball, bat, club, or racquet and then focus on techniques and strategies.

Let's look at valid forms of deductive argument and then consider invalid (incorrect) forms. Remember that valid forms reflect logical reasoning. Once the reasoning can be established as logical, we can then move on to content and see if the reasoning is true.

An important framework for deductive reasoning is the syllogism. A syllogism is a deductive argument in which a conclusion is inferred from two premises. Let's look at the classic example of a syllogism given by Aristotle more than two thousand years ago:

All men are mortal. (Major premise)
Socrates is a man. (Minor premise)
Therefore, Socrates is mortal. (Conclusion)

This form of deductive reasoning can be coded in letters as follows:

All As are Bs.
m is A.
Therefore, m is B.

In this deductive argument, the first premise (All As are Bs) is a ***universal*** or ***categorical*** statement, a statement in which members of one class are said to be included in another class.

This statement is called the major premise. The second statement is called the minor premise. The final statement is the conclusion that can be logically inferred from the major and minor premises.

Let's look at some other common examples of deductive reasoning, noting their specific forms. The next three begin with **conditional,** or **hypothetical,** statements. In a conditional (hypothetical) statement, we are asserting that if the first part of the statement is true, then the second part is also true. We call the first part (represented by A) the antecedent and the second part (represented by B) the consequent.

1. **Modus Ponens** (this name means "the way of affirmation" or affirming the antecedent).

> **If A, then B,** (Major premise; we are stating that the antecedent leads to the consequent).
> **A.** (Minor premise; we are asserting that the antecedent is true.)
> **Therefore, B.** (conclusion; if the antecedent is true, the consequent is also true).

Example:
> If our team wins the playoff game, it will be in the championship game.
> Our team won the playoff game.
> Therefore, our team will be in the championship game.

Or, in the case of Tom's reasoning, which was discussd at the beginning of this section:

> If the weather person says that it will rain today, I will need my raincoat.
> The weather person says that it will rain today.
> Therefore, I will need my raincoat.

Notice that underlying Tom's reasoning is the assumption that the weather channel is accurate.

REMINDER

Keep in mind the difference between a statement or assertion and an argument. Remember that in a deductive argument, the conclusion is inferred (understood) from the premises that are given. A common error is to take one premise alone as constituting an argument. The first premise given above, "If our team wins the playoff game, it will be in the championship game" is only a statement. This statement, called a hypothetical statement, sets up a condition. The condition needs to be fulfilled (or fail to be fulfilled) for the argument to be complete. Conditional (or hypothetical) statements are used commonly in our lives in the form of warranties, contracts, threats, or predictions.

Your instructor may have given you a contract at the beginning of the semester that states:

If A, then B. If you get 80 percent of the points required, you will receive a B.

This is a conditional or hypothetical statement. It doesn't assert that you have 80 percent of the points in the class or that you have a B. But suppose you add another statement:

A. You have 80 percent of the points required.
If that statement is true, then we arrive at the conclusion that:
Therefore B. You will receive a B in the class.

Note that if the first two statements in this format are true, then the conclusion must be true. When the conclusion must be true, we have deductive certainty.

STOP AND THINK

What are some examples of hypothetical statements you have heard?

---

2. Modus Tollens (Denying the consequent).

> If A, then B.
> not B.
> Therefore, not A.

Example:

> If I have strep throat, then the culture would be positive.
> But the culture was not positive.
> So, I don't have strep throat.

In the case of Tom, our student in the previous example, we can follow his possible reasoning about sleeping longer when he first pressed his snooze button.

> If I have to get up now, my alarm will go off again.
> But my alarm hasn't gone off again.
> Therefore, I don't have to get up now.

3. Chain argument.

> If A, then B.
> If B, then C.
> Therefore, if A, then C.

Examples:

> If you lower the fat in your diet, you will lower your cholesterol.
> If you lower your cholesterol, you will reduce the risk of heart disease.

Therefore, if you lower the fat in your diet, you will reduce your risk of heart disease.

If the defendant's blood is found at the crime scene, then we can connect him with the crime.
If we can connect him with the crime, then we can have him stand trial.
Therefore, if the defendant's blood is found at the crime scene, then we can have him stand trial.

And, in Tom's case:

If I want to get a good grade in this class, I need high quiz points.
If I need high quiz points, I need to get to class on time.
Therefore, if I want to get a good grade in this class, I need to get to class on time.

Remember that deductive arguments must be structured to be considered valid. If our reasoning follows the steps outlined in these forms, our arguments are considered valid. If they do not follow the correct form, we have not provided adequate support for the conclusion, even if the conclusion happens to be true.

CHALLENGE EXERCISE

What's wrong with this picture?
Purpose: To be aware of patterns of argument that are invalid.

Consider the following *invalid* forms and state why they are invalid. If we follow the reasoning pattern they suggest, why is our conclusion still questionable? How could a *valid* deductive argument be made, given the same information?

1. "Affirming the consequent":

    If A, then B.
    B.
    Therefore, A.

Example:
    If Katie didn't take a humanities class, then she didn't graduate.
    Katie didn't graduate.
    Therefore, she didn't take a humanities class.

2. "Denying the antecedent":

    If A, then B.
    not A.
    Therefore, not B.

Example:
    If Jason asks Tonya, she will go to the dance.
    But Jason didn't ask Tonya,
    so she won't go to the dance.

3. "Broken chain argument":

    If A, then B.
    If C, then D.
    Therefore, if A, then D.

Example:
    If the defendant's blood is found at the crime scene, then we can connect him with the crime.
    If the defendant is proven to have committed the crime, then he will face life imprisonment or the death penalty.
    Therefore, if the defendant's blood is found at the crime scene, he will face life imprisonment or the death penalty.

We use deductive reasoning on a daily basis, usually in the form of an *enthymeme*. An enthymeme is a syllogism with a key part or parts implied rather than directly stated. The missing parts—the assumptions of the speaker or writer—are expected to be supplied by the listener or reader. For example, you may say, "We need to stop and get gas on the way to the movies." (This preceding statement is the enthymeme). Written as a syllogism, the reasoning would be:

> If we want to go to the movies in your car, we need to get gas.
> We want to go to the movies in your car.
> Therefore, we need to get gas.

Let's say, though, that your friend responds to your "We need to stop and get gas on the way to the movies" by stating "No we don't; we're fine." His reasoning would look like this:

> If we already have enough gas to get to the movies, we don't need to stop for more.
> We already have enough gas to get to the movies.
> Therefore, we don't need to stop for more.

Truth in Deductive Arguments

The sample disagreement in the preceding paragraph points out an important element of deductive reasoning; a deductive argument may be *valid* (that is, fit the correct form) without being *true*. The conclusion may follow from the premises, but one or both of the premises may not be true, and of course the truth factor is essential to argumentation. What happens if you have a perfect syllogism that states the following?

> All students in this classroom are mice.
> Marcus is a student in this class.
> Therefore, Marcus is a mouse.

Because this syllogism follows the correct format, the conclusion does follow logically from the premises. But are the premises true? Obviously not!

Once you have found a deductive argument to be valid, you evaluate the premises to see if they are true. If the argument is valid *and* the premises are true, then the argument is considered to be **sound.**

When we know that an argument is sound, we can accept the conclusion of that argument with confidence. We can make good decisions based upon the information given in a sound argument.

In short, a good argument needs to have both correct form and reliable content. The chart below illustrates the criteria for a sound argument.

	True	**False**
Valid	Sound Argument: Correct Form True Premises	Unsound Argument: Correct Form, Untrue Premises
Invalid	Unsound Argument: Incorrect Form, True Premises	Unsound Argument: Incorrect Form, Untrue Premises

STOP AND THINK

There is a famous story of a man who goes to visit his doctor because he thinks he is dead. The doctor tries in many ways to reassure the patient that he is indeed alive, but to no avail. Finally, in desperation, the doctor gets a needle, pricks the finger of his patient and says, "Look at that! You're bleeding. That proves you are really alive." The patient looks at his finger in amazement and says, "Well, what do you know. Dead men can bleed!"

Outline the arguments of both the doctor and patient in this story to clearly distinguish between a **valid** *argument and a* **sound** *one.*

REMINDER
1. *Understanding the process of deductive reasoning helps you realize what you are assuming to be true when you state your position on issues.*
2. *When an argument is valid and the premises are true, the conclusion must be true and the argument is called sound.*

The Uses of Deductive Reasoning

Why is it useful to learn the patterns of deductive reasoning? Using deductive reasoning can illuminate our beliefs and help us consider whether those beliefs are reasonable. For example, someone we'll call Linda might say, "I can't take that speech class." Her friend Lavelle asks why and she responds, "I can't take the class because I'd have to give speeches." Linda's confident friend says "So what?" to which Linda says with great emotion "If I have to take a speech class, I'll just fall apart and die!" Lavelle, knowing the principles of deductive reasoning, helps Linda to look at her logic through the pattern of chain argument.

If I take a speech class, I'll have to give speeches.
If I have to give speeches, I'll get nervous.
If I get nervous, I'll fall apart and die.
Therefore, if I take a speech class, I'll fall apart and die.

Considered in this light, Linda is able to see that, although her reasoning is valid, it is not true. She is "catastrophizing" her situation, making it much more serious than it is. Certainly, it may be uncomfortable for her to give a speech, but it is not a life-threatening situation. She can see that discomfort need not be catastrophic. The way we speak sometimes both reveals and creates our thoughts about situations. Using the tools of deductive reasoning to objectify her thoughts, Linda may be able to adjust her thinking to reality, rather than continuing to function with exaggerated fears.

Understanding deductive reasoning patterns is also useful in more formal situations. As an example, consider a prosecutor and a defender presenting arguments to a jury. The Menendez case involved two young men who shot and killed their parents. Everyone agreed that the boys committed the crime. The argument in their trial centered around their motivation: Was the killing a premeditated act by two children hoping to receive an inheritance, or was it an act motivated by years of abuse and a desperate sense of helplessness and rage? Reconstructing the positions of both the prosecution and the defense in simple terms, we might note the following dialogue. The prosecutor's basic argument could be outlined as follows:

If children murder their parents, they deserve to receive life imprisonment or the death penalty.
These children murdered their parents.
Therefore, they deserve to receive life imprisonment or the death penalty.

The defending attorney did not object to the claim that the children murdered their parents, but she added information that brought her to a different conclusion about sentencing:

If children murder parents who abuse them, they deserve a lighter sentence than life imprisonment or the death penalty.
These children murdered parents who abused them.
Therefore, these children deserve a lighter sentence.

To which the prosecutor would reply:

If children are old enough to leave home but choose to stay and murder their parents, they deserve to receive life imprisonment or the death penalty.
These children were old enough to leave home but chose to stay and murder their parents.

Therefore, these children deserve life imprisonment or the death penalty.

To which the defending attorney would argue:

If the children's parents have threatened to find and continue to abuse them and have the money and influence to do so, the children would see no other way to stop the abuse than to murder their parents.
If the children see no other way to stop the abuse other than to murder their parents, then the murder involves extenuating circumstances.
If the murder involves extenuating circumstances, then the children deserve a lighter sentence for murdering their parents.
Therefore, if the children's parents threatened to find and continue to abuse them and had the money and influence to do so, then the children deserve a lighter sentence for murdering them.

When jurors can follow the logic of the arguments presented, they can examine the evidence for both the prosecution and the defense in order to make better determinations.

Summary

When you are confronted with an argument to analyze, take the following steps:

1. First try to phrase the argument in one of the valid forms we have discussed. If the argument does not fit into a proper form, then we say that it is not valid (regardless of whether it is true). If the argument does fit the form (is valid), then
2. Consider the premises to see whether they are true. In the previous example about getting gas for the movies, we can see that both arguments are valid. But one of them is not true; either they have enough gas to make it or they don't.

The person whose premises are true and whose reasoning is valid has presented a **sound** argument.

USING DEDUCTIVE REASONING TO COMBAT PREJUDICE

Prejudicial statements often involve deductive reasoning that is untrue and unproved, but logically valid. Let's say that you hear someone comment: "Of course Lisa's a terrible driver—she's a woman!" This enthymeme could be placed into a syllogistic format as follows:

All women are terrible drivers.
Lisa is a woman.
Therefore, Lisa is a terrible driver.

You can see that if the premises of this syllogism are true, then the conclusion would be true. But the major premise given here could never be proven true; we can't know *all* about any group of individuals.

 EXERCISE

Purpose: To construct syllogisms from prejudicial statements.

Most prejudicial statements can be unraveled as valid arguments with false premises. Think of a prejudicial statement that has been directed at you (or a friend) in the past. Reconstruct that statement into syllogistic form.

Example:
"My friend is on welfare because her husband left her and her two children. She can't find a job that would make enough money for her to afford childcare. When people find out she is on welfare, they tell her she should be working and not sponging off of society. Their reasoning is:

All people on welfare are lazy.
You are on welfare.
Therefore, you are lazy.

There might be some people who fit into this description, but it's unfair to put all people who need welfare into this category. I think if people understood my friend's situation, they would be less judgmental and more sympathetic."

The Premise of Contention

> *"What eludes logic is the most precious element in us, and one can draw nothing from a syllogism that the mind has not put there in advance."*
>
> Andre Gide, *Journals*, June, 1927

Deductive arguments are most reliable in the realm of proven fact. There are some As that do fit into an all-encompassing category (B) and give us valuable information. For example, all women with an HCG (human chorionic gonadotropin) level above 5 are pregnant, and all persons with a blood-alcohol level of .10 in the state of Illinois are legally drunk. You might discover that all members of your immediate family have type O blood. Because of these known "alls," solid conclusions can be drawn; doctors can tell a woman if she is pregnant, police officers in Illinois can give solid evidence to justify a drunk driving arrest, and, if you need a blood transfusion, family members can be approached to volunteer.

However, as soon as we move out of the realm of proven fact, deductive premises can be argued in terms of the *truth* factor. An issue involves controversy, that is, more than one plausible side of an argument. Understanding the process of deduction helps us to outline our own reasoning and the reasoning of others, so that we can see if it is first of all logical (following correct form), and secondly, grounded in truth. Let's look at the reasoning from our previous article, "Acquittal Outrages Women"; we can use our

understanding of deduction to clearly outline the argument of the
defense attorneys:

> All women who dress in a revealing manner are asking to
> be raped.
> A Georgia woman was dressed in a revealing manner.
> Therefore, this woman was asking to be raped.

This syllogism passes the validity test: The conclusion logically follows from the premises. And the woman was dressed in
a manner that revealed her body, so the minor premise is true.
But is the major premise true?

Now consider this syllogism:

> All drivers who speed are subject to a fine.
> You are speeding.
> Therefore, you are subject to a fine.

In this example, you might agree with the major premise, but
question the minor premise.

For our purposes, we will call the questionable premise the
premise of contention. Critical thinkers will argue about the
premise of contention rather than arguing about the conclusion.

When people argue about conclusions, stalemates are in-
evitable. Adults end up sounding like children arguing over who
left the door open.

> "You did it."
> "No, I didn't."
> "Yes, you did."
> "No, I didn't." etc. etc.

Parents who weren't at the scene of the crime have little basis
for a rational judgment in an issue like this. Only real evidence
(fingerprints, videotapes, or witnesses) would help them get to the
truth.

The same frustrating process occurs in some sexual harassment cases, often called "he said, she said" issues. If there are no

witnesses, tapes, letters, or other forms of evidence, then the accuser has no proof of being a victim and the accused has no proof of being innocent. Focusing on conclusions without accompanying evidence statements creates no-win arguments.

So what can we reasonably do in arguments that seem to lead to stalemates? Let's take the highly charged issue of abortion. At demonstrations, we may witness a scene that is hardly more sophisticated than the one between children noted previously, as the advocates for both sides focus on conclusions.

"Unborn children are worthy of protection."
"No, they're not."
"Yes, they are."
"No, they're not." etc. etc.

If we can use deductive reasoning to uncover the beliefs of both sides, we can then focus our efforts on fruitful areas of inquiry. For example, we might outline the "pro-life" argument as follows:

All human life is valuable and worthy of protection.
An unborn child is a human life.
Therefore, an unborn child deserves protection.

Those who are "pro-choice" would find the minor premise the premise of contention; the contentious factor is whether or not an unborn child is a human life. In a similar manner, we might outline the "pro-choice" reasoning:

Tissue masses have no civil rights.
A fetus is a tissue mass.
Therefore, a fetus has no civil rights.

Which is the premise of contention in this syllogism?
Both syllogisms are valid since the conclusions follow from the premises. But the premise of contention in both cases is the minor one. So, each side needs to focus efforts on proving that their minor premise is true.

Note here that the arguments sound different depending on the terminology used—unborn child, fetus, product of conception. Chapter 7 will focus on the power of words to shape our perceptions of an issue.

THE BORN LOSER reprinted by permission of Newspaper Enterprise Association, Inc.

 REMINDER

In deductive arguments, a critical thinker will (1) outline his or her argument and the argument of the other person, (2) determine if the arguments are valid, (3) find the premise(s) of contention, and then (4) argue that his or her premises are correct.

Game: Valid or Invalid, Sound or Unsound

Valid forms used
Modus Ponens
Modus Tollens
Chain Argument
Categorical/Universal Syllogism

Invalid forms used
Affirming the consequent
Denying the antecedent
Broken chain

GAME RULES

Object of the game: to accumulate points by correctly identifying the valid and invalid deductive arguments of the other teams; to gain a clearer understanding of valid and invalid forms by an examination of many examples; to evaluate the soundness of valid arguments.

Form class teams of 3–5 persons each.

Each team should create several deductive arguments that are valid and several that are invalid and put them randomly on paper or index cards; this step may be done as homework before class or in groups during class.

Each team needs: 1 reader, 1 scorekeeper, 1–2 referees.

SCORING

Each team must have at least 8 deductive arguments; some of the arguments should be valid and some invalid.

The lead team (each team is the lead team when they stand in front of the class to read their arguments) earns 1 point for each appropriate example and loses 1 point for each inappropriate example. (In other words, if the lead team presents an invalid argument as valid, they lose 1 point).

Guessing teams win 2 points for each correct answer and lose 1 point for each wrong answer.

In order to receive 2 full points for a correct answer, the guessing team must be recognized by the referee of the lead team and say why the argument is valid or invalid. The answer must satisfy both the lead team and the instructor.

Your instructor may decide to award points toward a grade for this exercise or just to use the game to help you recognize valid and invalid arguments when you see them.

Ideally, a good discussion of what distinguishes valid from invalid arguments will occur as a result of this exercise.

For 2 more points, distinguish the sound from the unsound valid arguments. Discuss which arguments are sound because the premises are true and which are not sound because the premises are not necessarily true (even though they are presented in a valid form).

EXERCISE EXPANDER

After the exercise, look for examples of both valid and invalid and sound and unsound arguments from editorials, political speeches, or your own personal life. Put these examples in syllogistic form and turn them in to your instructor for extra credit or class discussion.

This game offers you another useful opportunity. In our era of competitive argumentation on television or radio talk shows, people often get loud and verbally abusive as they vie for the best "sound bite." When you play this game, try to use only your ability to reason to win the argument, not your ability to be loud or combative.

Introduction to Inductive Reasoning

We have looked at the concept of deductive certainty and the criteria for developing a sound deductive argument. Ideally, all of the issues that we face could be resolved with certainty by following correct reasoning. In our human state, however, there are very few conclusions that can be proven beyond a shadow of a doubt. Even our court system only asks that a conclusion be proven "beyond a *reasonable* doubt." That means the evidence does offer strong support for the conclusion with the reservation that there may be an *unusual* exception. When we offer evidence that gives weight (but not complete certainty) to a conclusion, we are reasoning inductively. We speak of deductive *certainty* (which occurs in a sound argument) and of inductive *strength*.

If we can present evidence to prove that a premise (assertion, statement) is very *likely* to be true, we have valuable information on which to base our decisions. In addition, if we know that there can be exceptions, we can understand them when they occur.

The process of induction occurs when we use facts or research findings to make generalizations. Stated in coded form, we offer proof that most As are Bs. Therefore, if I encounter an A, it is probably a B. However, I realize that there are exceptions.

Inductive arguments are evaluated on the basis of their strength. A strong inductive argument does not guarantee the truth of the conclusion, but rather provides strong support for the conclusion.

> Two kinds of logic are used, inductive and deductive. . . .
> If the cycle goes over a bump and the engine misfires, and
> then goes over another bump and the engine misfires,
> and then goes over a long smooth stretch of road and
> there is no misfiring, and then goes over a fourth bump
> and the engine misfires again, one can logically conclude
> that the misfiring is caused by the bumps. That is induc-
> tion. . . .
> If, from reading the hierarchy of facts about the ma-
> chine, the mechanic knows the horn of the cycle is pow-
> ered exclusively by electricity from the battery, then he can
> logically infer that if the battery is dead the horn will not
> work. That is deduction.

From *Zen and the Art of Motorcycle Maintenance: An Inquiry into Values.*
(New York: William Morrow, 1974), p. 99.

REMINDER
Critical thinkers use the process of induction to draw rea-sonable conclusions and to make thoughtful decisions.

Most of the issues we face on a daily basis involve inductive reasoning. We gather facts from our background experiences and our reading and research—experiential and empirical data—to come to conclusions that make sense to us because of their strength. We then use these conclusions to guide our actions. For example, let's say a woman receives a call from her sister who tells her that she has developed breast cancer. The woman does some research and talks to her own doctor. Her inductive reasoning sounds like this:

Researchers claim that most women who have a family history of breast cancer (A) will develop breast cancer (B). (Most As are Bs.)

My mother (m1) developed breast cancer (Q).
My sister (m2) developed breast cancer (Q).
My two aunts (m3 and m4) died of breast cancer (Q).
Since m1, m2, m3, and m4 are family members, I have a family history (P); I (m5) am P.
Therefore, it is likely that I (m5) will also develop breast cancer (Q).
(Conclusion—m5 will probably be Q, because most Ps are Q).

Can you see that the conclusion "It is likely that I will also develop breast cancer" is not a certainty but a strong possibility? The woman who reasons in this way can now examine her choices in a logical manner. She can do a reasonable risk assessment about her chances of developing cancer and also her chances of recovery if she were to develop this form of cancer. Some women faced with this family history have had healthy breasts removed before cancer could develop. These women will never know if they might have "dodged the bullet" and avoided the disease without having taken these measures. But they reasoned that, in their individual cases, the probability was high enough and the consequences grave enough to justify their actions.

When you reason inductively, you look at evidence and draw conclusions that are not certain, but likely. These conclusions are called inductive generalizations. All inductive generalizations are *possible*, but within the range of possibility, some are much more *probable* than others because they are based on good evidence (see Fig 3.1).

Figure 3.1

Some scholars believe that many deductive premises are derived from previous inductive arguments. For example, a parent may present the following major premise of a deductive argument to a son or daughter heading off to college:

"If you charge more on your credit card than you can afford, you will get yourself into debt."

The student—let's call him David—leaves for school and is suddenly faced with the responsibility of handling finances above the tuition and housing which his parents have paid and a small scholarship which covers books. David gets a part-time job at a video store to cover the expenses of clothing, entertainment, gas, insurance and repairs for his car, and any other goodies he may wish to buy.

David has been careful not to use the credit card that was sent to him, but he does keep it in his wallet, just in case. As the school year goes by, some unexpected expenses use up most of his salary and David starts using the credit card: he has to have a brake job on his car, he wants new clothes for a dance, and he meets someone that he'd like to take out for dinner and a movie once a week.

When some of David's friends ask him to join them on a vacation during the winter break, he knows he can't afford to go, but decides to charge the trip anyway. When he returns from his vacation, a bill from his credit card company reveals that his monthly payment has gone up for the third time.

If he took the time, David might reason:

The first time I overcharged, I owed more to the credit card company each month.
The second time I overcharged, I owed so much that I had to extend my working hours to pay the credit card bill.
The third time I overcharged, I realized that my monthly payment will be used just to pay the finance charge and it will take several years to pay off what I owe.
Because of all of these incidents, I'm in debt.
Therefore, if I overcharge on credit cards, I will be in debt.

David has come to this conclusion inductively, through a series of experiences. He has learned from his mistakes that it is harmful to overcharge on his credit cards. Probably, David will pass his wisdom on to his future children, in the form of a deductive argument:

> If people overcharge on their credit cards, they will be in debt.
> I overcharged on my credit card.
> Therefore, I was in debt.

His children may be wise enough to take his word for it, to learn from the truth of the general principle. But they may be like many of us and only come to the truth inductively, through trial and error. Inductive generalizations, such as those discovered in David's case are also foundational to more formal decision-making situations.

For example, once a jury in a criminal trial understands the arguments of both prosecution and defense, they proceed to use inductive reasoning to examine the evidence. They receive some information which is definitely true; for example, they may know that a murder has been committed. They may also receive undeniably factual information about the blood type of the victim and of the defendant and about the legal issues involved in the case. These facts can be presented in sound deductive arguments.

However, the jury will also hear different interpretations about what may be concluded from the given factual information. Both sides will try to convince the jury of the strength of their arguments by presenting the statements of experts and of witnesses, by presenting research and statistics, by using examples of similar cases, and offering a pattern that would (or would not) cause the defendant to commit the crime. These interpretations are expressed as inductive generalizations.

In the following chapters, we will focus on methods of examining and assessing the strength of evidence used to support conclusions in inductive arguments, whether the issue is the guilt or innocence of a defendant, the qualifications of a political candidate, the usefulness of a product or service, or the importance of a social cause.

When you understand these forms of inductive reasoning, you are better equipped to evaluate the quality of the support people give for their conclusions. You can then defend against poorly supported arguments and also know why you are accepting good arguments. You will be ready to strengthen your own reasoning and make wiser decisions based on that reasoning.

Chapter Highlights

1. Reality assumptions are beliefs about what is true and false; these beliefs are often taken for granted, and they are part of the foundation of a person's argument.
2. Reality assumptions need to be brought to light and examined so that those who make them do not build arguments on untrue or unconsidered premises.
3. In deductive reasoning, the conclusion is inferred from the premises. When the premises follow correct syllogistic form, the argument is considered valid. When an argument is valid and the premises are true, the conclusion must be true and the argument is called sound.

Articles for Discussion

Just Walk on By

A Black Man Ponders His Power to Alter
Public Space

by Brent Staples
Ms. Magazine, 1986

My first victim was a woman—white, well dressed, probably in her early twenties. I came upon her late one evening on a deserted street in Hyde Park, a relatively affluent neighborhood in an otherwise mean, impoverished section of Chicago. As I swung onto the avenue behind her, there seemed to be a discreet, uninflammatory distance between us. Not so. She cast back a worried glance. To her, the youngish, black man—a broad six feet two inches with a beard and billowing hair, both hands shoved into the pockets of a bulky military jacket—seemed menacingly close. After a few more quick glimpses, she picked up her pace and was soon running in earnest. Within seconds she disappeared into a cross street.

That was more than a decade ago. I was twenty-two years old, a graduate student newly arrived at the University of Chicago. It was in the echo of that terrified woman's footfalls that I first began to know the unwieldy inheritance I'd come into—the ability to alter public space in ugly ways. It was clear that she thought herself the quarry of a mugger, a rapist, or worse. Suffering a bout of insomnia, however, I was stalking sleep, not defenseless wayfarers. As a softy who is scarcely able to take a knife to a raw chicken—let alone hold it to a person's throat—I was surprised, embarrassed, and dismayed all at once. Her flight made me feel like an accomplice in tyranny. It also made it clear that I was indistinguishable from the muggers who occasionally seeped into the area from the surrounding ghetto. That first encounter, and those that followed, signified that a vast, unnerving gulf lay between nighttime pedestrians—particularly women—and me. And I soon gathered that being perceived as dangerous is a hazard in itself. I only needed to turn a corner into a dicey situation, or crowd some frightened, armed person in a foyer somewhere, or make an errant move after being pulled over by a policeman. Where fear and weapons meet—and they often do in urban America—there is always the possibility of death.

In that first year, my first away from my hometown, I was to become thoroughly familiar with the language of fear. At dark, shadowy intersections in Chicago, I could cross in front of a car stopped at a traffic light and elicit the thunk, thunk, thunk, thunk of the driver—black, white, male, or female—hammering down the door locks. On less traveled streets after dark, I grew accustomed to but never comfortable with people who crossed to the other side of the street rather than pass me. Then there were the standard unpleasantries with police, doormen, bouncers, cabdrivers, and others whose business is to screen out troublesome individuals *before* there is any nastiness.

I moved to New York nearly two years ago and I have remained an avid night walker. In central Manhattan, the near-constant crowd cover minimizes tense one-on-one street encounters. Elsewhere—visiting friends in SoHo, where sidewalks are narrow and tightly spaced buildings shut out the sky—things can get very taut indeed.

Black men have a firm place in New York mugging literature. Norman Podhoretz in his famed (or infamous) 1963 essay, "My Negro Problem—And Ours," recalls growing up in terror of black males; they "were tougher than we were, more ruthless," he writes—and as an adult on the Upper West Side of Manhattan, he continues, he cannot constrain his nervousness when he meets black men on certain streets. Similarly, a decade later, the essayist and novelist Edward Hoagland extols a New York where once "Negro bitterness bore down mainly on other Negroes." Where some see mere panhandlers, Hoagland sees "a mugger who is clearly screwing up his nerve to do more than just *ask* for money." But Hoagland has "the New Yorker's quick-hunch posture for broken-field maneuvering," and the bad guy swerves away.

I often witness that "hunch posture," from women after dark on the warrenlike streets of Brooklyn where I live. They seem to set their faces on neutral and, with their purse straps strung across their chests bandolier style, they forge ahead as though bracing themselves against being tackled. I understand, of course, that the danger they perceive is not a hallucination. Women are particularly vulnerable to street violence, and young black males are drastically overrepresented among the perpetrators of that violence. Yet these truths are no solace against the kind of alienation that comes of being ever the suspect, against being set apart, a fearsome entity with whom pedestrians avoid making eye contact.

It is not altogether clear to me how I reached the ripe old age of twenty-two without being conscious of the lethality nighttime pedestrians attributed to me. Perhaps it was because in Chester, Pennsylvania, the small, angry industrial town where I came of age in the 1960s, I was scarcely noticeable against a backdrop of gang warfare, street knifings, and murders. I grew up one of the good boys, had perhaps a half-dozen fistfights. In retrospect, my shyness of combat has clear sources.

Many things go into the making of a young thug. One of those things is the consummation of the male romance with the power to intimidate. An infant discovers that random flailings send the baby bottle flying out of the crib and crashing to the floor. Delighted, the joyful babe repeats those motions again and again, seeking to duplicate the feat. Just so, I recall the points at which some of my boyhood friends were finally seduced by the perception of themselves as tough guys. When a mark cowered and surrendered his money without resistance, myth and reality merged—and paid off. It is, after all, only manly to embrace the power to frighten and intimidate. We, as men, are not supposed to give an inch of our lane on the highway; we are to seize the fighter's edge in work and in play and even in love; we are to be valiant in the face of hostile forces.

Unfortunately, poor and powerless young men seem to take all this nonsense literally. As a boy, I saw countless tough guys locked away; I have since buried several, too. They were babies, really—a teenage cousin, a brother of twenty-two, a childhood friend in his mid-twenties—all gone down in episodes of bravado played out in the streets. I came to doubt the virtues of intimidation early on. I chose, perhaps even unconsciously, to remain a shadow—timid, but a survivor.

The fearsomeness mistakenly attributed to me in public places often has a perilous flavor. The most frightening of these confusions occurred in the late 1970s and early 1980s when I worked as a journalist in Chicago. One day, rushing into the office of a magazine I was writing for with a deadline story in hand, I was mistaken for a burglar. The office manager called security and, with an ad hoc posse, pursued me through the labyrinthine halls, nearly to my editor's door. I had no way of proving who I was. I could only move briskly toward the company of someone who knew me.

Another time I was on assignment for a local paper and killing time before an interview. I entered a jewelry store on the city's affluent Near North Side. The proprietor excused herself and returned with an enormous red Doberman pinscher straining at the end of a leash. She stood, the dog extended toward me, silent to my questions, her eyes bulging nearly out of her head. I took a cursory look around, nodded, and bade her good night. Relatively speaking, however, I never fared as badly as another black male journalist. He went to nearby Waukegan, Illinois, a couple of summers ago to work on a story about a murderer who was born there. Mistaking the reporter for the killer, police hauled him from his car at gunpoint and but for his press credentials would probably have tried to book him. Such episodes are not uncommon. Black men trade tales like this all the time.

In "My Negro Problem—And Ours," Podhoretz writes that the hatred he feels for blacks makes itself known to him through a variety of avenues—one being his discomfort with that "special brand of paranoid touchiness" to which he says blacks are prone. No doubt he is speaking here of black men. In time, I learned to smother the rage I felt at so often being taken for a criminal. Not to do so would surely have led to madness—via that special "paranoid touchiness" that so annoyed Podhoretz at the time he wrote the essay.

I began to take precautions to make myself less threatening. I move about with care, particularly late in the evening. I give a wide berth to nervous people on subway platforms during the wee hours, particularly when I have exchanged business clothes for jeans. If I happen to be entering a building behind some people who appear skittish, I may walk by, letting them clear the lobby before I return, so as not to seem to be following them. I have been calm and extremely congenial on those rare occasions when I've been pulled over by the police.

And on late-evening constitutionals along streets less traveled by, I employ what has proved to be an excellent tension-reducing measure: I whistle melodies from Beethoven and Vivaldi and the more popular classical composers. Even steely New Yorkers hunching toward night-time destinations seem to relax, and occasionally they even join in the tune. Virtually everybody seems to sense that a mugger wouldn't be warbling bright, sunny selections from Vivaldi's *Four Seasons*. It is my equivalent of the cowbell that hikers wear when they know they are in bear country.

Brent Staples is the author of the memoir *Parallel Time: Growing Up in Black and White*. He writes editorials for The *New York Times*.

Questions for Discussion

1. What reality assumptions were made about the author of this essay that made him uncomfortable? Why do you think these assumptions were made?
2. Brent Staples cites articles written years ago by Norman Podhoretz and Edward Hoagland. Do you believe the comments of these writers would be published today? Do you think the assumptions made years ago by these writers are still widely held or not?
3. Toward the end of the essay, Staples discusses the method he uses to diffuse anxiety among fellow pedestrians. What assumptions is he hoping they will make about him?
4. All of us have a unique personal appearance. People make assumptions about us because of our race, gender, weight, height, and clothing style. John Molloy, author of *Dress for Success*, and other researchers have discovered that a person is judged on dimensions of competence, authority, and affability based on these superficial characteristics. "Clothing engineers" make a living advising politicians, engineers, and aspiring professionals on how to package themselves for maximum impact on their desired audiences.

    How has your personal appearance been judged by others who do not know you? What assumptions have been made

about you because of your race, sex, height, weight, or style?
Were these assumptions correct? If not, why do you think they
were made?

Is This the Promised Land?

by Hector Martin
A California community college student from Mexico

It was a beautiful evening, that Friday, March 26 in 1985, when I arrived at the Los Angeles Airport. That was when I took my first steps in
the United States. From the L.A. airport to my cousin's house, I was ad-
miring the beauty of the city. I was very amused by the magnificent
buildings, the beautiful houses and the modern freeways.

A feeling of joy filled my heart. Everything was as great as I had heard
from my friends. They said that the United States was one of the most
beautiful places on earth, that it was a land of opportunities just waiting to be taken advantage of, and that there I could fulfill all my dreams.
Yes, it was beautiful and I was there to conquer that land. I felt a real
happiness about being in the United States.

The evening of the next day, my cousin took me to visit some of his
friends who were having a party. I was very happy to know, before anything else, what a party was like in this country. Unfortunately, in a few
minutes my happiness turned into confusion. At the party, most of the
people were celebrating because three of them had just turned eighteen
years old, and would be able to leave their parents' homes to go to live
with their friends.

I asked my cousin why they were leaving their parents' homes and he
told me that it was common in the United States to do so. My mind
sought a more logical answer that would excuse their actions, but I
could not find one. My mind was struck with a very strong fear, the fear
of not being able to understand their customs, and the fear of not fit-
ting into their society.

To become part of a society in a different culture requires much more
than the willingness of the individual because of the existence of invisible and unavoidable intercultural barriers. Some of these barriers are
discussed by Laray M. Barna in her article "Intercultural Communication Stumbling Blocks." This article examines the obstacles faced by foreigners in communicating with people from a different culture.

As a person who has experienced the difficulties of adapting to a new
culture, I believe that cultural and behavioral differences often create

barriers that block the adaptation of foreigners. The first barrier arises when the foreigner faces customs that are strange to him. Since I came from a traditional and conservative family, I found unacceptable the American tradition that after turning eighteen years old, many young Americans leave their parents' homes to live on their own.

Unconsciously, I developed the "tendency to evaluate," a term defined in Barna's article as the tendency to disapprove or approve the actions of others based on one's own culture instead of trying to understand, with an open mind, the thoughts and actions of people in the new culture.

The practice of leaving home at such an age was very strange to me because I never saw that in Mexico, my native country. I felt that the children, who left their parents' homes after all that their parents had done for them, were being ungrateful. In my own mind, because of my experience in Mexico, I could not find an acceptable reason to justify such a decision, so I labeled this action as insensitive.

However, a couple of years after I arrived in the United States, I changed my way of thinking about that custom. I had a conversation with an American girl whose brothers had left their parents' home. She told me that her brothers were attending school out of state and that they had begun to live independently.

In response to my question about her parents' opinion on this matter, she told me that they were very proud of their children because they were not dependent or irresponsible. She said that her parents were actually very happy that their sons were standing on their own two feet and were learning to face life's problems on their own.

Upon hearing these opinions, I realized that the custom which I had labeled as insensitive was actually a reflection of the American value of independence and was not considered an insensitive act by American parents. They perceived that custom as a sign of personal growth and maturity of their children. From that time on, I learned not to evaluate American customs too quickly. I became more aware of the fact that the Mexican and American cultures differ greatly from each other, and I learned to respect and tolerate the factors which make them different.

The difference in the rhythm of life is another factor that can block the adaptation of a foreigner to a new culture. Robert Levine, in his article "Social Time: The Heartbeat of Culture," informs us of how the pace of life differs from country to country.

When people from a country with a more relaxed pace of life come to the United States and take notice of the fast rhythm of American life, they may become disconcerted at the difference. Usually foreigners defend themselves against this confusion by using criticism. For example, some Latin people who are not accustomed to living a life which is ruled by the watch do not understand why Americans are always tied to busy schedules and are always answering to their main boss, the clock.

This confusion is revealed in what happened one day when a friend of mine and I were enjoying breakfast in a cafe near the U.C. Berkeley campus. We took notice of the tables around us that were occupied by students from the university. On the tables, the students had their meals, but each had also brought a pile of books. A couple sitting next to us, who had their books open, were writing notes and eating at the same time. The people at the other tables were also reading and eating simultaneously.

My friend wondered why these people did not have enough time to eat normally. He felt that their incredibly rapid way of eating and studying reflected the American saying of "time is money." Then he said to me, "I can't believe these people. Their materialism makes them so obsessed with the idea of succeeding in school, which will prepare them for a job that will help them make a lot of money, that they spend their lives running all the time. These people are so wrapped up in their time limits that they cannot even allow themselves to sit down and enjoy a meal as they should."

I understood my friend's point because I knew that he came from a country ranch where the people's main concern was to finish their daily tasks so that they could spend the rest of the day hunting animals or visiting friends.

Although foreigners use criticism to defend themselves in an unfamiliar environment, they are not the only ones who have the tendency to evaluate. Criticism also comes from the members of the host culture who are unaware of how they are different from the foreigners. As explained earlier, time is a concept that is perceived differently by American and Latin people. Latin people are not very concerned about punctuality, but on the other hand, this is of major importance to Americans. Therefore, when Americans notice the disregard of time by Latin people, they may tend to consider Latins as lazy and irresponsible.

Levine, in his article, provides facts that clearly illustrate the difference of time concepts in different countries. In research which compared Brazilians to Americans regarding their personal sense of "lateness," Levine notes that Brazilians define lateness for a lunch date with a friend as arriving 33.5 minutes after the time arranged, while Americans only allow a 19 minute grace period.

Obviously, this difference in the perception of punctuality as seen from the viewpoint of an American would only reinforce the stereotype that Latin people are lazy and irresponsible. But if judged from a Latin person's point of view, it would only reinforce his belief that Americans are materialistic people who believe that time means money. These differences block the ability of foreigners and Americans to understand each other and this often leads to discomfort between the two groups, which may in turn eventually prevent social interaction between them.

Adaptation to another culture is not an easy task. In many cases, such as my own, it may take several years. I had to learn to break down my old preconceptions about Americans and also to learn to understand others' customs and ways of thinking.

I have come to realize that intercultural differences are easily misunderstood. Does the fast rhythm of American life prove that Americans are materialistic? Does the fact that the Brazilian concept of punctuality, by being not as strict as that of American standards, prove that Brazilians are lazy?

As I think back to the day when I arrived in the United States, I remember how my excitement turned into fear when I was faced with such unexpected intercultural differences. I felt as if a huge ocean was interposed between me and that new and different world. I remember how my dream of conquering that world began to crumble away as I collided with those barriers of misunderstandings, and also how much it hurt to realize that I would be unable to become part of that society.

Fortunately, with the help of day-to-day experiences which have given me insights into this new culture, I have come to understand the world around me and to discover the beauty of its cities, customs, traditions, people, and most importantly, of life.

In order to adjust to a new culture, foreigners should remember that their own flexibility is imperative. They need to accept and respect the customs and ways of living of the culture in which they hope to be integrated. They have to remember that every culture is unique. After all, wouldn't this world be boring if we all thought and acted the same way?

Questions for Discussion

1. The friend of the author is quoted as saying, "I can't believe these people. Their materialism makes them so obsessed with the idea of succeeding in school, which will prepare them for a job that will help them make a lot of money, that they spend their lives running all the time. These people are so wrapped up in their time limits that they cannot even allow themselves to sit down and enjoy a meal as they should." To what extent do you believe his assumption is justified? What other

interpretations could be made about the behavior of students who are eating and reading or eating and taking notes?

2. In explaining the different interpretations that Americans and Latins make about the others' use of time, Martin states, "These differences block the ability of foreigners and Americans to understand each other and this often leads to discomfort between the two groups, which may in turn eventually prevent social interaction between them." What are some other examples of different interpretations made by members of different cultures or subcultures that prevent or affect social interaction?

3. Martin speaks of the "tendency to evaluate . . . to disapprove or approve the actions of others based on one's own culture instead of trying to understand, with an open mind, the thoughts and actions of people in the new culture." Can you think of times when you or others have made judgments about the actions of members of other cultures without attempting to understand those actions?

A Turn in the "Asian Way"

Editorial from *The New York Times*, November 17, 1996

A look at the numbers at this week's Asia Pacific Economic Cooperation summit meeting in the Philippines provides the latest indication that Asian political leaders need not control their citizens so markets can be free. The new growth statistics challenge a familiar argument made by several Asian rulers that political freedom hurts economic growth and, more broadly, is alien to Asian values.

The argument, advanced principally by leaders of Singapore, Malaysia, Indonesia and China, came to prominence at the 1993 World Conference on Human Rights in Vienna. It was an angry reply to the Clinton Administration's early promise to make the promotion of democracy a foundation of its foreign policy. Armed with the new growth figures, President Clinton has an opportunity to re-emphasize that goal during his visit to Asia this week.

The Asian assertion goes like this. Asians value social order and family over individual rights. Economic growth and social harmony require a strong government that can make unpopular choices. It must be able to control the press and arrest strikers, protesters and dissenters. The decadent West, torn by crime, racial tensions, drug abuse and other so-cial disorders, should mind its own affairs.

Rapid growth rates in East Asia gave this proposition a veneer of in-tellectual respectability. Until recently, Asia's economic tigers were all authoritarian nations, like Singapore, Indonesia and Malaysia, or coun-tries only recently lifted from autocracy, like Taiwan and South Korea.

But the theory that political repression is good for economic growth was always dubious. There are a dozen impoverished dictatorships for every case like Chile under Gen. Augusto Pinochet or Singapore under Lee Kuan Yew. Recent growth figures show there is even less reason to believe the theory today. In 1992, Mr. Lee, the most articulate propo-nent of Asian values, called the Philippines a "sick man" and recom-mended more discipline and less democracy. This year, the Philippines, more democratic than ever, is growing faster than Singapore. Of all the Asian nations, only China is growing more rapidly than Thailand, an-other democracy.

As South Korea and Taiwan become freer, their growth remains as high as that of Singapore and Indonesia.

The advantages of freedom should be self-evident. Free speech helps identify failed policies and exposes the corruption that often rots the economy in authoritarian societies like Indonesia. As information-based industries replace manufacturing as the foundation of Asian economies, nations will find it increasingly difficult to compete without free access to foreign media and the Internet.

Recent statements by Asian leaders show more respect for human rights.

Pressure from the Philippines and Thailand has provoked the Association of South East Asian Nations, whose other members are authoritarian, to reverse its earlier embrace of Myanmar and delay its membership. In Malaysia, Anwar Ibrahim, who is Deputy Prime Minister and heir apparent to the top job, has openly and eloquently criticized leaders who justify oppression in the name of order.

Japan, which treats its citizens with respect, has begun to push for human rights in the rest of Asia.

The last word in the debate should go to Asia's increasingly vocal citizens. During the summer, Indonesians poured into the streets to protest the crackdown on an opposition party. A recent meeting of Asian non-governmental organizations applauded the pressure Europe and the United States were putting on Myanmar. It was one of many endorsements of human rights from the members of Asia's growing civil society, who believe that governments that de-clare their people want orderly silence might do well to consult them first.

Questions for Discussion

1. The editorial writer asserts that new growth statistics in Asian countries "challenge a familiar argument made by several Asian rulers." What is the familiar argument that is being challenged?
2. What evidence does the writer offer to support his statement, "The theory that political repression is good for economic growth was always dubious"?
3. What advantages of freedom are cited in this article?
4. If social order and family are valued over individual rights, can a society still honor human rights? To what extent can these values coexist harmoniously? Give reasons for your answer.

Ideas for Writing or Speaking

1. Explain three or four assumptions made by your culture, subculture, or family. These assumptions can be about use of time and/or resources, holiday traditions, the role of men, women, and/or children, or the place of work, family, and citizenship.

Example:
"One assumption of my family is that everyone will go to college. My parents were expected to go to college by their parents, even though their parents didn't have the money to go themselves. It was never directly stated that we had to go to college; it was just taken for granted that we would. My parents would start sentences by saying, 'When you go to college . . .' or 'After you finish college. . . .' When my little brother decided to get a job right after high school, everyone was in shock. It never occurred to us that we wouldn't all go straight to college. After he worked two years in a warehouse, my brother did decide to attend college. Maybe he was living up to the family's expectations, but I think he was hoping for an easier life!"

2. Choose a social, political, or religious movement or group and write about three assumptions that guide this group. Take a position, agreeing or disagreeing with the assumptions of this group. Begin with an introductory paragraph that contains your conclusion (thesis statement). Then write a paragraph for each assumption you discuss. End with a paragraph that summarizes your beliefs about the underlying assumptions of this group. Some possible topics for this assignment: Greenpeace, The Young Republicans, The Democratic Party, The Libertarian Party, Buddhism, Judaism, Islam, Feminism, Action for Children's Television, The National Rifle Association, Mothers Against Drunk Drivers, The Society for the Prevention of Cruelty to Animals.

3. Using the same organizational format as Idea 2, explore the assumptions made by both sides of a controversial issue. For example, you might explore the assumptions of people who support and people who are against tuition for community colleges. One assumption of those who support tuition might be that people work harder when they have to pay for education; an assumption of those against tuition might be that fees are an unnecessary and prohibitive burden on the poor and that they are therefore "classist." Find several assumptions on both sides of your issue. Then explain which assumptions are the most reasonable and why.

4

Inductive Arguments: Statistical & Causal Generalizations

Prove It to Me.   What Are the Statistics?

A critical thinker understands the basics of polling and the legitimate uses of statistical research in supporting conclusions.

A critical thinker understands the basics of causal generalizations.

This chapter will cover:

◆ The use of statistical evidence in arguments
◆ The reporting of statistical data
◆ The use of causal generalizations

In the last two chapters, we focused on the foundations of arguments, including the basic reasoning patterns of deduction and induction. In this chapter and the next, we will consider the kinds of evidence and the quality of the evidence used to support inductive generalizations.

As discussed in the first chapter, anyone can have an opinion (conclusion) and give reasons for that opinion. But the critical thinker evaluates the quality and credibility of the reasons before offering or accepting a conclusion. Inductive arguments aim at establishing strong, if not absolutely certain, conclusions. Inductive strength is based on good evidence from which we can draw useful generalizations.

In this chapter, we will learn principles for evaluating both statistical generalizations and causal generalizations.

Statistical Evidence

Statistical evidence, the first subject of this chapter, refers to data collected by polling and research studies. Polltakers and researchers use systematic methods to get results with great predictive value, that is, they can tell us what probably will happen. For example, a Gallup poll or Harris poll generally reflects how people will vote and who will be elected to political office.

Why do we carry out research aimed at generating accurate statistics? One motivation for doing research is to have a sense of control over our individual and collective futures; as critically thinking people, we want to act clearly, deliberately, and responsibly. We want to be prepared for future events. One way we can anticipate the future, which is unknown, is to reason from known facts and observations; in other words, we reason inductively.

On a daily basis, we use inductive generalizations to make predictions and decisions in our personal lives. For example, if you've been on three blind dates arranged by your cousin and they have all been terrible, you will probably predict that a fourth date arranged by this person will turn out the same way. If you have noticed that a particular route home from school is usually congested during commute hours, you might choose to take another route or schedule your classes for less busy times. Or, you might watch a baseball game and predict that because the batter has a .350 average and has been doing well the last few games, he will make at least a base hit right now. You're surprised if he strikes out. On the other hand, a batter with a .220 average who has just recovered from an injury would not be likely to get a good hit. If he does, you are again surprised.

As individuals, we reason inductively by generalizing from observations we make about our own circumstances and experiences. As a society, we use more formal research methods to get accurate information about social issues such as rates of disease, drug and alcohol use, likely election results, and public opinion about government policies. We use this information to make decisions about our future direction; statistical research helps us decide which programs should be funded or denied funding, which should be modified, and what goals we wish to achieve.

The Use of Statistics

Statistics are used in numerous professions in our culture. Lending companies use statistics on interest rates to support their arguments that people should get car and home loans or refinance existing loans. Real estate agents show statistics on public school test scores to clients to convince them to move into a new neighborhood. Weather forecasters use statistics to help them make predictions and seismologists use statistics about past earthquakes to predict the progression of future earthquakes. Political advisors use statistics to decide the popularity of candidates and policies. Advertisers collect evidence on the size and nature of magazine and newspaper audiences to decide where to place their advertisements. The Nielsen ratings give commercial advertisers a good idea of what television channels are being watched for a given period.

New ways to gather statistics are also being discovered. One new method, called a "Q" score is described in the following excerpt from a daily television column by Jon Burlingame:

The research into who watches television, when and why, has produced an entire sub-industry of pollsters and numbers-crunchers. One of the best-kept secrets, and at the same time one of the most valued tools of network executives, is the so-called "Q" score.

That's short for TvQ, the periodic report's title, with the "Q" standing for qualitative. Essentially, average viewers are asked which stars and shows they recognize, then asked to rate them in terms of best-liked personalities and programs. The results are invariably hush-hush, but they are prized by network execs as a measurement of what shows create audience favorites, even if they're low-rated.[7]

STOP AND THINK

How might advertisers or television or film producers use some of the information gathered from "Q" scores?

Just as the Nielson company helps television executives decide which programs are worth keeping, government agencies conduct statistical studies to determine the best use of taxpayer dollars. If the statistics tell us that the rate of teenage pregnancy is down but the rate of teenage drug use is up, then government and community efforts can be focused on current drug problems. If student scores in math and science are declining but scores in English and history are high according to international criteria, then more attention can be usefully directed to improving education in math and science.

Sometimes the results of the research offer evidence that spending priorities need to be changed. Such is the conclusion suggested by the following article:

[7] Jonathan Burlingame, "Television," *Contra Costa Times*, January 12, 1990, p. 10-c. Reprinted by permission of the author.

Sexual Diseases Are a Growing Scourge in the U.S.

Hidden Epidemic Costs $10 Billion a Year,
Excluding Tab for AIDS

by Lauran Neergaard, *Associated Press*

Contra Costa Times, November 20, 1996

WASHINGTON. Sexually transmitted diseases are diagnosed 12 million times a year in the United States—including a staggering 3 million cases among teen-agers, the Institute of Medicine reported Tuesday.

The institute urged a national attack to wipe out the largely hidden epidemic.

The nation spends just $1 to prevent sexually transmitted illnesses for every $43 spent treating them, the report found. The tab reaches $10 billion a year not counting the massive costs of AIDS, the best known of these diseases.

Left untreated, sexually transmitted diseases can cause infertility, cancer, birth defects and miscarriages, even death.

And Americans suffer 10 to 50 times more sexually transmitted diseases than people in other developed countries, concluded the Institute of Medicine, an arm of the National Academy of Sciences.

Sexually transmitted diseases are "far more common than most Americans are aware," said report co-author Dr. Edward Hook III of the University of Alabama.

"They attack people early in their life but . . . these diseases change people's lives and affect them for the rest of their lives."

. . . A separate Kaiser Family Foundation survey Tuesday found one in 10 Americans cannot even name a sexually transmitted disease.

And only 23 percent know about chlamydia, the most common sexual disease, striking an estimated 4 million Americans a year, the survey found.

Chlamydia is easily cured, but often goes undiagnosed because it seldom causes symptoms—and ultimately as many as one in 10 infected women become infertile from advanced disease.

The federal Centers for Disease Control and Prevention is spending $106 million this year to fight sexually transmitted diseases other than AIDS, and the Clinton administration already is wrangling with whether to increase that funding.

The CDC hopes for additional money next year to expand nationwide a chlamydia screening program that has cut cases up to 60 percent among women who visit family planning clinics in 20 states.

CDC will re-examine how it fights sexual disease in light of the Institute of Medicine report, said the agency's chief scientist for sexually transmitted diseases, Dr. Helene Gayle.

Questions for Discussion

1. The Institute of Medicine is quoted as urging an attack on the largely hidden epidemic of sexually transmitted diseases. What was the evidence upon which they came to the conclusion that there was an epidemic?
2. Why do you think the epidemic was "largely hidden?" How does the knowledge of the extent and damage of the epidemic help both the government and individuals to make better decisions?
3. Why do you think that Americans suffer ten to fifty times more sexually transmitted diseases than people in other developed countries? To what extent is it helpful to compare our rates of disease with that of other nations?

How the Research Is Done

In this age of the proliferation of statistical information, most people and professions are influenced by the findings of research studies; as we have discussed, these studies are frequently used as a basis for making significant decisions. Check your local or national newspaper on any given day, and you will probably notice several articles on recent studies. How do we determine the quality of the statistical evidence we hear or read? To answer this question, we need to have a basic understanding of how the research is carried out.

When someone creates a research study, he or she needs to consider three questions:

1. What do I want to find out? This is called the *characteristic of interest*.
2. Who do I want to know about? This is called the *target population*.
3. Who can I study to get accurate answers about my entire target population? This is called the *sample*. We usually can't study everyone in a given target population, so we have to observe some representative members of the population. For polling, the adequate sample size is usually 1,000.

SKILL

Understand the basic structure of statistical research.

Examples

Characteristic of interest: What are the most popular television programs in the United States?
Target population: Residents of the United States who watch television.
Sample: At least 1,000 randomly selected Americans who watch television.

Characteristic of interest: Who will win the next presidential election?
Target population: Americans who are eligible to vote.
Sample: At least 1,000 randomly selected Americans who are eligible to vote.

Characteristic of interest: Whether Canadian parents want warning screens that inform of violent or sexual content on all Internet sites.
Target population: Canadians who are parents.
Sample: 1,000 randomly selected Canadian parents.

The characteristic of interest and target population are fairly easy to identify. The quality of statistical research depends largely on the **sample** drawn from the target population. For a study to be accurate and reliable, several things must be true about this sample.

THE SAMPLE MUST BE LARGE ENOUGH

Any sample studied must be sufficiently large to justify the generalizations drawn from the research. Otherwise, we are dealing in poor experimental design or even stereotyping. If someone says, "Men are terrible cooks—both my brother and my boyfriend have burned dinners this year," she is generalizing from a few cases. Her outline would look like this:

> *Characteristic of interest:* Whether men can cook well.
> *Target population:* One-half of the human race.
> *Sample:* My brother and my boyfriend.

Sometimes when we stand back and look at what someone is claiming and the evidence they use, we can see how inadequate the argument is. Yet how often do we talk like this or agree when others talk like this?

A real problem in both statistical and experimental research is having the resources to study a sufficiently large sample. This problem is discussed by researcher Frank Sulloway:

> Small studies are less reliable than large studies. The typical behavioral study involves about 70 subjects. Owing to statistical error, studies routinely fail to confirm relationships that are known to be true for larger populations. . . . Everyone knows that girls, at age eighteen, are taller than they are at age fourteen. In samples of only 70 subjects, this lawful relationship will be validated statistically less than half the time! Common sense dictates that findings should count more if they are based on 10,000 subjects than if they are based on 100.

Sulloway suggests that when only small samples can be studied, researchers combine the results of several studies in order to draw more reliable generalizations.

EXERCISE

Purpose: To assess the adequacy of sample size relative to a target population.

Outline the following claims based on inadequate samples. State the target population, the characteristic of interest, and the sample.

> "Asians are so good at math; there are four of them in my algebra class and they have the top scores."

> "People who live in that part of town are such freaks —I saw two women with purple hair there last week."

> "Men have such a hard time showing their feelings—my dad has never cried in front of us."

There are many theories about why we so easily jump to hasty conclusions about a whole group of people (target population) based on a small sample of people. One theory is that we feel more secure about ourselves and our relations to others when we can place everyone in a neat category.

Another theory is that we are too lazy or untrained to be careful about our generalizations. Most of us enjoy giving our opinions but we're not willing to find the data that is required to prove our opinions. So we "mouth off" on topics we really are just guessing about; other people do the same thing and we call it "conversing" and "socializing" and everybody's happy. If we happen to hear about a really well-done study on a topic of interest to us, we add that to our conversation too.

This author has known only one person who consistently asked people to tell him why they believe the statements they make; he was clear-minded, fair, precise, and extremely unpopular! We get defensive about our pet stereotypes and indefensible positions and don't like people to shake us up. However, as we become critical thinkers, our positions will be taken more carefully and backed up with the kind of evidence that gives us real confidence about the opinions we share with others.

REMINDER

The sample must be large enough—that is, enough people must be studied—to justify the generalizations made by the researchers.

THE SAMPLE MUST REPRESENT THE TARGET AUDIENCE

The people studied must be like the people about whom you wish to generalize. For example, if you want to study the effects of fluoride on children in the United States, it would not be enough to only study children who live in the Northeast. If you draw a conclusion from your research, it must reflect the entire target group.

For a sample to be representative, it must have the same significant characteristics in the same proportions as the target group; this principle is illustrated in Figure 4.1. If the sample does not have these characteristics, then it is called *biased*. A biased sample does not provide adequate evidence to support a conclusion.

A common problem with modern social science research is that some researchers are college professors who use their students as "volunteers" for their studies. While some extrapolations from

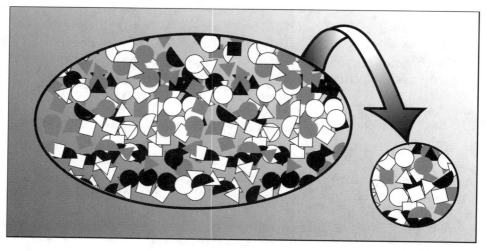

Figure 4.1

student samples to the general population are reasonable, other findings may relate more specifically to college students on a particular campus rather than to larger segments of the population. Student populations generally reflect a limited age grouping, and students on a given campus may be more politically liberal or conservative than the general population. Their ideas about an upcoming election can't be generalized to the larger public. And if the sample studied comes from only one class, say, political science, they may not even be representative of the college as a whole.

THE SAMPLE MUST BE RANDOM

Randomness is closely linked to the representativeness of a sample. It has been found that you can draw solid conclusions about a large target population by using a much smaller, but representative and randomly selected, segment of that population. Randomness means that every member of the target population has an equal chance of being chosen as part of the sample. For example, pollsters might choose a random method of interviewing residents of a particular city by calling every tenth name in the local directory. Statisticians have discovered that a truly random sample is generally representative of the target population.

Using random samples of the target population makes the results of a study accurate within a small percentage of possible error. Polls could show that a certain candidate will get approximately 25 percent of a vote with a "margin of error" of 5 percent, which means he or she will probably get 20 to 30 percent of the vote. This margin of error will decrease as the random, representative sample increases in size.

QUESTIONS TO ASK ABOUT STATISTICAL REPORTS

You might think, at this point, that the requirements of a good statistical study are very hard to meet; yet, despite the difficulties involved with the need to find random, representative, and sufficiently large samples of a target population, it can be and is done frequently. For example, you can review polling predictions about election results and find them to be quite accurate.

SKILL

Analyze the quality of statistical evidence by noting the size, representation, and randomness of the sample.

When you need to critically evaluate reports of statistical studies, consider the following questions:

1. What is the sample size? For national public opinion polls, it is a general principle that at least 1,000 randomly selected individuals who are representative of the target population will give reliable results. When a research study involves carefully supervised testing and training of subjects or expensive material (like the studies discussed in Chapter 5), a much smaller sample might be necessary. For example, it is unreasonable and undesirable to have hundreds of subjects test an experimental drug that may be helpful in treating a particular disease but may also have significant side effects.
2. Is the sample representative both in all significant characteristics and in the proportion of those characteristics? For example, if 10 percent of a state's voters are 65 or older, are 10 percent of the sample voters in this age range? If the sample is not representative, then the study is considered biased.
3. Have all significant characteristics been considered? Sometimes it is hard to know exactly which factors about the target population are significant. Does the sex and age of the target matter? What about race and educational level?
4. If the study is a poll, are the questions biased? In other words, are they slanted to bring about a particular response? For example, consider the following "loaded" questions:
    a. Do you believe that the government has a right to invade private lives by taking a census?
    b. Do you approve of preventing thousands of senior citizens from enjoying a safe, affordable, and lovely retirement home in order to protect a moth?

Because these questions are biased towards the obviously "correct" answer, the information gathered from them is unreliable.

5. What is the credibility of the polling organization or research institute? In most cases, we read about a study in a magazine, newspaper, or textbook. Since we get an abridged version of research from these sources, it is helpful to note whether polls were conducted by credible organizations like Gallup, Harris, and Roper and whether research studies were done under the auspices of universities or reliable "think tanks."

The preceding checklist can be used to help you feel more confident about using statistical evidence to support conclusions. It can also be used to help you refute unreliable and inadequate evidence.

Calvin and Hobbes by Bill Watterson
CALVIN AND HOBBES © Watterson. Dist. by UNIVERSAL PRESS SYNDICATE.
Reprinted with permission. All rights reserved.

Using Surveys as Evidence

Sometimes the use of surveys can yield helpful, accurate information. Consider the following excerpt from an article on store-issued credit cards:

A survey of 62 retailers across the nation concluded that major department and specialty stores are more likely to saddle their credit card customers with finance charges in the 20 percent range than the traditional bank lenders that issue Visa cards and MasterCards.

Consumer Action, a San Francisco-based advocacy group, found that all but two of the retailers imposed interest rates of 19.8 percent or higher on credit card purchases that aren't paid off each month.

In contrast, a Consumer Action survey of 73 bank credit card lenders earlier this year found 32 lenders offering interest rates below 16 percent.[8]

Straightforward surveys like this one can be beneficial in helping consumers make decisions about which, if any, credit cards to use. The findings in this survey could easily be corroborated with calls to banks and department stores.

In contrast, one method of research that may lead to interesting speculations but is not generally considered accurate is the mail-in survey. Let's imagine that a magazine asks its readers to respond to questions about how they spend their money. If the magazine has a circulation of 10,000 and they receive only 2,000 replies (which would be a high response rate), they can't really draw any information from those 2,000 answers because the sample is no longer random. Those who answered are a select group—they have something in common, which is that they are readers of this particular magazine who had the time and inclination to answer the questions and send them in. You can't use this survey to generalize about how most people spend money. Another problem is that survey questions often do not reflect what people would really do in a given situation; they only reflect what people would like to think they would do. If you ask someone if they use money for necessities first and luxuries second, they might answer yes, but their checkbook could reveal a completely different reality.

In addition, it's possible for someone to send in several surveys to skew the results or just for fun. Survey results can be more controlled than these examples indicate, but you are safe to con-

---

[8]   Michael Liedtke, "Store Issued Credit Comes at a High Price," *Contra Costa Times*, November 20, 1996, p. C-1.

clude that most mail-in surveys you read about in magazines and newspapers are not representative and therefore don't provide reliable support for your conclusions.

REMINDER

Arguments using statistical evidence need an adequate sample that is randomly selected from a representative group in the target population. When you find studies like this, you can accept them as accurate and use them for your personal decision making and argumentation.

Statistical Generalizations

Keep in mind that although you may get information from a well-conducted study, the conclusion will not be true in every case. Statistical evidence reflects only what can *generally* be expected; conclusions about such evidence are called *statistical generalizations*. They add strength, not certainty, to your conclusions. For example, it might be discovered that most hyperactive children in a study responded well to dietary changes; this finding does not mean that every child will respond in the same way. Or, we might read about a study showing that most sports magazine readers are men, but that does not mean every reader is male. Knowing that *most* of the readers are men helps the magazine recruit the most appropriate advertisers.

Remember that inductive strength is based on good evidence from which we can draw useful generalizations. (See Figure 4.2.) In short, we can get important information from statistical research that helps us make decisions or gain knowledge in a general way. Still, we need to allow room for the complexities of individual people and not expect that what is *generally* true will be true for everyone.

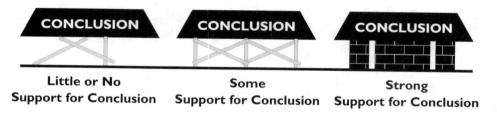

Figure 4.2

EXERCISE

Purpose: To analyze the quality of one reported study.

Read the following report of a research study, keeping the following questions in mind:

1. What is the conclusion of the researcher?
2. How representative of the target population was his sample? Was the sample size adequate?
3. What methods did he use to gather his data? Are these methods reliable?
4. In the second paragraph the reporter implies that these research results would be duplicated in other classrooms. Do you agree or disagree, and why?
5. To what extent is the headline given to this article a responsible one?

At a Lecture—Only 12 Percent Listen

Bright-eyed college students in lecture halls aren't necessarily listening to the professor, the American Psychological Association was told yesterday.

If you shot off a gun at sporadic intervals and asked the students to encode their thoughts and moods at that moment, you would discover that:

- About 20 percent of the students, men and women, are pursuing erotic thoughts.

- Another 20 percent are reminiscing about something.

- Only 20 percent are actually paying attention to the lecture. 12 percent are actively listening.

- The others are worrying, daydreaming, thinking about lunch or—surprise—religion (8 percent).

This confirmation of the lecturer's worst fears was reported by Paul Cameron, 28, an assistant professor at Wayne State University in Detroit. The annual convention, which ends Tuesday, includes about 2,000 such reports to 10,000 psychologists in a variety of meetings.

Cameron's results were based on a nine-week course in introductory psychology for 85 college sophomores. A gun was fired 21 times at random intervals, usually when Cameron was in the middle of a sentence.

Reprinted from *San Francisco Sunday Examiner Chronicle* by permission.

The Reporting of Statistical Studies

As we have noted, studies are not usually reported in the popular media in their complete context. Instead, excerpts from a study are given, and sometimes the reader or listener gets an incomplete or distorted picture of what was really discovered by the research.

One of the most important responsibilities of those reporting studies is to give us a true picture of what was discovered so that we can draw reasonable generalizations. Both raw numbers and percentages should be used so that we can assess the significance of any findings; for example, a report might claim that a new study shows a 50 percent drop in the rate of teenage pregnancies. But on closer examination, we might discover that the sample was taken from only one high school in which the number of pregnant girls went from 4 to 2. Obviously, the sample size is too small to make any relevant claim about teenage pregnancy rates. Conversely, a large sample size may find 200 more teenage pregnancies for a given year across a particular state, yet the researcher could claim only a 10 percent increase in pregnancies if 2,000 had occurred in the previous year.

Advertisers may also "lie with statistics." For example, a business, let's say a bicycle store, could place an ad thanking the public for "doubling" the volume of sales this year. That ad could mean, in reality, that sales of the bicycles went from 5,000 to 10,000 for the year or that sales went from 1 to 2.

The following article is an example of a study that was reported responsibly. Unfortunately, the headline (which is often the only part noticed by those who "scan" the news) distorts the information in a dangerous way.

Family Members, Not Strangers, Abduct Most Children

Times Wire Services, *Contra Costa Times*, Friday, May 4, 1990

WASHINGTON—As many as 4,600 children were abducted nationwide by non-family members in 1988, and more than 100,000 were the targets of attempted abductions, primarily by passing motorists, according to the first comprehensive study of the number of children missing in the United States.

The study, released Thursday by the Justice Department, also estimated that more than 350,000 children were abducted by family members during the same time, most often in connection with child-custody cases. The number was at least three times as great as previous estimates, according to the report.

Many of the abductions involving non-family members ended within hours, often after sexual assaults, but 200 to 300 children disappeared for longer periods or were killed, according to the study.

The fact that only 1.4 percent of all abductions of children are committed by strangers should ease parents' fears of strangers, said Ernie Allen, president of the National Center for Missing and Exploited Children.

"We don't want parents to be paralyzed by fear," he said, adding, however, the total still represents "10 elementary school classrooms full. That's a tremendous concern."

Despite widespread publicity about specific child-abduction cases—including the Bay Area kidnappings of Amber Swartz-Garcia of Pinole and Michaela Garecht of Hayward in 1988 and the 1989 abduction of Ilene Misheloff of Dublin—efforts to develop public policy and allocate funds have been severely hampered by a lack of knowledge about the problem.

Police generally do not categorize crimes by the age of the victim, and most nationwide data on child abductions have been compiled by private child-welfare organizations.

The study, called "Missing, Abducted, Runaway, and Thrownaway Children in America," was mandated by Congress in 1984. Prepared by the Office of Juvenile Justice and Delinquency Prevention, it attempted to compile the number of crimes in one year against all children younger than 18.

Although most child abductions involve family members, the estimated 3,200 to 4,600 cases involving non-family members were significant, researchers and child-welfare advocates said.

"That's the size of a small town," said John Walsh, host of the TV show "America's Most Wanted" and father of Adam, a 6-year old boy abducted from a Florida store and slain. "The Justice Department had some guts to come out and do what they did. It finally puts a handle on the fact that kids are exploited in this country."

Questions for Discussion

1. How does the headline that an editor put on this article summarize the content of the article? Is this summary fair? If so, why? If not, why not?

2. What is the difference in your thoughts and feelings when you read "only 1.4 percent of all abductions of children are committed by strangers" versus "as many as 4,600 children were abducted nationwide by non-family members in 1988 and more than 100,000 were the targets of attempted abductions"? Why is it important for a report to include both percentages and raw numbers?

3. Why do you think that "efforts to develop public policy and allocate funds have been severely hampered by a lack of knowledge about the problem"?

Causal Generalizations

Statistics and controlled studies (which will be discussed in the next chapter) are often used to draw inductive generalizations about the causes of conditions or events. We attempt to determine causal connections for several reasons: First, we seek to eliminate current difficulties and prevent future problems that arise for individuals; secondly, we want to resolve general problems that affect groups of people; and finally, much great investigation is motivated by sheer human curiosity.

On an individual level, we look for causes in order to eliminate problems that arise in daily life. We might seek to understand why our car is making a certain sound, why our checkbook doesn't balance, why our dog seems lethargic, or why we lost a job or an important relationship. If we find a cause, then we hope we will find a cure for our current difficulties, as exemplified by the following Ann Landers column.

Ann Landers

Contra Costa Times, October 10, 1996

Dear Ann Landers: If it weren't for one of your recent columns, I might be either dead or paralyzed. I owe you a large debt of gratitude.

For about a week, I had been experiencing temporary numbness in my left arm and hand. The numbness was sometimes accompanied by periodic paralysis of my left hand. My first thoughts were that I either hit my crazy bone or had perhaps been using my computer too much.

As I read your column describing the symptoms of a stroke, I immediately recognized that my numbness matched the early warning signs you had mentioned. I dropped the newspaper and went directly to the emergency room. The CAT scan revealed a large mass of blood in the crevice between my brain and my skull.

Fortunately, the operation to drain the fluid was a complete success and the doctors say there should be no lasting effects. For this, I am extremely thankful. Please know I am enormously grateful to you, Ann, for the perfect timing of that column.[9]

Permission granted by Ann Landers/Creators Syndicate.

[9]   Ann Landers column, *Contra Costa Times*, October 10, 1996.

We look for causes of societal problems in our efforts to en-sure that these problems do not occur again. This search for causes occurs when we have car, train, and plane accidents, out-breaks of food poisoning, a trend of lower test scores, or a dis-ease that is becoming an epidemic.

In addition, we seek causes in order to eliminate *potential* problems that affect the general public: Seat belts were created and altered as a result of understanding the causes of the kinds of human injury that can occur after the impact of a collision; baby furniture and toys are modified based on our understand-ing of their harmfulness to children; the government may look at inflationary trends caused by the infusion of more money into the country before they take action to stimulate a failing economy; and premarital counselors can advise engaged couples about the major causes of divorce and help them address important issues before they get married.

Philosophers and scientists have developed theories of cause and effect over the last few centuries. These theories are used to help us make causal generalizations, which can then be used as evidence to support a conclusion. Keep in mind, however, that what is believed and accepted as causal today may change as new information becomes available. This section will review the most common theories of causation.

Hume's Conditions for Cause and Effect

One definition of cause and effect was put forth by the British philosopher David Hume (1711–1776). He reasoned that we are justified in saying that one thing is the cause (**X**) of an effect (**Y**) if the following three conditions are met:

(1) **X,** the cause, *preceded* **Y,** the effect, in time.
(2) **X** and **Y** are *contiguous* (in contact with one another) in time and place.
(3) There is a *history* of (1) and (2); that is, there is a his-tory of **X** preceding **Y** and of **X** and **Y** being related in time and place.

The first condition is clear; if one thing causes another, the cause must come before the effect. But we should also note that sometimes the cause and effect appear to occur at the same time; for example, as soon as I pull the plug on my lamp, the light goes out.

The second condition specifies the need for a relationship in time and space between a cause and an effect. In outbreaks of diseases caused by "sick buildings," a connection is made between workers (often on particular floors) and the onset of the same illness. The reminder that causes and effects must be connected wards against superstition and against unlikely causes.

The third condition helps us to justify a causal effect by pointing to a regular tendency. A florist can reason that every year, on certain holidays, the demand for flowers goes up. A public school teacher can chart a tendency for a consistent reduction in math skills over summer vacation. A doctor can anticipate that a patient will be nauseated as a side effect of many types of chemotherapy. A driver can note which roads are regularly jammed during the week because of rush hour. Conversely, if there is no history of regularity between a particular cause and a particular effect, then a critical thinker should wait for such a trend to surface before accepting an alleged causal connection.

Even when all of Hume's criteria are met, it is hard to distinguish between a correlation (two events occurring together in a regular pattern) and a specific causation. We can, for example, look at studies that show a connection (correlation) between violent criminals and their abusive parents. But it is difficult to explain fully why some of these violent criminals from abusive homes have siblings who are nonviolent, productive, and functioning members of society. In other words, it is easier to see *connections* in time and space between two conditions than it is to prove that one of the conditions was *caused* by the other.

However, when we come across a strong correlation between two conditions or activities, we should consider whether there is a possible area of causation to be explored. Consider these statements by MIT research scholar and author Frank Sulloway:

There is an old maxim that "correlation is not causation." Although this is certainly true, it is also true that, under some circumstances, correlations provide a reasonably reliable guide to causation. For example, the correlation between winning a million dollars in the lottery and having more money to spend is very high, and these two outcomes are obviously related in a causal manner. We must employ common sense in deciding whether, and to what extent, correlations suggest a causal relationship. Even when correlations do not warrant the assumption of causality, they generally suggest that *some other variable, itself associated with the two correlated variable*s, is causally involved in the observed relationship. As we introduce additional variables into a statistical analysis, we can often pinpoint the most likely source of "causation."[10]

Theories of technical causation, which we turn to now, can help us better understand causal connections between conditions.

Technical Causation

Another format for determining causation specifies two different types of conditions between causes and effects:

A *necessary condition* is a condition (state of affairs, thing, process, etc.) that must be present if the effect is present. Equivalently, if the necessary condition is absent, then the effect cannot occur.

One of the necessary conditions of life as we know it is oxygen. Some of the necessary conditions of a fire are oxygen, a flammable material, and a form of ignition. If we know the necessary conditions of an event then we can *prevent* it from happening. Remove any of the necessary conditions and the effect does not take place. A necessary condition is a prerequisite for the effect. Thus we can speak of a necessary condition as a cause, or one of the causes, of an event.[11]

---

[10] Frank Sulloway, *Born to Rebel* (New York: Pantheon Books, Random House, Inc., 1996).
[11] Nicholas Capaldi, *The Art of Deception* (Buffalo: Prometheus Books, 1987), p. 158.

A *sufficient condition* is a condition (state of affairs, thing, process, etc.) that automatically leads to the production of another event. If the condition is present, then the effect will definitely occur. The sufficient condition creates the effect.

Swallowing cyanide is a sufficient condition for death. The difference between a necessary and a sufficient condition is that although a necessary condition must be present, it will not produce the effect by itself. The sufficient condition is "sufficient" by itself to produce the effect. Usually the sufficient condition is really a set of necessary conditions, all of which must be present at the same time and place. For instance, a combustible material, oxygen, and the combustion point are all necessary conditions for a fire. Together all three constitute the sufficient condition for a fire. If we know the sufficient condition of an event, then we can produce it at will. Thus we can speak of a sufficient condition as a cause of an event.[12]

Finding the exact cause of an event or an effect can be very difficult, even in technical matters. We often must look at *multiple causes,* a combination of causes leading to a specific effect. A particular business might be successful because of a *combination* of the needs of the community, the location of the store, and the advertising campaign. A person may die because of a combination of a weak heart, a diet with a large proportion of fat, and an overexertion in exercise. The weak heart could be further traced back to a family history of heart disease. Taken in combination, these factors may be sufficient to cause death.

The phenomenon of multiple causes makes it difficult to provide evidence beyond a reasonable doubt in many cases. For example, over the years people have tried to sue tobacco companies because, they claim, the tobacco caused them to develop lung cancer. However, despite convincing evidence on the harmfulness of tobacco, people have had difficulty proving that tobacco is the *only* cause, sufficient by itself, for the development of lung cancer. Until recently, lawyers for the tobacco companies argued that there are, in any given case, other possible causes for a person's susceptibility to lung cancer and that other people who smoke a similar amount of tobacco have not contracted the disease.

---

[12]   Ibid.

The difficulty of establishing causal connections and then proving them in court is chronicled by Jonathan Harr in his book *A Civil Action,* which he spent eight years researching and writing. The book deals with the case of eight children in Woburn, Massachusetts, who contracted leukemia as the result, their families claim, of toxic pollution from industrial plants near their homes. The lawyer, Jan Schlictmann, who took on the corporations in court, believed in the truth of his clients' case, but also knew it would be a difficult case to prove.

> The children's illnesses and the contamination of two water wells that served their homes had been documented. What was missing was proof that the two industrial plants, owned by Beatrice Foods Co. and W.R. Grace and Co., were responsible for the contamination and that the chemicals had caused the children's illnesses. . . .
>
> He hired geologists to prove that Beatrice and Grace had contaminated the wells. And he hired medical experts to establish a link between leukemia, the cause of which was unknown, and the contaminated water.
>
> The millions spent in preparing for trial virtually bankrupted Schlictmann and his firm. . . . [In court], he had to confront an unsympathetic judge and high-paid corporate attorneys who used every motion and procedural sleight of hand to block his way.
>
> A split decision that absolved Beatrice of responsibility and held little promise of final victory over Grace forced Schlictmann to settle the case for $8 million. The settlement gave a measure of satisfaction and compensation to the Woburn families, but it wasn't enough to pay Schlictmann's bills.[13]

The Woburn case, which generated 159 volumes of depositions and trial testimony, is a good example of the difficulty in proving a causal connection against the doubts generated by good defense lawyers. In gathering the necessary expertise to

---

[13] Willy Morris, " 'Civil' Author Nearly Beaten by Case," *Contra Costa Times*, October 10, 1996, pp. F-2, 3.

make a case, Schlictmann spent so much money that his car and furniture were repossessed and the bank foreclosed on his home. Lawyers have to believe that they can prove their cases with a "preponderance of the evidence" before they will take such risks.

The new practice of allowing juries to assign a portion of blame for an injury to the plaintiff and a portion to the defendant is a recognition of the difficulty in determining the precise cause of a problem. In one recent case, a male psychologist was accused of causing pain, suffering, and suicidal tendencies in a female patient with whom he had had sexual relations. The psychologist admitted to having had sex with his patient, but he produced explicit love letters she had sent to him. In addition, his attorneys presented information about the patient's previous sexual history; the psychologist, as defendant, was not required to reveal details of his own sexual history. As a result of the evidence presented by the defense, the jury softened the verdict by assigning 18 percent of the blame to the patient and 82 percent of the blame to the psychologist. They reasoned that, although he had broken his professional ethics, she had contributed to that breakdown.

In the case of Jonathan Schmitz, who killed a gay man who revealed a crush on him during a television talk show, the argument for multiple causes led a jury to conclude that the defendant committed second-degree murder. Note the citing of multiple causes for this decision in the following excerpt:

> In deciding against a first-degree murder conviction, the jury found that 26-year-old Jonathan Schmitz acted without premeditation in the 1995 slaying of Scott Amedure, 32.
>
> Schmitz could get from eight years to life in prison, with the possibility of parole. First-degree murder carries no hope of parole.
>
> Jurors said they concentrated almost entirely on Schmitz's state of mind when he shot Amedure, who revealed an attraction to Schmitz three days earlier as a studio audience whooped and hollered.
>
> Juror Joyce O'Brien said that for Schmitz it was like "someone pulls the rug out from under you. Even a sane person might have trouble dealing with all that stuff."
>
> The case had focused attention on "ambush" television and titillating daytime TV tactics, with Schmitz's lawyers

arguing that the show misled him into believing he was going to meet the woman of his dreams.

They said he was publicly humiliated when his secret admirer turned out to be a man. That, coupled with his history of depression, suicide attempts, a thyroid ailment and other problems, left him incapable of forming the intent necessary to commit first-degree murder, his lawyers said.[14]

EXERCISE

Purpose: To understand the need to consider multiple causes when addressing social problems.

Read the following excerpts from articles on various issues: For each one, isolate the multiple causes of the problem as given in the article; discuss what policies are currently addressing these causes. If no policies are mentioned, come up with your own suggestions for dealing with the various causative factors.

Asian Women in U.S. Face Higher Cancer Risk

by Eileen Glanton, *Associated Press*
Contra Costa Times, June 25, 1996

For 49 years, Rose Hsu lived a dream.

The daughter of Chinese immigrants, she coasted through childhood in San Francisco's Chinatown, excelled in school, married a doctor and moved to the suburbs.

Then, in 1994, Hsu got breast cancer and discovered a medical truth doctors already knew: Although Asian nations have the world's lowest incidence of breast cancer, Asian women in the United States have the

---

[14]   Greta Guest, Associated Press, *Contra Costa Times*, November 13, 1996, p. B-1.

same risk as white women. An Asian woman's chance of getting breast cancer increases by more than 80 percent within a decade of arriving in this country.

The biological factors are abundantly clear, says Regina Zeigler, a National Cancer Institute physician who led a 1993 study on Asians and breast cancer.

"A woman coming to the U.S. from Asia probably gives up a naturally healthy diet for American processed foods," Zeigler said. She may exercise less and undergo stress in navigating a new culture. And a language barrier may prevent her from seeking medical help or understanding public service announcements.

More elusive, though, are a host of cultural factors—modesty, day-to-day philosophy—that narrow Asian women's odds of beating the disease.

Health officials are learning that the best way to battle those factors is to step out of the doctor's office and into the community.

The American-Italian Cancer Foundation, based in Manhattan, does most of its work in the city's poorer minority neighborhoods. Staff members drive a mammography van to churches, community centers and health fairs, where they perform free mammograms.

"We seek out underserved, uninsured women, and those in culturally cloistered neighborhoods," says Gilda Zane, the group's executive director. "Immigrant women have their own language, their own culture, and they don't go out. So we have to try to get in."

Mei Tsing recently visited the Chinatown Health Clinic in Manhattan for her second mammogram in four years.

Experts would say the 63-year-old woman should have first had the test 20 years ago, and should receive it every year or two. But before Tsing trades her oversized Columbia University sweatshirt for a paper robe, she discounts the idea of visiting any doctor that often.

"I have other things that worry me more", says Tsing, whose mammogram turned up no problems.

That's a common, and dangerous, philosophy among immigrant women.

"They worry about making a life for their family, not about a lump that doesn't hurt," Zane says.

But finding such a lump is critical. Breast cancer is the most common type of cancer among adult women, but its sufferers boast strong survival rates—more than 70 percent live at least five years after diagnosis. The most likely survivors are the women who catch the disease before it can spread.

After several years of gentle pestering by her family physician, Hsu had her first mammogram in March, 1994. The test turned up a cancerous tumor, tiny enough to remove through a lumpectomy.

"I was lucky, really," Hsu reflects.

Study: U.S. Is Abusing Its Future

Neglect, Mistreatment of Children
Nearly Doubles

Staff and wire reports, *Contra Costa Times*, September 19, 1996

WASHINGTON. The abuse and neglect of America's young nearly doubled between 1986 and 1993, a federal study says.

The increase is so dramatic, the study says, that it reflects a "true rise" in the severity of the problem rather than one based solely on heightened awareness.

The study, issued Wednesday by the Department of Health and Human Services, says the estimated number of children abused and neglected rose to 2.81 million in 1993—up 98 percent from 1.42 million in 1986.

Child welfare workers say the upward trend is continuing.

Many blame drug and alcohol abuse and a breakdown of the family.

Renita David, a case manager at an early childhood program in Laurel, Miss., said she thinks unemployment is partly to blame for a rise in abuse and neglect.

"The jobs that you get pay little or nothing so you have two choices: Either you go on unemployment, or you sell drugs or you turn to alcohol" and this leads to stress in the home, which leads to violence, she said.

The estimated number of seriously injured children nearly quadrupled from 141,700 in 1986 to 565,000 in 1993, the report said. It said those statistics appear to "herald a true rise in the scope and severity of child abuse and neglect in the United States."

It is unreasonable to suppose that so many more seriously injured victims of abuse and neglect existed at the time of the last report and somehow were not noticed by community professionals, the report says.

In California, child abuse reports did not rise as rapidly during the seven-year study period as elsewhere in the country.

The number of reports rose by 33 percent to 455,526 during that time, according to state reports.

"It could be the actual number of abuse cases are going up or that people are becoming more aware of it and reporting it," said Eileen DeMaria, executive director of the Child Abuse Prevention Council of Contra Costa County.

"My own individual view is that it's both."

. . . DeMaria predicted that the reduced welfare benefits and the accompanying economic desperation will lead to more abuse in coming years.

Health and Human Services Secretary Donna Shalala released the report at the National Conference on Child Abuse and Neglect.

She also announced $23 million in state grants will provide additional resources to community organizations that will use the money to teach parenting skills and provide other services aimed at preventing abuse.

Self-Segregation

Students Stick with Same-Race Groups

by Gina Pera
USA Weekend, August 18–20, 1996

Why do most teens hang out with friends of the same race? It's just "more comfortable" to be with people who share your background, say thousands of teens in essays submitted to USA WEEKEND. In fact, we got more mail on this topic than any other in the survey. Most also agree that adolescents possess a strong need to belong, and race provides the most obvious visual identity. At the same time, seven in 10 say they have a close friend of another race.

Here are the other reasons survey respondents cite most often:

Peer Pressure.
At some schools, making friends of another race creates problems with same-race friends. "If I talk to a person of another race, some black friends will say, " 'You're stuck up,' " says Chavonda Pighet, 15, a black student at South Robeson High School in Rowland, N.C. Her friends tell Chavonda that she should pick one group or the other. "But that's not right. I try to spend time with both."

Fear of Rejection.
Venturing beyond the comfort of a familiar group is a risk. For some, it comes at too high a price. "People of other races ask too many questions about my culture, which is Mexican-Indian and Native American," says Swift Sanchez, 14, of Forks (Wash.) High School. "They try to watch what they say, but they slip and say racial things." Twin sister Fawn agrees. "If I make a mistake around some white people, they say 'Look at that stupid Indian.' "

Safety in Numbers.

Some kids fear for their safety, says Anthony Harris, 14, of Chicago's Luther High School South. "They think all black people sell drugs, all Mexicans carry knives, all white people listen to heavy metal," says Harris, who is black. As a result, teens seek the protection of the group "just in case something happens, like a fight."

Ignorance.

Teens, who face big changes as they grow up, want to feel secure, says Luke Kozikowski, 13, of St. Stanislaus School in Chicopee, Mass. So the races separate to avoid conflict. "But then they feed on each other's fears." The only way to really feel comfortable with different kinds of people, says Kozikowski: "Take a chance and get to know them one at a time."

Curb Teen Smoking by Valuing Kids

by Caroline Allison Wolter, Walnut Creek, California
Contra Costa Times editorial, October 3, 1996, p. A-17
Contra Costa Times

There is no universal reason why young people smoke. However, before trying to discourage those who are already smoking, we need to understand what motivates them to begin. Discontent, boredom, peer pressure and escape are only the beginning. Deeper issues are likely to be at the root of this self-destructive behavior. Kids aren't born with these issues. They are learned and integrated from the day they are born.

I feel it is a difficult, if not nearly an impossible task to discourage teenagers from smoking once they have begun. They may cut back or sneak cigarettes, but chances are they won't quit. Why? Because smoking is only a symptom of deeper feelings of low self-esteem and inadequacy, which are more likely the root causes.

If we can't help teen smokers now, we should focus on what we can do. Parents, teachers and society must value children from the day they are born. Their behavior needs to change before the teens have a chance of not smoking. This means we must allow kids to be kids. People need to be more honest with themselves and their children.

In searching for causes, we should also consider the notion of an immediate or situational cause of a problem. We can ask, "What is the factor that makes the difference between an event happening or not happening?" (In folk wisdom, this might be expressed as "the straw that broke the camel's back.)"

The immediate cause is preceded by other factors that led up to the effect. If someone causes an accident because of driving drunk after a party, we have the immediate cause of the collision. However if no liquor had been served at the party, the accident probably would not have happened, or if the driver's father or mother had not been an alcoholic, the driver might not have been predisposed to drink. The driver's predisposition to drink would be termed a remote cause of the accident. In many cases, critical thinkers have to ask the question, "Where do we draw the line in our search for causes?"

 EXERCISE

Purpose: To distinguish immediate from remote causes of an event or effect.

1. Do some research on a social or national event and try to isolate the causes, both immediate and remote, of this event. For example, if you researched the United States' entry into World War II, you would go beyond the attack on Pearl Harbor, as far back as World War I to see all the influences that both compelled and restrained U.S. involvement. Another example would be the rioting in Los Angeles in 1992. You might find the immediate cause of the rioting to be the verdict acquitting the police officers of beating Rodney King; however, in your research, you would also discover deeper, although less immediate, causes for these events.

2. Study the arguments used by the prosecution or by defense attorneys in a trial that attempts to prove a cause-effect relationship between events. Examples would be trials against manufacturers of faulty products, such as breast implants or dangerous toys, or trials in which one person claims damage done to them by another person or by a company, such as com-

plaints about the effects of second-hand cigarette smoke or video display terminals. Investigative news programs, such as *Frontline*, *60 Minutes*, *48 Hours*, and *20/20*, often feature stories about such trials, and they make transcripts of their programs available to the public.

In looking at the statements made by the attorneys for both the prosecution and the defense, find examples of arguments claiming or denying a cause-effect relationship. Summarize these arguments and comment on their persuasiveness both to the jury and to you as a critical thinker.

Mill's Analysis of Cause and Effect

Another British philosopher, John Stuart Mill (1806–1873) formulated several specific methods (which he called *canons*) to help us systematically discover causes. Let's look at two of these methods, the method of difference and the method of agreement (or similarity).

METHOD OF DIFFERENCE

Using this method, the cause is found by noting that the only difference between the event or effect (called **Y**) happening or not happening is whether one element—**X**—is present.

Let's say a family of four goes to 'Chicken King' for lunch. Dad orders the fried chicken, while Mom and the kids have nuggets. All of them order root beer to drink. That night, Dad wakes up with painful cramps and stays up most of the night dealing with an upset stomach. At this point, Dad concludes that he probably got sick from the fried chicken, since it was the only thing he had that the rest of the family did not have. The fried chicken is the element (**X**) that caused the upset stomach (**Y**).

If a patient reports to a psychologist that he is depressed, he might be asked to keep a journal, detailing the times of most and least depression. If the psychologist discovers the most and highest depression (**Y**) occurring on Sunday night and Monday morning, then he or she might conclude that the depression is related to a return to work (**X**) after the weekend. Although the return to work may not turn out to be the cause, it provides a useful avenue of inquiry.

A famous example of looking for a difference occurred when Edward Jenner, a nineteenth-century British physician, was investigating a cure for smallpox. He discovered that there was a group of people who rarely got the disease—dairy maids. What was the difference between the dairy maids and the larger population?

On further investigation, Jenner discovered that most of the dairy maids had had cowpox, which is similar to smallpox but not usually deadly to human beings. Because they had had cowpox, they were immune to the smallpox; the cowpox had "vaccinated" them against smallpox. So cowpox (**X**) caused the positive effect (**Y**) of immunization from the illness. From this discovery, Jenner came upon the notion of 'vaccinating' people against smallpox.

METHOD OF AGREEMENT

Using this method, the cause is found by noting that **X** is the only factor always present when **Y** (the problem or the good effect) occurs; therefore, **X** causes **Y**.

Let's look at our family example again. This time, the family gets up and has plain bagels and cream cheese for breakfast. They then go to a carnival and all share a pizza for lunch. Then, after a few hours, the children have some cotton candy. Later that night, both of the children develop upset stomachs. Using the method of agreement, the parents conclude that since both children had cotton candy, cotton candy is the cause of the problem.

Using Difference and Similarity Together to Determine Cause

Often, we are able to use both the method of agreement (similarity) and the method of difference together. In our previous example about the Chicken King incident, let's imagine that the next day, while Dad sleeps in, Mom goes outside to do some yardwork.

She chats with a passing neighbor, and tells how her husband got an upset stomach, which she suspects came from his meal at Chicken King. The neighbor relates how, several days ago, she also got sick from eating the same meal, whereas her children, who had nuggets, were okay. In this case, **X** is the only difference between what Dad ate and what Mom and the kids ate. **X** is also the only similarity among the people in the neighborhood who got sick.

If a patient is having allergic reactions, a doctor may begin a systematic search for the causes of the ailment. The patient might be told to stop eating food typically involved in allergies (for example, wheat, sugar, and dairy products). Then, after a period of time, the suspected allergens are introduced one at a time; if the allergic reactions reoccur, the patient is advised to eliminate the food that triggered the reactions. If the patient continues to eliminate this food and finds that the allergic reactions are gone, then the process of reasoning from evidence to a cause has been successful in this case. **X** is the only food that caused the reaction (**Y**); and in every case in which **X** is eaten, the reaction occurs.

Mills' basic concepts are foundational to the scientific method in which experiments are conducted in order to discover or eliminate strong support for causal connections. The data from these studies can help us to make reliable causal generalizations, as we will see in the next chapter.

Chapter Highlights

1. The strength of a conclusion is based on the quality of evidence used to support the conclusion.
2. Statistical evidence can be gathered from polling a sample of a target population about a given topic, which is called the characteristic of interest.
3. Samples used to collect data must be sufficiently large, randomly chosen, and representative of the target population. When a sample is not representative, the study is biased.

4. Surveys can yield useful information when they are based on statistical research; however, mail-in surveys usually yield inadequate statistical evidence because they do not reflect a random and representative sample.

5. Studies reported in both print and electronic media are abridged; critical thinkers will read them carefully and do further investigation of the findings before using them to support conclusions or decisions.

6. Several theories of causation have been developed by philosophers and scientists; among these are Hume's conditions for cause and effect, theories of technical causation, and Mill's canons of cause and effect.

Articles for Discussion

Black, White, or Other

by Michael K. Frisby, *Ethnic NewsWatch*
© SoftLine Information, Inc., Stamford, CT

As Laurie Gantt filled out a form for her daughter's Social Security card, suddenly she paused. She was stumped by the boxes marked "race." Gantt is White, her husband is African-American; that made 3-year- old Madeleine neither White nor Black. So her mom wrote "biracial." But that didn't please the grizzled, White bureaucrat behind the counter in suburban Atlanta.

"What's this?" he barked. "None of the categories apply," explained Gantt. "She's not any one of these. She's biracial." Abruptly, the government man scratched out the word "biracial," glared at the infant and wrote an X in the box marked "Black." "She's got to be one of them," he grumbled and went on with his work. A dejected Gantt walked away, but mothers facing the same dilemma in the future may not have to endure that scene.

The federal government, as well as some states, are under siege by people of mixed race who don't want to be boxed in as simply Black or White. They want their identities recorded more accurately; and who can blame them? As America approaches a new century, biracial people lie trapped in a vortex with contradictory voices blaring, trying to fit themselves and their children into society's melting pot.

The government is wrestling with how to handle this hot-button issue. At its heart is Statistical Policy Directive No. 15, a rule established in 1977 setting the guidelines for racial and ethnic standards on all federal forms. The policy dictates that America should be broken down into four racial categories: American Indian or Alaskan Native, Asian or Pacific Islander, Black, and White. Then, the government tries to determine ethnicity by asking people to check off "Hispanic origin" or "not of Hispanic origin." These categories are used on federal surveys, such as the census and the monthly Current Population Survey completed by the Census Bureau for the Bureau of Labor Statistics. They are also used to monitor civil rights laws and the Voting Rights Act and are found on various forms at state and local levels, from public school enrollments to mortgage loans and scholarship applications.

Besieged by complaints, the Office of Management and Budget (OMB) is considering changes. Congressional hearings were held in 1993 and OMB held administrative hearings last year. Some 800 people wrote letters offering their views, and the suggestions for updates go far beyond just adding a "multiracial" category. Some Europeans, such as German-Americans, argue that they have suffered discrimination, but without data on their plight, the complaints aren't recognized, so they want their own category; Hispanics feel slighted, and some want race to be distinguished within their ethnic classification; Hawaiians want to be shifted from Pacific Islanders to the Native American slot, maintaining they are not immigrants; Arabs from the Middle East don't want to be White and seek their own identity.

In 1996, the Census Bureau plans to test categories on a sample survey to about 50,000 homes. It will compare the new information with numbers gathered from past forms and analyze the impact before OMB makes changes to Directive 15 in 1997, well in time for the 2000 census.

Giving mixed-race citizens a new category may help clarify their identities, but it almost certainly will muddy issues of fairness and compliance with anti-discrimination and civil rights legislation.

On one hand, civil rights groups proclaim that discrimination in many aspects of society remains strong; Blacks can't find jobs and are pummeled and disgraced by police, as officer Mark Fuhrman's taped statements demonstrated at the O.J. Simpson trial, and Black communities are ravaged by drugs and violence.

On the other hand, the nation puts a fresh spin on de-emphasizing race, as society denies its racism and spouts that skin color no longer makes a difference. The U.S. Supreme Court feeds this notion, repeatedly unleashing rhetoric about a color-blind society, moving affirmative action from chic to passé.

Undeniably, recent years have brought new levels of racial and ethnic diversity. In fact, according to 1995 census figures, the number of non-Whites now stretches to 27 percent of the population and is rapidly growing. The once illegal unions between the races have spread like wildfire—in 1960 approximately 149,000 interracial marriages existed; by 1990 there were almost 964,000, a 547 percent increase. And who can miss the Calvin Klein ads with a bare-chested, White male embracing a nappy-haired, dark-hued woman, or the Guess clothing ad that shows a brother with his hands around the waist of a blond White woman. Or the television cameras at the U.S. Open tennis match frequently panning Boris Becker's wife, Barbara Feltus, who is Black, among spectators in the stands.

So, with these signs that racial tolerance is vogue, why can't people like Gantt have "multiracial" boxes added to surveys so their families can take pride in their heritage?

That's a question on the mind of 12-year-old Kaleena Crafton, of Redford, Mich. A year ago, she wrote a passionate plea to federal officials: "I find something wrong with how people define my racial category," she said. "To them, I'm either 'black,' 'white' or 'Native American/Pacific Islander.' Well, I'm really European, African and Native American. To me (and others), this is a problem. . . . When someone says I'm white or black, it is really lying about my heritage. Yes, lying. Because my race is not black, not white, and not Native American. It is multiracial. This category is important to me, so that I leave out none of my races."

But allowing Kaleena the comfort of a government-recognized identity isn't as innocent as it might appear. It means dramatically altering this nation's ancient mind-set toward race. For more than 200 years, White America has put society in Black and White terms, with Black always valued as less than White. In the 1790 census, the nation's first head count, free Blacks and taxable Indians (those who lived on settlements and paid taxes) were dismissed as "all other persons." And when determining each state's representation in Congress, the Founding Fathers decided slaves would be counted as three-fifths of a free person; later, the "one drop" mandate took hold—a single Black in one's ancestry determined race, regardless of how White one might have looked. If that standard is implemented today, most African-Americans could claim to be "multiracial."

But despite assertions that race doesn't matter, this could harden the subtle caste system already in place among African-Americans. Ask darker sisters and brothers whether light-skinned Blacks have social and employment advantages because of their complexion, and the answer likely will be a resounding yes. A "multiracial" category would, in a way, codify that difference. In Brazil, a multiracial class means few people are "Black."

The reality for some African-American leaders is the concern that Blacks as a people would inevitably lose political and economic clout because their group numbers would shrink. Privately, some Black leaders contend the multiracial families pushing this movement are pawns for racists, whose real goal is to eliminate racial categories altogether, pushing the nation toward this delusion of a color-blind society. Such a move towards this fraud would dissolve the safeguards the government constructed to promote equal opportunities for Blacks.

On Capitol Hill, Rep. Tom Sawyer (D-Ohio), who, as chairman of the House Subcommittee on Census, Statistics and Postal Personnel, held hearings on the ethnic categories two years ago, acknowledges a root of the confusion if categories are not based on science or anthropology.

"The categories are social and political creations that have changed over our history," he says. "The irony is that at a time when the fundamental character of our age may be change itself, that the categories would remain unchanged." But he disagrees with attempts to eliminate them, saying categories should change to document shifts in perceptions but are still needed as tools to fight discrimination. They present "a shifting view of who we are," he says.

Most experts agree that some people listing themselves as Black will indeed opt for a "multiracial" category if it is available. On the surface, such a change could be perceived as progress in race relations. According to a February 1995 *Newsweek* survey, 49 percent of Blacks support a "multiracial" category, compared with 36 percent of Whites.

The best estimate is that 10 percent of African-Americans will go that route, but as multiculturalism grows in popularity that could be just a starting point. After all, various estimates say that at least 75 percent of Blacks have some mixed ancestry, and many may decide that now is the opportune time to claim it. That possibility troubles Arthur A. Fletcher, a member of the U.S. Commission on Civil Rights.

"I can see a whole host of light-skinned Black Americans running for the door the minute they have another choice," he told the House Subcommittee on Census, Statistics and Postal Personnel. "Black, White or whatever, but all of a sudden they have a way of saying, 'In this discriminatory culture of ours . . . I am something other than Black.' . . . In the employment field and, in some instances, the education field, the lighter skin[ned] the Black person is, the easier it is to hire them. . . . I know in the Black community, a large number of people who . . . think the economic opportunities that would flow from being identified as 'other,' whatever other is, in this culture is an advantage and not a liability."

Others now harbor the same fears expressed by Fletcher when he first addressed the issue in 1993. Barbara R. Arnwine, executive director of the Lawyers' Committee for Civil Rights Under Law in Washington, cautions that the new category would have "the practical effect of giving people who are less than positively inclined toward civil rights arguments for trying to disaggregate the population of African-Americans." She says, for instance, that the change would undermine civil rights enforcement such as voting rights and anti-redlining laws. "There are benefits and there are harms," Arnwine says. "I think the harms strongly outweigh any kind of positive benefit for children wanting to acknowledge their mixed parents."

Moreover, William Strickland, a visiting lecturer in Afro-American Studies at the University of Massachusetts at Amherst, argues that Blacks will pay a political price if splintered by the multiracial classification. "It's understandable that people want to honor both of their parents," Strickland explains, "but politically, it is deleterious. Even though we may redefine ourselves in a certain way, the system does not. Folks have to ask themselves if the right wing will see them any differently." More bluntly, he says of those pushing for the change, it's silly "to pretend that this system doesn't see all of us as niggers."

Of course, civil rights groups have weighed in. "We believe strongly that the OMB should not rush to institute the "multiracial" category when there is this clear potential for increasing the racial segregation, discrimination and stigmatization of Black Americans," says a statement from the Lawyers' Committee for Civil Rights Under Law, the NAACP, the National Urban League and the Joint Center for Political and Economic Studies.

But they face a determined opponent, and emotions run high on this issue. Susan Graham, a White Georgian, leads the crusade to identify multiracials. The executive director of Project Race, a support organization for multiracial children, Graham got involved when she was confronted with the 1990 census: Like Laurie Gantt, there was no slot for her children. When Graham talked to census officials, she was told her children should be classified as the mother's race "because in cases like these, we always know who the mother is and not always the father." At school in Roswell, Ga., meanwhile, she left the race space blank when her son, Ryan, entered kindergarten. The teacher filled it in. "Ironically, my child has been White on the United States census, Black at school and multiracial at home, all at the same time," Graham says.

Soon, she was contacted by a Cincinnati mother, Chris Ashe, who confronted similar problems because the Ohio school district in 1990–91 listed only five racial categories: Black, White, Asian, American Indian and Hispanic. Though the district added "other" in 1991–92, Graham and Ashe lobbied Ohio legislators until in 1992, the state passed a law adding the "multiracial" category, and removing "other" from school forms for the 1992–93 school year. That year, 527, or 1.05 percent, of the district's nearly 50,000 students marked the "multiracial" category, compared with 489, or less than 0.98 percent, who chose "other" the year before.

Legislatures in Georgia, Illinois, Indiana and Michigan have approved similar requirements for multiracial designations, while Florida and North Carolina did so through administrative rulings.

Ramona E. Douglass, president of the California-based Association of MultiEthnic Americans, is exasperated with the opposition from civil rights groups. Her mother is Italian, her father is Black and American Indian. She touts her civil rights credentials, marching in the South with the Ku Klux Klan "dancing in my face," and working with the defense team for 1960s activist Angela Davis. Now, she's ticked off at being given an anti-Black tag. "I'm real upset that the African-American community has taken a stand against us, saying, 'We want to step out of the Black box.' Let's get real, that's infuriating."

To Douglass, this is indeed a civil rights battle. "It's our way of saying, excuse me, we are not invisible," she says. "Part of being a full American is saying who you are. I refuse to have someone pick for me." Douglass argues that medical reasons exist for wanting people to be classified more specifically. For instance, she says people from different regions of the world are prone to illnesses that can be missed if they are classified simply as White or Black.

Still, the other side presents an equally compelling case for not changing the classifications.

Census data is used for studying changes in social demographics, health and economic characteristics of various groups. And of particular interest to Blacks, since the dawning of the Civil Rights Movement, it has been used for monitoring and reporting in areas such as housing, voting rights, credit protection, school desegregation, law enforcement and mortgage lending. For example, the Department of Housing and Urban Development (HUD) keeps records on mortgage lending, making sure Blacks aren't discriminated against. It caused havoc when "other" was added to the department's racial classes. In 1991, 35,000 were reported as "other" on mortgage papers used under the Home Mortgage Disclosure Act to determine if lenders were discriminating. HUD says that made it difficult, if not impossible, to monitor their cases.

And the Office of Federal Contract Compliance Programs says the change could force a decrease in the number of federal contracts to Blacks because some affirmative action programs are based on the percentage of Blacks in a given area. The U.S. Equal Employment Opportunity Commission would face similar problems because the pool of Blacks available for jobs in an area would appear to decrease, making it harder to prosecute companies for hiring discrimination.

Wade Henderson, head of the Washington bureau of the NAACP, warns that the census is not the place to make a social statement. Says Henderson: "Those of us who oppose creation of a "multiracial" category in no way seek to deny the self-expression of those who are of bi-racial heritage, but we think the census is not the appropriate venue for what is a social and political statement."

Questions for Discussion

1. How are statistics about racial categories used by various agencies?
2. Why do people who are of mixed race want a new category created on government forms? To what extent do you agree with their position?
3. The head of the Washington bureau of the NAACP "warns that the census is not the place to make a social statement." Why are some African-American leaders concerned about the impact of a new multiracial category on census forms?

The general public does not understand the art of public opinion polling, according to Janice Ballou, who is quoted in the following article by Ellen K. Coughlin. The following article provides a good 'state-of-the-art' review of statistical research, giving guidelines for understanding the numbers that are presented to us.

Researchers Practice the Science and Art of Public-Opinion Polling

by Ellen K. Coughlin
The Chronicle of Higher Education, February 7, 1990

Public-opinion polling sometimes appears to be the engine that drives American society. Ever since computers made the juggling of hundreds of numbers the work of an instant, opinion surveys have become ubiquitous, and so influential that they seem to play a part in deciding everything from what breakfast cereals we eat to what Presidential candidates we get to vote for.

Yet polling is so little understood by the general public, says Janice Ballou, director of Rutgers University's Eagleton Center for Public Interest Polling, that few people know enough to question the numbers they read. In fact, she adds, "it's actually a little frightening" how easily those numbers can be misleading, even when they are collected and reported in the best of faith.

It's Ms. Ballou's job to question the numbers.

As a researcher, she has taken a particular interest in an area known as "interviewer effects," or the ways in which the interaction between interviewer and respondent can influence the answers to questions.

A Little-Understood Tool

Ms. Ballou has spent some 20 years in survey research, working her way up from telephone interviewing to running a polling organization. As an experienced pollster, she will be part of a commission that will travel later this month to investigate public-opinion polls in Nicaragua—where, in anticipation of forthcoming elections, a great deal of polling has been taking place, she says, and "nobody believes the results."

The center Ms. Ballou directs, which is part of the Eagleton Institute of Politics at Rutgers, is both a polling organization and an academic-research center. In addition to running surveys under contract to clients, many of them state agencies in New Jersey, the Eagleton center is part of a national network of more than three dozen "state polls" that regularly canvass residents on issues of public interest. The center is also devoted in part to investigating the methodological problems that can cause error and bias in opinion surveys.

As such a hybrid, encompassing both polling and research on polling, the work of Ms. Ballou and her colleagues at the center illustrates some of the ways in which researchers have been trying to understand and improve what has come to be one of the most important and least understood *tools for designing social policy.* [My emphasis.]

Laws of Probability

Survey researchers like to say that public-opinion polling is both a science and an art.

The sampling part—deciding who and how many to survey—falls mostly on the science side.

Laws of probability, for example, have shown that a sample of 1,000 randomly selected respondents, no matter how big the total population, comes close to yielding an ideal balance of precision and economy.

Polls can be costly, and the more respondents, the greater the expense, Ms. Ballou says. Beyond 1,000 respondents, she explains, the precision of the results (or the likelihood that they will match opinion in the general population) usually does not improve enough to warrant the extra cost.

The design and execution of a questionnaire—deciding how to ask the questions and then actually putting them to people—are where most of the art comes in. The human interaction that must take place in any public-opinion poll is probably the area least reducible to rules or theories about how best to conduct a survey.

Something as simple as an introduction or the way in which a person is persuaded to take part in the survey, Ms. Ballou says, can cause error in the responses. Once engaged, most respondents are cooperative, and what researchers call "item non-response"—or a person's refusal to answer particular questions—is not a big problem.

"Besides," she says, "you'd be absolutely shocked about the kinds of things people will talk to you about. It's incredible what people will tell you on the phone."

Whether what people tell you is the truth, or whether it's an accurate account of what they believe, is something about which "we all scratch our heads," Ms. Ballou says.

Just last fall, for example, preference polls in elections involving black candidates for Mayor of New York and for Governor of Virginia turned out, when votes were actually cast, to have been significantly wide of the mark. Researchers speculated that white voters might have feared they would appear racist if they admitted to interviewers that they preferred a white candidate.

"It's one of those sources of error that we don't always understand," Ms. Ballou says.

Another example of the problem is a set of polls conducted by the Eagleton center on the subject of abortion.

As a major part of its work, the center runs what is known as the *Star Ledger*/Eagleton Poll, a survey sponsored by the Newark *Star Ledger* on issues of public interest in New Jersey. Established in 1971 as the Eagleton Poll, the survey is well known and highly regarded in the state; the newspaper took over its sponsorship in 1982, when the center became financially strapped. The poll is conducted four times a year; each one covers four or five topics, posing from 5 to 10 questions on each topic. Interviews are conducted over the telephone; that part of the work is subcontracted to a company in New York.

Responses Almost Identical

Twice last year, in March and September, the poll included questions on the subject of abortion. The September poll placed the issue in the context of the race for Governor then taking place in New Jersey. Both polls asked the same basic question: "Do you agree or disagree with the following statement: The decision to have an abortion is a private matter that should be left to the woman to decide without government intervention?"

The two surveys elicited almost identical responses on that key item. In March, 80 percent agreed; in September, 79 percent of all the respondents and 77 percent of the likely voters among them. Other questions that framed the same issue in somewhat different ways showed lower percentages but a similar sentiment—mostly in favor of a woman's right to choose abortion. The September poll revealed that the issue of abortion would probably not be a major factor in most voters' choice for Governor.

Both polls thus showed a decided "pro-choice" sentiment in New Jersey, and researchers at the Eagleton center are confident about that finding. An analysis of the answers that specific respondents gave to specific interviewers, however, revealed an intriguing pattern: Women talking to female interviewers and—oddly enough—men talking to male interviewers tended to give more "pro-choice" responses to the questions than did women talking to men or men talking to women.

So long as such biases are random, Ms. Ballou says, there's no problem. The trick is to keep them from becoming systematic.

In the profession at large, she says, "We're trying to begin to understand where that kind of thing is more likely to happen."

"We're starting to develop a sense of that, but it's far from a theory or a set of rules. But it is important to know that the possibility of that kind of error exists."

A Choice of Answers

Deciding how to word the questions that are asked in a survey is another area of opinion polling that is more art than science. A significant body of research has shown that changes in such things as phrasing, the amount of information offered, and the choice of answers available to respondents can influence the outcome of a survey to a greater or lesser degree.

"One of the rules in this business," says Ms. Ballou, "is that the question determines the answer."

The matter of question wording is particularly tricky on an issue like abortion, which has become so polarized the two sides don't even ask the same questions about it. "Pro-life" adherents think in terms of morality, "pro-choice" people in terms of rights. For one side, abortion is murder; for the other, it is a matter of personal freedom.

For their abortion polls, researchers at the Eagleton center made a difficult decision. None of the questions they asked even suggested that the issue of abortion might have a moral dimension to it, an omission that could have influenced the outcome of the poll.

"That would be a valid criticism," Ms. Ballou says. She says she would have preferred to cover both dimensions of the issue, but she argues that the center made the kind of "trade-off" that survey researchers are often forced to make—a sacrifice of a degree of comprehensiveness in favor of increased economy.

Order Can Affect Responses

"We can't do a whole survey on the abortion issue," Ms. Ballou says. "What do you ask when you can only ask 10 questions?"

By skirting the morality side of the abortion issue, the Eagleton researchers did lessen the possible consequences of another pitfall in polling: the effect that the order in which questions are asked can have on responses.

Studies have shown that the placement of a given question in a survey can change the proportion of people answering it a certain way by as much as 30 percent. That's why, for example, election polls sponsored by a particular candidate will sometimes solicit the respondent's opinion about the candidate at the end of the interview, after having, in effect, primed the respondent with a series of questions on issues the candidate is pushing.

On the issue of abortion, the so-called "personal choice" question— the one posed by the Eagleton center and asked first and in exactly the same way on both its polls—has been shown to elicit a markedly lower "pro-choice" response when it is asked immediately following questions about the morality of abortion.

The Eagleton researchers considered experimenting with the placement of their "personal choice" question between the first and second abortion polls, Ms. Ballou says. But they also wanted to test whatever change in public opinion may have occurred over the six months—in the intervening period, the Supreme Court had issued its decision in Webster v. Reproductive Health Services—and decided that the measurement might be skewed by a change in question order.

The question about a woman's right to make her own decision about abortion has been asked, pretty much in the way the Eagleton poll asked it, in countless surveys since 1973, Ms. Ballou says, and has consistently yielded responses similar to the one Eagleton got.

Such data about trends in public opinion are invaluable to survey researchers, Ms. Ballou says. Any researcher who has done his or her homework, is familiar with the trend data, and understands the issues, generally knows what to expect from the survey.

"You usually aren't surprised," she says. A result that surprises the researcher, she adds, is an indication that something may be wrong.

By the same token, public-opinion surveys rarely hit the nail on the head. In fact, when researchers report, for example, that 80 percent of the people surveyed agree that the decision to abort should be up to the woman, the figure really represents the midpoint on a range that may extend several percentage points in either direction.

Last fall, the Eagleton poll projected the percentage of votes each candidate for Governor of New Jersey would receive—and turned out to be precisely on target.

"We were exactly right, which is unusual," Ms. Ballou says. "There are some cases where you have the opportunity for external validation, but not that often."

Copyright 1990, *The Chronicle of Higher Education.* Reprinted with permission.

Questions for Discussion

1. What are some of the benefits of a well-done study as cited in this article?
2. What are important characteristics of valid statistical research?
3. What are some obstacles to good statistical research?
4. How does the order and the wording of questions affect the results of statistical research?

Ideas for Writing or Speaking

Using the following format, create a persuasive speech or essay on an issue of your choice. Use statistical research to support your conclusion.

1. Find an issue that interests you. The more interest you have in the issue, the more conviction you will have in your writing or speaking.

2. Write out your conclusion about the issue. Your position on the issue should be clearly articulated and will form your thesis statement.

3. Begin your essay or speech with an introduction that provides a context for your issue and your position. You may also use important statistics to gain the attention of your readers or listeners. Put your thesis statement at the end of your introduction.

4. Identify and expand upon the reasons that support your conclusion. Present these reasons in the body of the essay or speech. Concentrate on statistical evidence. You may also include examples and expert testimony to complete your support.

5. Use the conclusion of your speech or essay to restate your major points and to reemphasize the importance of your conclusion. Remind your readers or listeners of the points you brought out in your introduction, bringing these points full circle in your closing thoughts.

Longer-Term Writing Assignment

The purpose of this assignment is to give you an in-depth understanding of a social, national, or international problem and the many factors that enter into changes in policy. This may be done as a long-term project for an individual or a group.

Begin by asking yourself "What is a continuing community, campus, national, or international problem that concerns me?" Or, take the advice of English professor Bruce Reeves of Diablo Valley College, California, and fill in the blank on the following question: "If we can send a man to the moon, why can't we_____?" For example, you might think, "If we can send a man to the moon, why can't we solve world hunger?" Or, "Why can't we stop the drug cartels?" "Why can't we provide jobs for everyone?" "Why can't we have peace in the Middle East [or somewhere else]" "Why can't we rid our town of pollution from the local factory?" "Why can't we balance the national budget?"

Then, begin researching the problem. You will learn more about research in the next chapter, but begin with the knowledge you have gained in this chapter. Look up statistics that relate to your problem, being careful to note how the research has been carried out.

After you read Chapter 5, begin the rest of your research, using a minimum of six sources of information, including studies done about this problem and the opinions of experts who have written or spoken about the problem. If the problem you are studying is local, try to interview officials who are in a position to address the problem or who have worked on the problem.

Take notes on the background of the problem, noting the history of the problem, the scope of the problem, and the impact or effect of the problem. Focus particularly on what may be multiple causes that have created the problem.

As you research this problem, consider past efforts to solve it. To what extent were those efforts successful? Where there have been failed policies, explain why they have failed.

Note also any current or recent proposals about this problem. For example, if you are writing on the difficulty of balancing the federal budget, consider why past proposals made by congresspersons have not been approved. Also, consider the chances of success for any current proposals.

When you have finished studying this problem, make a proposal for a solution to this problem. Support your proposal, showing how it will resolve the difficulties that previous proposals have come up against. Also, explain how it will not create more problems than it solves.

If you find that you can't come up with a solution to the problem, then explain what variables make it too difficult to solve. State what would have to change for a resolution to be possible.

In sum, your paper or speech should include a complete explanation of the background of the problem, the scope, the harm it creates, the policies that have not worked against this problem, and your proposed solution to the problem or analysis of why it can't currently be solved. Also, include a bibliography of all sources you used in researching this problem.

5

Inductive Generalizations: Controlled Studies, Expert Testimony, & Analogies

Who Said So?
And Who Are *They* Anyway?

A critical thinker understands the proper use of controlled studies, expert testimony, and generalizations from analogies in supporting arguments.

This chapter will cover:

◆ The use of controlled studies in arguments
◆ The criteria for credibility of controlled studies
◆ The use and misuse of expert testimony in supporting conclusions
◆ The use of analogies in inductive generalizations

In the previous chapter, we considered the use of statistical studies and causal generalizations as evidence (reasons) to support conclusions. In this chapter, we will focus most of our attention on examining *controlled studies* and *expert testimony*. We will then look at another commonly used form of inductive reasoning, that of generalizing from *analogies*.

Researchers use controlled studies to make observations and draw conclusions about many subjects, including animal and human behavior, solutions to medical problems, and other scientific discoveries. The studies are called *controlled* because they use specific methods for comparing groups of subjects and can be duplicated by other researchers. In this way, the truth of the findings can be verified.

The conclusions drawn in carefully controlled scientific studies are inductive generalizations; a good study shows us what will *probably* or *usually* occur in a given circumstance.

Some of the elements of controlled studies are the same as those used by polling organizations. A researcher still works with the three questions discussed in Chapter 4:

1. What do I want to find out? (the characteristic of interest)
2. Who do I want to know about? (the target population)
3. Who can I study to get accurate answers about my entire target population? (the sample)

As with polling, researchers usually can't study everyone in a given target population, so they have to observe *some* members of the population. The number of subjects depends on how precise an answer is needed by the researcher. Preliminary results leading to *additional* studies can be gathered by a very small sample. For example, if a researcher discovers that twenty women with kidney problems have a negative reaction to the drug ibuprofen, his findings may be used to justify the funds for a larger study.

In medical research, the design of a study is called the **protocol.** Two groups of **subjects** (people or animals) who are alike in all important (relevant) aspects need to be studied in order for the research to have the element of **control.** Control involves weeding out extraneous factors that could affect the outcome of a study.

Research Design

A good research design includes:

1. A **question** to answer. This is the characteristic of interest concerning a targeted population. A researcher begins with a question, such as, "What is the effect of the new drug Z on migraine headaches?"
2. A **hypothesis,** which is a speculation about what will be discovered from the research. For example, "The drug Z will shorten migraine headaches caused by restricted blood vessels."
3. A **sample** of individuals to study. The sample should be randomly selected and representative of the target population. The sample is divided into two groups (see Figure 5.1):
   a. A **control group:** a group of subjects from the sample who get no treatment or a placebo (sugar pill).
   b. An **experimental group:** a group of subjects from the sample who are exposed to a special treatment; for example, this group might be given the drug to assess its effects in comparison with similar people who are not given the drug or who are given a placebo.
4. **Data:** The observations made by the researcher as he or she completes the study.

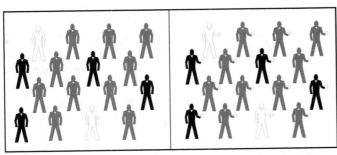

Control Group   Experimental Group

Figure 5.1

5. **Conclusions:** After the study is carried out, the researcher compiles the data and draws conclusions; the researcher interprets the meaning and significance of the data.

In addition, researchers carefully consider the implications of the findings, which means that they speculate about further research that can be done to answer questions related to the study.

Significant results may be discovered when the only significant difference between the control group and the experimental group is that the experimental group is exposed to special treatment, like a new drug. Researchers can draw accurate conclusions and eliminate alternate explanations for the results of their research if the studies are carefully designed. The generalizations they draw may be used as evidence in inductive arguments.

SKILL

Understand the basic components of a controlled study.

Criteria for Evaluating Research Findings

> *"Science is always simple and always profound. It is only the half-truths that are dangerous."*
>
> George Bernard Shaw, *The Doctor's Dilemma* (1913)

> *"Junk science makes junk law."*
>
> Dr. James Dobson

Interesting findings from research studies are often reported in newspapers and magazines or on television programs. Most of these reports don't give complete information about the research design. Before accepting the results of research as reliable, the following questions should be asked.

1. How large was the sample? As we discussed in the previous chapter, a small sample can suggest areas for further research, but should not be accepted as establishing factual information.

Sometimes, studies with an inadequate sample are reported in the news media because of the interesting results claimed by the researchers. If you read about a controversial report, be especially careful to listen for information about the sample used by the researcher. Consider the following study reported under the heading "FYI, True Love Is the Best Drug." Was the sample large enough to justify the conclusion expressed by the headline?

> While the verdict may still be out on whether love is stronger than hate, new research suggests it is at least healthier. In a study of older, happily married couples, Ohio State University researchers found that abrasive arguments weakened the couples' immune systems, making them more vulnerable to illnesses and infectious diseases. Scientists had asked 31 couples ages 55 to 75 to discuss the issues that caused problems in their marriage. Blood samples were taken at regular intervals and monitored for changes in hormone levels and immune function. The more negativity the couples expressed toward each other, the more their immune systems weakened.[15]

Remember that newspapers, magazines, and television programs want to present interesting information to their readers and viewers. Most reporters are not trained in research design any more than their audience members, so they are not usually skilled at examining methodology; their primary job is to create a good story.

2. Is the study reliable? As we discussed in Chapter 4, if a sample is not representative of the target group, then the study is biased and not reliable; the results cannot be generalized to a larger population. In the previous example about married couples, the reporter generalized about all couples from a small group of couples ages fifty-five to seventy-five. Remember that being representative means having the same characteristics in the

---

[15]　Staff and wire reports, "FYI, True Love is the Best Drug," *Contra Costa Times*, September 10, 1996, p. E-1.

same proportion as the target population. Consider the following claim made in an article entitled "Tea May Cut Stroke Risk"; notice that the conclusion is presented in the first sentence. Does the sample studied justify the conclusion?

> Drinking tea on a regular basis may help reduce your risk of stroke.
>
> That's the conclusion of scientists at the National Institute of Public Health in the Netherlands after they tracked the diets of 552 men, ages 50 to 69, for 15 years. The researchers were trying to see if flavonoids—a compound found in plant foods, such as black tea (the kind most Americans drink), and fruits—protected people from strokes. Flavonoids act like antioxidants, which prevent LDL or "bad" cholesterol from oxidizing, and help reduce the risk of heart disease and stroke.
>
> According to their findings, published in the *Archives of Internal Medicine,* men who drank more than 4 1/2 cups of tea a day had a reduced risk of stroke by 69 percent compared with men who drank less than three cups a day.
>
> The scientists also found a lower stroke rate among men who ate a lot of fruit, mostly apples. But that difference, they wrote, is "insignificant" until more studies are done.[16]

3. Have all of the important factors of the data been considered? There might be explanations for findings in research other than the ones given by the researchers. For example, if part of the sample knows they are receiving the treatment, they may report positive changes based solely on their expectations (that is, if Joanne knows she received the new drug that cures headaches, she may *expect* to feel better and then actually feel better). To control for this kind of error, researchers generally try to conduct *blind* studies, in which the participants are not told whether they belong to the experimental or control group.

Also, researchers may unconsciously exaggerate the improvement they see in the experimental group, especially if the

---

[16] "Tea May Cut Stroke Risk," *Better Homes and Gardens,* July, 1996, p. 66.

study results are very important to them. For this reason, *double-blind* studies are often conducted; in these studies, neither the experimenter nor the participants knows which is the control and which is the experimental group.

In addition, it is often difficult to do research studies that might help us discover causal factors. For example, we wouldn't want to take identical twins and encourage one to become a smoker to see if her lungs deteriorated over time while her non-smoking sister's lungs remained clear. So we often are hampered by limited information, evidence we can collect from past connections, as we seek to discover reasonable causal generalizations. There are also sample groups that are difficult to study, as discussed by columnist Linda Seebach in the following excerpt:

> American education suffers from an excess of experiment and a shortage of research. The difference is that research studies are carefully designed to test an educational theory by comparing one group of students who have tried a new method with a similar group who have not.
>
> The difficulty is that such research is expensive and complicated. New medicines are tested for safety and efficacy by "double-blind" tests in which neither doctors nor patients know who is getting the experimental drug. But education can't be conducted blind; children, and their parents, know perfectly well what is going on in their classrooms.
>
> Recruiting children for a research study can lead to errors, if the parents who consent are unlike those who don't in some way the researchers don't know about.
>
> So the staple fare of education journals is success stories told by enthusiastic teachers reporting on their own classroom experiments. The stories are true, they may even be inspiring, but they don't prove any general principles.[17]

4. Are the results statistically significant? When a finding is labeled *statistically significant*, it is probable that the reported

---

[17] Linda Seebach, "Education Lacks Enough Research," *Contra Costa Times*, September 1, 1996.

effect will occur again in similar circumstances. For example, let's say there are 100 persons in an experimental group and 100 persons in a control group, and thirteen more in the experimental group react to the treatment (the variable). With that proportion of difference in reaction, researchers can conclude that there is a 95 percent probability that the variable (and not a chance occurrence) caused the effect, and they can call their study *statistically significant.*

5. Have other researchers been able to duplicate the results? There is always a first discovery of a link between a variable and an effect on people. However, if a study reveals an important finding, then other researchers may try similar experiments to verify the results of the research and look for applications of the discovery. When others have tried to do the same experiment and failed, the results are considered unreliable, as exemplified by the following excerpt:

> In 1986, scientists reported that extremely gifted 12- and 13-year-olds were especially likely to be left-handed and to suffer from allergies. They proposed that the kids, while in the womb, had been overexposed to testosterone, which might have triggered both the allergies and the intellectual excellence. But this exotic idea vaporized in the summer of 1990 when different researchers—Jennifer Wiley and David Goldstein of Duke University—did a follow-up study; they found no evidence of a link between giftedness and left-handedness and allergies in children.[18]

6. Does the researcher claim that the study proves more than it was designed to prove? Some researchers may be too hopeful or excited about the implications of a study they conducted; if a small sample of cancer patients have been helped by an experimental drug, the researcher needs to limit the report of results to the findings of this particular study. A news organization may also report the results of a study in such a way as to magnify its significance. For example, a recent headline read "Lab helps find

---

[18]   Keay Davidson, "Nature vs. Nurture," *Image,* January 20, 1991, p. 15.

gene link to migraine. Research connects defect on chromosome 19 to familial headaches." In the opening paragraph, the results are summarized as follows:

> Scientists have for the first time linked a form of migraine headache to a defective gene by using DNA snippets supplied by Lawrence Livermore Laboratory and a lab-developed "map" of the gene's chromosome.[19]

The article goes on to discuss the fact that 20 million people in the United States suffer from migraine headaches; the traits of a migraine headache are described in detail. The reader is not told that this research may not be directly relevant to finding cures for typical migraine headaches until the ninth paragraph:

> But the finding, published in Friday's issue of the journal *Cell*, applies to a type of migraine that is "exceedingly rare" and atypical because it involves attacks of paralysis and brain deterioration, according to Neil Raskin, a UC-San Francisco neurology professor and immediate past president of the American Association for the Study of Headache. "I've only seen two patients (with that disorder) ever and I'm an old man," he said.[20]

When a study is promising, the researcher can suggest research that would be needed to make further discoveries about the effectiveness of a treatment. As critical thinkers, we need to "read the fine print" in an article that pulls us in with promises of more of a research breakthrough than has actually occurred.

7. Has the research been done by a respected institution? Research from a well-established institution such as the National Institute of Health or Stanford University is generally considered credible. Be careful in your judgments, however, if research from one reliable source contradicts research from another reliable

---

[19] Peter Weiss, "Lab Helps Find Gene Link to Migraine," *Contra Costa Times*, November 5, 1996, p. A-7.

[20] Ibid.

source; it is best to withhold judgment or to accept conclusions tentatively in these cases.

8. Are the researchers biased? Even if the research organization is well respected, it may have a vested interest in the outcome of the study. In a recent study on the effects of prostate medicines, note how one of the pharmaceutical companies that funded the research found fault with it. Do you think the criticism of the study they funded reflects bias?

> The first head-to-head comparison of the nation's two most popular medicines for prostate trouble found that one gives significant relief while the other is virtually worthless.
>
> The two medicines, Hytrin and Proscar, are taken by millions of older men to relieve the symptoms of an enlarged prostate gland.
>
> The study found that Hytrin eases men's discomfort by about one-third, while Proscar works no better than dummy sugar pills.
>
> Prostate drugs generally cost $30 to $45 a month.
>
> The study was financed by Merck & Co., which makes Proscar, and Abbott Laboratories Inc., the maker of Hytrin.
>
> Although both companies approved the study's design, Merck discounted its significance as publication approached in today's issue of the *New England Journal of Medicine*.
>
> Dr. Glenn Gormley, a Merck research official, said that in hindsight, the study was not set up properly to answer the question of which drug is better.[21]

REMINDER

Inductive reasoning is the process of making generalizations on the basis of specific observations.

---

[21]   Daniel Q. Haney, "The Battle of Prostate Medicines," Associated Press, *Contra Costa Times,* August 22, 1996, p. B-1.

EXERCISE

Purpose: To understand and utilize criteria for evaluating research.

Analyze the following examples in light of the criteria given for evaluating research findings. Then, answer the following questions:

1. To what extent did each study meet the criteria for evaluating research? What are the strengths and weaknesses of each design?
2. Are there factors the researchers overlooked in designing their studies? If so, what is needed to improve the design?
3. Does one study have a better design than the other? If so, how?

A researcher is interested in a new treatment for controlling the effects of the AIDS virus. He designs a study, called the *protocol*, which involves two groups of patients who have recently (within the past six months) tested positively for the virus. One group receives the new drug and the other group receives a placebo. There are no special dietary changes and no other treatments are given to the two groups. The only difference between the groups is that one is taking the drug and the other is not. The subjects in the experiment don't know whether they have the real drug or the placebo; that way the alternate explanation that they felt better because they expected to feel better (the placebo effect) is eliminated. As progress with the two groups is monitored, the researchers should be able to determine whether the new drug has had any positive effect.

A researcher wants to find out if test performance in college is improved when students eat a breakfast that is high in carbohydrates. She chooses two randomly selected groups of students and asks them to follow a breakfast plan for a semester. Because she does not want them to know that she is trying to discover the effect of diet on test scores, she tells them the test is for cholesterol ratings.

The control group is given a skimpy breakfast of a low-carbohydrate drink. The experimental group is given a breakfast loaded with carbohydrates like toast and cereal. Each subject keeps a diary of what they had for breakfast. Teachers are asked to report on the morning test scores of the groups of students. At the conclusion of the semester, the test scores are compared to see if the experimental group did better than their peers in the control group.

 EXERCISE

Purpose: To give you a hands-on sense of how research is done (that is, to give you experience in designing a study).

Design a study of your own. Pretend you have unlimited money and people and decide what you want to find out. Then create a study with a control group and an experimental group. You can be serious or humorous—the research topic is not important. The only important thing is your understanding of the scientific method.

This is a good exercise to do with a partner, because you can get more ideas on how to control against alternative explanations for your results.

You might also try to carry out your study with a small sample and to report your results to the class, telling them your design, your results, and your conclusions. Remember that a small sample can point to an interesting study to be carried out with a larger, more representative group.

Examples of Questions to Study:

- Does garlic cure the common cold?

- At what time of day are people more likely to answer the phone and talk to a salesperson?

- Would more people buy a green or a maroon camera case?

- Do people get more or less work done when they are sitting in an attractive room versus an unattractive room?

- Do young children learn math better if they work with real items (coins or beads) or with dittos?

- Do people who have no seasickness when sailing also have no seasickness when on a motorboat?

- Do people who have not eaten for a few hours buy more food at a supermarket than those who have just eaten?

- Do people who have a list buy less food at a supermarket than people without a list?

- Do athletes perform better after watching comedians?

As you can see, the possibilities of what inquiring minds would like to know are endless. Once you decide on your question and determine your hypothesis, state how you would find a control group and an experimental group, how you would guard for error, and how you would analyze your results.

Controversy in Research Findings

If you have studied the previous section and completed the exercises, you should have an appreciation of how difficult it is to do an accurate study. Good studies require time and money to complete. Even studies that use the scientific method and produce clear results are sometimes criticized by scientists or others who find flaws in the researcher's methods or conclusions. You may be familiar with studies of the effects of a substance (like saccharin) on rats that showed that the substance causes cancer. These studies were criticized on the basis that researchers were comparing human and rodent metabolism when they drew their conclusions; the findings were also criticized because the doses given to the rats were much higher than most humans would ingest.

Read the following excerpt from an article about another controversial research study that has been criticized by some groups and praised by others:

Two recent studies that conclude that abortions have little negative psychological impact on women have renewed debate over a politically charged issue that, many researchers concede, appears unlikely to be resolved soon.

Representatives of anti-abortion groups contend that the studies are methodologically flawed and biased because the researchers favor abortion.

In particular, the critics say the studies did not follow women for a sufficiently long time after their abortions to assess accurately the occurrence of delayed effects; that they used a sample of women unrepresentative of the general population; or that they employed inappropriate measures of psychological distress.[22]

The problem of divided opinion about the validity of a study is a difficult one, but as consumers of information, we can either withhold judgment until more conclusive evidence is presented or give credence to a study with evidence we believe is strong enough to influence our current decisions. For example, if we read that one study showed that a low-fat diet contributed to reduced cholesterol rates and another study showed no significant relationship, we may still choose to believe that there might be a chance of reducing cholesterol with the low-fat diet. The critical thinker realizes that researchers are not in agreement about the ultimate prevention and cure of elevated cholesterol levels, but he chooses to make some dietary changes based on limited research because "It can't hurt and it might actually help my heart."

A more difficult problem with research is avoiding errors that could affect the results of a study. Consider the following commentary on the subject of research studies conducted by young scientists:

Errors may occur through improper laboratory practices, faulty equipment, accidental mix-ups, poorly designed experiments, inadequate replication of research results, or any number of other reasons, some involving negligence and others occurring through no fault of the scientist.

---

[22]   Chris Raymond, *The Chronicle of Higher Education*, February 7, 1990, p. A6.

. . . error is, in fact, inherent in any endeavor carried out by fallible human beings. The great possibility of error is one of the reasons why judgment is so important in science and why a scientist who has avoided error, designed good experiments, exercised good judgment, and discovered something new about the nature of things in the universe can experience such a thrill of achievement.[23]

Given the possibility of error in experimentation, the question arises: "Whom should I believe?"

As critical thinkers, we must live between two extremes. One extreme is an attitude of cynicism and anti-intellectualism that says, "Scientific research studies can never be trusted because there are too many possibilities for error." The other extreme is an attitude of passive reverence for the scientific method that says, "Scientists are geniuses who are trained to carry out the studies that have brought us so many great advances, so I am not intelligent or educated enough to question any research I read." Both of these attitudes are inappropriate for the critically thinking individual. Research can be trusted if it is carried out in the correct manner, and you are quite capable of understanding the basic elements of research and evaluating specific studies you read or hear about. You can use the factors we have discussed in this chapter to evaluate the credibility of research studies and implications for any decisions you may need to make.

Remember that when we evaluate new or controversial findings, we also need to consider the credibility of the publication or news station reporting the study. Do the reporters have a reputation for being thorough and careful before they report on a study? Is there a science editor for the newspaper or magazine who knows which studies deserve to be reported? We also need to consider the credibility of the institution who did the study: Was it carried out by a questionable sex researcher who spends a lot of time on the talk show circuit? Was there possible bias in the research, as in a tobacco company finding that cigarettes

[23] Francisco J. Ayala, "Point of View: For Young Scientists, Questions of Protocol and Propriety Can Be Bewildering," *The Chronicle of Higher Education,* November 22, 1989, A36.

improve lung capacity? Or was it done by a reputable research institution with no known biases?

Consider the following article, by a consultant pharmacist who writes a well-researched, nationally syndicated column.

Study Implies Nicotine Prevents Alzheimer's

by Richard Harkness
Contra Costa Times, November 19, 1996

. . . Now, a new study suggests that smokers may be less likely to get Alzheimer's disease, and that nicotine could actually prevent the disease.

The study was published in the journal *Biochemistry* and was partly funded by the Philip Morris Company, a maker of cigarettes.

Keep in mind, though, that nobody is suggesting that you smoke to get the possible benefits of nicotine. In smoking, the bad far outweighs any good one might get from nicotine.

In the study, a chemist at Case Western Reserve University in Ohio created a "model" of the brain's chemistry and found that nicotine might stop the development of damaging beta amyloid plaques, which are characteristic of Alzheimer's disease.

The researcher theorized that it might be possible to prevent Alzheimer's if a nicotine-like drug was started around age 40.

The Alzheimer's Association called the research interesting, but very preliminary.

Georgetown University researchers are doubtful that nicotine can stop the disease, but say that it might slow its progression. "Not only would all these people continue to interact with their families and live independently, but there would be a significant financial impact of not having to admit them to chronic-care facilities."

Reprinted with permission.

In a casual scanning of this article, some people might conclude that a cure for Alzheimer's is just around the corner. Others might dismiss the findings completely and wait for more definitive research findings.

As critical thinkers with some knowledge of what makes good evidence, we would note that the study was done by a researcher from a respected university and that it was published in a professional journal. We would also note that a tobacco company, which could profit substantially from positive findings, funded the research. In addition, we might conclude that, given the research linking lung cancer and other diseases to smoking, it would not be wise to start smoking to prevent Alzheimer's disease.

Now let's imagine that you have more than a passing interest in this research. What if you have to do a report on developments in Alzheimer's disease research, or perhaps your parents or grandparents have the disease and are losing not only memory, but also responsiveness?

SKILL

Read and discuss original studies before making decisions based on controversial research findings.

Let's say you have to do a report. If you are going to state that significant research is being done on the effects of nicotine on Alzheimer's patients, you should get the original study from the journal in which it was published, so that you know exactly what was done and what was discovered. You could check on similar studies concerning nicotine and brain function that have been done by other universities, such as the University of California at San Diego and Reading University in England. You can also ask a professor, doctor, nurse, librarian, or group concerned with the issue to help you understand the importance of a particular study.

In your research, you may find that health care professionals don't give much credence to the study, or you may find that it was an exciting breakthrough that would greatly enhance your report. The general rule of thumb is, if you are going to report information to others, you need to verify your sources, just as a good journalist would.

If you have a personal interest in research that is reported in an abridged manner in a magazine, newspaper, or televised segment, you can, as we have discussed, get more complete information by going to the source of the research. You might find the study detailed in full by a scientific journal, or you may be able to contact the researcher through the institution that sponsored the research. In addition, you can ask physicians who are treating your friends or relatives for their opinions concerning the relevance of the research findings to your specific situation.

In short, we can't possibly keep up with all advances in any given field of research. As critical thinkers, we can look at the credibility of the reports we hear or read and we can choose to do more intensive study of those reports that are relevant to our situations.

 EXERCISE

Purpose: To explore the effect of reported research on decision making.

For a few days, consider how decisions you have made are based on information you've read about or heard about. Did you choose to have or not have a surgical procedure because of research findings you read? Have you invested in a particular stock or mutual fund based on reports of a successful track record? Are any of your decisions about the food you eat (fat content, cholesterol content, sugar or salt content, balance of food groups) based on research? If so, do you remember what the research said and where you read or heard about it? If you take vitamins, ask yourself why you take them and what research led you to make vitamin supplementation a daily habit.

What about exercise options? Do you regularly exercise, and if so, have your decisions about what kind to do and what equipment or clothing to wear been based on research studies? Do you read consumer magazines before making purchases, or listen to friends or salespeople, or do you buy impulsively?

To complete this exercise, answer the following:

1. What is the habit you have acquired, the action you have taken, or the item you have purchased?
2. What factors led you to make the decision to acquire the habit, take the action, or buy the item?

3. What have been the effects (if any) of your decision? To what extent has your life been enhanced by your decision? How might your life be different if you had not made the decision?

Read the following humorous article as a review of some basic elements of controlled studies:

Sickening Experiment on Human Subjects

by Steve Rubenstein
San Francisco Chronicle, Friday May 25, 1990

Scientists were paying people $200 to throw up in San Francisco this week. It was too good a deal to miss.

They do these sorts of things at the University of California at San Francisco. Researchers are always looking for guinea pigs willing to try experimental drugs. In this case, the drug was a new anti-seasickness pill. The ad said you could make $200 for popping the pill and taking an eight-hour boat ride.

There was only one condition. You had to be the nauseous type. Somehow I qualified.

Dozens of people, many with holes in their pants, signed up for the voyage. It was encouraging to see so many selfless people pitching in for science.

"People will do anything for $200," explained one researcher. "Even this."

Before sailing away, we had to take a physical. It was a snap. The main thing the doc seemed interested in was whether I was the throw-up type. It's no good testing seasickness pills on people who don't get seasick.

"How do you feel on boats?" the doc asked, in that concerned demeanor of his calling.

"Terrible," I said. "Lousy. I head straight for the rail."

It was the right answer. The doc's face lit up like the penlight in his breast pocket. He put my chart in the active file. I was in.

On the appointed day, we men and women of science assembled at the hospital to take our pills. Since it was a scientific study, only half of us would be getting capsules containing the actual drug. The other half would receive capsules containing sugar, a placebo. A researcher handed out the pills randomly.

We weren't supposed to know which capsule was which, of course. That wouldn't be scientific. But the capsules, made of clear plastic, were easy to tell apart. The drug looked like tiny time pills, and the placebo looked like sugar. Someone sure screwed up, the doc said, especially because many people believe seasickness is a state of mind.

"What did you get?" we guinea pigs asked each other.

"Placebo," said one sad-eyed soul. "Darn. I'm a goner."

We were to swallow the pill precisely at 8 a.m. The researcher took out her digital watch.

"Place the pill in your right hand," she said. "Prepare to swallow."

We three dozen strangers stood abreast, pills in hand, united in time and place.

"Five, four, three, two, one. Swallow."

Gulp.

Into the buses we marched, and off to Fisherman's Wharf. We had a job to do.

The seas looked calm, which did not sit well with one of the passengers on the boat. His name was Kirt, and he turned out to be the president of the company that was trying to market the new drug. He had paid $80,000 to UCSF to conduct the impartial study—which he cheerily denied would be any less impartial because of his busybody presence on the boat—said the last thing he wanted to see was calm seas. Sick people is what he wanted.

"I don't want everyone to throw up," he said. "I just want the right people to throw up. The placebo people."

And then we shoved off on our mission. Eight nauseating hours on the high seas.

"Don't worry," the skipper told Kirt. "I'm going to get these people sick for you."

© *San Francisco Chronicle*. Reprinted with permission.

Questions for Discussion

1. What controls did the researchers use for this study?
2. Since this article was humorous, and probably exaggerated, we can't claim it as factual evidence of faulty research. Given that

disclaimer, what areas of potential error in results did the author point out?
3. If you were to set up a study to test a new anti-seasickness pill, how would you design your research?

EXERCISE

Purpose: To gather data from personal research.

Choose one of the following options for a personal experiment.

1. Chart your study habits for a week or two. Note if you have a regular time and place for studying. Is the equipment you need readily available (pens, paper)? Do you review notes shortly after class? Do you study alone or with others? What distractions intrude upon your study time (television, radio, phone, snack breaks, visitors)? After you have charted your habits, look at your record and draw conclusions about where time is well used, where it is wasted, and how it could be put to better use.
2. Chart your eating and exercise habits for a week or two. Then look at your record and draw some conclusions about your lifestyle. Does your record reflect healthy, nutritional choices, a rushed, erratic schedule, or a combination of both? Do you exercise regularly? Try to predict what will happen to your health if you continue to eat and exercise in this way.
3. Try a lifestyle experiment on yourself. Change an aspect of your daily life: Set and stick to consistent study habits, do a certain aerobic or bodybuilding exercise, reduce your intake of fat or sugar, or eliminate caffeine, tobacco, or a food you crave (some nutritionists believe that people are allergic to foods that they crave). Keep a record of how you feel after adhering to your new program for two weeks or a month, and

report the results to your instructor. (It might also be interesting for several people to work together on this, forming an experimental group.)

Use of Authority: Expert Testimony

In addition to drawing generalizations from controlled studies, writers and speakers frequently find strong support for their conclusions from the testimony of experts. An expert is an individual who has education, significant experience, or both in a given area. We turn to experts in many areas of our daily lives: We consult doctors, dentists, lawyers, mechanics, counselors, and salespersons who are supposed to have more knowledge and experience in their fields than we do.

We also rely on friends and acquaintances who have become knowledgeable about various subjects because they spend time on and keep up with these subjects; for example, we might consult a friend we respect who has read all about the local candidates for an upcoming election. We listen to what she says because she has credibility as an informed voter. When we buy a car or a stereo, we might consult a friend who works a lot on his car or who has had several stereos because we see him as more of an expert than we are. Even for small purchases, like clothing, we may ask a friend to help us if we believe this person has more knowledge of fashion trends than we do.

The phenomenon of consulting acquaintances before we make decisions has been called the *two-step flow* of information (see Figure 5.2). Our expert friends, who are called **opinion** leaders, first (step 1) get their information from the media (television, radio, the Internet, magazines, newspapers, and books) and then (step 2) they pass this information on to us. In our information-saturated age, this method makes sense; we can't be informed about everything, so we become experts in the areas we spend our time on and others become experts in other areas, and we share information. We learn from one another's experiences, mistakes, and successes and save time (and sometimes money) in the process.

Advertisers and campaign managers are well aware of this two-step phenomenon as they carefully choose the magazines

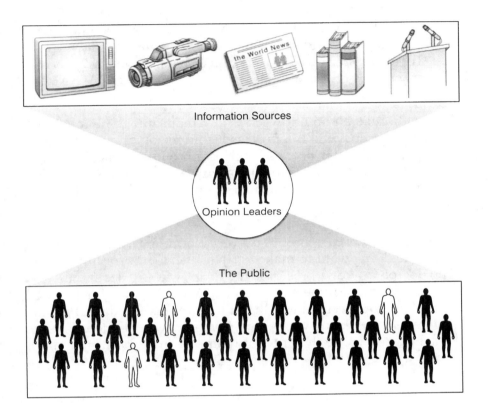

Figure 5.2

and television shows to best reach their target audiences. If they can get the opinion leaders to vote for them or to use their products, the rest of us will follow. News of the person or product will travel by word of mouth to the secondary audiences.

EXERCISE

Purpose: To find examples of how the two-step flow influences decision making.

Consider some voting or buying decisions you've made lately or some decisions about medical treatment. Did you consult an expert or a knowledgeable friend before making your choices? If not, on what basis did you make your decisions?

Try to list your three most recent decisions and trace any outside influences on those decisions.

Examples:

"I used to read a popular weekly newsmagazine to be informed. A friend of mine who is a professor told me about another magazine he likes better because it gives more in-depth coverage on issues. I switched to this other magazine and I really like it. I enjoy getting a broader report on current events." (from a retired student)

"I developed a breast infection—very common for nursing mothers—and didn't want to make a trip to the doctor for antibiotics. The doctor wouldn't prescribe the drugs without seeing me, so I called a friend of mine who is an expert in the use of herbs. She suggested home remedies which I took for several days; they did keep me from getting worse. But I wanted to get better faster, so I gave in and made the appointment." (from a mother of an infant)

Use of a network of friends may work well for personal decision making, but it won't work to quote these friends in papers or speeches. You can't say "Vote for Candidate X for senator; my friend Mark, who reads all the major newsmagazines, thinks he has the best foreign policy" and expect your audience to be convinced.

Nor can you say "I know a woman who works for a pharmacy and she thinks that 80 percent of the people who get prescriptions for Valium are drug addicts" as evidence that Valium users are addicted to drugs. It may be true that this drug is carelessly prescribed and it may be true that Candidate X is the best person for senator; however, the writer or speaker needs to use support that is generally recognized as valid in order to present a strong argument.

An expert who can be used to add strength to arguments has relevant academic credentials and/or significant experience in the area in question. People who are seen as experts in a field have been recognized by their colleagues or by the general public, or both. This recognition often comes as a result of publishing articles or books, earning advanced degrees, or attaining success or acclaim.

People who fit these categories have credibility, and their opinions are generally considered reliable sources of evidence for a particular argument.

The author of the following passage is a professional tracker. Trackers like Tom Brown, Jr., are experts in deciphering markings like footprints; often, they are called upon to study crime scenes. After years of intense observation, Tom Brown is able to recognize whether a person who left footprints is right- or left-handed; he can also determine their approximate weight, among other factors. Tom can even discern accurate information from a crime scene after rain has covered the area.

An Opinion With Substance

Excerpted from *The Search* by Tom Brown Jr.
He founded a survival school and teaches from coast to coast.

I took the class into the woods and stopped by a drainage ditch. The bottom was covered with soft sandy soil. It was also covered with animal prints. I asked the class to notice all the prints that were visible. They named two animals and guessed at two more. There were eleven, not counting the dog.

When I ask for prints, I'm not just looking for clear sharp markings of large well-known animals. I'm searching for an explanation of every mark on the ground. . . . As I study the markings a picture begins to form in my mind of what passed the spot I am checking before I arrived. My mind begins to place animals in space and time.

Something began to take shape as I noticed the age of the different tracks . . .

"Wow!" I yelled. "Look at that." It had all come together, and I began to explain the scene to the class as I pointed to the markings that were the tracks of a dog and a rabbit, which had been on this spot at the same time.

"Dog came down, saw the rabbit before it smelled him. Maybe a cross wind. He jumped after the rabbit. Here is his first set of four running prints." I pointed. "Here, here, here, and here. Here is the rabbit moving up the side of the ditch to that sweet new grass." Again I pointed to markings that looked almost as if someone had scraped the dirt with a branch. "The rabbit sees the dog, does a boogie here, and races down the hill. He made two gigantic leaps. See where he jumped? See where the dog leaped for him and missed? Skidded here, regained his balance, and followed up the other side, there." . . .

"How did you do that?" Kay asked.

"I sat for days on the edge of a field and watched rabbits feed, breed, bear young, and avoid danger. After each happening, I would study the marks that had been left in the earth. I can tell when a rabbit is sitting or standing, agitated or calm. Whenever a dog came through the field and happened on a chase, I would follow its every marking, remembering what my eyes had seen just moments before. After a great amount of time, I began to recognize those signs as I happened onto them."[24]

SKILL

Recognize legitimate and illegitimate uses of expert testimony.

Problems with Expert Testimony

There are some common problems associated with expert testimony that a critical thinker should consider when listening to an argument. These problems are:

1. Use of experts in the wrong field of expertise.
2. Use of experts who are not recognized as experts.
3. Use of experts who are paid for their opinions.
4. Use of experts who are biased.
5. Expert testimony that is contradicted by equally expert testimony.

[24] Tom Brown, Jr., with William Owen, *The Search: The Continuing Story of the Tracker* (Englewood Cliffs, NJ: Prentice-Hall, 1980), pp. 215–216.

1. Use of experts in the wrong field of expertise: The most visible form of this problem occurs in advertisements in which a person who is respected in one field is used to endorse a product out of his or her area of expertise. It is a legitimate use of authority for an athlete to promote sports equipment, but some ads capitalize on handsome or popular athletes by using them to promote cars, shampoos, or cereals.

When the television program *Marcus Welby M.D.* was popular, Robert Young, who played Dr. Welby, was used to promote a brand of decaffeinated coffee; the advertisers hoped consumers would think of him as a doctor dispensing medical advice (or that older viewers would remember Robert Young as the wise father in *Father Knows Best*). It seems that advertisers have recognized our increasing sophistication as thinkers by having a new TV doctor announce, "I'm not a doctor, but I play one on TV" The way the actor states this fact implies that "playing one on TV" makes him *sort* of a doctor, maybe even *more* than a doctor, especially since he looks so impressive in the white coat he wears on the commercial. And why else would he be dispensing medical advice on prime-time television!?

Be careful of slick expert advertisements by nonexperts, which are generally accompanied by impressive costumes and backgrounds. If real credentials aren't mentioned in an endorsement, don't assume there are credentials lurking somewhere in the person's background.

2. Use of experts who are not recognized as experts: Most areas of expertise today are in the midst of increasingly new discoveries. If someone is used as an expert based on experience or education completed years ago and if the person has not kept up with his field, then he is questionable as an expert. When someone quotes a finding by an expert, a date should accompany the quotation so we know when the discovery was made.

The importance of current information accounts for your instructors' advice to look up recent journal articles when you want to support a position. Books are good sources of support; still, in some fields, a book that is even a few years old is obsolete due to new information. The fact that some of your textbooks are in the fifth or sixth edition reflects the need for updating information in all areas. For example, history books that end with George Bush as President of the United States are missing vital information. Although foundational theories are essential, current ideas and events in any field are just as important.

Sometimes a person's credentials are distorted. Having *Doctor* in front of one's name can mean that one is a physician, a dentist, a recipient of a doctoral degree in an academic field, a chiropractor, or a psychologist. As a critical thinker, you need to understand what a title means, the reputation of the institution that conferred the title, and, if possible, the credibility the titled person has with his colleagues. The claims made by this person are then considered in the light of his or her position as an expert.

3. Use of experts who are paid for their testimony: One fairly obvious consideration in listening to evidence based on expertise is to find out whether the authority is paid for the testimony or endorsement. Some people, particularly salespeople, are paid to promote products. A salesperson may genuinely believe that a brand new truck will meet your needs, but he is not the only person to ask about it because of the conflict of interest built into his role. Similarly, an expert witness, such as a psychologist, who is called to testify on behalf of a defendant in a trial may lose credibility if she is paid for her testimony. If you suspect that an expert may be advising you based on what's in it for him, get a second opinion, as did columnist Thomas Sowell in the following excerpt:

The other day, the lights suddenly went out in the bathroom. After our amateur attempts to find out what was wrong got us nowhere, my wife found an electrician in the yellow pages and had him come over.

He did all kinds of investigating in all kinds of places and came up with the bad news: None of the usual things was wrong. What was wrong was probably that a wire had gone bad somewhere in the walls.

He conjured up a picture of a broken live wire dangling somewhere in those walls, ready to ignite something, so that we could wake up in the middle of the night with the place engulfed in flames. My wife was upset and

I didn't find the prospect all that great myself. What could we do?

The electrician said that he would have to open up the walls and just track down the place where this dangerous wire was. His estimate of how much it would cost was not cheap.

I thanked him and paid him for his time, but said that obviously we would have to get a second opinion before undertaking something that drastic. He said he understood, but urged that we get that opinion very soon—today—because of the danger involved.

This time I decided that the yellow pages were not the way to go. I phoned a very reputable contractor I know who had done some work for us a couple of years earlier and asked for his recommendation of an electrician.

Enter electrician number two—and exit electrician number two less than five minutes later. The lights were back on and not a wall had been touched. What was wrong was so simple that the first electrician undoubtedly realized immediately that we must not know anything about electrical systems if we had not fixed it ourselves.[25]

4. Use of experts who are clearly biased: Many people feel so strongly about an issue that they join with others who have similar beliefs, forming clubs, unions, and associations. They often are or become experts in their areas of interest, but their expertise is sometimes accompanied by a strong bias.

For example, those who lobby together for gun control may become highly knowledgeable of laws and regulations across the various states; similarly, members of the National Rifle Association gain expertise on the various statutes. Neither of these groups can be considered impartial and unbiased in a discussion of gun control. This does not mean a critical thinker should not listen to them; in fact, most editorials and televised debates on this issue and other controversial issues involve individuals with strong biases, and many of these individuals try to present a balanced viewpoint. However, critical thinkers keep in mind that they are

---

[25] Thomas Sowell, "Who Do Poor Turn to in a Pinch," *Contra Costa Times*, July 29, 1996, p. A-10.

hearing the facts from particular points of view, and they listen for possible exaggeration of the benefits of, or problems with, proposed policies.

 EXERCISE

Purposes: To discover examples of bias in books, magazines, or televised programs; to consider biased viewpoints.

1. Try to isolate an incident of possible bias in your reading or viewing. You might go through your textbooks and note that examples given seem to support a particular viewpoint or political stand. When you watch a television interview show, note whether the host gives equal time and courtesy to all points of view, or whether he or she seems to favor one side over the other. Many newsmagazines are considered to have a bias, conservative or liberal, or radically left or right; find an issue that is covered by two magazines with different biases and contrast the presentation of the issue.

   Example:
   This passage is from an English composition textbook. In a chapter about being fair to many points of view, the author begins with these statements:

   > Yvonne is a first-year college student of eighteen . . . among other lessons, her parents taught her that no man likes a woman with brains, that tears make a woman appealing, and that motherhood is a woman's sacred duty.
   > When Yvonne left home for college, her worried parents warned her to watch out for radical young college instructors who would try to put wrong ideas in her head. Yvonne really didn't pay much attention, though she dutifully promised to watch out. But then, the very first day she walked into her English composition class, there was the young instructor she had been warned about. And sure enough, after the instructor checked the roll, she as-

signed an essay on, of all things, the subject "runaway mothers"![26]

The chapter continues with a dialogue in which Yvonne's unreasonable words are contrasted with the instructor's wisdom. Yvonne is described as being impulsive, as crying, as waving her fist in her instructor's face, as not understanding the instructor's simple explanations, and as calling people who need social workers "icky." Later in the text, Yvonne's father is portrayed as a boob from another century who feels that women are only good enough to make coffee on the job.

This text is biased in its presentation of parents as stupid and behind the times. They are portrayed as backward, while the instructor is seen as progressive; they are old and the instructor is young; they are worried and controlling and the instructor is calm and reasonable. It doesn't make sense that such controlling parents as those described here would even allow their daughter to go to college.

Throughout the book, the instructor is seen as the person with all truth, and the parents are seen as bigoted and judgmental with no sense of reality or fairness. The first paragraph quoted lists three lessons taught by Yvonne's parents. Since the first two lessons are ridiculous, the third teaching—seeing motherhood as sacred, if not a duty—becomes crazy by association with the first two reasons. Downgrading of motherhood could be intimidating to a student who considered it an important profession.

What is really unfair is that all of these comments and many more like them are put in a book claiming to teach fairness and empathy and to warn against hasty moral judgments and stereotypes. I wonder if this author is aware of his own bias.

2. Take an issue and create viewpoints for several characters. For example, you could imagine the responses of a police officer, an addict, a drug pusher, a parent, and a politician to the notion of legalizing drugs. What natural biases might influence their responses? Working alone or in groups, write out each of their possible responses and see where the similarities and differences are. This exercise works well as a role-play followed by a class discussion.

---

[26] Ray Kytle, *Clear Thinking for Composition* (New York: McGraw-Hill, 1987), p. 7.

5. Expert testimony that is contradicted by equally expert testimony: One characteristic of the "age of information" is the proliferation of research that is carried out by individuals, corporations, universities, and think tanks. The outcome of one study may be diametrically or partially opposed to the findings of another study done by an equally prestigious person or group. In addition, we are seeing that today's discovery can sometimes be tomorrow's mistake; that is, current research often makes research of a few years ago obsolete, and even dangerous. Such was the case for the pregnant women of the 1950s who were given the drug DES to prevent miscarriages; this drug was later found to have done significant damage to their daughters and grandchildren.

When we consider these problems, we can understand why some people have become cynical about all medical pronouncements; they may fear catching hepatitis from drinking fountains because "next year, they'll find out that hepatitis is transmitted through water." This attitude is not reasonable, but there is wisdom in choosing a *healthy* skepticism.

A healthy skepticism looks at pronouncements from authorities and considers their credentials, whether they have support from their colleagues (which is not necessarily important as a factor by itself—consider Copernicus), and whether their ideas make sense.

There is a useful way to interpret contradictory research findings, as explained by researcher Frank Sulloway. In his book on birth order and personality, he discusses why we can trust his findings about the personalities of first-born children, despite some studies whose results contradict these findings:

The question we need to ask about any topic of research is whether significant results exceed "chance" expectations, especially in well-designed studies. *Meta-analysis* allows us to answer this question.

. . . 72 of the 196 studies on birth order display significant results that are consistent with my psychodynamic hypotheses. Fourteen studies yield contrary results. The remaining 110 studies are not statistically significant in either direction. What does this mean? In any group of 196 studies, chance will produce about 10 spurious confirmations, give or take a random fluctuation in the error rate. We can be 99 percent confident that chance will produce no more than 21 spurious confirmations. The likelihood of obtaining 72 spurious findings is less than 1 in a billion billion! In spite of occasional negative findings, the literature on birth order exhibits consistent trends that overwhelmingly exceed chance expectations."[27]

Sulloway's statistical analysis, summarized in Table 1,[28] shows us that when many studies are combined, we can draw good generalizations about the meaning of the research.

Summary of 196 Controlled Birth-Order Studies, Classified According to the Big Five Personality Dimensions

Behavioral Domain (by Degree of Confirmation)	Outcome[a]	Likelihood of Outcome by Chance[b]
OPENNESS TO EXPERIENCE Firstborns are more conforming, traditional, and closely identified with parents	*21 confirming (2.2 expected) 2 negating 20 no difference*	*Less than 1 in a billion*
CONSCIENTIOUSNESS Firstborns are more responsible, achievement oriented, organized, and planful	*20 confirming (2.3 expected) 0 negating 25 no difference*	*Less than 1 in a billion*
AGREEABLENESS/ANTAGONISM Laterborns are more easygoing, cooperative, and popular	*12 confirming (1.6 expected) 1 negating 18 no difference*	*Less than 1 in a billion*

(continued)

---

27 Frank Sulloway, *Born to Rebel* (New York: Random House, Inc., 1996).
28 Ibid. p. 73

Summary of 196 Controlled Birth-Order Studies, Classified According to the Big Five Personality Dimensions (continued)

Behavioral Domain (by Degree of Confirmation)	Outcome[a]	Likelihood of Outcome by Chance[b]
NEUROTICISM (OR EMOTIONAL INSTABILITY) Firstborns are more jealous, anxious, neurotic, fearful, and likely to affiliate under stress	*14 confirming (2.4 expected)* 5 negating 29 no difference	Less than 1 in a billion
EXTROVERSION Firstborns are more extroverted, assertive, and likely to exhibit leadership	*5 confirming (1.5 expected)* 6 negating 18 no difference	Less than 1 in a million (but studies conflict)[c]
All Results Pooled	*72 confirming (9.8 expected)* 14 negating 110 no difference	Less than 1 in a billion billion

NOTE: Data are tabulated from Ernst and Angst (1983:93–189), using only those studies controlled for social class or sibship size. Each reported finding constitutes a "study."
a. Based on a "chance" confirmation rate of 5 percent.
b. Based on the meta-analytic procedure of counting confirming studies versus all other outcomes (Rosenthal 1987:213); one-tailed tests. With the expected number of confirming studies set to a minimum of 5, all statistical comparisons are significant at $p < .005$. For Openness, $z = 13.19$; for Conscientiousness, $z = 12.14$; for Agreeableness, $z = 8.44$; for Neuroticism, $z = 7.68$; for Extroversion, $z = 5.01$; for all results pooled, $z = 20.39$.
c. In this one instance I have compared positive and negative studies together, versus those showing no difference, and employ a two-tailed test.

Table 5.1

Copyright © Springer-Verlag New York, Inc. Reprinted with permission.

In contrast, when two respectable experts or institutions disagree and there is no clear-cut weight of evidence, critical thinkers have two options: They can remain neutral until more confirming studies are completed or they can do more personal research. Personal research includes going to libraries for relevant journal articles, interviewing people in the field, and calling the institutions that have done the studies and asking for copies of their findings (because, as previously discussed, they are usually summarized only briefly by the standard media sources).

Consider this excerpt from American Health magazine:

Circumcision's Comeback?

Now Pediatricians Say the Surgery May
Be More than Cosmetic

by Vicki Brower
American Health Magazine, September, 1989

Circumcision has been controversial more than once during its 3500-year history. Recently, an American Academy of Pediatrics' (AAP) task force reversed its earlier position that there is no valid medical rationale for routine circumcision of newborns. The AAP now says the procedure "has potential medical benefits and advantages."

The AAP's more positive stand is largely based on studies by Army pediatrician Thomas Wiswell, which show that uncircumcised male infants suffer 11 times more urinary tract infections (UTI's). Researchers suspect bacteria get trapped under the foreskin and move up the urethra to the kidneys. UTI's can be serious and may even have lifetime consequences.

The AAP also notes that circumcision virtually eliminates cancer of the penis, and may reduce sexually transmitted diseases and cervical cancer in women.

Not all pediatricians and urologists agree with the AAP's new position. Dr. Howard Snyder, associate director of urology at Children's Hospital of Philadelphia, calls circumcision "unnecessary surgery and unnatural," pointing out that post-circumcision rates of infection and other complications run about 1 percent to 3 percent.

Reprinted by permission of the publisher.

If you have a son or if you someday might have a son, you will decide one way or the other about circumcision. How would you know what to believe when you discover that experts genuinely differ on the subject? All you may know is that there is disagreement among pediatricians about the medical value of this procedure.

You might, in frustration, forget the medical aspect of the operation and focus on other factors, such as choosing to circumcise so the child will look like his father or friends. Another option might be to first consider personal religious beliefs, then medical benefits; you might look up the studies cited and/or discuss the findings with one or more pediatricians.

Being thoughtful takes time and effort and that's why we can't be thorough about every decision. Each of us needs to choose our priorities according to individual values. Once we have determined something is really important, we can do the homework necessary to make sound judgments and to avoid decisions we will later regret.

The preceding article included the story of one mother who had made a hasty decision to circumcise, given her approval to the doctor, and is now suing him for performing the surgery—because, she claims, it was done against her son's will! If only she had poured her energy into the initial decision, she wouldn't be wasting time and energy and experiencing personal agony over her choice. Clear thinking has emotional benefits!

EXERCISE

Purpose: To recognize controversial expert testimony.

Find an example of expert testimony contradicted by equally expert testimony; editorial pages sometimes contain pro-con arguments of this nature, or you can find them in *U.S.A Today* on the debate page or on programs such as public broadcasting's *The Jim Lehrer Report* or ABC's *Nightline*. State the basic areas of disagreement and the reasons given for each side's conclusion. Then decide which of the arguments you would support and explain why.

Reasoning by Analogy

Another interesting and common form of inductive generalization involves reasoning from analogies. When someone uses analogies to support an argument, he or she is drawing a comparison, saying in essence: I have evidence that this policy works well in one or more cases; therefore, I infer that it will work well in other, similar situations.

Have you ever taken a test with questions like these?

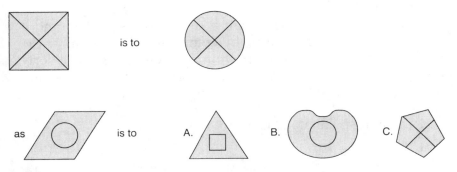

Figure 5.3

This test measures the ability to reason by analogy. If you answered "B" you correctly identified the analogous drawing; both drawings contain two figures (X and 0) that have the same relationship to the figure that encloses them.

When speakers or writers use analogies, they describe something (an object, event, idea, or process) and compare it to something else. The *claim* is that the two things are alike in important ways. Reasoning by analogy can be coded as follows:

A is to B as C is to D.

Reasoning by analogy, comparing one idea or plan to another, is one of the major forms of evidence used by speakers and writers. For example, schoolteachers, police officers, firefighters, city planners, and other professionals often share ideas with others who do similar work, because they know that what worked in one community might work in another. Conferences and conventions for people in the same profession are focused on sharing what is useful in one context, under the assumption that it will also be useful in another.

We will consider effective reasoning by analogy for the remainder of this chapter. In the next chapter, we will focus on faulty analogies and other errors in reasoning.

The human mind's ability to reason by analogy begins at an early age and continues throughout life. A child may reason, "Camp is just like school—I have to get up early and do what the counselors tell me." A friend may help parents understand a child's jealousy of a new baby by comparing the arrival of the new baby to a spouse bringing home a new mate. An elderly person may complain "This nursing home is like prison—the food is lousy, I have to follow strict rules, and no one comes to visit me."

Reasoning by analogy is useful in two ways:

1. We are able to explain a new or difficult idea, situation, phenomenon, or process by comparing it to a similar idea or process that is more familiar.
2. We are able to give reasons for a conclusion by showing that our idea or program has worked at another time or in another place. We are also able to show that an idea or policy we don't favor has not worked well in another context.

REMINDER

When we reason by analogy, we assume that since something holds true for one thing, it will also hold true for another, similar thing.

Reasoning by analogy is commonly used in argumentation. Good analogies add inductive strength; if an idea or policy has been shown to be useful in some situations, we can argue that it will also be useful in other similar situations. When we report studies of experiments on animals and draw conclusions about humans, we are reasoning by analogy.

Example

A researcher may report that when rats are confined to an overcrowded cage, they exhibit antisocial behavior; a conclusion is then drawn about humans, comparing crowded rats to city dwellers. The researcher may imply that crime is a result of overcrowded conditions.

When we look at a specific past event to get a clue about what is likely to happen in a similar present situation, we are reasoning by analogy.

Example

Someone may argue that prohibition didn't work in the 1920s—people still found a way to make alcohol and an underground criminal network was supported. In the same way, it is argued, making drugs illegal today only forces people to get them from pushers at a high price.

When we compare one condition to another, in order to justify attention to the condition, we are reasoning by analogy.

Example

A lobbyist for a recovery group may claim, "Addiction to shopping is like addiction to drugs; the shopaholic can no more change his behavior than can the drug addict. Therefore, we should spend federal funds on the prevention and cure of shopaholism."

When we compare a system in one place to a system in another, we are reasoning by analogy.

Example

Employees may cite the generous maternity leave policies of European countries as a way to argue for better leave packages in the United States and Canada.

In a commentary on teen curfews, law professor Dan M. Kahan challenges criminologists "who ridicule curfews as empty gestures that do little to address the root causes of juvenile delinquency." Kahan believes that curfews are effective because they free juveniles from the pressure to appear tough by hanging out at night and breaking the law to impress their peer group. Using inductive reasoning by analogy, Kahan states: "Many cities that have adopted curfews, including New Orleans, San Antonio and Dallas, have reported dramatic drops in both juvenile criminal activity and juvenile criminal victimization."[29]

When you notice someone supporting a position by comparing one idea, situation, or plan to another, stop and evaluate whether the comparison is valid. If it is, you have a good analogy, which may be used to add inductive strength to your conclusions.

 EXERCISE

Purpose: to understand the usefulness of analogies as learning tools; to increase familiarity with the use of analogies.

Although we are considering analogies as they relate to persuasion, analogies are also useful in understanding information. Ask a teacher you respect how he or she has used analogies to explain a difficult process to students. Find two or three examples of these kinds of analogies and share them with the class.

 Chapter Highlights

1. Scientific discoveries are often made through controlled studies; a good study can be repeated by other researchers and thus can lead us closer to the truth about an issue.

---

[29] Dan M. Kahan, Commentary for *The Washington Post,* reprinted *Contra Costa Times,* November 17, 1996, p. A-17.

2. A good research design includes a characteristic of interest, a hypothesis, and a sample that is divided randomly into a control group and an experimental group.
3. The only difference between a control group and an experimental group is the treatment received by the experimental group.
4. The data gathered from a study is used to draw conclusions and to suggest areas for further study.
5. A critical thinker will review a study according to specific criteria to determine the extent to which the study is valid or biased.
6. The findings of many studies are considered controversial by experts in the field. When studies are controversial, critical thinkers withhold judgment or accept findings provisionally.
7. When using authoritative testimony as a support for conclusions, critical thinkers should consider whether the expert is educated and/or experienced in a field that is relevant to the issue under discussion.
8. Problems with using expert testimony include the use of experts in the wrong field of expertise, the use of experts who are not recognized as experts, the use of experts who are paid or biased, and the use of expert testimony that is contradicted by equally expert testimony.
9. Reasoning by analogy, comparing one idea or plan to another, is a form of inductive evidence used both to explain and to persuade.

Articles for Discussion

Food News Blues

by Anthony Schmitz
In Health, November, 1991

Not long ago I set a coffee cup on the table and opened the newspaper to a piece of good news. "New Study Finds Coffee Unlikely to Cause Heart Ills," read the headline. One thing less to worry about, I thought, until I remembered a story from a few weeks before. That morning the headline warned, "Study: Heart Risk Rises on 4, More Cups Coffee Daily." My paper does this all the time. Concerning the latest dietary findings, it flips and flops like a fish thrown to shore.

"Medical research," it declared one Wednesday, "repeatedly has linked the soluble fiber in oats with reductions in serum cholesterol." By Thursday of the next week all that had changed. "Studies Cast Doubt on Benefits From Oat Bran," the headline cried. Once again the paper offered its readers a familiar choice. Which story to believe? This week's, or last week's, or none at all?

The paper in question is the *St. Paul Pioneer Press*. It's a respectable provincial daily, not unlike the papers in Houston, Detroit and dozens of other cities. One day, recently, the news editor, Mike Peluso, said he'd take a crack at explaining his paper's flip-flops.

Peluso is compact, graying, more grave than jocular. He met me at the newsroom door. "You want a cup of coffee?" he asked, pointing at a vending machine. No, I said, trying to recall whether this week coffee was good or bad. Peluso shrugged and headed for his cluttered cubicle. Beyond its flimsy walls reporters jabbered into phones.

I arranged the coffee and oat bran clippings on a paper-strewn table. Peluso examined them one by one. He grimaced. He sighed. He swallowed black coffee from a paper cup.

"How do you reconcile the conflicting claims?" he asked himself. "One month coffee can't hurt you, the next month quit coffee and your heart will tick forever."

Exactly.

Peluso shook his head. "I don't know, I don't have any answers for that. You've got to talk about the real world here."

For Peluso, the real world looks something like this: News of a hot nutrition study gets beamed into the newsroom from wire services such as Associated Press, the *New York Times* or the *Baltimore Sun*. Peluso and his staff poke at the story, trying to find flaws that argue against putting it in the paper. By and large it's a hamstrung effort. Never mind that the reporter who wrote the piece is thousands of miles away. She'd defend the story anyway. The paper's own health reporter is scant help; he's been on the beat two months.

Meanwhile, Peluso knows that his competitors—another daily paper, plus radio and television news—won't spend a week analyzing the study. They'll run it today. Which is to say Peluso will, too. But the story the reader sees won't be as detailed as the piece that came over the wire. Compared with the *New York Times* or the *Washington Post*, the *Pioneer Press* is something of a dwarf. Stories get trimmed to fit. Subtleties and equivocations—the messy business of research—don't always make the cut.

"Look," said Peluso, "we're not medical authorities. We're just your normal skeptics. And it's not like we're inventing the research. We're simply reporting on it. We present what's there and let people draw their own conclusions."

"So what should readers make of all the contradictory advice you offer them?"

Peluso sighed again. "I don't know," he said. "You've got to take everything with a grain of salt until the last word comes in. I hate to tell people I don't believe everything I read, but the fact is anybody who believes everything they read is nuts."

Researchers whose work makes news soon learn that the match between science and journalism wasn't made in heaven. Richard Greenberg, a microbiologist who directs the office of scientific and public affairs at the Institute of Food Technologists, has watched what happens when the scientific method collides with journalistic technique.

"The first thing you've got to remember," says Greenberg, "is that science is not fact. It is not truth. It is not holy scripture. It's a compendium of information. You try to put all the research together and come to a consensus. Just because somebody runs a study that comes to a particular conclusion doesn't change everything that's gone before."

Scientists don't generally reach consensus in time for the next deadline. After 30 years of study, coffee's link to heart disease remains an open question. Four plus cups a day may slightly increase the risk, though some research suggests only decaf is linked to heart problems. Similarly, a decade's worth of oat bran experiments have served only to get a good argument going. Some studies suggest oat bran isn't any better at lowering cholesterol than white bread. If you eat enough of either, the message goes, you won't have room for fatty food. Others say oat bran has innate—though so far inexplicable—cholesterol-lowering properties.

While on their way to answering the big questions about fat or cholesterol or fiber, researchers often pause and dicker merrily about the design flaws in one study or the dicey statistical analysis in another. "Among ourselves," says one epidemiologist, "we're more interested in the detail of how things are done than in saying right now whether oat bran's good for you."

For journalists it's exactly the opposite. The arcana of statistical analysis and research design are boring at best, baffling at worst. The big question is whether oat bran will keep your heart ticking.

"The reporter and headline writer are trying to distill the meaning of the latest piece of research," says Greenberg. "They're trying to grab the eye of the reader. They're searching for absolutes where there are no absolutes. And this is what happens. One day you read caffeine is bad. Then you read that if you take the caffeine out, coffee is OK. Then you hear that the solvent that takes out the caffeine is dangerous. Then you find out the caffeine isn't dangerous after all. It so confuses the public they don't know whom to believe. And the truth is, there wasn't really any news in any of these studies. Each of them was just another micromillimeter step toward scientific consensus."

For Greenberg, news exists in those rare moments when scientists weigh the evidence and agree to agree—when the American Heart Association, the National Cancer Institute or the National Academy of Sciences pronounces that you ought to eat less fat, or more vegetables.

But by the terms of journalism, scientific consensus is a dead-letter file. If everybody agrees, there's no conflict, there's no news. In comparison, debates such as those about coffee or oat bran are a newsroom gold mine. Contradictions and conflict abound. Better still, almost everyone has oatmeal or coffee in the cupboard.

"You can't convince an editor not to run this stuff," says Howard Lewis, editor of the newsletter *Science Writers*. "My advice is that they do it for the same reason they run the comic strips and the astrological columns. But I feel it's all a hoax. Usually they're not accomplishing anything except sowing panic or crying wolf."

A Purdue communications professor raised a stir few years back when he suggested that research news might be more harmful than helpful. Writing in the journal *Science, Technology and Human Values*, Leon Trachtman observed that 90 percent of the new drugs touted in newspaper reports never reached the market or were driven from it because they were ineffective, too toxic or both. Readers relying on this information would have made wrong choices nine times out of 10.

So who's served, Trachtman asked, by publicizing these drugs before there's a scientific consensus on them? "When there's no consensus, why broadcast contradictory reports?" Ultimately, he said, readers are paralyzed by the pros and cons. He asked whether the result will be contempt for research, followed by demands to stop wasting money on it.

Not surprisingly, Leon Trachtman got blasted for implying that a scholastic elite ought to be making decisions for us. Among the critics was David Perlman, a science editor who writes regularly about health and nutrition. Often, Perlman says, research leads to public debates. Will avoiding fatty foods really lengthen your life? Should government experts try persuading people to change their eating habits? It's debatable. But citizens can hardly take part if they're capable of nothing more than numbly accepting expert advice. "To abdicate an interest in science," says Perlman, citing mathematician Jacob Bronowsky, "is to walk with open eyes toward slavery." Perlman trusts people's ability to sort through well-written news.

"It's not just the masses who are confused," says Trachtman. "It's the same for well-trained scientists once they're out of their field. I think people ought to establish a sensible, moderate course of action, and then not be deflected from it every morning by what they read in the paper."

But let's face facts. Do you have the resolve to ignore a headline that declares, "Sugar, Alzheimer's Linked"? If you can't help but play the game, you can at least try to defend yourself from nonsense by following these rules:

Count the Legs.

First, ask if the group studied bears any relation to you. Don't let research done only on four-legged subjects worry you. Pregnant rats, for instance, are more likely to bear offspring with missing toes after getting extremely high jolts of caffeine. What's this mean for humans? Probably nothing. There's no evidence that drinking moderate amounts of caffeine causes human birth defects.

If research subjects have two legs, read closely to see if they're anything like you. Early research that helped launch the oat bran fad involved only men, most of whom were middle-aged. All had dangerously high blood cholesterol, which reportedly fell after they ate a daily cup-plus of oat bran—enough for a half-dozen muffins. Fine, unless you're female, have low cholesterol already, or can't stand the thought of eating half a dozen bran muffins every day.

Check for Perspective.

Even if you're a match for the group being studied, don't assume the results are significant. "Check if the journalist gets the perspective of other people in the field," says Harvard epidemiologist Walter Willett. "People who have watched the overall flow of information are in a good position to say, 'Well, this really nails it down,' or 'That's interesting, but it needs confirmation.' "

Ask How Many Guinea Pigs.

Quaker Oats research manager Steven Ink, who's written a guide to nutrition studies, says the best research uses at least 50 subjects. By this standard, we should look askance at the recent study showing that eating 17 tiny meals a day lowers cholesterol. Only seven people took part. But rules of thumb don't always work. A small number can be meaningful if the effect observed is large and consistent. You don't need to feed 50 people cyanide to figure out that it's going to be bad for everyone.

What's more, Ink advises, subjects shouldn't be fed quantities of food that no one in his right mind would eat. One example is the recent study showing that trans fatty acids such as those in margarine may be bad for your heart. Subjects ate three times more trans fatty acids than the average American.

Finally, any group tested should be compared to a similar group. Early studies that linked coffee to heart disease were skewed because coffee drinkers differed greatly from the control group. The coffee drinkers were more likely to smoke and eat a high-fat, high-cholesterol diet. Both habits carry bigger heart risks than does drinking coffee.

Wait for Confirmation.

"Don't let one study change your life," says Jane Brody, the *New York Times* health writer. She waits for three types of food research to agree before changing her eating habits.

First, she looks for studies of large groups that show a link between a food and good or bad health—Italy's big appetite for olive oil and its low rate of heart disease for instance. Then she watches for lab evidence in test animals that suggests how the food causes its effect in people. Finally, she considers human experiments in which two groups are compared—one eating the food, the other not eating it, with neither group knowing which is which.

Applying this rule to her own meals, Brody skimps on butter and favors olive oil. She eats plenty of fruits and vegetables, lots of potatoes, rice, beans and pasta, and modest amounts of lean meat. "This plan won't make you sick, has a good chance of keeping you well, and is immune to these fads that are here today and gone tomorrow," Brody says.

Hunt for Holes.

No matter how carefully you read, you'll have to rely on the information your newspaper chooses to supply. If the big mattress ad on an inside page gets dropped at the last minute, the editors may suddenly have room for an exhaustive treatment of the latest coffee study. But if a candidate for national office gets caught with his pants down, the space required for a thorough expose may mean the coffee piece gets gutted.

When editors at the *St. Paul Pioneer Press* got hold of a wire service report debunking oat bran, they found room for the first two-thirds. The third that didn't fit held a stern critique by other experts. They charged that the study contained too few people (20 female dietitians), didn't control the rest of what they ate, and started with subjects who had unusually low cholesterol.

"The reader really has to be skeptical," says Frank Sacks, the Harvard researcher whose oat bran study was under attack. "Take my case, for instance. The reporter really ought to say that this is a new finding, that it needs to be replicated. This is a warning sign that you have to wait a while. Reporters hate that when you say it. They call it waffling. But the truth is your hot new finding might not be confirmed down the line. You hate it when that happens, but it happens time and again.

"The real conservative advice is not to take any of this stuff in the newspaper with a whole lot of credence," says Sacks. "You could just wait for the conservative health organizations like the American Heart

Association to make their recommendations and then follow their advice."

I called the American Heart Association to get its line on oat bran and coffee. "We don't have an opinion," said John Weeks somewhat plaintively.

"We get calls every day from the media," said Weeks. "They want to know what we think about every new study that comes out. And we don't have an opinion. We don't try to assimilate every new study. Our dietary guidelines would be bouncing all over the place if we did. Once the evidence is there, we move on it. Until then, we don't."

The Heart Association is sticking with the same dietary advice it's dispensed since 1988, when it last revised its model diet. Eat less fat. Eat more grains, vegetables and fruit. The evidence that oat bran lowers cholesterol is so limited that the association makes no specific recommendations about it. Concerning coffee, the group has nothing to say.

Weeks' advice for whipsawed newspaper readers has a familiar ring. "What people need to keep in mind," he said, "is that one study does not a finding make."

"You mean," I asked, quoting Mike Peluso's newsroom wisdom, "I'm nuts to believe everything I read?"

Said Weeks, "That's exactly correct."

Reprinted from *In Health*, November 1991, © 1991.

Questions for Discussion

1. Comment on the following paragraph from the article: "But by the terms of journalism, scientific consensus is a dead-letter file. If everybody agrees, there's no conflict, there's no news. In comparison, debates such as those about coffee or oat bran are a newsroom gold mine. Contradictions and conflict abound. Better still, almost everyone has oatmeal or coffee in the cupboard." Should newspapers and magazines report controversial studies or wait until there is scientific consensus for the findings of the studies? What are your reasons for your answer?

2. What habits, if any, have you changed because of research that was reported by the popular media? (Consider dietary and exercise habits as well as advice on car safety, crib safety,

durability of consumer goods, and so on.) To what extent has the advice been helpful?

3. What is the best approach to the reading of research in the popular press? Should you believe nothing, everything, or some things? Do you agree with the guidelines for reading research that are given in this article?

4. Do you believe that scientific journals such as the *New England Journal of Medicine* should be more readily available to the public by being sold in bookstores and supermarkets? Would people buy these publications, and if so, would they be capable of understanding them? Give reasons for your answers.

Study: Educational TV Truly Makes Kids Smarter

Findings Also Show Children Who
Regularly Watch Commercial Programs
Are Less Motivated to Learn

by Eric Adler

Kansas City Star, reprinted *Contra Costa Times,* July 25, 1995

KANSAS CITY, MO. We interrupt this program to bring you an important news flash regarding kids and cartoons:

Kids who watch Big Bird get big brains.

Kids who watch Beavis become Butt-heads.

OK, it's not really that simple. But that's the essence of a new study, conducted by two researchers at the University of Kansas at Lawrence, that strongly links good school performance, especially in math and English, to kids who watch educational TV programs such as "Sesame Street" and less-than-stellar performance to kids who don't.

You say you're not shocked?

Well, maybe not. It probably does seem obvious that kids who watch Kermit the Frog will be smarter, or at least be better prepared for school, than kids who watch Ninja Turtles.

Filtering Other Influences

But the recently released study is somewhat more significant because it is also among the first to try to statistically control for a host of other social variables—parents' education, preschool attendance, family income, home environment—that powerfully influence a child's academic success.

Such factors have long clouded the issue of whether educational TV really helped create smarter kids or whether good grades and the like were more a matter of upbringing.

But after four years of following 2-year-olds and 4-year-olds from more than 250 low-income families in the Kansas City area, researchers say that even when other factors are statistically controlled, educational TV programs definitely have a positive effect.

"Watching 25 minutes of educational programming per day at ages 2 and 3 will be the cause of about a five-point advantage (on standardized tests) at age 4 or 5," said John C. Wright, who conducted the study with his wife, Aletha Houston, at KU's Center for Research on the Influence of Television on Children.

"The first 25 minutes is five points," Wright said. "If you watch 50 minutes a day, you have about a seven-point advantage."

But Wright said what was most surprising to him and Houston, both professors of human development, "was that we were able to find a negative effect of watching commercial entertainment programming."

By "commercial programming," Wright generally means commercial cartoons, "Bugs Bunny" instead of "Beakman's World," "Mighty Morphin Power Rangers" instead of "Barney and Friends."

Originally a Skeptic

Indeed, despite TV's "boob tube" reputation, Wright said he went into his study scoffing at the idea that TV was to blame for the perceived dumbing-down of America. He still thinks it's a ridiculous notion. Just like he thinks it's wrongheaded to lay violence and other cultural ills at the feet of television.

But still, Wright said, their study did find that just as preschoolers who watched educational TV tended to do well on standardized math, spelling, vocabulary and other tests, kids who didn't watch much educational TV didn't do as well.

The study also showed that, the more kids watched educational TV, the more apt they were in their off hours to read, be read to or to engage in educational play such as taking music lessons or working in puzzle books.

Kids who watched commercial cartoons, meantime, were less likely to spend time reading and more time playing video games.

"Nintendo and Sega go with cartoons," Wright said.

Reprinted with permission of the *Kansas City Star*.

Questions for Discussion

1. Why did the researchers in this study control for such social variables as "parents' education, preschool attendance, family income, home environment"? What problems in generalizing from these studies would have occurred if these factors had not been controlled?
2. What information about the design of this study has been left out of this article? Would you need this information to draw conclusions about the importance of this study?

 ## Ideas for Writing or Speaking

Research Paper or Speech

1. The purpose of this assignment is to help you to become familiar with using research to support your conclusions. Many highly intelligent people will give good reasons for their conclusions; however, they may not take the time to study current research findings to support their reasons.

   Your objective for this paper or speech is to find out how well you can substantiate the reasons for your conclusion.

   Since the issue you choose will be controversial, there will be opinions on both sides. You need to show, with your research, that your reasons are stronger than the reasons given by the opposition.

   The steps to take to prepare this essay or speech are as follows:

   a. Choose a controversial issue that you can research. It is important that the issue has been studied by researchers and discussed by experts.
   b. Take a stand on the issue, or formulate a tentative **hypothesis.** A hypothesis states what you believe your conclusion will be after you conduct your research.

c. Find at least four sources of research to support your conclusion. These sources include reports of studies done on the issue and articles and comments by experts that can be culled from professional journals, newsmagazines, or broadcast interviews. If you know an expert, you can arrange for an interview and record the comments as authoritative testimony.

    Also, find some experts arguing for the opposing side of the issue, so that you can address their reasoning in your essay or speech.

d. Complete a rough draft of your essay or speech, which should include your issue, conclusion, reasons, and evidence to support your reasons. Also, in the body of the essay or speech, address the strongest reasons given by those who draw the opposite conclusion, and say why these reasons are not strong enough to justify that conclusion.

e. Write the final form of your speech or essay, adding an introduction and conclusion. The introduction should highlight the importance of your issue; you can use quotes, statistics, analogies, or anecdotes to gain the attention of your audience. The conclusion should summarize your reasons and reemphasize the importance of your issue and the validity of your conclusion.

Pro-Con Paper Speech

2. The purpose of this assignment is to have you understand, firsthand, that issues are controversial because there is usually valid reasoning on both sides. In addition, when you complete this assignment, you will be a more experienced researcher and a more discerning thinker about the quality of reasoning given to support conclusions.

    To complete this assignment, do the following:

a. Choose a controversial issue. For this assignment, it is best if you do not feel strongly about the issue because you need to be objective about the good reasons on both sides. However, do choose an issue that is interesting to you, so you are motivated to read about it.

b. Write your issue in question form, so you can clearly see the pro and con side of the issue by answering "yes" or "no" to the question. For example, you might write: "Should high-school principals be able to censor articles from student newspapers?" Those who answer yes are on the "pro" side of this issue; those who say "no" are on the con side.

3. Find eight sources of research on your issue. Four should be pro and four should be con. The sources may be journal articles, newspaper or magazine articles, books, transcripts of radio or television broadcasts in which experts testify, or personal interviews you conduct with an expert on the issue. (Some experts will give you their time, so don't hesitate to call for an interview.) A bibliography of these sources should be handed in with your finished product; use standard bibliographical form.

4. Study the research that you compile and choose three reasons for supporting the "pro" side of the issue and three reasons for supporting the "con" side. These reasons should be the best you can find for each side. Write out the reasons for each side, using evidence to support each reason.

5. Finally, take a position on the issue and state why you found the reasons for that position to be the most sound. (You can see now why you should start off being as neutral as possible on this issue). Acknowledge the strengths of the other side while explaining why you found your chosen side's position to be stronger. Conclude your essay or speech by commenting on what you learned in the process of studying both sides of an issue.

CHAPTER SIX

Reasoning Errors

I Know What I Think.
Don't Confuse Me With Facts.

*A critical thinker recognizes
errors in reasoning.*

This chapter will cover:

- Fallacies (errors in reasoning) as reasons that do not provide adequate support for conclusions
- Fallacies in the form of statements that lead listeners away from the real issue
- A reasonable approach to handling fallacies

Understanding an argument is a complex process, as we have seen. We need to know what someone is concluding (claiming) about a particular issue or problem and the reasons for his or her beliefs. And we need to assess the strength of an argument by considering the quality of evidence used to support a conclusion.

When we look at an individual's support for his beliefs, we may perceive that something doesn't make sense, but we may not have words for whatever seems faulty in the reasoning. This chapter will teach you some terms that are used to characterize typical errors in reasoning. These errors occur so often that they have acquired a name of their own: **fallacies.**

Keep in mind, as you read this chapter, that the fallacies discussed are simply labels we give to faulty reasoning. Don't be concerned about labeling every faulty reason perfectly. Instead, use this discussion of fallacies as a general tool to help you analyze the quality of reasons given for a conclusion.

Fallacies can be seen as (1) reasons that seem logical but don't necessarily support the conclusion, or (2) statements that distract listeners from the real issue.

Inadequate Reasons as Fallacies

Reasons that sound good and logical but are not adequate support for the conclusion are the first fallacies to consider. These are tricky because they use the form of good reasoning, but they don't have real substance.

The major categories for insufficient reasons are: **faulty analogies, false cause, ad hominem, slippery slope, and hasty conclusions.**

FAULTY ANALOGIES

As we discussed in the last chapter, analogies can be legitimately used to create inductive strength for an argument. If we can show that an idea or policy has been useful in some instances, we can generalize that it will be useful in another, similar situation.

Because analogies are used commonly, we must be careful not to accept them uncritically. The key to an accurate analogy is that *the two things being compared are alike in all significant aspects.* If there are significant differences between the items being compared, then we have a **faulty analogy.**

Sometimes the comparison is easy for a critical thinker to make. Let's look at a typical use of analogy in advertising, that of comparing a product to an experience:

"Springsoft fabric softener smells great. It's like hanging your clothes out in the fresh air."

Similarities:

Both are used in getting clothes dry and both presumably smell good.

Differences:

Springsoft	*Fresh Air*
smell induced by chemicals	smell from fresh air
clothes feel soft	clothes feel rough
recurrent cost involved	one-time clothesline cost
quick when used with dryer	time-consuming

You can see that comparing Springsoft with fresh air is not accurate in all of the dimensions that are significant to a consumer. It would be more accurate to ask consumers to buy Springsoft because it has a nice fragrance and makes clothes feel softer. So why don't advertisers just state the facts?

Advertisers, politicians, teachers, and other advocates usually realize that a powerful picture is worth more than a detailed argument. A swim instructor may know that asking children to put their arms out straight is more effective when she adds "like Superman does." Campaign managers realize that a powerful negative image leveled against an opposing candidate may have greater impact than a reasoned case against him. Likewise, parents who want to feel that they are doing the best for their children may respond to the idea of infusing fresh air and sunshine into their clothes, especially since the fresh air and sunshine come in an easy-to-use product.

Faulty analogies occur when we compare one situation or idea to another and disregard significant differences that make this comparison invalid. For example, to compare plans for overcoming racism in the United States to plans that work for the Finnish people would be fallacious: there are very few races in Finland compared to the United States. Or, someone might suggest that we look at the low rate of theft in some Middle Eastern countries and adopt a similar prevention plan. The problem is that in those countries, the punishment for stealing is the removal of a hand—that method is not likely to be adopted by North American voters and legislators.

Faulty analogies are used frequently when social issues are discussed. You might hear someone claim there is no problem with violence on television or in movies. The person taking this position might say, "I watched cowboy shows all of my life and I turned out just fine." Besides the ambiguity in the term *just fine,* the problem with this reasoning is that G.I. Joe and the Lone Ranger are quite different from Power Rangers. The speaker may or may not be right about the effect of televised violence, but this comparison does nothing to prove his or her point.

You might note that faulty analogies are often accompanied by a poor understanding of history, that is, the fact that our current world is different in significant ways from the world of previous generations.

You can often see faulty analogies in personal relationships when one person gives advice to another. For example, if a grandparent tells you that he or she used to walk five miles in the snow to get to school, implying that you or your children should do the same, you would have to consider the difficulty of implementing this plan in a culture where parents are afraid to even let their children play in the front yard alone.

Or let's say a friend of yours is advising you about how to prepare for a speech you have to give for a class. He or she might say, "Just relax and don't prepare too many notes. That's what I did and I got an A." That method may work for your friend but may be totally inappropriate for you; you may be the kind of person (like most of us) who needs to have good notes and to practice a speech before giving it to a class.

A common problem with people who give advice is their assumption that what worked for them will work for you—a classic case of faulty analogy.

When you see someone supporting a position by comparing one idea, situation, or plan to another, stop and evaluate whether the comparison is valid. If it is, you have a good analogy and a good reason to listen to the speaker. If it is not a valid comparison in some important way, then you have a faulty analogy.

EXERCISE

Purpose: To utilize criteria for evaluating reasoning by analogy.

Consider the following analogies and evaluate their validity. Note similarities that make the analogy useful and persuasive and/or significant differences between what is being compared that make the analogy misleading.

1. This excerpt is from an introduction given by Ted Koppel of ABC's *Nightline* when he did a program on 1992 presidential candidate Ross Perot.

> *Koppel:* How do you figure the phenomenon of Ross Perot? Why do so many people who know next to nothing about the man seem so enchanted by him? A few years ago, I mulled over the same question with regard to the enormous popularity of Vanna White. She of *Wheel of Fortune,* you ask? The very one. She is, after all, a lovely woman with an engaging manner and a charming smile, and no one, but no one, lights up letters on a board better than she. But that still doesn't explain the depth and breadth of Vanna's popularity. The world is full, after all, of thousands of equally lovely, engaging, and charming women. What is it, then, about Vanna?
>
> And then it struck me. Of all the people on television whose names we know who are not playing somebody else, we probably know less about Vanna, that is, what she thinks and believes, than almost anyone else, and so we can project onto her what we would like her to believe.

So, too, with Ross Perot. He is enjoying the support of conservatives, liberals, and moderates precisely because, like Vanna, Ross doesn't go into much detail.[30]

2. Homosexual men and women have been traditionally excluded from the armed forces, and the "don't ask, don't tell" policy did not foster an atmosphere of acceptance. When this topic was first debated in Congress, one argument for completely lifting an exclusionary policy is that gay men and women are a minority group just like Hispanic Americans and African Americans, and that no other minority group is banned from the military.

   In an argument given for keeping gays out of the military, the assertion was made that separate living quarters would have to be provided to keep straight and gay personnel apart, just as similar policies provide separate living quarters for heterosexual men and women in the military.

3. A couple sued a landlord for refusing to rent to them because of their sloppy appearance; they claimed discrimination in the form of "lookism" (prejudice against someone because of how they look). In defending himself, the landlord stated, "You wouldn't hire someone who was out of shape as an employee in a health spa, and you wouldn't want a receptionist for an investment firm who had purple hair. So why should you have to rent an apartment to people who look sloppy?"

FALSE CAUSE:
POST HOC ERGO PROCTER HOC

Post Hoc Ergo Procter Hoc, also called **False Cause,** is an interesting fallacy which is committed frequently in reasoning about personal, social, and political issues.

The Latin translates to "after this, therefore because of this," and refers to the practice of stating that because one event fol-

---

[30] Ted Koppel, "The Unknown Ross Perot," *Nightline*, April 23, 1992.

lowed another, the first event caused the second event. As we discussed in Chapter 4, cause-effect reasoning is sometimes relevant and valid; it is used extensively in psychology (a person may have a fear of abandonment because he or she was abandoned as a child), history (Jewish people became a merchant class in parts of Europe because they were not allowed to purchase land), business (sales have increased since we've been using the new advertising campaign), medicine (you are tired and run down because of low blood sugar), politics (she had 70 percent of the votes and lost 50 percent after the last minute smear campaign of her opponent), and economics (the economy began to recover when interest rates were lowered).

In all the cases listed above, research and reasoning could prove one event came after another and that, in all probability, the first event caused the second event. The fallacy of post hoc occurs when there is no real proof that one event *caused* another event; there is only evidence that one event came *after* another event.

The clearest example of false cause occurs in superstition. Superstitious thinking is noncritical thinking. A superstitious person may reason fallaciously, "I got fired because I walked under that ladder yesterday," or, "The reason I failed the test is because a black cat crossed my path right before I got to class." What's especially dangerous about superstitious thinking is that if someone really believes he is somehow "cursed," he may act as if he is cursed and make the curse come true because of his expectations.

However, the post hoc fallacy is more subtle than mere superstition; it consists of reasons that are not supported by evidence or that are supported by an inadequate sample. For example, politicians are fond of blaming budget deficits and unemployment rates on their predecessors ("I didn't get us into this mess—the previous administration did"). The problem with this reasoning is that it ignores the more complicated causal factors that need to be understood in order to change the current situation for the better. The blaming process is often at the root of a post hoc fallacy and it stops constructive action that could alleviate a problem.

Here are some examples of post hoc fallacies based on shifting the blame and therefore not taking responsibility:

"The reason our team lost is because we weren't playing at home."

"I failed the class because the teacher hated me."

"I saw how you put your television set in the car. The reason it doesn't work is that it was poorly placed in your car after you left our repair shop."

"I ate three pieces of pie at Joanne's house because I didn't want to hurt her mother's feelings."

"I can't find my soccer ball because a large green and brown monster came and ate it while I was sleeping." (Who says small children can't use the reasoning process?)

Although many post hoc fallacies are based on blame and use rationalization (why is it so hard for us to admit error?), some are based on a lack of information to substantiate a valid reason—that is, we don't know the real cause of a particular problem.

In our frustration to find reasons and therefore solutions or explanations for situations, we may rush to assign blame without fair and careful analysis. Then we are in trouble, because we may be tempted to address surface and not deeper causes for problems; we may look for singular rather than multiple causes.

For example, if we say that homelessness is usually the result of a lack of desire to work (false cause in most cases), then we look for a solution to fit the false cause. So homeless people are given jobs, training, and motivational lectures. A year later, we still have the basic problem of the homeless, although some individuals have been helped. We would do better to get at the root causes and the diverse causes of social problems, rather than to try to find quick fixes to what may not be the complete problem.

For example, some of the homeless may be mentally unfit for employment or seminars; some may be displaced homemakers who would rather be in the parks with their children than shuffled off to training; some may be perfectly happy in a homeless condition, in which case communities need to plan what to do about them; and some may welcome job training but find it difficult to get hired. Problems are complex and a single cause doesn't address them accurately.

EXERCISE

Purpose: To discover diverse causes for a given phenomenon.

1. Look at the problem of substance abuse in our culture and answer the following questions: What are some of the simplistic (post hoc) reasons given for the problem? What might be some of the deeper causes of this problem, and what solutions are implied by these causes?
2. If you completed the research suggested at the end of Chapter 4 concerning a social, national, or international problem, do a short paper or speech on the causes of this problem. Take a position on which causes were immediate, which remote, which sufficient, and which necessary for the problem to develop. If some analysts of your problem commit the fallacy of assigning a false cause, say how. Support your position with evidence.

ATTACKING THE PERSON

Ad hominem is a Latin term meaning "to the man" or **attacking the person.** Ad hominem arguments occur when a person is attacked on a personal quality that is irrelevant to the issue under discussion. For example, someone might say that a woman is not qualified for a position on a city council because she's a homemaker; or someone might say that an actor has no right to take a position about environmental issues.

In these cases, the people should not be judged because of their professional affiliations: A homemaker could do as well as anyone else in city government and an actor is also a citizen who has the right to speak out (even if he or she does have the advantage of a larger audience than the average person).

The use of ad hominem arguments has been a staple of political rhetoric for a long time. Consider the following accusations that were used in the presidential campaign of 1800, which is said to have been characterized by "ugly insults coming from both sides": "President John Adams: 'a fool, a gross hypocrite and an unprincipled oppressor.' His opponent, Thomas Jefferson: 'an uncivilized atheist, anti-American, a tool for the godless French.' "[31]

Many logicians believe that discussing an opponent is always a diversionary tactic. However, there are times when attacking the person is valid, because the area of attack is pertinent to the position the person is taking. For example, it is relevant to say that you won't vote for someone for class treasurer (or Congress) because you know he can't balance his checkbook and has overspent his credit cards. It is relevant to refuse to vote for a certain person to be a deacon in your church if he is continually gossiping about other church members. It is relevant to refuse to vote for a candidate who promises to care about the homeless, but who lacks a record of supporting legislation aimed at helping homeless citizens. In these cases, personal character *is* relevant to the position being sought.

It is hard to determine the relevance of some aspects of personal character. A frequent point of discussion in the 1996 presidential election was whether or not the character of a candidate was an important factor for voters to consider. The debate generated interesting speculations about what traits and behaviors constitute the character of a leader. For example, many asked whether a candidate who has had extramarital affairs or who has initiated divorce proceedings can be trusted. Interestingly, in one famous case, that of Gary Hart running for the democratic presidential candidacy in 1988, many claimed they wouldn't support him, not because he was sexually immoral but because he was so indiscreet as to be caught with another woman while in the midst of campaigning. The reader can decipher what this says about our culture and about ad hominem reasoning!

If someone attacks the character, appearance, personality, or behavior of another person, ask yourself, "Is this aspect of the person an important part of the issue?" If not, you have an ad hominem fallacy.

---

[31] Abby Collins-Sears, "Shortcomings of Founding Fathers Studied," *Contra Costa Times*, 1996, p. A-3.

EXERCISE

Purpose: To determine whether there are cases in which personal qualities are relevant reasons for rejecting political candidates.

List the elements of personal character that are important for a president or congressional representative. What in a candidate's background, if anything, would prevent you from voting for him or her? Are there things about a person that would bother you if they had occurred recently, but that you would overlook if they occurred in his or her past? How far back into someone's background would you look when making your voting decision?

THE SLIPPERY SLOPE

Slippery slope refers to the domino effect. If you push one domino in a pattern, then all the others will fall. A slippery slope argument states that if one event occurs, then others will follow, usually in an uncontrollable way. If you think about it, any domino effect argument is based on a prediction about the future, and is therefore based on speculation. Still, this form of reasoning can be valid, even when opponents call it a slippery slope, if the interpretations are soundly based on existing facts and reasonable probabilities. For example, in the 1970s people used to discuss the possibility of a domino effect in Southeast Asia; they believed that if the United States left Vietnam, then not only Vietnam but also Cambodia would fall to the communists. This concern proved to be valid.

When school-based health clinics were introduced, some parents complained that this was the first step in birth control devices being distributed by schools. This argument, which was dismissed as a "slippery slope" argument, did prove to be valid. Many school-based health clinics now offer birth control and reproductive counseling.

There are also cases in which an individual is refused a reasonable privilege because it would probably call for the privilege to be extended to too many others. For example, let's say you are

a day late paying your auto registration. The clerk would probably still have to charge you a penalty because "If I make an exception for you, I would need to make an exception for everyone."

The slippery slope fallacy occurs when the consequences of
a single act are predicted and not substantiated by evidence. For
example, many people fight the idea of making tobacco advertisements illegal despite overwhelming evidence concerning the
harmfulness of this substance. The slippery slope argument given
is that if tobacco advertising is made illegal because tobacco
hurts people, then pretty soon advertising for eggs and milk
would be curtailed because of their cholesterol content.

The problem with this argument is that eggs and milk are not
analogous to tobacco; although there is a high cholesterol content in these products, they are also extremely nutritious in other
ways, whereas no nutritional or health value has been found for
tobacco. Therefore, it's not likely that advertisements for eggs or
other healthy products would be disallowed just because tobacco
ads would be.

Another example of the use of the slippery slope fallacy concerns Gregory K., a severely abused child in Florida who successfully sued to "divorce" his parents so that he could live with
his foster family, who wanted to adopt him. The boy's parents
were divorced, the father was an abusive alcoholic, and the
mother was so neglectful of the child that he had been placed in
foster homes for several years. Lawyers for the boy feared for his
life should he return to this enviroment. Lawyers for the state social workers, however, claimed that allowing a boy in this circumstance to sue his parents could lead to other children suing
to leave their parents because they were denied the latest style of
shoes or video games. As one writer stated in revealing the fallacious nature of this argument:

If the lawyers really believe that, it doesn't say much for
their own profession. Are there attorneys who would handle some brat's Ninja Turtle–deprivation case? Not likely,
especially if the kid didn't have a fat retainer fee in his
piggy bank. And are the lawyers saying there are judges
who would take a frivolous suit seriously, and not toss it
out as nonsense?

No, if the Florida boy wins his case what we'll probably see are other suits filed by kids who will be saying that they have had it with parents who are dope heads, drunks, sadists; parents who don't know how to take care of children and are unwilling or incapable of learning. And that they've had it with social service agencies that don't provide real social services.[32]

There are also examples in personal communication in which the slippery slope fallacy occurs. If you ask for a day off work to take your sick dog to the vet and your employer says, "I can't give you the day off because then everyone would want the day off," you have probably encountered this fallacy. Not everyone is going to want the day off and most people would not take advantage of your situation to ask for similar time off. Your need for time off is not based on negligence (as is the case with people who pay bills late and are penalized); your need is based on an emergency.

HASTY CONCLUSIONS

> *"Labels are devices for saving talkative persons the trouble of thinking."*
>
> John Morley, "Carlyle," *Critical Miscellanies* (1871–1908)

When we want to know the answer to a serious problem or event, we may be tempted to draw a **hasty conclusion,** that is to draw a conclusion on the basis of insufficient information. An example of such a hasty conclusion occurred shortly after the bombing at the 1996 Summer Olympics in Atlanta, Georgia. Writing about this story in the *American Journalism Review,* Alicia Shepard notes the following chain of events that led to the character assassination of someone who was under investigation by the FBI

---

[32] Mike Royko, "When Mother and Father Don't Know Best," *This World*, May 3, 1992, p. 4.

(and was subsequently cleared of suspicion because no evidence was found to link him with the bombing):

Reprinted by permission of American Journalism Review and NewsLink Associates.

Three days after the bombing at Centennial Olympic Park, Christina Headrick, an intern at the *Atlanta Journal and Constitution*, drove to security guard Richard A. Jewell's apartment in northeast Atlanta.

Her assignment was to stake out Jewell, the man hailed for discovering the bomb and evacuating hundreds of people from the area. The paper had heard the law enforcement authorities were beginning to have doubts about Jewell's story, and her mission was to watch what he did and check out who came or left his apartment. When she arrived at the apartment complex she spotted three cars, all occupied by men in sunglasses watching Jewell's apartment. By the pool, other men had their binoculars trained on the same target.

Headrick called in several times to report that Jewell—who had been treated as a hero during an interview with Katie Couric only hours before—was clearly under surveillance.

Headrick's discovery, buttressed by the fact that the FBI had interviewed one of Jewell's former employers that morning and by off-the-record information from several law enforcement sources, led the *Atlanta Journal* to tear up its afternoon Olympics special edition on July 30. The new banner story proclaimed that Jewell had become "the focus of the federal investigation" in the bombing that killed one person and injured 111 others.

The new edition hit the streets around 4:30 p.m. Half an hour later, a CNN announcer was reading the *Journal* story aloud on the air. The networks led with the development that night. The next day, almost all major newspapers—with the notable exception of the *New York Times*—carried stories about Jewell's suspect status on page one, above the fold.

A day later, the public knew more about Jewell's life than most people know about their own neighbors. Jewell, 33, was publicly psychoanalyzed as a victim of the "hero syndrome," a condition in which a person creates a dangerous, life-threatening situation and then comes to the rescue. The security guard was tagged a police "wannabe."

"This much was clear: He had a driving desire, even a need, to be a cop," concluded *Boston Globe* reporters Brian McGrory and Bob Hohler in a profile of Jewel on July 31.

The unattributed 378-word *Journal* story naming Jewell as a suspect before he had been detained, arrested, charged or indicted triggered a media frenzy. The prominent play and exhaustive, often unflattering, detail that characterized the coverage left the widespread impression that law enforcement officials had swiftly nabbed the culprit behind the terrible Olympic tragedy. But were the media being manipulated by authorities? And in their zeal to respond quickly to a competitive, high-interest story, did the media go too far, inalterably tarnishing Jewell in the process?

"The news media's focus on the background and character of the suspect at this stage of the investigation is entirely out of line," says Deni Elliott, an ethics professor at the University of Montana. "Unless news organizations can provide some good reason why we need to have this information, which is a violation of his privacy, at this stage it's illegitimate to give out this information."

Says *Village Voice* media critic James Ledbetter, "I don't mean to portray any of this as an easy call in an extraordinarily competitive environment." But, he adds, "there's a way in which you can report that he's a suspect that doesn't constitute the massive character assassination and invasion of privacy that happened to him. There's a world of difference in reporting he's a suspect and camping out at his apartment, writing detailed profiles and having psychologists on the air talking about him."

As Ledbetter notes, it was not easy for journalists—print or electronic—to merely report a limited number of facts and to wait for the FBI to make a statement about whether they have evidence with which to charge this suspect. The facts alone in this case did not make for an interesting story; on the other hand, the idea of the "hero complex" provided fodder for news features and psychologists to create a fascinating story.

In defending the need to report information on Jewell, a reporter for the *Atlanta Journal and Constitution* said:

"I don't think we did (Jewell) wrong . . . We did not say he was guilty. We said the FBI was investigating him, and that was very obvious from the fact that they were questioning him and had a search warrant for his apartment."

This reporter, Ron Martz, also discussed the pressures of being the only newspaper in Atlanta, the source people were relying on to get information about the investigation. However, Martz and a colleague also wrote about the "hero syndrome."

"This profile generally includes a frustrated white man who is a former police officer, member of the military or police 'wannabe' who seeks to become a hero."[33]

We may also jump to conclusions without the influence of media when we hear a few facts or make a few observations and then make a sweeping generalization. For example, someone may be treated poorly by a few people in St. Louis and jump to the conclusion that all people in St. Louis are rude. Or someone may have spoken to a Republican who has no sympathy for the homeless and jump to the conclusion that all Republicans are cold and heartless.

Drawing generalizations on a small sample of information is the basis of stereotyping. When we are prejudiced, we are prejudging people and situations instead of taking responsibility for considering the realities of each situation. The antidote to prejudice is more information and experience, but we sometimes fail to get more information; we draw hasty conclusions because it is the easiest route to take. It's easier to just take someone's word for it when he or she says "this soup is nu-

---

[33] Alicia Shepard, "Going to Extremes," *American Journalism Review*, October 1, 1996.

tritious" or "this candidate cares about the environment" than it is to do research for ourselves. Other times, we are more comfortable living with our noncritical assumptions because they have become a part of our thinking patterns; if we stereotype people and situations, then we think we know what to expect from them.

If we believe that only Republicans or Democrats or Independents can govern the best, then we know who to vote for without having to think about individual qualifications. A teacher may classify students as good, mediocre, or poor based on a few assignments, rather than giving them the chance to succeed over time. You can see how uncritical interpretations can have lasting negative effects for both individuals and society.

One important effect of making hasty conclusions is called the self-fulfilling prophecy. When someone makes a self-fulfilling prophecy, he or she starts with an unproven conclusion, such as "I'm no good in math," and then acts as if this inference is a fact (he or she doesn't bother to study math and fails the tests), proving the inference that he or she is poor in math.

There are two types of self-fulfilling prophecies—those that other people make about us and those we make about ourselves or others. If you think back to labels given to you by teachers, peers, or parents in early years, you may find that they have become fulfilled in your life.

For example, if you were told that you were going to do well in sports, you probably assumed that was true and had the confidence to succeed; on the other hand, if you were told that you were a terrible artist by an art teacher, you probably accepted his evaluation and gave up on art. You assumed that the conclusion was true and then acted as if it were true. Finally it *became* true.

Examples
"You'll never be able to learn geometry."
"I always strike out."
"He's a really selfish guy."
"I'll never learn to swim."
"You can't talk to those Yuppies."

"That textbook is too hard to understand."
"You'll love new Bolger's instant crystals!!!"

The self-fulfilling prophecy has been operative on a societal level in such forms as bank runs and escalating tensions between ethnic and political groups. On personal levels, self-fulfilling prophecies are responsible for limitations we place on ourselves and our abilities.

As critical thinkers, we are responsible for knowing if personal or group limitations are the results of careless predictions. Then we are empowered to change ourselves or our attitudes.

 ## EXERCISE

Purpose: To analyze the effect of hasty conclusions and self-fulfilling prophecies.

Think of some personal and some cultural hasty conclusions and self-fulfilling prophecies. How did they come about and how did they become "fulfilled"? What could be done to change attitudes and/or actions now?

Example:

During a recent Winter Olympics, one of the medal contenders for pairs figure skating fell during a crucial performance. The commentator for CBS said that a reporter had once written that this skater seemed to be having trouble with jumps. The commentator explained that after she read this article, the skater continually had trouble with her jumps:

> I noticed that this skater seemed hesitant about her jumps during the Olympics. I wondered if a sports psychologist could help her get over what seemed to be a self-fulfilling prophecy. Her coach and her psychologist could help her to form a positive attitude. She could come to believe she's good at jumping by practicing and watching her jumps. The evidence of many successful jumps completed in practice sessions would change her negative expectation and she would perform better in competition.

EXERCISE

Purpose: To think of ways to respond to situations more critically; to consider how to avoid hasty conclusions.

Read each situation, noting what the noncritical thinking response would do. Then give an example of what a critical thinking response might be.

Example:

A candidate for your state assembly is campaigning door-to-door and asks for your vote. You tell her that your major concern is waste-water management. She tells you that she is very concerned about this problem also and has given it much consideration.

Noncritical thinking response: Votes for the candidate.

Critical thinking response: Asks the candidate about her specific concerns and the solutions she proposes; follows up with questions about the details of the candidate's proposal. Asks about the sources of funding for any programs the candidate proposes. May ask her to comment on the proposals of other candidates. Checks out the plans of other candidates and weighs them carefully before voting. Also considers the general platform of other candidates to assess the overall consequences of voting for a given candidate.

1. Your friend from your 10:00 class tells you to meet her at the cafeteria early.

   Noncritical thinking response: Arrives at the cafeteria at 9:45, assuming the friend wants to tell her something or to walk to class together.

   Critical thinking response:

2. You are depressed because you seem to be balding before your time. While switching channels on your television set one night, you catch a promotional show on anti-balding medication. There are several testimonies from the audience about how well this medication works to restore hair. Also, a famous actor is endorsing the product.

   Noncritical thinking response: Dials the 800 number on the screen and charges the product.

Critical thinking response:

3. You are invited to a birthday party at your friend's house. He is a good friend, but each time you have attended a party at his house you have had a bad time. Once, you got food poisoning from the fried chicken; another time, it seemed as though everyone had a date except you. You've started to predict that you'll have a terrible time at his parties. What do you do?

    Noncritical thinking response: Stays at home.
    Critical thinking response:

Add any other situations to which you responded noncritically. What could you have done differently?

SKILL

Recognize when reasons given to justify a conclusion are not sufficient.

Fallacies that Mislead

To this point, we have examined errors that occur when the reasons given for a particular conclusion do not clearly support the conclusion. The second type of fallacies are those characterized by reasons that lead the listener away from the real issue. Common examples of this type of fallacy are **red herrings, ad populum, appeal to tradition, false dilemma,** and **begging the question.**

THE RED HERRING

The red herring fallacy gets its name from the old practice of drawing a herring—a smoked fish—across a trail to distract hunting dogs from following the trail. In this manner, the hounds were led away from finding their prey; this technique was used by criminals who didn't want to be found and had access to smoked fish. Similarly, when someone can distract your attention by getting you on the defensive about a different issue than the one under discussion, that person has taken you off track of the real, or original, issue.

Children are particularly skillful at using red herrings; it's one of their best defense mechanisms against parental demands.

Example

   Mother: Get that sharp stick out of here!
   Child: That's not a stick. It's a laser beam. I need it to perform surgery on some space aliens.

   Or,

   Father: Joey, it's time to brush your teeth and get into bed.
   Joey: You didn't tell that to Suzy.
   Father: (getting off track) Suzy's older than you.
   Joey: But I'm taller than she is.

If this child is successful, he will have gained extra time, and he might even be able to stall long enough for his parent to forget what time it is!

What a child does purely in the pursuit of having his way, he may learn to do as an adult in defense of a larger cause.

Example

   Presidential candidate H. Ross Perot was questioned at a conference of newspaper editors. *Philadelphia Inquirer* columnist Acel Moore wanted specific answers about Perot's proposals concerning the drug problem in the United States.

Acel Moore: Let this audience know. I haven't heard it.

Mr. Perot: Do we have to be rude and adversarial? Can't we just talk?

Mr. Moore: If you're going to be a candidate for the President of the United States, I think you should have to go through that process. And part of the process is being asked questions of a very specific nature, and coming forth with some responses.[34]

Or, consider this fictional example:

Reporter: Mr. Secretary, why won't the president admit that he wrote those memos with his signature on them?

Secretary: Why are you reporters always attacking this president and defending his opponents?

If the secretary can get the reporters to defend themselves, they will have been led away from the issue of whether the president wrote the memos. Red herrings serve to move the dialogue away from an uncomfortable topic to a topic that can be more easily discussed.

AD POPULUM: JUMPING ON THE BANDWAGON

The **ad populum** fallacy is another one we seem to learn from early childhood. This fallacy consists of a false appeal to the authority of "everyone." We are told that a course of action should be taken or an idea should be supported because "everyone" is doing it or believes it.

American society has been said to produce individuals who are *other-directed*, which means the opinions and approval of others are important motivating factors for Americans. (The other-directed person is contrasted with the individual who is inner-

---

[34] Ted Koppel, "The Unknown Ross Perot," *Nightline*, April 23, 1992.

directed and derives his motivation and approval mostly from in-ternalized sources.)[35] Some of our societal clichés reveal this ten-dency, with popular phrases being "keeping up with the Joneses," "the in-crowd," or simply "everybody's doing it."

Advertisers capitalize on our tendency to jump on the band-wagon and follow the crowd by using such slogans as, "Who wants Trident? I do, I do!" "The Pepsi Generation," and "He's a pepper, she's a pepper, be a pepper." Or, assertions are made with-out any proof, such as, "This is the way America vacuums" or "This is where America goes for dinner." Sometimes advertisers don't even use words; they just show large numbers of people who are happily using their products. If you stop and think about these "reasons" for buying products, they seem silly. So why do advertisers continue to use them? Because they work; many peo-ple want to identify with the right products, to be cool and be ac-cepted.

Examples

"Join the millions of satisfied customers who have purchased a Crocodile pick-up. What are you waiting for?"

"That's not fair. All the other kids get to go to the Dis-membered Junkies concert!"

"Hey, America: Introducing your new turkey stuffing mix!"

APPEAL TO TRADITION: "WE'VE ALWAYS DONE IT THIS WAY"

Closely related in its logic to the ad populum fallacy is the **appeal to tradition,** which occurs when a belief or action is supported simply because it conforms to traditional ideas or practices. In both ad populum and appeal to tradition arguments, the conclu-sions of the speakers or writers may be fine, but the reasons are not relevant to the conclusions. You should drink Pepsi or Coke because you like the taste, not because "everyone

---

[35] David Riesman, *The Lonely Crowd* (New Haven: Yale University Press, 1950), pp. 19–26.

The Far Side by Gary Larson

4-5   © 1985 Universal Press Syndicate

"As if we all knew where we were going."

THE FAR SIDE © FARWORKS, INC. Used by permission of UNIVERSAL PRESS SYNDICATE. All rights reserved.

is drinking it." Similarly, you may not want to change the way you are doing something because it works well for you, not because it has always been done that way; the folk wisdom on that is "if it ain't broke, don't fix it."

Yet, there are times for a reasonable discussion about whether something should be done a different way or with a different person. In such cases, it is not useful to say that "we need to do it this way because we've always done it this way." That statement is an appeal to tradition that short-circuits useful dialogue or needed change.

Examples
"Vote for Smith. We've always had a member of the Smith family in our state legislature."
"All the men in our family are lawyers; you will be too."
"Our workers have always been happy working 9 to 5; there's no need to change that schedule."

Traditions held by families, organizations, and nations are wonderful in their ability to bind us together and give us a sense of belonging. These traditions are not what we are suggesting when we discuss "appeal to tradition" as a fallacy. In fact, in our "new and improved" society, we might note the fallacy of "appeal to change" or "appeal to the novel."

Sometimes a newly elected candidate or manager in a corporation may make changes without considering the reasons why a particular system is in place. Often, non-incumbents campaign on the idea that we need change, but they don't tell us what that change will involve or how the change will be an improvement over the current situation. Neither tradition nor novelty is an adequate reason to vote for a candidate, support legislation, or buy a product.

As noted by the above examples, the fallacious appeal to tradition gives an irrelevant and distracting reason for an opinion. It may very well be that the company mentioned in the last example should not change their working hours or create flex-time for their employees; they may find they need all the workers available at the same time. However, to offer "we've always done it this way" as a reason does nothing to engender a meaningful discussion of the possibilities of useful change, and in fact, obscures the issue.

THE FALSE DILEMMA

Another error in reasoning, common in both personal and political communication, is the **false dilemma,** or the **either-or fallacy.** When someone makes this error, he or she polarizes a situation by presenting only two alternatives, at two extremes of the spectrum of possibilities. Any other reasonable possibilities besides these two extremes are left out of the statement, and the careless listener may believe that the issue is limited to the two choices given.

Hagar the Horrible by Chris Browne. Reprinted with special permission of King Features Syndicate.

Examples

"Do you want four more years of overspending and poor priorities or do you want four years of prosperity and sensible spending?"

(Note: you may be able to prove that the incumbent candidate can be fairly criticized on his spending priorities, but does that mean the only alternative is the new candidate or that the new candidate will be as flawless as is implied?)

"Do you want to give your family the same, boring potatoes for dinner tonight, or do you want to give them the exciting taste of Instant Stuffing?"

"Sure, you can go ahead and date Terry and end up with a broken heart and bad memories; but wouldn't it be better to go out with me since I know how to treat you right and show you a good time?"

"If you don't go to college and make something of yourself, you'll end up as an unhappy street person."

The false dilemma leads a listener away from a reasonable consideration of the complex problems involved in most decision-making situations and presents one conclusion as perfect while the other is seen as disastrous.

This is a dangerous fallacy because it leads us to simplistic solutions and it encourages us to give our allegiance to a person or idea above a fair consideration of a solution that would address all concerns.

The error of false dilemma is easy to make for two reasons:

- We like to think solutions are clear-cut and simple; a simple solution saves us time and effort in understanding all the complexities of a situation.

- Our language encourages polarized thinking by including few words to describe a middle ground between extremes. Look at this list:

Beautiful .... Ugly
Strong .... Weak
Extroverted .... Introverted
Brave .... Cowardly
Happy .... Sad

Although we have words that describe the extremes (poles) of a state of being, we have no words describing a middle ground. To put yourself in the middle of these adjectives, you have to say "sort of happy," "somewhat happy," "average," or "medium."

Since our language is polarized, our thinking tends to be polarized if we don't make the effort to be more accurate. In our statistically oriented culture, we tend to use numbers to let us know where things stand on a polarized continuum. We might say "On a scale of one to ten, how happy are you with our relationship?" or "On a scale of one to ten, how close are we to closing this deal?" We use numbers to fill in where words are lacking.

As a critical thinker, you can tell someone who is creating a false dilemma that you see the situation as more complex than it is being described. You can then draw attention back to the issues by asking questions such as, "What specific changes does your candidate propose to make if she is elected?" or "What is so good about Instant Stuffing?"

BEGGING THE QUESTION

The fallacy of **begging the question** is one of the more subtle ways a speaker or writer distracts attention from an issue. Begging the question takes place in two ways:

1. The speaker asks you to prove that his or her belief is not correct. Instead of giving reasons for a conclusion, he or she places the burden of proof on the listener or on the person he or she is debating. For example:

   "How do you know I can't do psychic surgery?"

   "Show me that space aliens don't exist!"

   "Why do you think they call it Up Close"?

   "Why wouldn't you call 1-800-DENTIST?"

   Don't be trapped into proving someone else's conclusion. It's hard enough to prove your own!

2. The second way a person can beg the question is by building on an unproven assumption in his or her argument as if it is a given fact. The classic example is: "Have you stopped beating your wife?" This question *assumes* the husband has beaten his wife. Notice how there is no way to answer this question with a "yes" or "no" without admitting that the speaker's assumption is correct.

Other Examples Are

"Why are you always so defensive?"

"How can you vote for a dump site that is going to destroy the environment?"

"Why are you supporting a team that is going to lose the Super Bowl?"

Begging the question does not always mean that a question is asked. People can beg the question when they give reasons to support their conclusions. For example, a speaker might say:

"Since legalizing drugs would reduce the crime rate, we have to consider where our legislative priorities are."

Can you see that the speaker here has made the assumption (interpretation, inference, guess) that the crime rate would be reduced if drugs are legalized and then has moved on to the next point? It could be that the legalization of drugs *would* reduce crime; but that possibility has to be proven before it can be used as a reason.

Begging the question is also called *circular reasoning:*

"If it's on television, it has to be a good show, because only good shows get on television."

The speaker in this example is using the assumption that only good shows get on television as proof that a particular show is good. The assumption that only good shows get on television has not been proven.

SKILL
Recognize reasons that are irrelevant and distract from the conclusion.

STOP AND THINK

You may find it hard to categorize errors in reasoning under one label or another; some speakers manage to use a whole group of fallacies at once!

Example
"Everyone knows the governor is unreliable; if we keep trusting him not to raise taxes, we could all be in debt by next year."

This statement could be an example of **begging the question,** since the speaker reasons from an unproven assumption that the governor is unreliable. It could also be **ad populum,** since the speaker uses the phrase "everyone knows" to support his claim. It could be seen as **ad hominem,** an attack on the character of a person that is unconnected to an issue. Finally, it could be called a **slippery slope** argument, because the speaker predicts catastrophic results from the action of trusting the governor.

The bad news is that speakers and writers who are not careful in their reasoning may lump several errors together and leave you to wade through the mess! The good news is that you don't need to be obsessed with finding the exact title of a fallacy and attacking your opponent with it. You only need to see that there are reasons people give to justify their conclusions that are insufficient or irrelevant. The labels we give to the reasoning errors are useful in helping us define and avoid inadequate and faulty support for our conclusions. These labels also provide guideposts for evaluating and refuting the reasons others give.

 EXERCISE

Purpose: To practice isolating errors in reasoning; to notice overlap in categories of fallacies.

1. Find errors in reasoning in magazine, newspaper, or television advertisements, or in letters to the editor. You may discover that a particular inadequate reason may fit the description of several fallacies. Share the errors you find with your class.
2. There are other common fallacies in reasoning. Find examples of other types of fallacies that are not listed in this chapter (from other instructors or textbooks). Explain these to your class.
3. In a class group, come up with two examples of each of the fallacies. Then, as a class, play the game explained below called "What's My Fallacy?"

What's My Fallacy?

FALLACIES INVOLVED

Faulty Analogy	Red Herring
Post Hoc (False Cause)	Appeal to Tradition
Begging the Question	Slippery Slope
Either-Or (False Dilemma)	Ad Populum
Ad Hominem (Attacking the Person)	Hasty Conclusion

GAME RULES

Object of the game: To accumulate points by correctly guessing the fallacies of the other teams.

Form class teams of 3 to 6 persons each.

Each team should put 20 fallacies (2 for each category) in random order on paper or cards; this step may be done in groups during class, or the team may assign several fallacies to each member to do at home. These fallacies should be no more than a few sentences. For example, a team might say, "How can you vote for him for student body president—he's a vegetarian!" This would obviously be an instance of attacking the person rather than his policies.

Each team needs: 1 reader, 1 scorekeeper, 1 to 2 referees.

SCORING

Each team must have 20 errors in reasoning to read to the other teams.

The lead team (each team is the lead team when they stand in front of the class to read their list of fallacies) earns 1 point for each appropriate example and loses 1 point for each inappropriate example.

Guessing teams win 2 points for each correct answer and lose 1 point for each wrong answer.

In order to get 2 full points for a right answer, the guessing team must be recognized by the referee of the lead team and say **why** the fallacy was chosen. The answer must satisfy the lead team and the instructor. The instructor may award 1 point for a close answer.

Your instructor may decide to award points toward a grade for this exercise, or may just use the game to help you practice recognizing fallacies.

In most classes, an interesting discussion of what distinguishes one fallacy from another will occur; this discussion will help you to recognize fallacious reasoning more easily.

Chapter Highlights

1. Errors in reasoning are called fallacies.
2. One type of fallacy involves reasons that sound logical, but are inadequate support for conclusions. These include: faulty analogies, false cause (post hoc), ad hominem, slippery slope, and hasty conclusions.
3. A second type of fallacy is found in reasons that lead listeners away from the real issue. These include: red herrings, ad populum, appeal to tradition, false dilemma, and begging the question.
4. Often, an error in reasoning may be hard to classify. The important point for the critical thinker is that the recognition of fallacies helps us to analyze the quality of reasons given to support conclusions.

Articles for Discussion

Discovering fallacies is sometimes a complicated process. If you think you've detected a fallacy, first stop and ask yourself, "What is the issue and conclusion of the writer?" Then, see if the statement in question fits one of the two criteria for fallacies. Is it an assertion that is irrelevant to the conclusion (and thus does not support the conclusion) or is it a statement that leads the listener away from the real issue under discussion? If the statement fits one of these criteria, then you can name the particular fallacy with confidence.

Consider the following examples, all from editorial pages. When you read two sides of an issue, try to distinguish which points genuinely support the writer's conclusion and which are fallacious. If you discover fallacious reasoning, think about whether the author could have made his or her point with better support.

Ashamed of Strug's Sacrifice

by Silvia Lacayo
Contra Costa Times, August 1996

I'd never been more ashamed to be American after I watched in horror the women's gymnastics competition in which Kerri Strug "sacrificed herself" for the team by vaulting on an injured ankle.

Then I saw the next morning's headline on the *Times*, which summarized the event as "Magnificent." To sacrifice children for the greediness of coach Bela Karolyi isn't magnificent. It's not magnificent to expect kids to peak at the age of 18.

Columnist Sam McManis, who reported the "magnificent" story, says they're adults and make their own choices. Strug's 18 years mean nothing, knowing that practically her entire life has been manipulated to please her coaches' desires. To please Karolyi is her only choice.

She may be an adult legally, but her squeaky, Mickey Mouse voice over the reporter's microphone proved she's no adult and her limited life proves she's never been a kid.

Gymnasts are neither kids nor adults. They're pawns in Karolyi's and NBC's ratings supervisors' game of greed and power. It's a game those adults choose to play, but don't say Strug chooses to play it. I'm 19 years old, and I know that leaving the Georgia Dome in a stretcher, crying in pain could never be my dream.

Reprinted with permission.

Kerri Struggles and Wins

by Terry Elgin

I watched a real American hero when Kerri Strug made her final run at the vault. Others would have had her quit but I thought she showed she had courage and heart.

The press had stories about the selfishness and greed of Bela Karolyi, forcing Kerri to continue.

Why would a great coach like Karolyi do anything that wasn't the best for one of his gymnasts? He was right behind her all the way, just like any good coach.

Kerri's voice has nothing to do with her ability to make an athlete's decision to compete. I stand with most Americans, and we were thrilled with the performance of the Olympic team and particularly with Kerri's contribution.

The following letter to the editor was written in response to the question put to readers: "What needs to be done to reduce the number of sex crimes and cases of sexual harassment of women in the military?"

Keep Women Off The Streets

by Larry Bunker

End the front line involvement of women in the police and firefighting departments. It has been a horrible experiment, and there is really only one solution. They can stay behind the desks and push all the paper they want, but get them off of street duty.

Placing female officers as partners in squad cars has not only endangered the lives of veteran policeman but also increased the cases of sexual harassment. Don't kid yourself, we, the taxpayers, are ultimately paying huge sums of awards resulting from integrating the sexes.

What examples do we have in history where women were shown to have the courage, strength, and stamina to fight crime or fight fires. Isn't this just another sad and dangerous way to get more votes?

To those who comment that women have been successful in these areas, I would say you haven't looked at the facts. Ask any training officer about the standards that are now in place. They have been lowered in every case; even men that would never have been allowed to serve the public are now given a uniform. So what is the price for this "reduced quality" equality? We, the public, are more than ever responsible for our own safety. I say, stock up all the guns and fire extinguishers you can. You're going to need them.

The following columns are more challenging. Both writers point out fallacies committed by others, and they each create interesting, extended arguments. Keep in mind, as you read, that the original question was "Are the salaries of basketball players anyone else's business?" With that question before you, think about the extent to which each writer takes a stand on that issue and offers relevant and adequate support for his stand. Your answers will vary, but an interesting and helpful class discussion should emerge.

Most of us commit fallacies in our arguments, especially when we discuss strongly held opinions; at the same time, we may make some excellent points that are well supported. Critical thinkers will be able to distinguish valid arguments from fallacious ones, even when they both occur in the same essay.

Who's To Say Who Earns Too Much?

Do You Really Want Our Government Involved in This?

by Thomas Sowell

An irate reader has denounced my observation that what Michael Jordan is paid is none of my business, except for the basketball franchise owner who pays for it. Her letter was a classic example of today's mindset.

She accused me of callousness toward the parent who cannot afford to take her child to a basketball game because of the inflated price of basketball tickets, presumably because the likes of Michael Jordan, Charles Barkley and the others are raking in big bucks. She puts me down as one of those people who are rich and cannot understand the poor.

Alas, I know a lot more about being poor than about being rich, though I am currently neither. But none of that is really relevant. If I am wrong I am wrong, and if I am right I am right, regardless of my income bracket.

What is truly appalling is how overwrought people can become over the price of a basketball ticket, when basketball games are broadcast free all the time. This is the "me" generation and the "now" generation, for whom the denial of anything they want is an outrage.

From an economic standpoint, it is very doubtful whether basketball players' salaries are covered by the sales of tickets. The big bucks are from television revenues, and the advertisers pay that. Let the beer companies and automobile companies complain.

Ah, but the price of advertising is added to our drinks or our cars, right? Wrong. Advertising can lower prices just as easily as it can raise them.

The cost of producing most goods varies with how many units are produced. If General Motors produced just one Chevrolet, it would probably cost more than a Cadillac. Mass production brings down the price and mass advertising makes mass production possible. Life is not a zero-sum game, especially not economic life, otherwise we would all still be living in caves.

Large salaries are spread out over millions of customers, if not in the basketball arena, then in the television audiences. If Michael Jordan played for free, it is doubtful whether a ticket to the game or an automobile that sponsors it on TV would be a dollar cheaper.

But let's say it would be. Is it right to force Michael Jordan to work for less than his employer is willing to pay him, so that more people can watch in person at the arena, instead of seeing the game at home on TV?

Would it be right to force you to work for less than your employer is willing to pay you, so that your product or service could be reduced in price and more people could then afford it? Right and wrong do not depend on how many zeroes there are after the dollar sign.

To the more modern sorts, to whom right and wrong are just quaint notions that old codgers like me talk about, let me ask a different question: Who is to be given the enormous power of deciding how much all of us are "really" worth? Anyone with that kind of power over you would be your master, however much he might call himself a "public servant."

Are you prepared to flirt with this kind of totalitarianism in order to get cheaper basketball tickets? Does freedom really mean so little?

Some of the rich may not deserve what they get. But, as Hamlet said, give every man what he deserves and how many would escape a whipping?

None of us deserves to live several times as long as the cave man and consume at least a hundred times as much wealth. We are just lucky to have been born at the right place at the right time. If our own ancestors of just a few generations ago could see us now, they would think that we were living like maharajahs.

What ingratitude to complain because a few others were even luckier than we are. We need only look around the world to see millions who are still not nearly so lucky, either in material things or in having what we consider basic human rights.

We are like the dog in an old fable, who had a bone in his mouth and looked down into a stream, where he saw the reflection of what he thought was another dog, who was also carrying a bone. The other dog's bone somehow seemed bigger, so he opened his mouth to try to get it—and dropped his own in the stream.

Some of the great horrors of the 20th century came from giving governments the power to right every wrong—which is of course also the power to create new wrongs that make the old ones look like child's play. The millions of innocent human beings slaughtered by the likes of Stalin, Mao and Pol Pot are monuments to this very real human folly, going far beyond the folly of envy of that dog in the fable.

Reprinted by permission.

Sowell Column Got It All Wrong

When Public Pays for Stadiums, the Whole Debate Changes

by Thomas M. Goetzl
Professor of Law, Golden Gate University School of Law.

In his September 30 column in the *Times*, Thomas Sowell undertook to respond to critics of the mega-million dollar salaries paid to superstar athletes. Titled, "Who's to say who earns too much? Do you really want our government involved in this?", his editorial insinuated that those of us who are offended by these astronomical salaries want government to set salaries.

Starting with this utterly incorrect premise, he then proceeded adroitly to demolish it. Having mischaracterized the issue, he easily can outwit his nonexistent opponents.

No one questions the talents of superstars like Michael Jordan. Certainly no one, not even a most ardent economic conservative, has ever asserted that any employee should be "forced" to work for less than an employer is willing to pay. And no one has recommended imposing caps on earnings.

Who Really Pays?

The issue is not whether Michael Jordan earns too much or even the price of basketball tickets. Rather three questions come to mind. Who is really paying these salaries? Is government playing an inappropriate role in affording public subsidies to the sports franchises without which they would not be willing or able to pay such high salaries? And, finally, what status ought to be accorded to the athletes who command such extreme salaries?

The first two questions will prove to be inextricably linked.

Sowell's superficial analysis displays a surprising naïveté about how public revenues from income taxes, property taxes and even utility taxes subsidize sports franchises, enabling them to provide multimillion dollar incomes to both athletes and owners.

Sowell writes that what revenues are not provided by ticket sales are furnished by television advertising, arguing that it is ungrateful of us to complain because a few others are luckier than we. After all, says Sowell, each of us is free to stay home. We need not buy either tickets to the game or the television sponsors' products.

This is simply not the whole story. Sowell conveniently ignores the fact that franchises often demand, on threat of abandoning a community, public financing for construction of new playing fields, inevitably with expanded luxury suites.

Those luxury suites are generally purchased by corporations as deductible business expenses, thereby reducing their income tax bills.

All of us, sports fans or not, contribute to the bloated monies available to the sports franchises. Hardly a stadium or sports arena has been built in this country without having been underwritten by taxpayers.

Recall how Santa Clara County proposed using its utility tax to finance a new stadium in its failed attempt to lure the San Francisco Giants to the South Bay.

Often accompanied by assurances from local politicians (themselves corrupted by the celebrity status of the players and by offers of complimentary box seats) that rents and other revenues from the franchise will repay the public indebtedness, these projects inevitably result in charges to the public.

In the highly unlikely event that everything proceeds better than optimistically projected, the public may escape without having taken a financial bath.

However, the scandal now simmering in Oakland offers some insight into who will bear much of the economic burden for returning the Raiders to Oakland.

Taxpayers of Oakland and Alameda County will have to cough up tens of millions of dollars to pay for the Oakland Coliseum expansion. This at a time when Oakland's schools and communities cry out for economic assistance. Neither raiders owner Al Davis nor any of the players will have to miss a meal to pay for the shortfall.

No, Sowell, this is not free enterprise. This is government interference of the most inappropriate kind. We hapless taxpayers are subsidizing the multimillion dollar payrolls of the franchises owned by rich playboys.

How right you are! Government should not be involved in this enterprise. If the owners of sports franchises would build their own new or expanded stadiums, risking their own money, no one would begrudge any profits they made or how much they chose to pay their athletes.

The third question, raised above is, perhaps, the most perplexing. Adult fans, as well as youngsters, revere super-athletes for their undeniable grace and prowess.

They Are Role Models

Such gifts, "God-given" some would say, are extraordinary to witness. Who is not amazed at the sight of Michael Jordan as he flies through the air? And yet, any heroic stature accorded them should reflect their character. Whether they like it or not, their fame makes them role models.

They can choose to be positive role models or not, but they cannot avoid being role models. Charles Barkley doesn't understand this. For others, like former Oakland A, Dave Stewart, being an exemplary role model comes naturally.

Even more difficult, however, is to pass judgment on Michael Jordan, Beneficiary of a salary of maybe $30 million this year alone, he chooses to earn yet more by endorsing shoes.

Those unnecessarily expensive shoes are then marketed (with Jordan's name) to adoring kids, many of whom are hard-pressed to raise the money to buy them.

Thus, rather than using his wealth and stature to benefit the community, Jordan only further impoverishes it.

Yes, that is clearly his right. But, Sowell, you self-confessed old codger who still talks of quaint notions like right and wrong, is it right that he do so?

Has it not been written: "Of those to whom much has been given, much is asked?"

Ideas for Writing or Speaking

1. Write an argumentative essay or speech about a current issue in which you include several examples of fallacious reasoning. At the end of the essay or speech, identify the fallacies you have committed. Share your papers or speeches with the class and see if they can isolate your errors in reasoning.

2. Write a critique of an editorial or essay from a newspaper or magazine. Point out the fallacies made by the writer of the editorial. Also, discuss valid reasoning on the part of the writer.

3. Choose an issue about which you have strong opinions. Read some viewpoints by people who oppose your viewpoint on this issue; errors in their reasoning will usually be obvious! List and explain several errors made by your opponents or one major error that weakens their argument. Next, look critically at your own viewpoint. What errors are committed by those who favor your position on this issue? List and explain these errors.

CHAPTER SEVEN

The Power of Language

Talk Is Not Cheap.
So Who Pays for It?

A critical thinker examines the power of language and how it can be used or misused in an argument.

This chapter will cover:

◆ The power of words in framing arguments
◆ How words influence perception
◆ Vagueness, ambiguity, doublespeak, and weasel words

263

> *"If language be not in accordance with the truth of things,*
> *affairs cannot be carried on to success."*
>
> Confucius, *Analects*, 6th century, B.C.

In his definition of man, Kenneth Burke said "Man is the symbol-using animal."[36] Language is the powerful system of symbols that enables us to communicate in ways no other creatures can. Speechwriters for politicians or businesspersons can be paid thousands of dollars for a short speech. Those who are willing to pay these enormous fees know that the words that are used and the way they are organized can make or break a campaign, a merger, or a crucial proposal.

On a smaller scale, many professionals attend workshops that focus on how to present ideas—how to sell stereos, clothing, or food by using the correct phrasing. Recently, a large supermarket chain trained its checkout clerks to ask, "Is plastic okay?" They assumed that if people are asked if they want paper or plastic, they would opt for the more expensive paper bags. By asking in a way that narrows the customers' responses to a polite yes or a less polite no, they hoped to cut down on the expenses of using paper.

Employees who work in front office positions are often trained to handle the public by speaking to them in ways that reflect courtesy and diffuse anger. You may have noticed that in a well-managed store, you can complain and receive sympathetic words from a clerk (if not your money back)!

In our personal lives, we think about phrasing things in such a way as to get the desired results. Teenagers and adults may rehearse their opening words carefully before calling a potential date. Children think about and practice how to ask their parents for treats or money. You may have experienced a time when you sat in your room or car rehearsing what you were going to say to someone; we usually engage in that kind of preparatory behavior when we are dealing with an emotional situation—a fight with a loved one, a proposal of marriage, a request for a change in salary or working hours. We believe, consciously or uncon-

---

[36] Kenneth Burke, *Language as Symbolic Action: Essays on Life, Literature, and Method* (Berkeley: University of California Press, 1966), p. 3.

sciously, that our choice of words and the way we say those words can influence others.

This chapter will explore the influence that words have on people, especially as citizens and consumers. We will look at the way words can help us to clarify issues and, conversely, how words can be used to make issues more obscure and difficult to understand.

Denotation and Connotation

The first principle to understand is that words, as symbols, are extremely powerful. To comprehend this idea, consider two terms, *denotation* and *connotation.*

Denotation is the specific object or act that a word points to or refers to. Words like "dog," "van," "walk," "swim," and proper nouns like "Marisa" all point to objects, actions, or persons; these objects, actions, or persons are the word's denotations.

Connotation refers to all the images—positive, negative, or neutral—that are associated with any given denotation. The connotations of words include their emotional meanings, which may be different for different individuals.*

If you think about those definitions, you might conclude that although denotations are the same for everyone, connotations vary from person to person. For example, for citizens of the United States, Thanksgiving denotes a national holiday that takes place on the fourth Thursday in November. According to this excerpt from an editorial writer, the holiday has diverse connotations:

> Thanksgiving has different and sometimes multiple images for each of us. The Pilgrims and Indians dining at Plymouth. A joyous (or stressful) gathering of family and friends. Travel. A day off work. Time away from school.

---

* For our purposes, we are adopting the definition of connotation used by general semanticists, who study the effects of words on thinking and behavior. Some scholars employ different meanings of this term; you may wish to consult a formal logic text for definitions of this term that are used in that context.

The beginning of the end for the American Indians. The official start of the shopping season. Soup kitchens and food banks.[37]

Another way to understand the difference between denotation and connotation is to consider names. Names that indicate group affiliations are very important to us; in Chapter 4, an article discussed the distress felt by people of mixed race who are not named on census forms. At the end of this chapter, a writer talks about his discomfort in calling himself "African-American." People write to advice columnists to get help in responding when they feel insulted by a label, as the following excerpt from a "Miss Manners" column illustrates:

Question: A group of women was giving testimony before a congressional committee regarding an issue of serious concern to them. When it came his turn to question them, a certain Southern senator said, "Mr. Chairman, we've got a lovely group of ladies here. We thank you for your presence. I have no questions."

The senator surely thought he was being gentlemanly, but the women felt they were being patronized and did not hide their displeasure at being referred to as "lovely ladies."

Is it ever correct for a government official, or anyone for that matter, to make such remarks? If not, what would be the proper response to discourage such offenses from being recommitted? This sort of thing seems to occur frequently.

Was the senator rude, or were the women overly sensitive?

Answer: The senator was rude, but not in the purposeful sense of delivering an insult. The manners he used were once considered gracious in any setting, although they are now widely recognized to suggest, when employed in a clearly nonsocial situation, that the chief contribution of ladies is to be decorative.

---

[37] Pat Craig, "Let's Not Forget the Little Things," *Contra Costa Times*, November 28, 1996, p. A-27.

There is, however, a grandfather clause, by which elderly people who are obviously unaware of changes are not taxed for mild offenses that are well-meant. Miss Manners is thinking of closing this down soon, because there has now been ample time for gentlemen to understand changes that began a quarter of a century ago. In any case, politicians usually do not wish to avail themselves of the excuse that they are unaware of what is going on in the modern world.

You did not tell Miss Manners which senator it was, so she will kindly presume that he was not being wily and purposely trivializing their appearance—and in such a way that they probably looked petty and ill-tempered in bristling. It would have been better to reply graciously, "How kind of you, Senator; we gather this means that you fully support what we are saying.[38]

In addition to having emotional reactions about how we are labeled as members of a group, we also have strong feelings about individual names. The name *Terry*, for example, simply refers to a given person (denotation); still, I may have a positive connotation for the name while you may dislike the name because of a negative experience you had with someone named Terry in your life. Try this exercise to see if you and another person have a disagreement about connotations of names.

EXERCISE

Purpose: To understand and experience the power of connotations.

1. Meet with a friend, family member, or ideally a "significant other" (boyfriend or girlfriend) and try together to pick out a

---

38 Judith Martin, "Time to Say Goodbye to Patronizing Phrases," *Contra Costa Times*, August 14, 1995, p. A-2.

name for a boy and for a girl that you would both be happy to give to a child. See if in your discussion you can isolate how the connotations of some names are different for both of you because of your memory of different people (denotations).

When you find a name that you can both agree on, state why. What are the positive connotations that you have for the name, either because of past associations or because of the sound or meaning of the name?

2. Ask your parents or someone else's parents what they had in mind when they chose a name for their son or daughter. Specifically, ask them how they decided upon the name and what connotations they associated with that name.

Since children often live up to parental expectations, try to assess whether the name had any effect on the child as he or she was growing up. Did the name imply strength, weakness, friendliness, masculinity, or femininity, or did it call forth images of a famous person? Interestingly, teachers in one study favored papers written by children who had typical names (like Mike and Jennifer) and reacted less favorably to papers signed by children with less common names (like Horace).

The Power of Connotation

We may have personal connotations that are based on our unique past experiences; we also have cultural connotations associated with names and words. When the child star Shirley Temple was at the height of her career, there were thousands of parents who named their daughters Shirley after her, but in the succeeding generation there were very few. In the 1960s, the name Bruce was associated with weakness or femininity, but in the 1980s the name Bruce (perhaps because of the Bruce Lee films) was seen as a strong, macho name.

Lawyers, generally aware of the power of connotations, will be careful about the words they use to make their cases to a jury. For example, the defense lawyer for Alex Kelly, who was accused of raping a 16-year-old girl "skillfully managed the information that was presented to the jurors. He often referred to Kelly's father, who has a plumbing business and real estate investments, and posted a $1 million bond for his son, as 'a plumber.' "[39]

Semanticists, who study the meaning of words, use a tool that allows them to assess the cultural connotations of a word. This tool is called a **semantic differential.** Researchers give a list like the following to groups of people in order to assess the connotative meaning of a word. The word is rated on a scale from one extreme to the other.

fast	...	...	...	...	...	slow
strong	...	...	...	...	...	weak
beautiful	...	...	...	...	...	ugly
active	...	...	...	...	...	passive
brave	...	...	...	...	...	cowardly
good	...	...	...	...	...	bad
powerful	...	...	...	...	...	powerless

Meaning is based upon three dimensions: Is the word good or bad? Is it active or passive? Is it powerful or weak? Note that all of the polar dimensions given in the semantic differential fit into one of these three categories.

In several classroom studies of the words *lady* versus *woman,* it was discovered that most students see the term *lady* as good, passive, and weak, while the word *woman* is seen as neither good nor bad, but as active and strong. Advertisers commission studies of words to discover whether the name they will give to a car, cola, or laundry detergent has positive connotations for their target audiences.

We can say that a name or word is just a label and has no effect on us, but consider the following examples:

- When you go into a gift or novelty store, you are likely to see a section of "over the hill" paraphernalia for persons who are turning 30, 40, 50, or 60. You know that, logically, when you have a birthday, you are essentially the same biochemical and emotional being you were the day before. Yet

---

[39] William Glabberson, "For Juries, the Truth Vs. the Whole Truth," *New York Times,* November 16, 1996.

when the label 30 or 40 is attached to you, you may suddenly experience a sense of despair, futility, or mild depression because of the connotations (images) associated with that age. Conversely, ask young children how old they are and they will usually be quite conscious of whether they are 5 or 5 1/2 or 5 3/4 and will use these minute distinctions as status symbols among their peers. People who reach the age of 21 in our country (the age of full adult privileges) will sometimes say with surprise, "I don't feel 21" or "I don't feel different." The main difference is in the label.

- If you believe that abortion is wrong, do you want to be described as *anti-abortion, anti-choice,* or *pro-life?* Do you want to use the word(s) *fetus, product of conception, unborn, pre-born,* or *baby?*

- If you believe that abortion is a right, do you want to be described as *pro-abortion, anti-life,* or *pro-choice?* Do you want to use the word(s) *fetus, product of conception, unborn, pre-born,* or *baby?*

- Colorado's governor vetoed a "lettuce libel" law that would have let farmers sue anyone who falsely insulted their agricultural products. Now, the produce police have struck in Louisiana, where a new law prohibits "disparagement of any perishable agricultural or aquacultural food product." Could this lead to a Crawfish Anti-Defamation League?[40]

- Leonore Hauck, a managing editor for the Random House dictionary division, discussed how definitions change to reflect current sensibilities: "One of the definitions of 'girl' in 1947 was 'a young, unmarried woman.' Today we say, 'a young, immature woman, esp. formerly, an unmarried one.' The word 'formerly' shows you how the meaning has changed, and a note warns the reader, 'Many women today resent being called girls.'"[41]

[40] Amy Bernstein, "Eye on the '90s," *U.S. News and World Report,* December 23, 1991, p. 17.
[41] Patricia Holt, "The Woman Who Decides What Goes in Webster's," *San Francisco Chronicle,* October 24, 1991, p. E-5.

- In late 1996, the Food and Drug Administration "ordered milk labels changed to give Americans a better idea of how much fat is in that glass. Those jugs of 2 percent milk that now are labeled 'low-fat' were to be renamed 'reduced fat.' Only 1 percent milk can be called 'low-fat,' while skim milk, the healthiest choice, can be advertised as 'fat-free' or 'nonfat' milk. The change came after consumer advocates complained that Americans were misled into believing milk with 2 percent fat was healthier than it actually is."[42]

- In a budget battle in the state of California, Governor Pete Wilson apologized to Americans of Welsh ancestry for using the term "welshing on his agreement":

  "If I have offended you or the Welsh community by my comments, I apologize," Wilson said, in an August 9 letter to Rees Lloyd, lawyer for the Twm Sion Cat-Welsh-American Legal Defense, Education & Development Fund.

  The term "welsh" is used in a derogatory manner to mean failure to pay what is owed, to go back on one's word, Lloyd said Sunday from the group's Glendale headquarters.

  "I recognize the distinct history and pride that makes the Welsh heritage unique, and can assure you that it was not my intention to offend you or your ancestry in any way," Wilson wrote.

  Lloyd said the governor's apology ends the dispute.[43]

Reification: When Words Take on More Power than Reality

Imagine yourself subject to a classroom experiment. You are sitting in class, about to see a film. To make the session more festive, your instructor gives you crackers and a homemade paté to

---

[42]   *Contra Costa Times* wire service, November 20, 1996, p. B1.
[43]   Associated Press report, *Contra Costa Times*, August 14, 1995, p. A-7.

munch as you view the movie. You enjoy the hearty taste of this snack, and when the film is over and the lights go back on, you ask for the recipe. Your teacher then informs you that you have been eating dog biscuits with canned cat food on top.

If you are like many people, you may experience a sense of nausea and disgust, though some cat food and dog food is perfectly edible for humans and is more nutritionally balanced than most fast food. But the labels put on this food, the words themselves, not the actual products, might make you sick.

In the same way, some people feel special when they are served expensive caviar or sweetbreads. The fact that they are eating fish eggs or cow organs has no jarring effect on them because there are such powerful, positive connotations associated with the names of these foods.

Reification occurs when the words themselves become more powerful and influential than objective reality. It leads to such human foibles as the following:

- Paying more money for "name brands" that may have the same ingredients as generic brands of products.

- Feeling confident when wearing designer label jeans or unworthy when wearing possibly higher-quality jeans that don't carry the popular label.

- Feeling like you can't succeed in a math or writing course because a teacher in fourth grade said you were "poor in math" or because of one previous grade.

- Feeling overweight even when you are at or below your ideal weight because you were called fat years ago. (Karen Carpenter, the singer who died from complications of anorexia nervosa, was reportedly very upset about a reviewer who referred to her as overweight, and that label may have contributed to her obsession with her weight.)

- In "primitive" cultures, being subject to stomach cramps because you know that someone is sticking needles in a doll with your name on it. Or in "sophisticated" cultures, having hotels with elevators that go from floor 12 to floor 14, because no one wants to stay on the (unlucky) 13th floor. (Note that this arrangement is especially true in ho-

CALVIN AND HOBBES © 1988 Watterson. Dist. by UNIVERSAL PRESS SYNDICATE. Reprinted with permission. All rights reserved.

tels that house gambling casinos, presumably filled with people concerned about maximizing their "luck.")

Sometimes reification can cause life-or-death consequences; our superstitious and confused thinking can get us into deep trouble. Consider the story of a 25-year-old Frenchman, Lucien Schlitz, and his 19-year-old first mate, Catherine Plessz, who set out on a long cruise for the tropics aboard a 26-foot steel cutter. They started in the Mediterranean Sea, which was so rough that it put the boat on its side. The boat righted itself, but later a freak wave swept over the boat and both Lucien and Catherine found themselves in the water. Through desperate efforts, both managed to get back on board, but they no longer had a rudder (steering mechanism), so they were adrift.

The boat was still whole even though it had been knocked around by the storm. It would seem, to our clear, dry heads, that the logical thing would be to remain on board with the comforts of food, water, and blankets and to wait for help. But Lucien's mind was stressed and fatigued and he began to think obsessively about the life raft. He was terribly concerned that it wouldn't inflate, so he pulled it open, nearly losing it to the wind in the process. Since it measured six feet across, he couldn't fit it in the cockpit, so he moored it to the back of his steel boat.

Soon after that, by mental processes that would surely be a feast for any psychologist, the only solution that seemed left to Lucien and Catherine was to take refuge in the *life* raft which represented safety [my emphasis]—still, as we see it, in a pattern of psychological aberration which explains the inevitability of everything they did. . . . On 14 September, 1972, Lucien and Catherine had now sought safety in their life raft after throwing into it some tinned food, some distress flares, two 20-litre jerricans of water, a compass and the leather sack with their money and their papers. Then the line linking them to the *Njord* parted.[44]

Over the next days, Lucien and Catherine needlessly suffered great thirst, hunger, sleep deprivation, and cold (from being frequently tossed into the water by the waves upsetting the raft). On the twelfth day, ". . . just as they had decided that survival was too difficult and they would make a quick end to it by drinking all the rest of their water at once for a last sensation of well-being, they were spotted at fifty yards, despite 8 foot troughs, and rescued by a cargo ship."[45]

This extended example reveals that we can give a word or phrase (in this case, *life raft*) power of its own and make faulty decisions based on that word or phrase.

SKILL

Recognize the power we can attach to words. Pause and consider the facts, knowing how labels can be deceiving.

Meanings Are in People

General semanticists, who study the effects of words on people, have articulated some key principles to guide our responsible use of words.

---

[44] Bernard Robin, *Survival at Sea* (Camden, Maine: International Marine Publishing Company, 1981), p. 112.
[45] Ibid., p. 114.

Their main principle is: *The word is not the thing.* They use the analogy of a map (the words) showing a particular territory (reality). The map can give us information about the territory, but it is only a visual representation of the territory and it can never show all the details of the territory. Our responsibility as thinkers is to realize that words are limited and to check out the territory before we draw hasty conclusions. If Lucien and Catherine, the sailors just discussed, had had the strength and wisdom to think over their options, they would have realized that, though their inflatable raft was *called* a life raft, their lives were more secure if they remained on board their cutter and sent up flares from there, saving the raft for a second vessel. In fact the sailboat *Njord* was found adrift, but sound and dry, many days before Lucien and Catherine were rescued.

The meaning of words lies in people and not, magically, in the words themselves. Misunderstandings of words and phrases can be clearly seen when people speak different languages, as illustrated in the following news feature.

CASE CLOSED: BLADDER THREAT, NOT BOMB

Drunken German Served 9 Months

by Warren Richey
Fort Lauderdale Sun-Sentinel

Fort Lauderdale, Florida. A drunk German tourist who triggered a bomb scare as he tried to tell a frightened flight attendant that he really, really, really had to go to the bathroom was a free man on Wednesday after more than nine months in prison.

Johann Peter Grzeganek, 23, told a judge in federal court in Fort Lauderdale that it was all a misunderstanding.

He said when he warned a flight attendant that when it was "going to explode," he was referring to his bladder, not the plane.

The pilot wasn't taking any chances. He turned the plane around, dumped his fuel, and returned to Fort Lauderdale airport.

The plane was searched. No bomb.

Grzeganek was charged with knowingly making a false bomb threat on an aircraft in flight, a crime that carries a 20-year minimum mandatory sentence with no parole.

Faced with the prospect of growing old in prison, Grzeganek agreed to plead guilty to four lesser charges.

Unable to make his bond, he remained in prison waiting for his day in court, which arrived Wednesday.

Prosecutors came to the sentence hearing prepared to ask Chief U.S. District Judge Norman Roettger to keep Grzeganek behind bars for two to three years.

Roettger had a different idea. The chief judge, who understands German, read in court a letter Grzeganek wrote from his cell.

Grzeganek, who speaks little English, admitted to having been drunk the night of the flight. He said he drank heavily in part because he fears flying.

He also said he needed to use a bathroom. When the need became an emergency, he sought relief. The plane was in a steep climb at the time. An English-speaking flight attendant stopped him. He told her in German, according to his letter, "I have to go to the bathroom, my bladder is full and going to explode."

The attendant, Beate Westerhouse, testified it appeared Grzeganek was drunk and preparing to urinate in the aisle.

Westerhouse told him to get back in his seat.

"He said 'No, no, no, the roof would go,'" Westerhouse said.

"I took this to mean that something would make the roof explode," she said.

Roettger asked if she had ever heard the German phrase: "Then the roof flies." It is a colloquialism, Roettger said, that means a person needs to use a bathroom.

Roettger sentenced Grzeganek to time served.

Reprinted with permission from the _Sun-Sentinel_, Fort Lauderdale, Florida.

Even when people speak the same language, misunderstandings frequently occur because of what words mean to different individuals. Dictionary definitions are useful for providing knowledge, but they often fall short in creating understanding among people. _Webster's New International Dictionary_ may define _love_ as "a deep and tender feeling of affection for, or attachment or devotion to, a person or persons," but we can't rely on that definition when a significant other says "I love you."

We need instead to find out what the word _love_ means to an individual (does it mean "I want to marry you," "I enjoy your company," "I love every person and you're a person," "I will always be with you no matter what happens," or something else?). If your friend wants you to meet her at class "early" and gives you no further explanation, there's a good chance that one of you may be there a few minutes before class starts and the other may be there an hour before, waiting impatiently.

SKILL

Realize that meanings are in people. Ask "What do you mean?" whenever a word or phrase is unclear or is a potential source of misunderstanding.

This skill may seem so simple as to be insulting to your intelligence, and yet it is one of the most valuable and underused skills we have. We tend to use a form of what psychologists term **projection*** when we hear a phrase, a political speech, or a commercial message; that is, we tend to assume that what the other person means is what we would mean if we had used those words.

Our tendency to project meaning explains why we are so often disappointed with blind dates ("This person is wonderful"), political candidates ("I care about the 'little people' in America"), or products ("Pimples virtually disappear!"). Sometimes we don't take time to question what the people who bring us these messages mean, because we really want to believe there is the perfect date, political solution, or pimple formula for us.

SURE I'M COMMITTED . . . OOPS . . . BYE-BYE

by Dr. Laura Schlessinger
How Could You Do That?

Simply saying words such as *committed* or *love* does not mean there actually is commitment or love. Then why say the words? Because of the

---

*   This term is used by those who study languages and perception. For an in-depth study of the meaning of projection in psychology, consult a psychology text or professor.

instant gratification brought upon by such declarations; gratifications like sex or enhanced (temporary, of course) sense of self. Listen to Cliff.

Cliff, thirty-nine, is in a difficult situation right now. He's been dating a twenty-seven-year-old woman for two and a half months. That's ten weeks of weekends they spent together, amounting to about twenty days of actual contact time.

"We had a committed relationship and it seemed like our relationship was made in heaven. Then she was diagnosed with lupus and I went over to talk with her and tried to explain my feelings."

"What feelings are those, Cliff?"

"That I can't marry her because of her health condition."

"I guess you only enjoy relationships when they look like they're made in heaven, and don't come burdened with the realities of earth."

"Well, I suppose. Maybe 'made in heaven' was a poor choice of words."

"No, I imagine it accurately expresses that you like your relationship pretty and neat."

"Well, yeah."

"Cliff, I don't know if you're ever going to find a perfect situation with nothing unpleasant or challenging to deal with, but I guess you could just move on and keep trying."

"If we were already married, it would be a life-long commitment and that would be different."

"You already used the word committed before. You said you were committed already."

"I didn't mean that really."

"I guess you really meant the sex was good and she was fun."

"Is there a way to explain my feelings to her?"

. . . "Realistically, there isn't much between you. Your predicament shows why infatuation and recreational sex should not be used as criteria for the notion of commitment. You are at the point of committed to good sex, good times, good fun, good feelings."

. . . Cliff had sex, which I think ought to be serious business, and told his lady he was committed; when there was an opportunity to show that the commitment meant something, he showed it meant nothing.[46]

Copyright © 1996 by Dr. Laura C. Schlessinger. Reprinted by permission of HarperCollins Publishers, Inc.

---

[46] Dr. Laura Schlessinger, *How Could You Do That?* (New York: HarperCollins Publishers, Inc., 1996) pp. 152–154.

Often, then, the cause of projection may lie in our emotional need to believe that something is true; other times, we are just untrained or too busy or lazy to pursue the reality of what is being said to us. And sometimes speakers or writers make things so confusing that it takes a grand effort to understand them. Consider a report that reads: "We have confirmed that the overturning of the presidential veto to create an amendment protecting the flag has been enforced."

In states where voters are given choices through propositions, there is often confusion in the wording of these propositions. For example, years ago, in California, if you voted *yes* on a particular proposition, that meant you were saying *no* to nuclear power plant expansion; if you voted *no* that meant you were saying *yes* to this expansion. Confused voters probably often cast votes they didn't really mean.

To help us defend against words that don't clearly represent reality, we will examine four common problems with language: **vagueness, ambiguity, doublespeak,** and **weasel** words. All are used by advertisers, salespersons, politicians, and others.

The Problem of Vagueness

A word or phrase is **vague** when its meaning is unclear. **Vagueness** is a common problem in public discourse. Some politicians will use only vague, abstract terms that have generally positive connotations and not define what they mean, hoping that each listener will like the sound of the promises being made. When asked for specific details about their plans, they may commit the fallacy of "ignoring the question" (see the following example). Conversely, a good politician will say he has a plan for "increased aid to the needy," and then define what he means by aid and what he means by the needy and then what, exactly, he has in mind.

Good reporters will notice vague language and press politicians to explain themselves. If the politicians explain using only more vague, abstract terms, be careful about supporting them (because you don't know what you're supporting).

Example

> *Reporter:* Mr. Candidate, you mentioned you have a comprehensive plan to deal with our terrible freeway delays. Can you tell us what is involved in this plan?
>
> *Candidate:* Gladly. I plan to use all available resources to create a wide range solution to this problem that has plagued us for years.
>
> *Reporter:* Can you be more specific? Are you planning expansions, and would these cause greater bridge tolls or taxes for the citizens?
>
> *Candidate:* As I've said, the program will be really comprehensive and each citizen will be considered and served. If I'm elected, you're going to see some incredibly positive changes.

This candidate appears bright enough to describe his program in glowing terms, but he is unwilling or unable to detail what he is actually proposing. Perhaps the candidate hasn't formulated a plan or perhaps he avoids giving details about his plans for fear of alienating special interest groups.

Example

> *Family:* Can you tell us if this operation on our mother's hip is dangerous and, also, will she have use of her leg afterwards?
>
> *Surgeon:* All surgery has risks and these things are always hard to predict.
>
> *Family:* Well, can you give us typical recovery rates and times?
>
> *Surgeon:* Each person is different, but you can rest assured we are doing everything in our power to help.

In this example, everything the surgeon said may be true, but he has not provided any statistics or details to help the family feel at ease. Health care professionals are busy people and they can't afford to make promises they can't keep; still, you need to press for information so you can make the best decisions for your health and the well-being of your loved ones.

Example

Darlene: Paul, I really love you, and I think it would be good for our relationship if we started seeing other people.

Paul: What are you saying? Do you want to break our engagement?

Darlene: No, nothing like that. I just think it would be healthy for us to date other people.

Paul: Are you interested in seeing someone else?

Darlene: No, not at all. I think we'd both just grow more if we were able to experience a variety of relationships.

Paul: What does that mean?

Darlene: Well, it means I still love you but I just think it would be great for our relationship if we saw other people too.

In this situation, Darlene is either confused about what she wants or is sure of what she wants but doesn't know how to tell Paul. He needs to keep pressing for specifics for the sake of his mental health!

Examples of Commercials with Vague Wording

Get your clothes a whiter white and a brighter bright!

Smoke Winters—with cool, smooth flavor!

It's the real thing!

The Hugo Company: We care about people.

By this time, you should be identifying vagueness in language, and, in this case, how advertisers, like politicians, use positive connotations to excite the audience. But the question is, what are they talking about?

The preceding examples are all meant to show how frustrating it can be to get people to move from the nonspecific to the concrete so that we can really understand what they are saying. Some people are purposefully vague; others just have a hard time expressing themselves or knowing exactly what they want to communicate. Still, critical thinkers need to persist in understanding what is meant by vague words and phrases; then, any decisions about voting, having surgery, buying a product, or continuing a relationship can be made rationally.

Ambiguity in Language

Ambiguity in language can also cause problems in communication. A word or expression is ambiguous when it has two or more different meanings. Often, riddles use ambiguity to create a puzzling situation; one common riddle asks you to turn the following drawing into a six by adding just one line.

IX

The answer, reflecting one of the two types of "sixes," is:

SIX

Ambiguity is also the problem in these humorous but real headlines compiled by Jay Leno:

"Drought turns coyotes to watermelons."[47]

"Need Plain Clothes Security. Must have shoplifting experience."[48]

"Foreclosure Listings: Entire state of New Jersey available."[49]

On a more serious note, ambiguity in language is confusing and causes numerous communication problems, as in the following example:

Former FBI director J. Edgar Hoover was reading a typed copy of a letter he had just dictated to his secretary. He didn't like the way she had formatted the letter, so he wrote on the bottom, "Watch the borders," and asked her to re-type it. The secretary did as she was instructed and

[47] Jay Leno, *Headlines* (New York: Warner Books, 1989) p. 99.
[48] Ibid., p. 148.
[49] Ibid., p. 48.

Drabble ® by Kevin Fagan
DRABBLE reprinted by permission of United Feature Syndicate, Inc.

sent it off to all top agents. For the next two weeks FBI agents were put out on special alert along the Canadian and Mexican borders.[50]

Ambiguous language is especially confusing between cultures. Many expressions that are common to speakers of one language group (or subculture) are misunderstood by members of other cultures. For example, when asked if they would like more coffee, some English-speaking people respond, "No, thanks. I'm fine." People who are learning the language can't understand what seems to be a report on the state of one's health as an answer to a question about more coffee.

As in all cases of possible confusion in language, a critical thinker should consider alternative meanings to words and phrases and clarify terms by asking "What do you mean?"

EXERCISES

Purpose: To recognize how vague or ambiguous terms can be misleading and how we can avoid the problems associated with projection. To realize that meanings are in people, not in words.

---

50 Roger von Oech, *A Whack on the Side of the Head* (New York: Warner Books, 1990), p. 114.

1. Give an extended example, or several examples, of the use of abstract, ambiguous, or vague terms that are not defined by the speaker or writer. You can find these examples in editorials, political speeches, advertisements, or, perhaps, when you converse with friends. List the abstract, vague, or ambiguous terms or phrases used and tell how different people could interpret these words in different ways. If possible, extend the exercise by asking someone who is using abstract terms to clarify what he or she means by those terms. For further practice, see the discussion questions and suggestions for essay or speech writing after the last article in this chapter.

2. Think of some examples of projection that have occurred in your life or in the life of someone you know. How could the problems associated with projection have been avoided? Consider a time when you misunderstood someone's words or instructions.

Example:
I missed an English class and called a friend to get the assignment. She said we had to turn in a copy of a resume that we might use to apply for a job. Then she said, "You also need a cover." I assumed she was using the word cover the way I use it, so I bought a report cover. What she really meant was that we were supposed to have a cover letter introducing ourselves to an employer. The cover letter goes with the resume. I could have avoided these problems by asking what she meant when she mentioned a cover. Or I could have repeated back to her what the assignment was; then she might have caught my error.

3. This exercise should be done in classroom groups. Assume you have been selected as a citizen's advisory committee to the Supreme Court. Your task is to form a clear definition of one (or more) of the following words or phrases: *obscenity, life, cruel and unusual punishment, competency,* or *adult.* Your definition will be used to guide future decisions on issues related to these terms.

In your discussion, try to come to a consensus. Whenever possible, resolve disagreements by presenting evidence to clarify positions. You may also give personal examples to increase the understanding of one another's viewpoints.

After you have used the time allotted (at least 30 minutes), choose a member of your group to present your results to the class as a whole. The spokesperson should discuss:

- The definitions the group agreed upon.

- The difficulties in coming to consensus and why they occurred. Consider especially the values of group members and their different experiences.

Article for Discussion

Read the following as an example of the power of words.

Federal Judge Orders Lawyer Not to Use Her Maiden Name

by Tara Bradley-Steck
Contra Costa Times, Thursday, July 14, 1988

PITTSBURGH—A federal judge told an attorney he doesn't allow anyone to "use that Ms." in his courtroom, ordered her to use her husband's name or go to jail and found her colleague in contempt for protesting.

"Do what I tell you or you're going to sleep in the county jail tonight. You can't tell me how to run my courtroom," Senior U.S. District Judge Hubert I. Teitelbaum told attorney Barbara Wolvowitz.

The judge told Wolvowitz, whose husband is University of Pittsburgh law professor Jules Lobel, that she must go by the name Mrs. Lobel in his courtroom.

When her co-counsel, Jon Pushinsky, protested, Teitelbaum found him in contempt of court for "officious intermeddling" and gave him a suspended sentence of 30 days in jail.

During a disjointed dialogue Friday that covered about 20 pages of court transcript, Teitelbaum told Wolvowitz that Mrs. Lobel is her legal name "under the laws of the state of Pennsylvania.

"And that's what I want you to be, to call yourself from here on in this courtroom." he said. "That's an intolerable kind of thing."

The judge claimed a married woman must petition Common Pleas Court for permission to use her maiden name. The Pennsylvania Family Law Practice and Procedure Handbook said no legal proceedings are required if a woman chooses to use her maiden name.

Teitelbaum, presiding over a race discrimination suit against PPG Industries Inc., also asked each of the six female jurors on Friday if she used her husband's name or maiden name. All used their husbands' names.

Wolvovitz, 36, said she was "in shock for two days."

"I've practiced for 10 years. I've gotten into arguments with judges but never over something like this. I can't quite understand what happened," said Wolvovitz, who had never previously argued a case before Teitelbaum. "After it was over and the jury left, I had tears in my eyes."

When the trial resumed Monday, Teitelbaum denied Wolvowitz's request for a mistrial, and the attorney again refused to be called Mrs. Lobel.

"What if I call you sweetie?" said Teitelbaum, 73, a former U.S. attorney appointed to the federal bench by President Nixon in 1970.

The judge declared he would refer to Wolvovitz only as "counselor."

Questions for Discussion

1. What's in a name? What significance do you think that each person gave to the use of the title "Ms" accompanied by a maiden name? In other words, what connotations does the title probably have for each person?

2. Why do you think the judge asked each of the six female jurors if she used her husband's name or her maiden name?

3. Analyze the judge's statement "And that's what I want you to be, to call yourself from here on in this courtroom."

4. What does the abstract term "officious intermeddling" mean in concrete terms?

Doublespeak, Including Weasel Words

We have seen how vagueness and ambiguity in language can be used either unintentionally or deliberately to make issues cloudy. Words can be used to deceive in other ways. In this section, we will look at doublespeak and its subcategory weasel words.

Doublespeak is "language used to lie or mislead while pretending to tell the truth . . . it is used by the highest elected officials, by bureaucrats in state and local government, by members of industry, academia, and other areas of society in order to deceive, to make the bad seem good, the negative appear positive, the disastrous seem tolerable."[51] If language is the map, as general semanticists like to say, and reality is the territory, then doublespeak is the creation of a map that distorts the territory. Those who hear doublespeak are misled about the territory because of the deceptive map.

In his popular book, *Doublespeak*, William Lutz claims that doublespeak is

> a very conscious use of language as a weapon or tool by those in power to achieve their ends at our expense. While some doublespeak is funny, much of it is frightening. We laugh and dismiss doublespeak as empty or meaningless words at our own peril, for, as George Orwell saw so clearly, the great weapon of power, exploitation, manipulation, and oppression is language. It is only by being aware of the pervasiveness of doublespeak and its function as a tool of social, economic and political control that we can begin to fight those who would use language against us.[52]

Doublespeak includes the use of **euphemism,** which means the use of a less direct but more acceptable term to describe an event, person, or object. In their daily use, euphemisms are not

---

[51] Position Paper, *National Council of Teachers of English*, 1988.
[52] William Lutz, *Doublespeak* (New York: HarperCollins, 1989), pp. xii–xiii.

usually meant to deceive and to distort, but to soften harsh realities. We use euphemisms to explain disease and death to children when we make such statements as, "Aunt Lily isn't feeling
well today, so she's in the hospital" or "Grandma passed away."
We may use euphemisms to sound better to ourselves or others
when we describe ourselves as *slender* (instead of skinny), *hefty*
(instead of fat), or *under a lot of stress* (instead of irritable).

A teacher might use the euphemism "We're going to have a
quiz" to announce a fifty-item exam, reasoning that people would
not panic studying for a "quiz" as much as they would for a "test"
and therefore they would do better. Yet, students might prefer a
10-point "test" to a 50-point "quiz."

Euphemism as doublespeak is common in business and government. In some cases, the euphemisms chosen become another category of doublespeak, which Lutz terms "inflated language." Inflated language is designed to make the commonplace
seem extraordinary or to make simple things more complex than
they are. Below are some examples compiled by the National
Council of Teachers of English.

Fired: dehired, nonrenewed, nonretained, selected out
Layoffs: negative employee retention, workforce adjust-
    ments, headcount reductions, career alternative en-
    hancement program
Pain: discomfort
Death: terminal living, negative patient care outcome (or
    "That person is no longer a patient at this hospital")
Classrooms: pupil stations
Poor: economically nonaffluent
Prisoner: client of the correctional system
Poor: economically marginalized
Lazy: motivationally dispossessed

Doublespeak is a form of personal and corporate denial of
painful realities. No company wants to be seen as "firing" employees because that term has negative, cruel connotations. They
want to be seen as compassionate, so they use terms that present
the company in the best possible light. Many professionals use euphemisms to soften or inflate reality. Psychologists refer to someone who regularly explodes into bursts of anger as a "borderline

personality." Real estate agents refer to tiny houses as "darling cottages" or "dollhouses"; they may describe dumps that are falling off of foundations as "needing a little tender loving care."

Doublespeak is used in our personal lives also. If you have children or siblings, you know that a fight is explained differently from each person's viewpoint. A "light tap" to one person ends up being a "big hit" when described by the other. Some women in the business world have complained that when they have made an unpopular decision they were labeled as "aggressive" whereas a favored male counterpart would have been labeled "assertive" or "a strong manager." We may describe a friend of ours who rants and raves at small provocations as "just excitable" or even "dynamic."

Sometimes it is suggested that we should change words to create better connotations. For example, Gail Sheehy, author of popular books on the stages of life, would like to eliminate the word "aging."

"Let's don't even call it aging anymore," Sheehy exclaims. "The very word carries pejorative baggage. Let's refer to successful aging as saging—the process by which men and women accumulate wisdom and grow into the culture's sages."[53]

EXERCISE

Purpose: To recognize euphemisms and how they are applied.

Try to think of euphemisms that you've heard or used. What are some euphemisms for the following: selfish, cheap, war, lies, kill. How about for a badly damaged car that someone wants to sell?

Now try an exercise that British philosopher Bertrand Russell created and called "Conjugating Irregular Verbs." Take a personal characteristic or action and express it favorably, neutrally, and unfavorably as follows:

I'm slender.	You're thin.	She's skinny.
I'm frugal.	You're careful with money.	He's cheap.

53   Gail Sheehy, *New Passages:* New York (Random House, 1995) p. 420.

Complete these conjugations:

1. I have high self-esteem.
2. I'm curious about my neighbors.
3. I like to relax.
4. I'm pleasantly plump.
5. I don't like to stifle my child's creativity.
6. I'm not a perfectionist about cleaning.
7. My car has a lot of character.

Other forms of doublespeak include *jargon,* the use of specialized language to exclude or impress people who don't understand the terminology, and *gobbledygook,* which is vague language used to confuse and overwhelm those who hear it. These forms of doublespeak have been labeled "crazy talk" by professor and semanticist Neil Postman. He defines *crazy talk* as talk that reflects "bad" purposes.[54] Postman cites Werner Erhard, the founder of the very successful Erhard Seminars Training (a self-help group), as using crazy talk in the following excerpt from a interview:

> Sometimes people get the notion that the purpose of Erhard Seminars Training is to make you better. It is not. I happen to think that you are perfect exactly the way you are. . . . The problem is that people get stuck acting the way they were instead of being the way they are. . . .
>
> The purpose of est training is to transform your ability to experience living so that the situations you have been trying to change or have been putting up with clear up just in the process of living.[55]

Another example of crazy talk is the wording given by telephone solicitors who tell you that they represent a popular charity. One ploy is to use the vague phrase "I am part of a commercial fundraiser for charitable purposes." In reality, these individuals are taking the lion's share of your donation for them-

[54] Neil Postman, *Crazy Talk, Stupid Talk* (New York: Delacorte, 1976), p. 83.
[55] Ibid.

selves and giving only a small percentage to the group they claim to represent. Critical thinkers should listen carefully to what is being said between the lines and ask questions before giving money to such solicitors.

Advertisers also use inflated language and gobbledygook to impress consumers. They want to present their products as necessary and in some cases even miraculous, and they have developed the tools to do so in the form of creative doublespeak. According to Carl Wrighter, an advertising copywriter, "Today's advertising industry is the most potent and powerful mass marketing and merchandising instrument ever devised by man."[56] He claims that, even if you think that you're smart enough to see through advertising tricks, you're really not because of the subtle power of **weasel words.**

A weasel word is "a word used in order to evade or retreat from a direct or forthright statement or position"(*Webster's New International Dictionary*).[57] Let's look at how advertisers use these words so that they can make great claims and not have to prove them.

According to Wrighter, the most commonly used weasel is the word *help* or *helps*. An ad might say "This cream will help prevent acne," or "Our new formula helps the pain to go away," "This mouthwash helps stop the germs," or "This pill helps you feel drowsy so you can sleep." Notice that no one is claiming that the products will prevent acne, make pain disappear, stop germs, or guarantee sleep. They only promise to *help* do those things.

By only promising to help, advertisers relieve the manufacturers of any responsibility for the actual effectiveness of their products. Wrighter says that we don't really hear the word *help;* we only hear the promise (perhaps because we want to believe there is a perfect product for our problem). He also believes that 75 percent of advertising uses the word *help*. If that's true, you should be able to detect this weasel word easily. Watch also for modifications of this word such as "significantly helps" or "greatly improves".

Another prominent weasel word is *like*—the word *like* is used to "romance the product," which means to make you think

---

[56] Carl Wrighter, *I Can Sell You Anything* (New York: Random House, 1972), p. 2.
[57] Ibid. p. 23.

about something bigger, better, or more interesting than the product and to associate the product with that better thing. You might think of "romancing the product" as creating a faulty analogy.

Wrighter gives several examples of "romancing the product." An old Mateus ad claims that drinking their wine is like taking a trip to Portugal. When the ad appears on television, depicting a romantic Portuguese holiday, the audience may forget that they'll be drinking it in their own homes—no beaches, music, or wonderful meals will accompany it like they do in the ad. Other powerful images from the past include "It cleans like a white tornado" and "It's like a great taste explosion in your mouth." Some products are romanced with a name, like Softique (for tissues) or Beverly Hills (for a perfume). Lipton specialty teas have names like Gentle Orange, Mountain Berry Apple, and Lemon Soother. One Lipton ad compares the tea to the experience of a deep massage.

 EXERCISE

Purpose: To identify gobbledygook and phrases that romance the product.

An ad for Mercury Sable automobiles featured a silhouette of a dancing couple behind a car.

1. Explain how the following words, which accompanied the ad, were used to romance the product.
2. Point out the vague gobbledygook that is used to describe the "new" changes in the car.
   We dressed in silence.
   And drove.
   When we walked in,
   she said something to the piano player.
   Next thing, I hear this song we used to love.
   She takes my hand. We dance. And something
   that was there before, was back. Only stronger.

Mercury Sable.
The new, remarkably sophisticated Sable.
Its body has been totally restyled.
Its interior so thoroughly redesigned
even the controls are easier to read and reach.
It has standard driver and optional passenger air bags.
It rides smoother. Quieter.
And makes driving more of a pleasure.
The car that started it all,
does it again.

Other weasel words cited by Wrighter include:

- *Virtual* or *virtually:* This word means "almost, but not in fact."
  "Virtually foolproof"
  "Virtually never needs service"
  "Virtually trouble-free"

An ad for a "medication tracking system" reads as follows:

Do you worry when a loved one forgets to take daily medication? Or takes too many pills because he or she loses track of the dosage schedule? You can help by giving Medi-Track™. This caring gift makes it virtually impossible for medication users to lose track of their schedule—no matter where they happen to be.

- *Acts* or *works:* This word is another form of *helps* and is often used with the word *help*.
  "Works like magic"
  "Works to help prevent"
  "Acts against . . ."
  "Acts on the cough control center"

- *Can be:* When advertisers say their product *can be* useful they make no definite claim that it *will be* useful. *Can be* simply means that it is possible. Variations are *could be*, *might be*, and *may be*.

"Shine toothpaste can be of significant value when used in a monitored dental program."

- *Up to: Up to* implies a range from zero to the figure that is given. Consumers tend to hear only the largest number.
"You may have won up to $500.00."
"Dude deodorant gives you protection for up to 12 hours."
"Come to our sale and get up to 50 percent off."

- *As much as:* Similar to *up to, as much as* means that you might get the ultimate benefit described, but you might not.
"As much as 20 percent greater mileage"
"Blabble gum gives you as much as an hour more chewing satisfaction than the leading brand."

Also, Wrighter suggests that you be aware of vague terms such as "refreshes," "comforts," "tackles," and "fights." These are vague terms with positive connotations that may or may not have a basis in reality when referring to a specific product. Some terms that are commonly used because of their appealing sound but that have no definite meaning include:

Fortified	Flavor and Taste
Style and Good Looks	Different, Special, Exclusive

Sometimes these terms are strung together:

Phitrin: New. Improved. Bigger. Better.

 SKILL

Recognize when words are used to deceive and confuse readers and listeners.

Recognizing the problem of misleading commercial claims, the federal government has been making attempts to set clear standards about the meaning of labels given to foods. Consumers have been confused about the meaning of terms such as "fresh," "light," "low-fat" and "cholesterol-free."

New regulations will set guidelines for categories of products, such as yogurt or cheese. Currently, food companies can determine the serving size given on the package. If they make it small enough, then their product can be called "lower in fat" than a similar product with a larger serving size.

We as consumers can't rely on government agencies to clarify our thinking about commercial messages. We need to recognize doublespeak in all of its forms and keep in mind William Lutz's admonishment about advertising:

Every word in an ad is there for a reason; no word is wasted. Your job is to figure out exactly what each word is doing in an ad—what each word really means, not what the advertiser wants you to think it means. Remember, the ad is trying to get you to buy a product, so it will put the product in the best possible light, using any device, trick, or means legally allowed. Your only defense against advertising is to develop and use a strong critical reading, listening, and looking ability.[58]

EXERCISE

Purpose: To discover weasel words in persuasive messages.

Analyze some television, radio, or magazine advertising, campaign literature, or junk mail, specifically looking for doublespeak and weasel words. Bring samples to share with your class.

Try to include campaign messages in your search. Look for literature that comes in the mail dealing with upcoming elections.

[58]   William Lutz, *Doublespeak* (New York: HarperCollins, 1989), p. 102.

What particular "weasels" did you find used the most? What effect did the weasel have on the message—that is, why do you think that the writer of the message used that weasel?

Use the following sample ads to get you started:

Having a party and don't know what to serve? Try Tony's Barbequed Party Wings for that spicy hot partytime action. Our secret sauce has 37 of the world's finest ingredients mixed to virtual perfection and applied with tender loving care to each piece. So, spice up your next party with Tony's Party Wings; you'll feel like you're flying high with satisfaction.

Is your smile an average dull white in an average dull world? Make the change and brighten your outlook. For that all-day smile, your teeth deserve the best. *Flash* toothpaste with ZX-19 can help whiten and brighten your teeth for up to 8 hours. Stand out from the crowd—join the *Flash* generation, and change your dull world into a *Flash* world.

Vote for Richmond for school board. She knows about the latest classroom technology and can help make our school district the most progressive in the state. As a parent herself, J. Richmond cares about excellence in education and she shares your concerns. Having J. Richmond on the board is like having a friend attending the meetings for you.

 Chapter Highlights

1. Critical thinkers should be aware of the power of words to both clarify and obscure issues.
2. Language has a persuasive impact on people because of connotations, the images associated with words and phrases.
3. Reification occurs when words take on more power than reality.

4. The meaning of words are in people.
5. Four common problems with language are vagueness, ambiguity, doublespeak, and weasel words.

More Articles for Discussion

'AFRICAN-AMERICAN' IS AN IMPRECISE, DEBATABLE TERM

by Leonard Pitts
Syndicated columnist, December 21, 1996

Today's topic: the trouble with being African-American. Meaning the term, not the people.

I refer to the January issue of Playboy, in which interviewee Whoopi Goldberg says she doesn't allow people to call her an African-American "because I'm not African-American. I'm purebred, New York raised. I'm not from Africa. Calling me an African-American divides us further."

Candidly, I am loath to agree with anything this woman has to say on the subject of race. She is, let us not forget, the same grinning ninny who saw nothing wrong when her white boyfriend, Ted Danson, performed a blackface sketch in her dishonor at a Friar's Club roast in 1993. Compared to Goldberg, Clarence Thomas is Malcolm X.

But for all that, she has a point here.

It's not that "African-American" is divisive, as Goldberg and many others claim it is. I'm at a loss to figure out how one can divide what was never together.

Nor is it that the reasoning behind the term is suspect. We call ourselves African-Americans because that ties us to our ancestral homeland and because in the public mind, "black" is synonymous with evil and filth.

And yet . . . 10 years after the term came into general use, I am still not able to make my peace with it. Ten years later, it still feels imperfect, drawing attention to itself by its very awkwardness. Ten years later, it still seems like a stretch by colored folks, black people, Negroes, whatever, to lay claim to this grand, iconographic African past. But we are so many centuries removed from Africa that the attempt feels suspect and forced.

A man just off a plane from Nigeria is an African-American. We are Americans of African heritage. There is a difference.

It's not that I'm opposed to "African-American." Just ambivalent. Hey, I use the term myself. It is, after all, the politically correct thing to say.

But saying it still feels not unlike a fashion statement masquerading as deeper truth. Because, yes, Africa is place of our origin, engine of our culture, foundation of our identity. But despite all that, it is not our home. We have been gone too long.

This reaching back, this searching for touchstone is only natural, I suppose, especially for a people that has been largely defined by rupture and dislocation. We have been separated, taken, removed, split apart, lost . . . and it's only to be expected that we would try till the end of our days to get back to who we were.

But it should not be at the expense of ignoring who we are. Nor of denying a compelling truth: that this is now home. Sometimes, we act as if it were not. Often, other people treat us the same way.

But the first indentured servants arrived in 1619, the year before the Mayflower. Two centuries before that, a black Spaniard named Esteban explored what are now the states of Arizona and New Mexico. And in his book *They Came Before Columbus*, anthropologist Ivan Van Sertima documented evidence of Africans who explored what is now south Texas in ancient times.

We forget sometimes that we are as American as Mom's sweet potato pie. We picked American cotton in the delta of the Mississippi. Fought American wars at Yorktown, Richmond, Normandy, and Saigon. Championed American ideals at the Mall in Washington and the jails of Birmingham. Created American music on a front porch in Selma, a whorehouse in New Orleans, a street corner in Brooklyn, a bungalow in Detroit. And every day, we teach American children, cook American meals, write American books, drive American buses, enforce American laws and make American history for generations yet unborn.

We are unalterably American.

But "African-American . . . ?"

Well, sure, if you insist. But know it for what it is: the latest chapter in a long, ongoing debate, the latest reflection of the duality W.E.B. DuBois once famously felt in his landmark work, *The Souls of Black Folk*. Meaning the schism in the midst of self that asks, Which am I? African or American?

The debate can't end, nor moving on begin, until we find a way to make peace with the obvious truth.

We are neither. And we are both.

Understand that, and what we are called will take care of itself.

Reprinted with permission of *The Miami Herald*.

Questions for Discussion

1. How would you summarize Leonard Pitts' discomfort with the term "African-American"?
2. Pitts talks about a connection felt to Africa as a "place of origin" and a "foundation of identity." Do you feel a connection to your ancestral homeland—whether it be Africa, Italy, Ireland, China, or somewhere else? If so, how does that connection affect your life and your perception?
3. Whoopi Goldberg is quoted as saying that the term African-American "divides us further." To what extent do you believe that hyphenated terms used to describe identity are useful or harmful?

The following article was written after the United States exerted its veto power to prevent Boutros Boutros-Ghali from serving a second term as secretary-general of the United Nations.

A Diplomatic Translation

Here's What the New U.N. President
Should Have Said

by Robert Mott, McClatchy Newspapers Associate Editor
The Contra Costa Times, December 21, 1996

After being confirmed by the General Assembly this week as the new secretary-general of the United Nations, Kofi Annan of Ghana made a few pertinent remarks.

As befits his station and his sense of decorum, the longtime U.N. official spoke in diplomatic terms. Among other things, that means not naming names.

Yet no one who has followed the unfolding U.N. drama over the past six months had any doubt about what his message was, or to whom it was addressed. It was, after all, the Clinton administration's full-bore campaign to deny Boutros Boutros-Ghali a second term that led to Annan's ascent to a post he might otherwise never have attained.

Herewith excerpts of Annan's remarks, and a wholly unauthorized rendition of what he may have meant, freely translated into the American vernacular.

"I wish to pay tribute to the vision and energy of Secretary-General Boutros Boutros-Ghali, an extraordinary statesman who led the United Nations through a turbulent period of transition. . . . All of us recognize and history will record with gratitude, his important contribution."

Translation: This man, granted that he has shortcomings, got a bum rap. His arrogance, his independent thinking and his failure to genuflect to the most powerful member state made him a perfect scapegoat for U.N failures—including those, as in Somalia, for which the United States bears much of the responsibility.

"If all of us in this hall, together with the participation of all nations, large and small . . . can make this organization leaner, more efficient and more effective, more responsive to the wishes and needs of its members and more realistic in its goals and commitments, then and only then will we serve both this organization's high purpose and the planet's best interests."

Translation: I will do my best to carry on in the best tradition of . . . well, whom did you have in mind? Could you please tell me whether you expect me to be a secretary-general who has his own ideas, such as Mr. Boutros-Ghali? Or would you prefer a functionary who devotes his every waking hour to satisfying the whims of his diverse clientele, but especially the major powers—as did Kurt Waldheim, whose servility caused some in the United Nations to refer to him as "that butler"?

"To the nations . . . assembled here today, I say simply this: The United Nations is your instrument for peace and justice. Use it, respect it, defend it. It can be no wiser, no more competent, and no more efficient than those member states that now comprise and guide it."

Translation: It was the Clinton administration that first touted "aggressive multilateralism" as the favored means of dealing with regional crises but later, after the disastrous event in Somalia in which 18 Americans died, tried to blame that failure—indeed, the whole concept of multilateral intervention—on my predecessor, even though America once embraced that concept. The operation in question was run by Americans and the lack of backup for the trapped Army Rangers resulted in part from indecisiveness in the Pentagon.

"We cannot succeed without your political, moral, financial and material support and participation. Applaud us when we prevail; correct us when we fail; but, above all, do not let this indispensable, irreplaceable institution wither, languish or perish as a result of member-state indifference, inattention or financial starvation."

Translation: As you know, the United Nations faces not only a financial crisis and a managerial crisis but a crisis of purpose. Washington demands budget cuts and internal reforms to cut out wasteful duplication among various U.N. agencies. Well and good, but what about peacekeeping, the prime reason for creating the institution in the first place? As the member that has done the most in the recent past to undermine the institution, the United States has a special obligation to propose ideas that will not only improve efficiency but set the United Nations on a more purposeful course. Will it?

I might not be here had there not been a U.S. presidential election this year. The attacks on Mr. Boutros-Ghali by Republicans goaded President Clinton and his surrogates into telling voters that failure at the United Nations had only one father and that it was Boutros-Ghali. That was unfair; so was the mocking pronunciation of the secretary-general's name by Sen. Bob Dole, which really transgressed the bounds of decency.

While Mr. Boutros-Ghali was often aloof and peremptory, lacked "people skills" and moved less quickly than Washington desired to streamline the U.N. bureaucracy, in fact he did more than any previous incumbent in this regard, to no avail. This confrontation was not so much about reform as about the fact that Mr. Boutros-Ghali refused to be a lapdog. So will I.

U.S. officials would have the world believe that firing my predecessor will induce Congress finally to pay the $1.5 billion in back dues it owes the United Nations. May I thus assume that the check will soon be in the mail and that the U.N.-U.S. relationship will then become harmonious? Forgive me if I do not hold my breath.

I accept the responsibility thrust upon me, and I await your instructions as to what kind of world you wish to shape and how you expect me and my thousands of dedicated colleagues to help bring this about. If I do not hear from you soon, however, I will take it as a sign that you wish me to proceed according to my own designs. If that in turn displeases you, you can have my resignation in a New York minute. Those who refuse either to pay the piper or call the tune are entitled only to one benefit of the doubt.

Copyright © *The Sacramento Bee*, 1996.

Questions for Discussion

1. The "diplomatic" language given in the real address quoted here can be considered vague, allowing for several different meanings to be perceived by the listener. To what extent do

you agree with Robert Mott's translation of the true meaning of the words spoken by Kofi Annan? What other meanings could be attributed to some of his phrases?

2. How common is it for people to be indirect in the meanings of their statements? Do you find this indirectness in both public and private life? What would be the purpose of stating something vaguely or indirectly? Use examples to clarify your answer.

Free-Range? Natural? Sorting Out the Poultry Labels

by Suzanne Hamlin
November 13, 1996 © 1996 *The New York Times*

So why did the chicken cross the road?

If it was a free-range chicken, it was probably trying to find the meaning of life.

Consumers, too, are looking for answers, along with lower-fat, higher-protein alternatives to red meat. Poultry consumption is at record levels. In 1993, the last year for which Agriculture Department figures are available, the typical American ate 47 pounds of chicken, up from 26 pounds in 1975. And chicken and turkey together accounted for 32 percent of the total amount of meat consumed in the United States in 1993, up from 19 percent in 1970.

Which raises more questions: What does "free range" mean anyway? Is there a difference between a free-range chicken and an all-natural bird? What qualifies as organic and what as farm-raised?

Welcome to the arcane world of federal labeling regulations, which apply to poultry processors who sell at least 20,000 birds a year. The widespread assumption is that a free-range chicken is a happy-go-lucky bird, gamboling about the barnyard at will, pecking at organic grains until its rendezvous with a wood-burning grill.

But to the labeling division of the Agriculture Department, which sets the definitions and standards for poultry, a free-range bird is one that has access to the outdoors. Period. So a free-range chicken, turkey or duck could be munching on potato chips and drinking antibiotic cocktails and still be legal.

"Free range" was originally a menu term and is generally attributed to Larry Forgione, the chef at An American Place, his restaurant in Manhattan. In the early 80s, when he was at the River Cafe in Brooklyn, he used the term "to describe healthy chickens that were raised on small, local farms," he said.

But Kathy Leddy, a spokeswoman for the agency's labeling division, said that as long as chickens have some way to get out of the coop, they can be considered "free-range" or "free-roaming." When asked how the agency knew if producers were in compliance, she said that they must provide drawings or photographs with arrows pointing to the coops' doors.

A half-dozen large processors contend that free-range may not be such a good thing after all. Randy Day, the vice president for quality assurance at Perdue Farms Inc. in Salisbury, Md., said that sanitary and heated housing and nutritionally balanced feed formulas were the best thing that had ever happened to chickens. "Chickens that roam around outside pecking for food grains in manure are not chickens I would want to eat," he said.

The free-range chicken may or may not be "all-natural," a term sanctioned by the Agriculture Department and now in wide use on package labels. Does "all natural" guarantee that a bird that has never been fed antibiotics or coloring agents and has not been injected with salt and water?

Ms. Leddy said that it does not.

"The term was first approved by the USDA in 1982 for processed food," she said. "It meant that if additives were part of the product, they could not be artificial."

"For poultry to be 'all natural,' it means that if anything is injected into the chicken at the processing plant, it must be natural," she said. "Salt and water can be added, but not something like sodium phosphate." But "all natural" does not cover a chicken's diet or living conditions before it reaches the processing plant. Many of the chickens sold in this country have been fed coloring agents like marigold petals to make their skin more yellow.

And the majority have had antibiotics added to their feed. They are taken off the antibiotics seven to 14 days before they are killed. Producers contend that this makes them "antibiotic free," a term that is not, incidentally, an official Agriculture Department designation. But if the chicken has never been fed antibiotics, the processor can note that on the package.

What about chickens labeled "no growth hormones used"? That is just stating the obvious. Although the Agriculture Department has approved the use of growth hormones in beef, it has not sanctioned their use in veal, pork or poultry. But drugs, as opposed to hormones, are another matter.

Bacitracin, an antibiotic that is also a growth drug, is part of the feed formula of many chickens, including those processed by Perdue and

Bell & Evans. The Agriculture Department, while acknowledging that bacitracin can be a growth drug, characterizes it as an antibiotic, which processors contend are necessary to eliminate disease.

Producers say that new big-breasted breeds, not growth drugs, are the reason birds are bigger these days. Perdue, for one, is proud of its big chickens, bred to grow faster and consume less feed.

"The American public wants more white breast meat," said Day of Perdue, "and we deliver 15 percent more on our birds." The Agriculture Department says that the average four-pound broiler needed 10 weeks and 10 pounds of feed to grow to maturity in 1960. By 1990, a four-pounder could be produced in six weeks with eight pounds of feed.

And why do some chickens and turkeys labeled "fresh" appear to have just come in from an Arctic storm? They have so many ice crystals in their cavities that pliers are needed just to remove the giblet bag.

To the Agriculture Department, "fresh" is a broad term; it can be applied to any bird that has been stored or transported at anywhere from 36 degrees to zero. It's only when poultry dips below zero that it is considered frozen.

In poultry, "organic" is a term that has no meaning, at least not to the Agriculture Department. Using the strict dictionary definition ("Having the characteristics of, or derived from, living organisms"), all poultry is organic. But neither the Agriculture Department nor any other federal agency has ever defined the term, so no national standard exists. On poultry labels, only the phrase "raised on feed without pesticides" can be used, the Agriculture Department says.

Stress brought on by harsh living conditions is not monitored by the Agriculture Department, although a chicken cooped up in very little space is probably going to be one tough bird. The poultry industry recommends—but does not require—that each bird be allotted seven-tenths of a square foot of floor space in the chicken coop. The Agriculture Department does not address that issue at all. Unlike laying hens, chickens raised for the table are not kept in individual cages; they can zip around in their seven-tenths of a square foot as freely as they want.

So what can consumers do? There are at least two options. They can write or call the poultry processor at the address given on package and ask, in depth, about the feed formula and living conditions. They can also trust their own sense of taste. A stressed-out, waterlogged, ice-covered chicken just isn't going to deliver in flavor, no matter how much extra-virgin olive oil it's cooked with.

Many poultry perfectionists, including the Manhattan chefs Eberhard Muller and Gray Kunz, like Murray's Chickens, a special breed raised in Shomokin, Pa., and processed in South Fallsburg, N.Y. Available in markets on the Eastern Seaboard for nine months now, Murray's look and taste like real chickens. They are given more space than most to roam, the processor says, and are fed a protein diet that contains no animal byproducts, no bacitracin and no coloring agents.

Murray's does not advertise its chickens as free-range or organic because, "they are neither," said Steve Gold, who owns the company with Murray Bresky.

"At present, there is no legal standard for organic chicken," he continued, "and if we put our chickens outside during a Pennsylvania winter, they would freeze to death."

Questions for Discussion

1. Suzanne Hamlin states that a free-range chicken, turkey, or duck "could be munching on potato chips and drinking antibiotic cocktails and still be legal," since free-range only means that a bird has access to the outdoors. Cite some other examples from this article that illustrate differences between consumer perception of the meanings of poultry labels and reality.
2. To what extent do you believe that labeling should be standardized more strictly? Should consumers be given more written information about products that contain labels like "free-range" and "organic"?

Ideas for Writing or Speaking

1. Respond to one of the following quotes from English novelist George Orwell's *Politics and the English Language*. Take a position on the quote and prove your position using essays, newspaper, magazine or journal articles, advertisements, books, films, videos, or interviews.
   a. "In our time, political speech and writing are largely the defense of the indefensible."

    b. "The whole tendency of modern prose is away from con-
creteness."

    c. "The great enemy of clear language is insincerity."

    d. "In our age, there is no such thing as 'keeping out of politics.' All issues are political issues, and politics itself is a mass of lies, evasions, folly, hatred, and schizophrenia."

    e. "Political language . . . is designed to make lies sound truthful and murder respectable, and to give an appearance of solidity to pure wind."

2. Write or speak about a proposal for change, using both abstract objectives and concrete proposals. The abstract terms should be used to express the ideals you seek to achieve with your proposal; the concrete explanations are used to let your readers or listeners know exactly what your proposal entails and the real-world impact you expect it to have. For example, you might state that you would like to see increased employment opportunities in the inner cities (abstract objective). Then you can explain exactly how you would go about increasing employment, detailing the programs and the way the programs would be organized, funded, maintained, and evaluated (concrete proposals). You may want to organize your speech or essay using one of the speech formats discussed in Chapter 10.

3. **Sales Pitch.** Listen to a "hard sell" sales pitch by a professional salesperson. You might go to a car lot or stereo store or just invite a door-to-door salesperson to speak with you. Then list and analyze the reasons that you are given in favor of buying the product or service. Some questions to answer are as follows:

    a. Were you given valid and well-documented reasons for buying the product or service?

    b. Did the salesperson use deception or mislead or confuse you with vagueness or any of the forms of doublespeak covered in this chapter?

    c. Which arguments were persuasive and which were not? Explain why.

4. **Useless Item Survey.** Find something that you bought and never or rarely used. Then answer the following questions.

    a. What motivated you to buy this item?

    b. Why have you never or rarely used it?

c. Why do you still have it?

d. Have you learned anything useful from this useless purchase?

5. **Ad Campaign.** In the October/November 1991 issue of *Investment Vision,* readers were advised to consider investing in
products with ad campaigns that created powerful positive images. They reminded readers that corporations spend $129
billion yearly on ads and that the most effective are those with
a clear concept. The best campaigns, they believe, focus on one
or two words associated with the product, like *overnight* for
Federal Express or *dependable* for Maytag. Assuming that companies desire positive connotations for their products, study
the ad campaigns of several companies.

a. Discuss each image and how it is achieved through the ads,
focusing especially on the words.

b. Decide which campaigns are more successful at creating
strong, positive connotations. Support your conclusions
with reasons.

CHAPTER EIGHT

Suggestion in Media

Is What You See
What You Get?
Do You Really Want It?

*A critical thinker is aware of the presence
and power of suggestion in electronic and print
media.*

This chapter will cover:

◆ Suggestion in electronic media
◆ Suggestion in print media
◆ Subliminal persuasion

> *"The hand that rules the press, the radio, the screen and the far-spread magazine, rules the country."*
>
> Learned Hand, memorial address for Justice Brandeis, December 21, 1942.

The Lost Art of the Public Speech

by Bob Greene
Chicago Tribune, April 24, 1992

Speeches—eloquent, painstakingly crafted, carefully thought out, and meticulously paced, full-length speeches—are an endangered American species.

The speech has historically been one of the most important means of serious communication. If a person had an essential message to deliver, that message was conveyed in a speech. That's what politicians and great thinkers did when they had something to say: They labored over a speech until it was ready, and then they delivered it out loud to an attentive audience.

No more. The speech is already an anachronism. Twenty or 30 years ago, the serious speech was still a routine part of American life, and now the serious, influential speech is so rare that it's startling when one comes along.

The people you would most expect to want to continue the tradition of the speech—politicians with a national audience—are rushing to help devalue the speech. Next time you watch network TV news, pay close attention to how national politicians talk. They have begun to speak almost exclusively in those cute little bursts expressly written to be picked up by television producers—predigested 8 to 12-second nuggets that don't resemble anything an actual person would ever say during a real-world conversation. . . .

This goes on especially on the floor of Congress. . . . Except in the most uncommon of circumstances, reporters and camera crews are only going to pick up the luminescent little word-pellets that have been custom-constructed for them. . . .

If Abraham Lincoln wanted to make a point today, he would deliver the Gettysburg Sound Bite.[59]

---

[59] Bob Greene, "The Lost Art of the Public Speech," *Chicago Tribune*, April 24, 1992. Reprinted by permission of the publisher.

Public arguments, formerly consisting largely of political speeches and debates, can now be found on commercials, talk shows, interview programs, segments of news programs, and sometimes even sitcoms and dramas. Arguments that appear in print include advertisements, essays, and editorials; they can also be found in abundance on the Internet. This chapter will consider how media influences, shapes, and alters the messages we receive.

There are two types of persuasive techniques used by the print and electronic media that every critical thinker should understand. These techniques are called *suggestion* and *subliminal (unconscious) persuasion.*

Suggestion in Daily Life

Suggestion means presenting ideas or images in such a way as to reveal certain ideas or qualities and to conceal others. We use the power of suggestion to create impressions in our personal lives, impressions that help us to look or seem better in some way than we actually are.

You might stuff any debris under the seat of your car if you are unexpectedly asked to drive an attractive person home, so that the car (and therefore you) look neater than you actually are. Women (and some men) use suggestion when they wear makeup to look older, younger, or prettier. Balding men might wear hats or comb their remaining hair so it looks thicker than it is. Most of us choose clothing that makes us look better by concealing flaws.

People use the power of suggestion in the professional world also, such as when a real estate agent tells a client to bake something sweet for an open house so the house will seem warm and inviting; or when salesclerks are told to look busy, even when there is no real work to do; or when a car salesperson asks you to sit inside a car and feel comfortable, hoping that the suggestion of ownership and the smell and feel of a new car will induce you to buy.

EXERCISE

Purpose: To discover and analyze examples of suggestion in personal and professional contexts.

1. For the brave and honest only: Think of five ways you use the power of suggestion in your life to create an impression on a boss, friend, mate, teacher, parent, or in general. Or, observe or interview someone else as to how they arrange their world to create impressions.
2. Interview a professional, telling him or her about the concept of suggestion and asking in what ways it is used in his or her business. Examples include asking a manager of a supermarket if certain products are arranged at kid level to appeal to children and if items at the checkout counter are chosen for a particular reason. Or ask stereo salespersons or department store managers how their stores are arranged to give the desired impression to customers.

   Another approach to this exercise is to begin by analyzing the layout of a store or office (supermarket, department store, stereo store, bank, doctor's office, or toy store). Come to some conclusions about why the business is laid out in a particular way; support your conclusions with reasons. After you have made some assumptions about the layout, interview the manager of the store to find out if the layout is meant to influence customers in any way.

Televised Suggestion

> *"The media does set the agenda about what will and will not get discussed."*
>
> Sherry Bebitch Jaffe, Center for Politics and Policy, Claremont Graduate School, addressing the Society for Professional Journalists, September, 1992.

Television producers, directors, editors, and advertisers have always used the power of suggestion. The following guidelines will help you to view television with an understanding of the subtle, but consciously detectable, use of suggestion.

For news programs and talk shows, be aware of:

1. The selection of issues
2. The use of time
3. Selection of guest and panel members
4. What is included or excluded on a set
5. The nonverbal element of clothing
6. Use of language
7. Use of camera angles and cuts
8. Camera distance and framing

THE SELECTION OF ISSUES

Hundreds of global and national issues could be covered on any given day. The average network and local newscast is 24 minutes long, including sports and weather (with 6 minutes of commercials). Many stories are written but not aired because of these time limitations. So the selection of which stories are important and the decision about the order in which they will be presented gives network news editors enormous power. The very fact that a story is on the morning or evening news makes it seem important to us; we never really know what other issues are not being covered.

Mike Wallace, host of CBS' popular *60 Minutes* (an investigative reporting program) stated that on news-related programs, the reporter's interest often decides whether a story is profiled. In other words, both reporters (by choosing stories) and editors (by deciding which stories are aired) have the power to decide what is worthy of coverage and what is not. Another important factor in determining the content of programming is called *number* or *ratings*. The shows that get the largest audiences (determined by independent research companies, such as Nielsen) also get the largest share of advertising revenue. In effect, if a program wants to stay on the air, it has to attract a large audience.

One method used to attract viewers is called **sensationalism.** When broadcasters use sensationalism, more exciting stories are chosen over less exciting but perhaps more newsworthy ones, and the most bizarre, visually interesting, or sensational elements of these stories are featured. For example, a local station might focus in on the day's fires and auto accidents, showing all the gory details and bypass stories on upcoming propositions or elections. In addition, a host of shows that reenact sensational stories has developed over the last several years.

The apparent success of sensational coverage of the news is one factor behind the claim that the primary purpose of television news is to entertain rather than to inform. Whatever the objectives of the media, we as critical thinkers can choose to view news broadcasts with discernment rather than to passively absorb a program.

THE TIME FACTOR

Two elements of time can influence listeners. One is the time placement of a story. A story given prime (early) coverage on a newscast will seem very important to the audience. On network news, when the worldwide events of the day are given only 24 minutes, any item rating coverage attains instant credibility with viewers.

Anchorman Dan Rather was interviewed about the power of network news and asked why CBS used some of its precious evening broadcast time to cover a frog who could jump 30 feet. Rather laughed and said that when a frog can jump 30 feet, that is news! He skirted the question gracefully, but the issue remains: What is worthy of national broadcast in a limited timeframe, and, more importantly, who decides?

David Brinkley addressed the question of who decides what to broadcast at a meeting of the Radio-Television News Directors Association. He commented on the fact that most Americans don't read newspapers to be informed, choosing to watch televi-

"THAT'S 73% WHO ARE DISGUSTED BY TABLOID JOURNALISM BUT CAN'T TALK TO US WHILE 'CURRENT AFFAIR' IS ON."

Dunagin's People by Ralph Dunagin © Tribune Media Services, Inc. All Rights Reserved. Reprinted with permission.

sion news instead. "All they know about public policy," he said, "is what we tell them."[60]

The quantity of time is also a factor on television and radio, especially on talk shows featuring guests who discuss different sides of the same issue. When one guest is given more time than another to make his or her points, that guest has a greater chance of influencing the audience.

In addition, we begin to feel better acquainted with the person who is given more time; the factor of familiarity may unconsciously persuade us to feel closer to that person's position, especially on a topic that is new to us.

[60] Marlin Maddoux, *Free Speech or Propaganda?* (Nashville: Thomas Nelson Publishers, 1990), p. 73.

EXERCISES

Purpose: To compare the effect of different selection and ordering of news stories.

1. Watch the evening news on several stations, either local or national, for one or two nights. You may have to switch back and forth from one channel to another if the coverage is simultaneous (unless you can hook up two sets in the same room or have a classmate watch a different station). Then, consider the following elements.

   Note the selection of issues, the order of the stories shown, and the time given to each story. If different stories were covered, which station covered the more important story, in your opinion? Note also any "slant" given to a story by the comments or facial expressions of the anchorpersons. Did some stations feature more sensational stories or more in-depth coverage of stories than others?

   You may not notice much difference in the selection of issues on the commercial networks; try comparing a commercial network with public television's or C-SPAN's coverage. Are there any major differences? After compiling your research, answer this question: If you were an editor on one of the broadcasts, what changes, if any, would you make in the coverage of the news? Which stories would you give more, less, or no coverage? Which stories would get top priority on your network?

2. In class groups, assume you are the program editors for a local edition of the evening news. Look at the story topics below and put them in order from most to least important. The most important will be covered at the top of the program and the least important may be cut in the interest of time.

   To make your task easier, set some criteria before you order the stories. Possible criteria include informational value, usefulness to the local populace, and relevance to the largest number of people. In essence, you are to decide what the people in your audience should know. Think about other important criteria and then list your criteria in order of the most to least important.

a. There is an update on hopeful signs in new Mideast peace talks.
b. A murder-suicide occurred at a downtown hotel.
c. Polls on an upcoming election show the frontrunner falling behind.
d. There is a serious drought in a neighboring country.
e. A death-row inmate has been executed and there was a protest involving 300 people.
f. Someone has written a book claiming that a famous star, thought dead for twenty years, is alive and well.
g. A major freeway accident is causing hour-long delays in the evening commute.
h. A local daycare center has been charged with child abuse.
i. A new drug for treating AIDS, which has been used with some good results in France, has been banned indefinitely, pending Food and Drug Administration approval.
j. There is massive starvation in another country and relief efforts are hindered by a lack of funds.

SELECTION OF GUEST AND PANEL MEMBERS

When you watch a debate or talk show on an issue, notice the credentials of the persons being interviewed. On programs where the producer or editor is either not careful or has a bias, one side may be represented by attractive, articulate spokespersons and the other by intensely emotional, abrasive people. Are the persons selected really in leadership positions in the causes they represent and are they respected by their colleagues? Does the professional on the panel (usually a doctor, psychologist, or lawyer) represent only one side of the controversy and therefore lend credibility only to that side?

Be fair by keeping in mind the principle that if a controversy rages for a long time, that usually means reasonable people are disagreeing about important definitions or principles. Don't judge an issue by an abrasive spokesperson who may or may not represent the norm of persons who support his or her side. The producer may have chosen a more colorful and interesting, but much less representative, person to discuss either side.

Related to the selection of panel members or others who are chosen to be interviewed about an issue is the treatment of the spokesperson(s) by the interviewer. Note whether the interviewer is equally positive (or negative) in his or her interrogation of the guests. Sometimes, a biased interviewer will direct positive, easily answered questions, often called "softball" questions, to one guest and more negative, probing, "hardball" questions to a guest who represents the other side of the issue. For example, if the interviewer likes the guest, he or she could say, "Some people seem confused by your stand on this particular issue; could you explain more about your current thinking on it?" On the other hand, if the interviewer doesn't like the guest, the question might sound like this: "How can you explain the obvious contradictions in your position on this issue?" You can see the power an interviewer has to make a guest feel (and thus seem to the audience) comfortable and respected or uncomfortable and defensive.

WHAT IS INCLUDED OR EXCLUDED ON A TELEVISED SET

When an interview is set up, you should note the environment in which it is set. For example, on a commercial for encyclopedias, we might be impressed by a "teacher" who is surrounded with books and diplomas.

The director of a commercial can create an academic background that may have nothing to do with anyone's credentials. The actress who introduces herself as a teacher on an encyclopedia commercial doesn't have to be a teacher. Advertisers know that the impression of authority—created by a setting of a doctor's office, a classroom, or a law library can have a positive impact on our response to the commercial message.

 EXERCISE

Purpose: To understand the altering of settings to create impressions on viewers.

1. Analyze the setting of a place that you frequent—it could be your classroom, the business you work for, a store, a restaurant, or your home. What impression does the room convey? If you put a camera in different places in the same room, what different impressions would be created? Do the people in charge of this environment consciously set it up the way it is? If so, what is their purpose?

2. Analyze the set of a commercial or television program—why do you think it looks the way it does? How have the set designers "framed" the environment and what impression does it convey?

THE NONVERBAL ELEMENT OF CLOTHING, INCLUDING MAKEUP AND ACCESSORIES

The way someone is dressed is an important factor in creating a suggestion of his or her character and appropriateness for a given role. For example, both the Republican and Democratic parties have "schools" for their candidates in which training is given on campaign techniques; part of this training covers proper dress in various situations. Spouses are also encouraged to attend sessions on how to dress themselves and how to help their mates dress to create the right impressions. Even small details such as appropriate length and color of socks are covered in these workshops.

Clothing style is an essential element of advertising as well. Actors who are portraying teachers, doctors, or other professionals are dressed to fit the part.

Several years ago, John Molloy wrote the best-selling books *Dress for Success for Men* and *The Woman's Dress for Success Book* about his extensive studies on how styles and colors create impressions. His books are filled with research about how changing the look or color of one's clothes, jewelry, accessories, and hairstyle has helped individuals perform better at job interviews, sales calls, or other difficult communication situations. Many advertisers, candidates, or spokespersons are familiar with techniques such as Molloy's and use them to create positive suggestions on their audiences.

EXERCISE

Purpose: To understand personal image-engineering for the larger purpose of viewing in a more discerning way political candidates, salespersons, or actors promoting products.

1. Stop and write down everything you are wearing that is visible to others. Include makeup, jewelry, and accessories and consider your choices of colors. What impression are you trying to convey to others with your "look"? If you generally dress while you're half-asleep, stop and think about how someone else might judge you based on your clothing.

   You can extend this exercise to the classroom by having a few classmates write down the impression they get from your appearance. Compare their answers with the impression you'd like to make. How did you do as an image engineer?
2. Note how the actors in some commercials are dressed; what impression are they trying to create? If you have access to a televised trial, or even to the program *People's Court,* you can note the appearance of the plaintiffs and defendants and draw conclusions about why they are dressed as they are. How does their image affect their credibility? How might a different image give viewers a different impression?

USE OF LANGUAGE

Setting and appearance send messages nonverbally; the use of a reporter's language can affect our perception of an issue. Some years ago, when a terrorist bombing would occur, news reporters would say, "Such and such a group takes *credit* for the bombing." Other reporters and the public took offense at the word credit, which has a positive connotation. The late Eric Severeid, a respected commentator, did a segment on the harm done by such words. Because of these protests, the commonly accepted statement is now "Such and such a group claimed *responsibility* for the bombing."

   One media critic gave this example of the distortion of facts by how a reporter chooses words:

I might say "I've been a journalist for thirty years." Now a newspaper could pick that up and report: "Charles Wiley said he has been a journalist for thirty years." That's fact. Just straight reporting. Or the reporter could say, "Marlin's guest *admitted* he's been a journalist for thirty years." Or he can say, "He has *conceded* he's been a journalist for thirty years." Or he could go to the final step and say, "Wiley *confessed* he's been a journalist for thirty years." You see how one word changes the whole meaning.[61]

SKILL

Recognize the techniques of suggestion used by electronic media.

CAMERA ANGLE AND CUTS

Sometimes, directors tell camerapersons to shoot a person from below; this angle gives the speaker more authority, as if the viewers are "looking up to" the individual. Some networks were accused of using this angle to enhance the image of Oliver North when he spoke about the Iran-Contra affair.[62] Commercials use this technique to command attention and respect for a particular actor who is telling us to buy something or to show how large and impressive an authority figure looks to a common person. One recent commercial used this technique to illustrate how big a parent looks to a toddler.

Conversely, when the camera angle is above the speaker, the impression is that the viewers are looking down on the speaker; in this case, the speaker may look insignificant or even shifty.

The ability to use cuts (switching from one camera to another) to create positive or negative impressions about a speaker

---

61   Ibid. p. 54.
62   John Splaine, "Critically Viewing the Social Studies: A New Literacy," *Louisiana Social Studies Journal*, Volume XVI, Number 1, Fall, 1989, p. 16.

during a debate or talk show, or even in a news report, gives television directors great power. For example, a director can cut to a shot of an audience member's reaction to a speaker, thereby giving the impression of approval or disapproval of what the speaker has said. Also, during convention coverage, directors can cut to one audience member who appears bored with a candidate and thus unfairly represent the majority of audience members. Conversely, C-SPAN has used wide-angle cuts to show the audience that while a congressperson or senator is making an impassioned speech, the chairs in the room are empty.

Cuts in editing are used to select a short segment of a longer interview for broadcast. Sometimes, these cuts distort the statements that have been made by taking them out of context. The *sound bite* is a brief selection of a longer speech, usually heard out of context; both politicians and editors use sound bites to create impressions on viewers.

Advertisers also use distorted camera angles and quick cuts from scene to scene in order to command attention. These unusual, quickly moving scenes, coupled with increased volume, make sure that viewers pay attention to commercials.

CAMERA DISTANCE AND FRAMING

Directors of programs may deliberately or unconsciously use camera shots to influence audiences. Closeups control our emotions by adding an element of intimacy. We feel closer to a person and identify more readily with the person's viewpoint when we can see him or her as, literally, close to us. We may believe that the speaker is telling us the truth because he appears to be looking us in the eye. In fact, the speaker is looking at the camera or at the interviewer and only appears to be making eye contact with us. Conversely, educator John Splaine writes, "A camera angle from the side will suggest that a pictured person, who is responding to an incriminating question, might not be telling the truth."[63]

A wide-angle shot can make us feel distant from an individual. We feel uncomfortable with someone who seems far away

---

[63]   Ibid.

from us, and that may translate into a lack of trust for his or her position on a given issue. When a scene is shot from a helicopter, the people below are seen as far away and alien, sometimes appearing more like ants than human beings.

In addition, **framing**—the deliberate or unconscious use of camera shots that influence audiences—can make a critical difference. One loud demonstrator shown close up at a rally can create a distorted image if there are hundreds of other people protesting quietly. During the coverage of the chaos in Los Angeles following the verdict of the Rodney King trial in the spring of 1992, television viewers saw two Korean men standing in front of their businesses pointing handguns; a Korean community leader criticized the reporters for leaving out the rest of the scene, which consisted of groups of looters heading for the stores. By showing only the two men with handguns, viewers were given a false impression and the storeowners were literally "framed."

Critical thinkers need to be vigilant in their awareness of the subtle impressions that can be created electronically.

EXERCISE

Purpose: To find examples of suggestive techniques used by broadcast media.

Watch an interview program and analyze the suggestive elements we've mentioned in this section: the selection of issues, the use of time, the selection of guest and panel members, what is included or excluded on a set, the nonverbal element of clothing, the use of language, the use of camera angles and cuts, and camera distance and framing. Is there anything about the presentation of the material that creates suggestions—if so, what do you think might be the motive of the producers, directors, or editors in charge of the broadcast?

Watch (or tape, if possible) several commercials. Using the list of techniques as a guide, isolate the ways in which the advertisers are trying to persuade you to buy their product or use their service.

Suggestion in Print Media

"Four hostile newspapers are more to be feared than a thousand bayonets."

Napoleon I, *Maxims* (1804–1815)

The broadcast media—television and radio—are subject to what is called the **fairness doctrine,** which means that if broadcasters allow air time for one side of an issue, they must allow time for other points of view as well. Because of the fairness doctrine, a talk show cannot allow people to speak against capital punishment and then refuse to air a program with panelists who favor capital punishment. Within that provision, however, broadcasters can choose which guests appear and can manipulate programs using the techniques detailed in the previous section.

The print media, however, are not under the same governmental pressure to be fair. In noting the need for some kind of fairness doctrine for the press, media scholar Ben Bagdikian stated that "most daily newspapers have not faced up to the fact that they are monopoly institutions and therefore have an obligation to speak for the entire community and to be sensitive to every segment of it."[64]

Different newspapers and magazines have reputations for being conservative or liberal. They may feature columnists who largely subscribe to the publisher's political and social viewpoints. As critical thinkers, we can be responsible readers when we consider the following:

1. Use of headlines
2. Balance of reporting on an issue
3. Fairness in editorial essays and letters
4. Photo composition

---

[64]   Ben Bagdikian, *The Media Monopoly* (Boston: Beacon Press, 1973).

USE OF HEADLINES

Most readers know that the sensational headlines featured on papers found in supermarket checkout lines are not credible. When we read a headline proclaiming that a famous star has "8 new babies," we can assume that her cat had a litter of kittens or another equally silly explanation for this amazing news. Few of us believe that a 13-year-old really did elope with a two-headed alien. Obviously, these tabloids have little credibility and should not be used as resource material for your term papers!

Less sensational headlines can also distort information and mislead readers in subtle ways. Headlines in respectable newspapers and magazines are important because many readers are scanners—that means that they skim the paper, reading headlines and then going back to read only the articles of interest to them.

A headline that is scanned and recorded in the memory of a reader can give a distorted picture of information without actually being false. For example, let's say a reporter did a detailed story about an antinuclear protest that was held at a local power plant. The story covers the issues brought up by the demonstrators and the responses made by the plant spokesperson.

An editor who did not approve of this protest could use the headline, "No one arrested at power plant demonstration." Bringing in the idea of arrest by stating that there were no arrests is a subtle way of implying there might have been arrests, that is, that the protesters were not peaceful.

Headlines are often read as summary statements about events or discoveries. Consider the following headline and the opening paragraphs that expand on it:

Report on Chocolate May Bring a Real High

Associated Press

NEW YORK. Chocolate contains substances that might mimic the effects of marijuana, boosting the pleasure you get from eating it, researchers say.

The ingredients might make the texture, smell and flavor of chocolate more enjoyable and combine with other ingredients like caffeine to make a person feel good, researcher Daniele Piomelli speculated.

Later in the article, we are given information that greatly diminishes the claim made in the headline and the opening paragraphs.

We are talking about something much, much, much, much milder than a high," said Piomelli, a researcher at the Neurosciences Institute of San Diego. He reported the work with colleagues in today's issue of the journal *Nature*.

But a researcher who studies the brain chemistry of marijuana said chocolate contains such low levels of the ingredients Piomelli identified that he doubts they have any effect.

Christian Felder of the National Institute of Mental Health estimated that a 130-pound person would have to ingest the equivalent of 25 pounds of chocolate in one sitting to get any marijuana-like effect.[65]

Consider also the titles editors give to letters written by readers of a newspaper or magazine. Sometimes these titles are representative of the position of the person who wrote the editorial, but sometimes they are used to distort or ridicule the position of the writer. In this way, an editorial page may appear balanced, but in reality is not.

BALANCE OF REPORTING ON AN ISSUE

Whereas network news and interview programs have a shortage of *time*, newspapers and newsmagazines have limited *space*. The editor decides which stories are important enough to cover and on what page. Generally, if a story is on the front page it is perceived by readers as more important than a story placed farther back in the paper.

---

[65] From the Associated Press report: "Chocolate May Bring a Real High," *Contra Costa Times*, August 22, 1996, B-1.

EXERCISE

Purpose: To note that news coverage varies depending on the source and to consider different priorities held by various sources.

1. Compare a local newspaper, a large city newspaper, and a national paper. What stories are covered on the first few pages? Why do you think different stories are featured by the various papers?
2. Choose an issue that is getting wide press coverage. Find articles on this issue in several different newspapers or magazines. Compare the coverage in each one, and then write an essay in which you address the following questions:
   a. What elements of coverage framed the story in different ways? Analyze the summary of the story given in the first one or two paragraphs, the quotes selected from the persons interviewed, the amount of coverage given to both sides of the issue, and the use of headlines and photographs.
   b. Which source reported the issue most fairly, in your view? Give examples to support your position.

FAIRNESS IN EDITORIAL ESSAYS AND LETTERS

Some newspapers and magazines get a reputation for being primarily liberal or conservative because of the stands taken by their editorial commentators. In addition, local newspapers often print their suggestions as to how readers should vote in an upcoming election. It is important for critical thinkers to realize that reporting is not always objective and fair and that the editorial pages are set aside to reflect the *opinions* of readers and essayists.

Notice whether the essays on the editorial page seem to favor one political viewpoint over another. In addition, examine the letters to the editor that are published. They should reflect differing, rather than homogeneous, opinions on the same issue.

SKILL

Recognize the use of suggestion in print media.

PHOTO COMPOSITION

If a picture is worth a thousand words, then photojournalists have a strong communicative advantage. They can influence our perceptions of people or events with the photographs they print.

Most of us would agree that outright lies using photographs are unethical; for example, when photographers for *TV Guide* used image processing to create a cover featuring the head of Oprah Winfrey with the body of Ann-Margret, readers and fellow journalists alike were disapproving. We don't like to be deceived by our technology. Similarly, people object to photographs being altered by computer graphics, especially when they create an unflattering image of the person who is being depicted.

But more subtle forms of manipulation can occur through photo composition. A responsible photographer could take a wide-angle shot of a rally, thus giving the viewer a sense of the general scene. A less scrupulous, or less careful, photographer could shoot instead a few unruly persons, which would discredit the general group of peaceful participants. Conversely, he or she could focus the camera on a fight between one police officer and one participant, which would give an impression of general police brutality. In addition, captions beneath photographs can influence our perceptions of a person or event.

Newspapers and newsmagazines should treat photographs as documentary information that helps us get the general feel of an event. When you sense that a photograph is making an editorial statement, stop and consider what viewpoint is being suggested through the picture.

 EXERCISE

Purpose: To gain awareness of misleading headlines and how they distort information; to find examples of imbalanced reporting and editorializing and of slanted photojournalism.

1. Look for examples of headlines that distort the meanings of stories. Bring the headlines to class for discussion or write a paper in which you explain the following:
   a. How does the headline distort the information in the story?
   b. Why do you think that headline was chosen?
   c. What would be a more appropriate headline for this story? Why do you think it was not chosen?
2. Look for examples of imbalanced reporting or editorializing, or use of misleading photographs. Bring the stories, photographs, or editorial essays to class or write a paper in which you explain the following:
   a. How is the story, photograph, or editorial biased?
   b. How could bias have been prevented? What would be a more fair representation of the information?

The Power of Media to Shape Information

Writers and producers of news and feature stories have enormous power to shape the information that is broadcast or published. As we have discussed, camera angles, questions asked, choice of wording, placement in a program or publication, balance of reporting, people interviewed, and choice of topics for coverage all have an effect on how we view the world.

Those who study the effects of media often debate the extent to which programs *create*, rather than *reflect*, reality for readers and viewers. Certainly, producers and directors of feature films use all of the technical and artistic elements available to them to bring audiences into their world. We attend movies to be entertained and sometimes enlightened; we expect to laugh, cry, or marvel at the special effects. We are aware that our emotions and perceptions are being manipulated, and we often want to be affected by what we see and hear on the screen.

But the interesting question for the media literate individual is, "To what extent are my thoughts and feelings being manipulated by what purports to be news?" Are reporters just giving us a window to the world or are they creating the scenes we are shown? Are they presenting "just the facts" or are they really shaping the facts so that news stories and features become a subtle form of argumentation?

William Dorman, professor of Journalism and Government at the California State University in Sacramento, believes that meaning is shaped by print and electronic journalists:

> Media manufacture meaning; they do not simply serve as a neutral conveyor belt for information about what happens in the world. The important word here is **manufacture.** In my view, journalism is as much a manufacturing process as, say, the shoe industry. To be sure, there are important political, ethical and even moral differences—but the idea of a manufacturing process in which choices are made about what gets produced and how is precisely the same. Journalists select what will be covered and determine *how* it will be presented, including what elements will be included or left out, what elements will be emphasized or left in the shadows, what language will be used, and so on. These are human choices made by human beings working in a social system in which there are punishments and rewards. Indeed, I encourage my students to use the label ***Representer*** synonymously with the term Reporter."[66]

One example of getting an angle or framing a story occurred in a feature for the *Contra Costa Times*. This newspaper serves a county close to Berkeley and San Francisco in northern California, and the community has a diverse population. The feature profiled a variety of middle-school students and the challenges of their lives. Two of the preteens had lost parents already, one had watched a mother survive addiction to cocaine, one struggles with attention-deficit disorder, and one is the child of immigrants. Following each child's story were suggestions of how people in the child's immediate community could volunteer to help preteens and make a difference in their communities.

---

[66] William Dorman, "Using Frame Analysis in the Classroom," handout.

The parents of one of these children felt that their daughter had been misrepresented. The headline for her story read: "Lorene: Chafing at the Bit."[67] Following are some of the quotes characterizing her:

> Lorene is popular. Tall and slender, with straight blonde hair, clear green eyes and perfect teeth, she's one of the most popular girls in the seventh grade class at Orinda Intermediate School. "The queen bee of her little hive of popular girls," one teacher said, scornfully . . . Lorene does well enough in her classes, but it is the social aspects that dominate her school hours."[68]

The article goes on to mention detentions, attitude problems, disrespect for family members, and a privileged life affected by divorce. A sub-headline at the bottom of the three-page spread on Lorene reads: "Affluent Teens: Money Can't Buy Them Emotional Security."[69] Although Lorene is not mentioned in this section, the implication is clear: she, and other "privileged" teens are at risk for depression and substance abuse when their families don't provide them with emotional security. Her parents expressed their dismay at this implication in a subsequent editorial:

"Kids" Section Portrays Lorene Unfairly

by Dennis and Sandy Carlston
Contra Costa Times editorial, November 27, 1996

In the "Kids at the Crossroads" insert in the November 17 edition of the *Times,* our daughter Lorene was the young person interviewed from Orinda.

When the *Times* reporter originally approached us, we were led to believe that the principal at Orinda Intermediate School had recom-

---

67 Pam King, "Kids at the Crossroads," *Contra Costa Times,* November 17, 1996, p. 15.
68 Ibid.
69 Ibid., p. 15

mended Lorene as an outgoing, communicative student who would be a good candidate for the interview. The principal has told us that the *Times* never contacted her for her recommendations.

We were led to believe that this was an honor and that the article would be upbeat and positive. Little did we realize that the *Times* had an agenda to portray an Orinda teenager as an overprivileged, callous, uncaring person.

Our family and friends were outraged by the article. Our daughter was in tears after reading the portrayal of her and her family. After hours and weeks of interviews, the *Times* chose to print only the comments that would support its preconceived notions.

The *Times* omitted most that was good about Lorene and the loving part that both her parents play in encouraging her self-confidence and quest for independence. Her father spent a portion of one interview explaining how most teenagers experience a brief period of aloofness with their parents as they make the transition from adolescence to adulthood. The thrust of this discussion was about the transitory nature of this phenomenon. The *Times* chose to portray this as a way of life for Lorene.

Let's set the record straight. Lorene is a well-adjusted, loving, intelligent, goal-oriented 12-year-old. She gets all A's and B's, is on two basketball teams, a soccer team and a volleyball team. She has a large cross-section of friends and is sensitive to the needs of the less fortunate. She spent last Thanksgiving serving dinners to the homeless at the Richmond Rescue Mission and adopted a family to help last Christmas.

She is an actress and has an impressive resume of training classes, modeling, stage performances and voice-overs. Rarely does someone so young feel this focused. The *Times* was well aware of Lorene's wonderful traits, yet in the "Kids at the Crossroads" article, Lorene's fine grades, concern for the needy, and aspiring goals are never once mentioned.

Lorene is an asset to her family, her school and her community. She does not use drugs or alcohol, she is not violent, she does not have problems in school and she has the comfort of a loving family. How dare the *Times* insensitively slant the reporting to suggest otherwise.

The *Times* has done a child and her community a disservice. Shame on the *Times* for discrediting the reputation of a "Kid at the Crossroads."

When this editorial was researched for purposes of publication, Lorene's mother was asked to give further incidences of the distortion of information. Sandy C. said that the reporter never directly lied in the story, but that she presented the facts in such a way as to create a false image of her daughter. As an example, she mentioned a quote that was highlighted at the top of one page in which Lorene stated, in reference to staying for several weeks at her father's home, "I probably won't miss my mother. I'm looking forward to the freedom. I can do anything I want."[70] Sandy said that those words were spoken in an obviously kidding, bantering voice. She and Lorene were joking and laughing together at the time; she felt that the reporter clearly understood the context of the quote, but presented it as something an arrogant, self-centered child would say. In fact, Sandy stated that when her daughter read the quote and several others talking about how she enjoys "putting one over on the adults in her life," Lorene was incredulous; she cried and said she felt betrayed by the reporter. She feels that she doesn't get away with any negative behavior.

In another incidence of framing, Lorene is characterized as being suspended for "slamming a classmate up against a wall." Her mother said that, in fact, a boy had hit Lorene in the face at which point she pushed him away hard and he hit the wall. Sandy agreed to the suspension and the need to punish any use of physical force; however, she is upset by the characterization of Lorene as a violent bully.

One of Lorene's teachers, Maureen W., wrote the following comments after she read the article:

I am disturbed by the insinuation that most Orinda children are rich, selfish snobs. As in all communities, we have individuals who may fit that description. I have taught at Orinda Intermediate School for seven years. I have taught in several other school districts in Contra Costa County over my twenty plus years of teaching. In my years of teaching at both high schools and the intermediate schools, I have met all types of individuals. To generalize that the Orinda individual is morally insensitive is astonishingly stereotypical. If this article's intention was to harm Orinda children, you have succeeded. How devastating for a young person and her family to read such a negative article. Shame on you.[71]

---

[70]   Ibid.
[71]   Maureen W., reprinted by permission of the author.

Maureen W.'s letter was sent to the editor but was not published. Another unpublished letter in response to the article on Lorene came from her soccer coach, Tom A, who stated:

> . . . My take on Lorene's part of this article was to portray Orinda as an enclave of spoiled, wealthy kids from dysfunctional families. That exists here; Orinda is an easy target. Certainly this will reinforce some peoples' opinions. Perhaps that was the reporter's goal.
>
> Lorene and her family, however, are not as they were presented, and I hope that folks in and around the area won't believe everything they read.[72]

Many stories, such as Lorene's, are reported factually, but with the particular frame the reporter wants to create. Certain elements are emphasized; other factors may be completely omitted. As a critical thinker, it is important for you to consider the way in which a story is presented and people are characterized. Whenever possible, read or watch a story from different sources before making interpretations about the information presented.

 EXERCISE

Purpose: To become aware of the subtle ways in which a story may be shaped to influence readers or viewers.

This exercise, created by Professor William Dorman, encourages what he calls "frame hunts."

Bring in a clipping from a newspaper or magazine or a segment from a story covered on television and try to convince other students that the story has a frame of some sort. The class should vote thumbs up or thumbs down on each case. At the end of the semester or of this section of the course, have a "Frame Off," in which the "Frame of the Year" is selected from all the frames submitted throughout the course.

---

[72] Tom A., reprinted by permission of the author.

Subliminal Persuasion

It takes an educated or very discerning person to be aware of the many methods used to persuade viewers to think or act in a certain way. The old saying "Let the buyer beware" means that when we are subjected to various pitches by advertisers and politicians, we should have the power to say no to their claims and to resist being persuaded against our will. Increasing our awareness of the persuasive techniques used by print and electronic media gives us more power as thinkers, voters, and consumers.

What if, however, we are being persuaded to think and act against our will by messages geared to affect us in ways our conscious minds cannot detect? This happens when we are exposed to *subliminal persuasion.*

For our purposes, we will consider two types of subliminal persuasion:

1. Information that is tangential to the main message given. This information can be perceived if we are made aware of it, but this perception usually requires training.
2. Information that cannot be registered by the conscious mind, despite training. This information takes the form of photographs altered under high magnification and messages embedded in film, audio tracks, and videotape, which are meant to be picked up by the unconscious mind.

The existence of this second form of subliminal persuasion is controversial; many respected scholars dismiss it as the stuff of urban legends; others believe it is done frequently, yet usually denied by commercial artists and technicians. Among those scholars who do believe that this form of subliminal persuasion exists, there is disagreement as to its effectiveness.

PERSUASION WE CAN DETECT

Information that can be perceived if we know what to look for can be considered a form of suggestion. Copywriters and graphic designers can use subtle phrasing and combinations of colors and formats to attract us to certain products.

Television advertisers get our attention with loud music or words and frequent camera cuts. You may have noticed that you can do homework during a television program, except when the commercials come on; they seem to grab your attention. This process happens to children too. The next time you are watching television with a young child, notice how alert the child becomes during almost any commercial. We respond to loud, fast-paced programming with frequent camera changes. Even public television programs like *Sesame Street* use this technique of fifteen- to thirty-second spots to keep attention levels high. Commercials shown on programs airing after midnight are particularly loud; people who fall asleep in front of a television set may be startled awake by the blaring of a commercial message (invariably advising late-night viewers to improve their lives by using their product or service). No advertiser wants to play to a sleeping audience.

In addition to using the initial attention-getting devices, advertisers (and political media coordinators) are keenly interested in holding attention, even for just a few seconds more than their competitors. To hold attention they have to "grab" the audience in some way, and many utilize the psychological principles of Gestalt theory.

The Gestalt Principle

Gestalt principle states that "the whole is greater than the sum of the parts." Our minds strive toward congruence and completion of information. If a message strikes us as incomplete, we will fill in the missing details ourselves. Consider the following Gestalt techniques that are commonly used but seldom questioned by the consumers of the message (us).

1. Questions or Slogans That the Consumer Is Taught to Answer

Years ago, Winston cigarettes used a simple jingle: "Winston tastes good like a cigarette should. Winston tastes good like a (clap, clap) cigarette should." For a long time, television and radio listeners heard this jingle sung in a joyful manner.

Then one day, the jingle proceeded as follows: "Winston tastes good like a cigarette should . . . Winston tastes good like a (clap, clap)." Listeners who had heard the jingle before could hardly help completing the song in their minds, thus joining in with the advertisers to laud the praises of this cigarette. They had been trained over time to know the ending of the commercial, and when the standard ending was left out, they filled it in.

We are generally taught as children that it is rude not to answer a question asked of us, and this carries over into adulthood. Assertiveness trainers sometimes spend much time and energy teaching clients that they don't need to answer every question they are asked.

Advertisers capitalize on our early training by asking us questions, knowing we probably will instinctively formulate answers in our minds. Here are some examples:

Aren't you hungry for King Burgers now?

Why do you think they call it Up Close?

Doesn't your child deserve a gift of love?

2. Images That Don't Make Sense

Again, our minds try to make sense out of things that are together but don't seem to go together. Leon Festinger's theory of cognitive dissonance, discussed further in Chapter 9, states that the need for "congruence" (consonance, harmony) is not only a human need but a *drive*, just as powerful as our drive for food and water. We are motivated by this drive and so we take action when things don't make sense. We try to make sense out of them.

For example, you may be disturbed by a couple who don't seem suited for each other; their presence together may cause you to try to figure out what they see in each other. Even children love challenges called "What is wrong with this picture?"

Advertisers capitalize on our fascination with the incongruent by sometimes putting things together that don't seem to go together. They know that if we are puzzled, we will give more attention to or spend more time on the ad, even if we aren't aware of doing so. They also know that if we become familiar with a product's brand name (because we've spent more time or given more attention to its claims), then we are more likely to buy the product.

Benson and Hedges had a series of print ads showing two scenes of people interacting; there was no clear indication of what was going on between these people or why they were together. Often, the people were shown laughing, but the readers were not told what they were laughing about.

Sometimes incongruous scenes are combined with sexual insinuations, making them doubly fascinating to viewers. For example, a few years ago Jantzen swim suits carried an ad showing a man and a woman who had just emerged from swimming and were sitting on the beach. Only their bodies were visible and the female was wearing the male suit as the bottom half of her suit while the male was wearing the female bottom suit as his swimsuit. The patterns were similar, but different enough to be detected.

PERSUASION WE CAN'T DETECT

Information that cannot be perceived by the conscious mind (but that is registered unconsciously) despite training is the more controversial form of subliminal persuasion.

You may remember hearing about the merchandising trick drive-in movies allegedly used to play on customers. During a movie, they would show one frame (remember that movies are shown on a frame-by-frame basis) of delicious-looking hot-buttered popcorn. It was said that this frame, shown beneath the level of the viewers' conscious awareness, was correlated with an increase in popcorn sales at intermission time.

Graphic artists who use subliminal persuasion assume the following:

- Brand name recognition is a key to selling a product.

- A product will be remembered if the advertisement for the product holds the attention of the viewer in as many ways as possible, including the use of loud or catchy music, colors, movements, and fascinating images.

- Among the fascinating images holding attention the most are suggestions of sex and death.

Advertisers have used these principles in a variety of ways: One toothpaste ad showed a cute, smiling baby; the word *sex* had been airbrushed (invisibly to the naked eye, but not to a microscope) on his arm. An ad for a popular cigarette had the word *can-cer* outlined on the gloves of a hockey player.

Words and other subliminal images can be discovered through magnification; yet, most of us don't have the time to devote to researching and scrutinizing every ad we see. So what can a critical thinker do to be more aware of suggestion and subtle persuasion and to act responsibly?

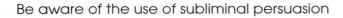

SKILL

Be aware of the use of subliminal persuasion

As a critical thinker you can:

- Understand the ways subliminal persuasion operates.

- Become aware of your attention span when you are listening to or viewing an advertisement. Are you drawn to a particular image, but can't explain why?

- When making decisions as a consumer, consider why you are buying a particular brand. Do you really believe this brand is the best or is it just a name you recognize? Read labels to see if the ingredients in your "brand" really differ from less expensive brands.

- When making decisions as a voter, be clear on the reasons you are supporting a particular candidate or proposition. Have you "bought into" a slogan or into someone's claims without thinking? Do you clearly understand the issues and the various conclusions about the issues?

The key to walking through the mines of print and electronic persuasion is to be armed with facts and logical reasoning about your decisions as a citizen and a consumer. Critical thinkers avoid basing their judgments on the consciously or unconsciously applied manipulations of campaign managers and advertisers. A good offense is your best defense.

EXERCISE

Purpose: To be able to detect subliminal persuasion in advertisements.

Find examples of television commercials or advertisements in magazines or newspapers that employ one or more of the forms of subliminal persuasion discussed in this chapter. Share your findings with class members. This is an exercise in which many heads are better than one because of the different perceptual abilities people have. One person may discover a musical trick used in a television commercial, while another may detect subtle images in a print ad.

EXERCISE

Purpose: To gain a deeper understanding of subliminal persuasion.

Read more about it! This chapter gives you a basic understanding of the principles of suggestion and persuasion. Many books and articles have been written on the subject. If you find these subjects interesting, do further research on them, including interviews with reporters, graphic designers, or instructors of journalism and broadcasting.

You may want to focus your research on the controversial questions associated with subliminal persuasion: Does it currently exist? If so, what are the influences on audiences? Share your research findings with your class.

Chapter Highlights

1. The power of suggestion is used by professionals to create impressions about products, ideas, or candidates.
2. To be more critical of televised suggestion, viewers should be aware of the selection of issues, the use of time, the selection of guest and panel members, the set, the clothing of television personalities, and the use of language, camera angles, camera cuts, camera distance, and framing.
3. To be more critical of suggestion in print media, readers should be aware of the use of headlines, the balance of reporting on an issue, the degree of fairness in editorial essays and letters, and photo composition. All of these elements taken together form the overall frame given to a particular story.
4. One form of subliminal persuasion involves information meant to affect people on an unconscious level. Messages of this kind can be detected with training.
5. A second form of subliminal persuasion, the existence and effectiveness of which are not agreed upon by experts, involves information that cannot be registered by the conscious mind, regardless of training.

Articles for Discussion

When Movies Go to War, Pentagon Tags Along

Not Every Story Gets Military OK, but
Some Need the Assistance

by Jennifer Brown, Associated Press
Contra Costa Times, November 10, 1996

In an early script for "Forrest Gump," the likable but dim character went to Vietnam in a unit full of slow-witted soldiers like himself.

"They had everybody of reduced intellect except the lieutenant," said Phil Strub, who coordinates the Pentagon's film liaison office. "And the Army said it never would have happened that way."

So Strub's office used some creative persuasion on the producers. And in the final version, Gump's fellow soldiers were smarter.

It was just one part of a big movie. But to the Defense Department, the things Americans learn in movie theaters endure, so it often uses the carrot of its cooperation to ensure that films reflect accurately, and positively, on the military.

"We feel strongly that the images people see of the military in Hollywood are the most formative images," said Major Nancy LaLuntas, director of Marine public affairs in Los Angeles.

"[We've] maintained all along that if we have the ability to accurately influence those images, the American public will have a better image of the military."

Of course, some filmmakers balk at the interference. For example, "A Few Good Men," starring Tom Cruise and Jack Nicholson, was made without help from the Pentagon, which had objected to the portrayals of some Marines.

The Pentagon gets a few hundred requests each year for tanks, aircraft carriers, active-duty officers to play extras, or just technical advice to make a story more accurate.

Filmmakers send scripts with wish lists to the military film offices— one in Washington, and four in Los Angeles for each of the military branches.

The Pentagon then uses its leverage to try to persuade filmmakers to change parts of the story deemed inaccurate or too negative.

How much filmmakers are willing to revise depends on how much help they need, Strub said. A movie like "Top Gun," about fighter pilots, could not have been made without the military—because "you can't just rent aircraft carriers."

Usually, he said, both sides bend.

"We say 'These are areas that are unrealistic. We know this isn't a documentary, we know this isn't news, but you've got to have some plausibility,'" said Strub.

Pentagon approval certainly makes life easier, said Amy Lemisch, who co-produced "Renaissance Man," starring Danny DeVito as an English teacher hired to educate U.S. troops.

"I've talked to a lot of people who didn't get approval . . . and we were lucky," Lemisch said. "They gave us the locations. They gave us the attention. They gave us military extras."

Filmmakers pay the Pentagon the costs of operating the expensive equipment, such as helicopters, planes, or tanks, that they use. The military says the charges cover only costs, and do not bring in a profit.

Moviemakers' demands for help from the Pentagon's film liaison office—opened in 1949—have increased since 1986's "Top Gun."

But while many get the Pentagon nod, scores did not, including "Crimson Tide," about an armed mutiny on a submarine. "Firing a gun on a submarine is stupid and would never happen," Strub said.

Of course, there may be more to the rejections than just being unrealistic, since the military helps with some extremely unrealistic movies if it likes the plot line.

The spy plane in 1996's "Executive Decision" has a tunnel that opens through the top, allowing heroes Steven Seagal and Kurt Russell to crawl through into a hijacked passenger plane.

"It couldn't have happened," Strub said. "But we'll say, 'Oh all right.' If that's a capability we can let bad guys think we have, why not?"

Questions for Discussion

1. To what extent do you agree with Major Nancy LaLuntas, who stated, "We feel strongly that the images people see of the military in Hollywood are the most formative images." What images of military life have you received from film?

2. Comment on the following statements from the article: "Filmmakers send scripts with wish lists to the military film offices—one in Washington, and four in Los Angeles for each of the military branches. The Pentagon then uses its leverage to try to persuade filmmakers to change parts of the story deemed inaccurate or too negative." ". . . to the Defense Department, the things Americans learn in movie theaters endure, so it often uses the carrot of its cooperation to ensure that films reflect accurately, and positively, on the military."

Survey Comes Clean About Sex on Soap Operas

Findings Show Numerous Erotic
Encounters, Little Depiction of Condoms
or Consequences

by Tim Whitmire, Associated Press
Contra Costa Times, September 8, 1996

NEW YORK. When, after weeks of smoldering glances, the male lead of a daytime soap opera finally ends up in bed with his brother's ex-wife, they are unlikely to discuss birth control.

Why does this matter, you ask?

Because soap sex and its consequences draw 40 million viewers likely to emulate those daytime dreamboats, said Katherine Heintz-Knowles, author of a study released Saturday on soap opera sex.

"We know that behavior performed by characters who are attractive, powerful and popular are much more likely to be imitated by viewers," said Heintz-Knowles, a University of Washington communications professor.

The survey found that, of 594 sexual behaviors shown during five weeks of soap operas, only 58 included the discussion or depiction of planning or consequences.

The study, released by the Henry J. Kaiser Family Foundation, a private health foundation, was presented to network executives and soap opera writers and producers meeting with reproductive health experts at "Soap Summit II."

The first Soap Summit was held in 1994; last year, the same group held a meeting on television talk shows.

The seminar is staged by Population Communications International, an organization that works with media around the world to encourage family planning and prevention of sexually transmitted diseases.

"The dilemma [soap opera producers] have is they have to provide entertainment," said Dr. Felicia Stewart, director of reproductive health programs for the Kaiser Foundation.

"The goal really here I think . . . is to try to figure out some way we can be more [educational]."

The survey of 97 hours of programming from the 10 nationally televised soap operas from May 27 to June 28 recorded 6.1 sexual behaviors per hour of programming. That compared to 6.6 sexual behaviors per hour recorded in a 1994 survey.

A sexual behavior was defined as any kissing, caressing, flirting or sexual intercourse that was shown, implied or discussed by characters.

Heintz-Knowles said this year's survey found a higher proportion of sexual behaviors being shown—rather than just talked about—than two years ago.

Of the sexual behaviors recorded in the survey, 73 percent were shown visually, compared to 27 percent verbally. In the 1994 survey, 67 percent of sexual behaviors were verbal, compared to 33 percent visual.

"This is not to imply, though, that soaps are getting more explicit," Heintz-Knowles said. What is being shown is more kissing, embracing and caressing, she said.

Soap sex generally is not casual and almost always is depicted as having a positive effect on a relationship, Heintz-Knowles said.

Researchers said messages about AIDS and condom use were more prominent this year than in their 1994 study.

Two soaps—"All My Children" and "General Hospital"—used condoms in major plots, while "General Hospital" featured an HIV-positive character and "The Young and the Restless" showed a woman deciding to get tested for HIV.

"But," Stewart said, "there is still a long way to go. The overwhelming message of sex without consequence is out of synch with reality and not a helpful model, especially for young people."

Questions for Discussion

1. Communications professor Katherine Heintz-Knowles states "We know that behavior performed by characters who are attractive, powerful and popular are much more likely to be imitated by viewers." Do you agree with her statement? If so, do the writers and producers of soap operas have an obligation to discuss birth control when their characters engage in sexual activities? Why or why not?

2. Given the fact that writers and producers of soap operas are hired to create a profitable product for their networks, do they have *any* moral obligations to viewers? Give reasons to support your answer.

3. Do you imitate the behavior of television personalities or do you know anyone who does?

The following excerpts are from an online interview of Professor Neil Postman, author and national expert on the impact of media on society. Postman was interviewed from Caesar's Palace about his perception that the line between information and entertainment is blurred by electronic media.

Prelude to Vegas

Neil Postman Gets Interviewed

by Stephen Marshall of Channel Zero.

"The dichotomy between education and entertainment has ended."

Marshall McLuhan

Neil: In one of my books *Amusing Ourselves to Death*, I use Las Vegas as the metaphor of America because it is a city devoted almost entirely to entertainment. It would seem that right now, Americans are more interested in entertainment than any other aspect of personal life. So that . . . culture today is in sharp contrast to earlier times when, . . . if you go back to the . . . 1870s and 80s . . . early twentieth century; I thought New York City and the Statue of Liberty would be the icons and metaphors of America. The nation of nations—the land of immigrants and then later the stockyards of Chicago, which symbolized the energy and entrepreneurial drive of Americans. So now I think Las Vegas would do just fine as a symbol.

To say that we have a culture that is obsessed at the moment with entertainment is also to say that there is a shallowness and a thinness to the culture which is most distressing, I think, to many serious people. I don't know that it will remain this way. America's always been a land of extreme change and one hopes that we'll see a time when this preoccupation with finding ways to entertain ourselves will dissipate and get more serious. This is why I have picked out Aldous Huxley and his book *Brave New World* as a better marker of the future than Orwell's *1984* because I see no signs that Big Brother, in the sense that Orwell talked about it, is our problem here. But I do see the "Brave New World" that Huxley talked about as the problem. See, in Orwell's vision, you controlled people by inflicting pain on them. In Huxley's vision, you controlled them by inflicting pleasure and that's why I picked out Las Vegas as the symbol and you used the word vapid—that's a good word—superficial, thin, distracting.

Steve: So you see a system of control being exerted over others . . .

Neil: Yes . . . well you see, all culture controls. I mean, any kind of culture you have has built into it a system of controls—which, in a way, is what we mean by culture. In fact, one could even define culture by saying that it is a sequence and pattern of no's. So, every culture controls the people who created it and who are subjected to it. What's interesting is the different ways in which cultures control people. Now by control I mean "organize" their behavior, provide them with their interests, turn their attention to certain arenas of human affairs. This is the sense in which I mean control and America right now is sated with media events that are maybe classified as entertainment and this is what people lust for and are controlled by and when I say controlled by I mean that this is where their attention is directed and, of course, they believe this is where they wish their attention to be directed.

Neil: I think McLuhan is right in saying at an earlier time there was a sharp division between what we meant by information and by entertainment, and I think he is also right in saying that now that distinction has been blurred. Now your question is: Do I think that we'll go back to a time when there is a distinction between the two? And I think that I must say that I hope that there will be. And in many of my books I always talk about this issue and try to define as carefully as I can the differences between what we normally call education and what we call entertainment. Among the differences is that what we mean by entertainment usually has no implications beyond itself . . . that is: you are entertained by a piece of music or a TV show or even a play—and that's the end of it. You're either amused or you may even be saddened but there are no implications of that for other aspects of your life . . . of course, great plays, I should say, are both entertaining and educational . . . in the best sense . . . in that they do have implications for how you go to live your life and in giving you moral guidance or sociological insights which then are useful to you.

But, generally speaking, what we mean by entertainment, at least here in America, is something that, in fact, has no implications beyond itself. Whereas education is something that will resonate in all sorts of directions in your life through space and time and unfortunately, perhaps, McLuhan is even implying in the quote you reread, that even in school now teachers are more and more trying to be entertaining because television has taught the young that learning, whatever it is, must always be fun. And if it's not fun, then it's not worthwhile and you should just change the dial . . . go to another station. Serious educators know that there are many things people really need to learn that may not be fun to learn . . . that are arduous and require levels of concentration and simple hard work that need to be done if you're to learn what it is. In addition to that, learning can be a great deal of fun—but it's a different meaning of fun from watching *Seinfeld*—it's a deeper kind of satisfaction that one feels when one's mind achieves an understanding or an insight or an accomplishment. Now that is, in quotes, fun of sorts but it's entirely different from what we normally mean by fun in association with entertainment.

Steve: "Poverty is a great educator"?

Neil: What I meant by that is: If one grows up poor, in any case, poor in the sense of today's world, there's a whole set of attitudes that is inculcated in one. Because one is poor—attitudes about the country one lives in, attitudes about one's neighbors and so on. So, what I meant when I said poverty is a great teacher—I meant teaching in that sense. People who grow up poor have a somewhat different world view from those who grow up in more affluent circumstances and some people—especially in today's world—are disabled, sad to say, from what they learn from their poverty—in part, by the way, because of television. If you went back to the early twentieth century and even well into the twentieth century there were probably more poor people then than there are now and my family would have been among them. Everyone was poor. And we didn't have television to raise our expectations to really quite unrealistic heights and so were able to endure our poverty and not exactly with equanimity but with a certain level of ease so that we were not angry all the time. But I imagine that if one is poor today and then sees on television a dazzling variety of goods and services that TV says every American is entitled to—"You can have it all," "You only go around once so live life with gusto . . ."—all that sort of stuff—I would imagine if I were a poor person—I would be very angry and bitter and disappointed, and so poverty teaches at all times but it will teach you different things depending on the surroundings in which you live.

Steve: Is television responsible (should it be) for representing reality to the world?

Neil: Well, that's a very complex question and I will answer it by just focusing on one thing which interests me the most. Television is a medium which lacks a *because*—what I mean by this is that language has embedded in it always "becauses": This happened because that happened. Television doesn't have a because, so that, for example—when you watch the news you get one story, and then another story and then another story and then another story—and if you would ask, "Well did this third story—this earthquake in Chile—did that happen because of the second story?—the rape in the Bronx or the fire in New Jersey?" The answer would be "of course not"—it's ridiculous even to ask it. There are no becauses on television—there are just "ands"—it's a world of "this happened and then this happened" and I think the result of that is to promote a world view that comes quite close to what I think the philosophers might call nihilism. And there aren't really connections in the world—things just happen—and to ask why do they happen or what are the historical precedents or what are the immediate causes seems irrelevant.

By the way, it's the same thing with shows—non-news shows—for example. . . . How many Americans think it's ridiculous to be seeing a very sad play on TV—even a soap opera—in which someone has just learned they have a terminal disease and then there's a commercial for United Airlines but truly a happy commercial or watching what television would consider a serious—even religious programs on Sunday and they're usually not interrupted by commercials but right as soon as they're over the commercial comes on for some detergent . . . some American Express—so that interspersed into anything that happens is always this absurd idea that whatever it is you just saw cannot be terribly important because now here is this happy commercial. So I think that goes a long way towards promoting this idea that there is no order anyplace, not only in the universe, not on the planet, not on your continent, not even your home or your town. And I think this is a very serious matter and not something that many people have paid attention to, how many people when seeing a newscast about, say, a serious earthquake or an airplane crash will actually start to cry or grow silent at the tragedies of life. Most of us don't because right after the story of the airplane crash there's going to be a thing for Burger King or, if not that, a story about the World Series or some other event that basically would say, "Now listen, don't take this thing about the airplane crash too seriously, it's just something to amuse you for the moment, and we certainly don't want you to be morose when we get to the United Airlines commercial because we'd like you to be in a sort of upbeat mood to sell you a trip to San Francisco." So I think this is part of what you might call almost the metaphysical point of view of television. There are no becauses. Nothing causes anything else and nothing has a connection to anything else, it's just a thing, an event. Don't get excited about it. Just sit back and in a couple of seconds there will be another event.

Steve: So you don't think television is bad? You don't think you should tell people not to watch it.

Neil: Well, I think it's nonsense to tell Americans not to watch television, but I think you could tell them every time you start to watch there are a whole bunch of questions you probably should know about and from time to time ask yourself about and you may find the answers to these questions will lead you to restrict how much you watch or will lead you to watch in a different way or will lead you to criticize what you watch in a somewhat more profound way.

Questions for Discussion

1. Neil Postman states that television hurts poor people by raising their expectations and creating the impression that other people have access to a "dazzling variety of goods and services." Student Lawrence James states the following: "To me hell is here on earth when you're constantly nagged by what you don't have and what you can't do. While the television teases you with the fake materialisms and good time fantasy life, you have nothing but your folks. Your female is looking from the TV to you, then at a nice car passing by, then back at you. Can you afford to take sweety out for a night on the town?"[73]

   What, if anything, can be done to help those who are poor "endure their poverty"; should televised images be more realistic and well-balanced?

2. Postman states that the line between information and entertainment has been blurred on television. Can you think of examples of this blurring? Do you believe that the blurring of information and entertainment creates problems for our society?

3. Do you believe it is harmful for news coverage of serious and tragic events to be followed by humorous stories or commercials? If so, what could be done to change this practice?

4. To what extent do you agree with Postman's view of Las Vegas as the metaphor of America?

 Ideas for Writing or Speaking

1. Respond to one of the following quotes from his book *Amusing Ourselves to Death* by Neil Postman. Support your thesis statement with evidence from radio, television, advertising, newspapers, magazines, journals, or books.

---

[73] Lawrence James, "Keeping It Real Until That Day Comes," *The Advocate*, October 4, 1996, p. 3.

"Indeed, we may have reached the point where cosmetics has replaced ideology as the field of expertise over which a politician must have competent control."[74]

"The shape of a man's body is largely irrelevant to the shape of his ideas when he is addressing a public in writing or on the radio or, for that matter, in smoke signals. But it is quite relevant on television."[75]

"The photograph presents the world as object; language, the world as idea."[76]

2. Analyze one of the more successful television programs and draw some specific conclusions about why it is successful. Support your conclusions with reasons. Consider the images the program projects about the people it represents.

    Another approach to this assignment would be to contrast programs that are popular now with shows (or films) that were popular in the past. Write about the different cultural, economic, or historical elements influencing these shows or films; it would be interesting to take programs from different decades for this assignment. Some questions to think about as you watch these programs are: What was acceptable in the past but is in some way politically incorrect now? What is acceptable now that would have been considered unacceptable in the past?

3. Discuss the influence of television programs on culture. To what extent does television *reflect* cultural norms and to what extent does it *create* them? Given your answer, what considerations, if any, should television producers make before approving new projects?

4. Consider the statement: "You can tell the ideals of a nation by its advertisements."[77] What does our current advertising say about our culture's ideals? Consider values, roles of men and women, the view of the elderly, the importance of technology, and the use of time and space. Support your position with at least six examples from both print and electronic media.

5. Writer Joseph Giordano states: "An important cause of distorted and damaging TV stereotypes is the tendency of some

74 Neil Postman, *Amusing Ourselves to Death* (New York: Viking Press, 1985), p. 4.
75 Ibid., p. 7.
76 Ibid., p. 72.
77 Norman Douglas, *South Wind* (London: Nartin Secker & Warburg, 1917), p. 64.

media executives to view ethnic culture as an 'immigrant phenomenon,' a transitional phase in the process of Americanization rather than a continuing influence on people's language, religious lives, arts, politics, food preferences and so on."[78] Should the media strive to emphasize our similarities, differences, or both? Provide reasons for your answer.

6. In discussing ethnic and religious traditions, Giordano also states: "At times, these traditions conflict with surrounding values, but they are also sources of strength and understanding. How they work in second-, third-, and fourth-generation families can provide a rich store of story ideas and authentic characterizations for writers, directors, and actors."[79] Write a proposal for a television program or a feature-length film centered around a tradition that provides strength and cultural understanding to an individual or group. How could a program like this be used to increase cultural understanding in a pluralistic society?

7. Critics have accused television news as functioning primarily as a form of entertainment. Watch several news programs and respond to these critics. To what extent do you agree or disagree with them and why? Give specific examples to support your answer.

8. Collect your junk mail for two or three weeks without opening it. Then analyze it by answering these questions:
   a. How did you recognize it as junk mail?
   b. What techniques does the sender use to entice you to open the envelope?
   c. Once opened, what techniques are used to prompt you to read farther than the first line?
   d. Are these techniques effective? Consider graphic design, placement of key words, the way you are addressed, special offers, enticements, and deadlines.

9. Take a position on one or both of the following statements:
   a. "The once slightly regarded talk shows and interview programs of radio and TV, the new hybrid media of American culture, are playing a powerful role in shaping who might be the next president. . . . The Establishment media, many

---

[78]　Joseph Giordano, *Media and Values*, Winter 1987.
[79]　Ibid.

analysts say, frame politics in language that many Americans do not identify with and around issues they do not consider important." Thomas B. Rosenstiel, journalist for the *Los Angeles Times*.

b. "Larry King . . . and talk radio and even Rush Limbaugh are interactive media. There is a way to get in. You can say your piece and vote. [However] In network TV, just like party politics, people are disenfranchised." Michael Deaver, Reagan media advisor.

10. Write an essay or speech about your viewpoint on the following quote by Senator John Danforth, Republican, of Missouri, taken from the "MacNeil-Lehrer Newshour," May 8, 1992.

What people see when they turn on the TV is violence. What they see is sex. What they see is total disrespect for family and for authority, and what they see is stereotypes. And this is, in my opinion, a very large part of the problem. The medium of television right now is disgusting. So are many of the movies that people see. And I think that one way to start on this problem is to have a summit meeting perhaps called by the President which brings together people who are leaders of broadcast, the broadcast networks, people who are leaders of cable television, of the motion picture industry, and ask them what responsibility they have for this country, other than squeezing every last dime they can out of it.[80]

---

[80] From the "MacNeil-Lehrer Newshour," televised May 8, 1992.

9

Fairmindedness

It's You and Me, Kid, and I'm Not So Sure About You

A critical thinker is aware of egocentrism, sociocentrism, and the role of emotions on judgment.

A critical thinker listens and responds to opposing viewpoints with empathy and fairmindedness.

This chapter will cover:

◆ Defense mechanisms that cloud our thinking
◆ Points of logical vulnerability
◆ Active listening techniques that foster openmindedness and empathy

Centuries ago, we learned, contrary to our previous beliefs, that the earth and therefore man, is not the center of the universe. We discovered that the sun did not revolve around the earth; instead our earth, along with the other planets, revolves around the sun.

The fact that we tended to see our earth as predominant reveals the self-centered (not necessarily selfish) nature of our perception of reality. That self-centered tendency did not die out with our ancestors; instead, it has taken on different, more subtle forms. Perhaps a self-centered shortsightedness has contributed to the Western use of a proportion of the earth's resources far outweighing our number of citizens.

Just as our ancestors made corrections to their theories and behaviors when confronted with inescapable facts, we as a culture are regularly changing our ideas and actions when new understanding warrants changes. For example, in the face of increasingly credible threats to our environment, we are rejecting the assumption that the earth is infinitely supplied with renewable resources. Instead, we are focusing on conservation and preservation of our environment as a crucial issue, viewing our resources as precious rather than expendable.

Increasing advances in media technology have enabled us to get a more complete picture of the global interdependence of not only our physical environment but also the world's people. When we see how others live and the problems they face, we can be less ethnocentric. **Ethnocentrism** or **sociocentrism** is the tendency to view one's own race or culture as central, based on the deepseated belief that one's own group is superior to all others.[81] We can only hold on to ethnocentrism when we can consider other cultures as less important or deserving than our own. Such an attitude of superiority is harmful to the dialogue that must proceed as decisions are made that involve a diverse and increasingly interdependent world.

A critical thinker can counter ethnocentrism by developing the trait of fairmindedness. **Fairmindedness** involves:

1. A respect for people whose ethnicities and traditions are different from our own,

---

[81]   Richard Paul, *Critical Thinking* (Rohnert Park, CA: Center for Critical Thinking and Moral Critique, 1990), p. 549.

Calvin and Hobbes by Bill Watterson
CALVIN AND HOBBES © Watterson. Dist by UNIVERSAL PRESS SYNDICATE.
Reprinted with permission. All rights reserved.

2. A willingness to hear and understand other viewpoints, and
3. An openness to change when new information or insight warrants that change

Egocentrism, the individual version of ethnocentrism, has been defined as a tendency to view everything else in relationship to oneself; one's desires, values, and beliefs (seeming to be self-evidently correct or superior to those of others) are often uncritically used as the norm of all judgment and experience. Egocentrism has been called one of the fundamental impediments to critical thinking.[82] To be a logical, fair, and less egocentric thinker, we can learn several skills. We can learn:

1. To recognize the basic defense mechanisms we use to distort reality and to deceive ourselves and others.
2. To recognize areas where we, for whatever reasons, have trouble being rational.
3. To understand and have empathy (the ability to share another's feelings and perspective) for someone else's viewpoint.

There is nothing wrong with taking strong, even immovable, stands on issues; we don't want to be so open-minded that we have no core beliefs or opinions at all! What is unfair is taking a

---

[82] Ibid., p. 548

strong stand without having thought carefully and honestly about all the relevant factors involved in an issue. And the most fair, ethical, and persuasive attitude is one of respect and politeness to those with whom we disagree.

 EXERCISE

Purpose: To understand differing points of view on global and national issues.

Fairmindedness is an important trait for critical thinkers to use when discussing any issue, but it is particularly crucial when the issues involve culture and therefore identity. Issues of culture, ethnicity, gender, and religion may surface when public policies are made. Many current issues involve the need to balance our separate identities as world citizens, citizens of a particular nation, and members of religious and ethnic groups within our nation and world. Individually, or in groups, consider some examples of these issues and come up with several different points of view for each. Who might hold these different viewpoints and why? How can we be more objective and fair about the viewpoints with which we disagree?

1. How should the United States and other nations work with the United Nations?
2. What kinds of measures should be taken against nations that violate human rights?
3. Under what circumstances, if any, should a soldier who has pledged allegiance to his own country take commands from an officer of the United Nations?
4. To what extent does being a superpower entail moral and practical obligations to less powerful countries?

Democratic nations are based on the delicate balance of the rule of the majority and the protection of the minority. Issues we face in our efforts to avoid ethnocentrism of both the majority and the minority include the following:

1. Can athletes refuse to stand for the national anthem of the country in which they are citizens when standing for the anthem violates a strongly held religious principle?
2. Can members of religious groups refuse to take part in the pledge of allegiance to their country's flag?
3. Should school districts allow spring and winter concerts that contain music from various religious traditions?
4. Can communities display religious symbols in public places?
5. Should national identity supersede ethnic or religious identity?

How We Defend Our Egos

> *"Are you thinking or are you just rearranging your prejudices?"*
>
> Walter Martin

The best place to start in understanding our weak points in reasoning is to examine human defense mechanisms. Defense mechanisms are "the clever ways we deceive ourselves, protect ourselves, and extract ourselves from uncomfortable situations—they are negative escape hatches that offer us temporary treatments for persistent problems."[83] For our purposes, we will consider two defense mechanisms that interfere with clear thinking.

Rationalization is a defense mechanism that underlies many others; it is our way of justifying or making sense of things that don't make sense. It's a way of explaining things away that should be brought under examination. When, for whatever reasons, we want to avoid an unpleasant truth or when we want to believe that something is true, we can come up with a justification for our desired belief. Note how we use our minds to distort reality in the following examples.

- Your favorite political candidate is found to have cheated on his taxes. You rationalize your continued support for

---

[83] Frank Minirth, MD, and Don Hawkins, ThM, *Worry Free Living* (Nashville: Thomas Nelson Publishers, 1989), p. 78.

this person by saying, "He may have cheated on his taxes, but he's made up for it by all the good budget cuts he helped pass."

- You find out that the car you just bought has been criticized by *Consumer Reports* for having a faulty transmission system. You rationalize by saying, "All cars are meant to fall apart in a few years."

- You continue to smoke cigarettes, although considerable evidence supports the fact that cigarettes are a causative factor in several diseases. You tell yourself and others, "I'm not going to worry about every habit I have. I could die tomorrow by slipping on a banana peel, so I might as well enjoy life today."

- Someone you'd like to get to know keeps refusing your requests for a date. You rationalize by saying, "He (or she) must be really busy this year."

- After committing yourself to a strict diet, you have a donut for breakfast. You then eat three more, rationalizing, "I already ruined the diet, so I may as well enjoy today and start again tomorrow."

- A clerk at a supermarket forgets to charge you for some sodas on the bottom of your cart. When you start to load them into your car and realize the mistake, you rationalize by thinking, "Oh, well. They're a big company and will never miss a few dollars."

 EXERCISE

Purpose: To understand why people rationalize rather than admit incongruities.

In a small group, take each of the examples of rationalization and discuss why someone might use that rationalization.

1. What need might they be trying to meet by rationalizing about that situation?
2. How is rationalization related to the attempt to preserve self-esteem?
3. How is rationalization harmful to the critical thinking process?

As you can see, rationalization can enter every area of our thinking. Leon Festinger, a sociologist, created a theory to explain why we use this mechanism so frequently. He said that as humans we are subject to a state of mind called **cognitive dissonance.** This state occurs whenever two ideas (or cognitions) are out of synch and create discomfort in our thinking patterns.

Festinger explained that when we are confronted by two clashing ideas, we try to make them harmonious by rationalizing. We explain away inconsistencies between our principles and our actions rather than face them and deal with them. Interestingly, Festinger believes that the need to resolve mentally inconsistent information is a basic drive, like the need for food; our minds strive to "survive" unpleasant incongruities.

A mentally healthy person is in a state of congruence; that is, the individual's behavior conforms to her beliefs and values. Unfortunately, many of us, instead of striving for true congruence by getting our behavior in line with our values when inconsistencies occur, will settle for a counterfeit peace of mind through rationalization. If we keep rationalizing, we can become psychologically unhealthy and removed from reality.

Consider the fate of many people who followed a cult leader named Jim Jones to Guyana and their death. When he passed himself off as a man of God and had sexual relations with many of his followers, he rationalized by calling it a form of ritual cleansing. When he humiliated young children for small infractions of his system, Jones (and some of the children's parents) must have rationalized that he had their best interests at heart.

The more we give up our critical thinking abilities, the harder it becomes to face our errors in judgment, and personal and social tragedies can be the result. As people who vote, buy products, influence others, and form relationships, we need to use information to help us learn and make decisions; rationalization is a form of sloppy thinking we can't afford to use.

BETTY by Gary Delainey and Gery Rasmussen
BETTY reprinted by permission of Newspaper Enterprise Association, Inc.

A defense mechanism closely related to rationalization is
denial. Denial is also a state of mind that blocks critical thinking, because it involves the repression of or refusal to recognize
any negative or threatening information. Some of us go into denial when we hear we've bounced a check or forgotten to make
a payment on a bill. We may tell our creditors they've made a mistake or that they never sent the bill, when the reality is that we've
made a mistake we choose not to face because of fear, pride, or
both. Another personal example of denial is summarized in an
anecdote from a call-in radio program excerpted from Dr. Laura
Schlessinger's book *How Could You Do That?*

> Nancy, forty-seven, called all bent out of shape because her
> "fella" of six months turns out to be married. Her ques-
> tion was about whether or not it was right for her to tell
> his wife of the affair . . . mostly, I thought to punish him,
> and only somewhat to warn her.
>
> That isn't the whole picture at all. I asked her if she'd
> been to his place of residence in the six months of their
> steamy sexual relationship: "No."
>
> I asked her if she'd even been given his home number
> or spoken to him at home on the phone in the evenings:
> "No."
>
> I suggested that she truly knew all along that he was
> probably living with someone, married or not, and that
> she ignored that because she didn't want to give up the im-
> mediate gratification: the passion and attention. Further-
> more, she had a fantasy going that she'd get him.

She begrudgingly acknowledged I was right.

Frighteningly, she couldn't seem to get with the idea that what she did wasn't right. She was too busy displacng all the blame for the current state of affairs on his adultery, not her own lack of conscience in getting involved with an attached fellow (the impact on his partner/wife/ kids) and her lack of courage in finding out truths up front and dealing with them. Motivation for this stupid behavior? Immediate gratification. She made a choice of "right now" over good sense or conscience.

Trying to avoid the self-examination, she calls to find out if it was right or not for her to blow the whistle on him. I told her, "That is a separate issue from what is my deeper concern about you, which is your denial that you made a choice, which got you to this point. If you tell on him, it doesn't change you, and you were not an innocent victim.

. . . There's no denying that sometimes choosing to own up to your own weakness, badness, selfishness, or evil is tough to do. But it's the only way finally to get control and some peace of mind."[84]

Denial, like other defense mechanisms, comes into play when we experience an emotional reaction to information. As a culture, we often deny certain warnings from environmentalists, like information about the ozone layer, the fossil fuel supply, or the effects of some pesticides. We may not only deny national problems; we also may rationalize that "you can't worry about every little thing."

Sometimes, denial is normal and helpful to our systems, as when we hear shocking news and give ourselves time, through denial of the facts, to cope with the information.

For example, if you are informed at a doctor's office that you have a life-threatening disease, it may be temporarily helpful for you not to digest this information completely until you are home with supportive family members or in the care of a good

---

[84]   Dr. Laura Schlessinger, *How Could You Do That?* (New York: HarperCollins Publishers, Inc., 1996) pp. 94–95.

counselor. In this case, it might be hard to drive home if you were fully immersed in the truth of your condition.

Denial becomes a problem for critical thinkers when they refuse to acknowledge the truth or the possible truth of an argument presented to them. This problem can be summed up in the cliché "I know what I believe. Don't confuse me with the facts." The facts may be complicated, but the critical thinker needs to sort through them in order to make a reasonable judgment on an issue, or at least to withhold judgment on a complex issue about which he is uninformed.

SKILL

Recognize defense mechanisms we use to deceive ourselves and others.

Denial and rationalization are often found together as defense mechanisms, when truth is denied and behavior is rationalized. Note both factors in another excerpt from the writings of Dr. Laura Schlessinger:

> I feel sorry for anyone's pain and problems. But when they are the result of betrayals and abandonments coming back to haunt, and the primary issue is not remediation of those actions, I don't feel it to be an ethical obligation to get personally involved.
>
> Trina, twenty-eight, has a sister, thirty-four, who split from her husband and has a new guy who dumped his wife. The sister kicked out her own seventeen-year-old daughter who wasn't going along agreeably with all this and is now living with Grandma. Trina is now wondering about not inviting the live-in guy to a family event.
>
> "Trina," I scolded, "you are displacing responsibility about this situation to him. You want to punish only him, but your sister is the one making the decisions; she chose him and she dumped her own daughter. Your sister's ac-

tions are being ignored so you can be appropriately, but safely, righteous? You don't want to upset the family applecart, right?"

"Right."

In discussing what her sister was actually doing wrong, Trina kept trying desperately to pardon her sister (by citing her traits as) low self-esteem, lonely, beguiled, not thinking straight, confused, lost, etc.

Sure, Trina says the guy is a bum, but she's just as sure her sister is merely weak and confused, not really bad. How is that again?

In psychological terminology, Trina is "splitting," i.e., ascribing ever so neatly all the bad behavior to one person and all the good to another. This is a means of coping with the difficult ambivalence of having love and attachment you feel for someone and not wanting that to be marred by ugly realities.

Well, in real life, all good people do some wrong things and all bad people do some right things. I've heard many women defend abusing men by saying, "But, other than that, he does good stuff!"[85]

On a personal level, we may see all of the shortcomings of people we don't like and deny and excuse the faults of people we care about, as illustrated in the preceding example. Similarly, we may see all of the negative aspects of people and policies we oppose and only good points in people and policies we support. By polarizing reality in this way, we leave out important considerations and hinder our ability to make the best decisions.

Critical thinkers take the time and energy required to recognize the weak points of their own side of an issue and the good points of their opponents. They search for truth rather than victory and are willing to change when presented with new information instead of insisting on maintaining a position that can no longer be supported.

Even when we are careful to give credit to the good points of all sides of an issue, we may still find that there are times when our emotional reactions cause us to lose rational perspective. When

[85] Ibid. pp. 183–184

that happens, we need to be aware of and adjust for our strong feelings, rather than denying that they have an impact on us.

Areas Where We Have Trouble Being Rational

Professor Zachary Seech has come up with a wonderful description of the trouble spots in our thinking. He calls them "points of logical vulnerability." We can be vulnerable to a general topic, like politics, or a specific one, such as our sister's choice of a husband.[86]

There are topics about which a person, we say, "just cannot be rational." What we mean is that this person has great difficulty being objective on these topics. He or she finds it difficult, in some cases, to consider the evidence impartially and draw a sensible, justified conclusion. These topics are the **points of logical vulnerability** for that person.[87]

Each person has different "sore spots" in his or her thinking and this fact further complicates the process of dialogue on a given issue. If you are a diehard fan of a particular team, you may be totally unobjective about how they will do in the next game. If fast food fits your lifestyle perfectly, you may not be open to any discussion of health problems associated with a steady diet of french fries and cheeseburgers. If you are upset because your roommate is getting married and moving out, you may find yourself disliking his or her new mate.

Points of logical vulnerability are topics affecting us so much on a personal level that we are likely to deny or rationalize any evidence that might disprove our opinions. For example, if you dislike a senator because of his views on the environment and then he supports an environmental bill you also support, you might rationalize that "he's just trying to appease environmentalists; he doesn't really care about the issues."

---

[86] Zachary Seech, *Logic in Everyday Life* (Belmont, CA: Wadsworth Publishing, 1988), pp. 2–3.

[87] Ibid., p. 2.

Conversely, if you like the senator and he does something you consider wrong, you might rationalize that he was forced into making concessions he would not have personally approved. Our points of logical vulnerability cause us to distort or deny information which goes against our deeply held opinions.

EXERCISE

Purpose: To recognize areas of logical vulnerability.

Discover some of your points of logical vulnerability. Think about people whose opinions are not credible for you. Consider political or social issues (capital punishment, drug legalization, euthanasia, gun control, or AIDS research policies) or choose an issue about which you frequently argue with other people.

Can you think of any ways in which you might not have been objective in hearing evidence from others about this issue? Do you use denial or rationalization when confronted with your points of logical vulnerability? How could you respond differently?

Example:
I don't like a congresswoman in my state. I heard her speak once and thought she was rude in the way she handled a question from the audience; also, she is against some of the legislation I consider important.

Once in a while, I'll hear her say something that makes sense, but I notice I discount whatever she says; if there's a negative way to look at her comments, I do. I guess I think she has some ulterior motive and I don't believe she has any positive contribution to make.

I don't like most of her positions and I'd never vote for her. But I could be more fair and admit that occasionally she does have a good idea and she might have real concern for the people in her district.

Keep in mind the difference between having strong, well-considered convictions about which you are not flexible (like your values) and opinions that have not been thought out, but that are based solely on emotions or identification with others who hold those opinions. The latter opinions are probably "points of logical vulnerability" for you.

Antidotes for Points of Logical Vulnerability

There are several effective ways to confront your points of logical vulnerability. The first approach is to apply certain techniques of rational thought to your opinions; the second is to learn to listen actively and accurately to people with differing opinions.

General semanticists study the relationship between words and behavior. They believe that we can improve our mental health by increasing the accuracy with which we speak, and they have come up with several "cures" for irrational statements.

A classic irrational statement stereotypes a whole group of people based on a limited sample of experience on the part of the speaker. Another term for a stereotypical statement is *sweeping generalization*.

Let's say a man named Harold has had several bad experiences in his relationships with women. The first woman he wanted to marry left him for another man; the second woman he wanted to marry told him she wasn't ready for a commitment and that she needed "space"; the third woman he wanted to marry left town with no forwarding address. In discussing his problems with his best friend, Harold makes the statement, "All women are cruel and selfish."

Now we can understand how anyone with this record of experience would be upset about his former relationships, but we also can see, as outside observers, that his statement is emotional and would not hold up to critical scrutiny. You can't study three women and then claim all women (about half of the human race) are cruel and selfish.

General semanticists, basing their work on the pioneering writing of Albert Korzypski, have come up with several cures for irrational statements. They would ask Harold to do a few things with his statement "All women are cruel and selfish."

- Eliminate the word *all* since no one can know every single woman. Change the general term *women* into specifics (Woman 1, Woman 2, and Woman 3 become Patty, Suzannah and Gina). Now Harold has: "Patty, Suzannah, and Gina are cruel and selfish." Not perfect, but more accurate; at least in this case he is not generalizing from three examples to half of the human race.

  Semanticists call this technique *indexing;* you take your general label (women, Catholics, Asians, Americans) and change it to actual people. You also delete the word *all* from your vocabulary when it precedes a general category. One can never know *all* about any given group.

- Next, a general semanticist would ask Harold to change his vague labels of "cruel" and "selfish" to specific behaviors. "Patty, Suzannah, and Gina did not marry me, although we were dating and I asked them to marry me. Patty married someone else, Suzannah told me she needed 'space,' and Gina left town without contacting me."

- For accuracy and perspective, our semanticist would also ask Harold to put a date on his statement. "Patty, Suzannah, and Gina did not marry me, though we were dating and I asked them to marry me. Patty married someone else, Suzannah told me she needed 'space,' and Gina left town without contacting me. These incidents happened when I was in my late teens and early twenties."

- The final addition to Harold's statement is called the etc. because it includes other realities that add balance and fairness to the original statement. Think of a young child who complains with all accuracy, "Joey pushed me!" This statement is clear and unambiguous, yet we don't know what else was going on in the situation. We don't have the total picture or the context in which the event occurred.

  To figure out what was going on, a parent or teacher might ask, "Did you push him too?" It could be that the child who complained was indeed the victim of Joey's aggressiveness, or maybe the complaining child pushed Joey first. Also, it could be that Joey was pushing to get somewhere and was unaware that he had pushed the other child. We can only know what happened in a situation when we get more information.

Think about the times you feel really annoyed with someone's behavior. In recounting your irritation to a friend, do you really try to be fair and objective or do you tend to present the details that best support your right to be annoyed?

When general semanticists recommend the use of the *etc.*, they are recognizing the complexity of situations and that we can rarely say all there is to say about the factors that create differences of opinion. They would suggest that Harold add information to his statement to give a more accurate picture of reality:

> Patty, Suzannah, and Gina did not marry me, though we were dating and I asked them to marry me. Patty married someone else, Suzannah told me she needed 'space,' and Gina left town without contacting me. These incidents happened when I was in my late teens and early twenties. I knew Patty was ready to get married, but I didn't ask her until she was involved with someone else; I could have still dated Suzannah as one of the men she was dating, but I wanted to be the only one; I don't know why Gina left town.

SKILL

Use rational thinking aids to overcome areas in which you have trouble being rational.

If you compare Harold's first statement with this last statement, you might understand why the use of semantic devices improves mental health. A counselor might help Harold arrive at the same kinds of rephrasings. If he continues to see all women as cruel and selfish, he might never try to interact with them again, but if he sees that he has had a few bad experiences, he can learn from his mistakes and continue to grow and develop relationships.

The semantic devices are useful in helping us to change irrational comments we make about people and issues to more truthful and fair-minded statements.

EXERCISE

Purpose: To practice using the semantic devices in order to make statements more accurate and rational.

1. Using the semantic devices, change the following irrational statements into logical statements. You may need to make up details.
    a. Women are terrible drivers. (Note the implied *all* before women).
    b. Wealthy people are greedy and materialistic
    c. Democrats are bleeding-heart liberals and can't be trusted.
    d. Republicans don't care about the poor and needy.
    e. Most people from ivy-league schools are elitists.
    f. People on welfare don't want to work.
        Can you add a statement that you've heard yourself (or a close friend) say?
2. Listen to yourself for a week and see if you tend to overgeneralize when confronted with your points of logical vulnerability. Try to stop yourself and to use the semantic devices to rephrase your opinions. What is the effect on your emotions and your conversations? You may note that if you try to get other people to be more specific and less prejudicial in their statements, you encounter some hostility. Why might that be?
        Write out several examples of instances in which you or someone else could have used the semantic devices to make more accurate statements.

Actively and Accurately Listening: Developing Empathy

Some psychologists believe that the ability to listen to another person, to empathize with, and to understand their point of view is one of the highest forms of intelligent behavior.

Edward DeBono

Many cultures place a high value on competition, and this competition is not restricted to sporting events—it also comes out in debates and discussions on issues. The desire to win and the enjoyment we find in having the most persuasive argument may limit our ability to be fair to opposing sides of issues.

The most persuasive speaker is one who can understand and address the points brought up by those who don't share his or her opinion. To understand an opposing argument, we must hear what the speaker for the opposition is saying.

Why do we find listening difficult, and why don't politicians listen more fairly in debates? Some of the reasons we don't listen are:

- The thrust of debate is to win; therefore we will tend to listen to the opposition's position only so we can find fault with it. The focus is on victory, not on understanding, especially in public debating forums.

- We are not trained to listen. Some of us have had training in speech, but few have had specific training in effective listening techniques.

- We fear if we really listen to the other person, we will lose our train of thought.

- We fear if we really listen to the other person, we might agree with him or her and that could be really uncomfortable.

- Effort and energy are required in order to understand the viewpoint of another person.

- For many of us, it is more rewarding to speak about our own ideas than to listen to others.

Listening accurately to an opposing position, however, gives us some clear advantages:

- We can learn what the opposition to our cause or issue believes and we can then address our opponents on specific issues.

- We can grow and adjust our position if new research or reasoning warrants the adjustment.

- When we are seen as secure enough in our position to listen to an opposing argument, our credibility increases.

- Our calm listening is often contagious; as we show our willingness to hear the other side fully, defenses are dropped and our opponents listen to us as well. We have a better chance of explaining our viewpoint and not having it distorted by interruptions.

- In an atmosphere of reduced hostility, areas of agreement can be found.

The Art of Listening Well

Years ago, a southern California psychologist, Carl Rogers, created a listening exercise that has become a staple for counselors and teachers of communications. Rogers' technique is simple and very effective; if done correctly, both sides will come out with a deeper understanding of the other's position.

Understanding does not necessarily mean agreement. We may know exactly what the other's position is and conclude that he is completely off base. The critical thinker is the one who draws conclusions based on understanding of both her and her opponent's position, not solely on an emotional commitment to her original position.

Here is Rogers' listening exercise:

1. Two people with opposing beliefs on an issue sit facing each other.
2. Person A begins with a brief statement about her opinion on an issue.
3. Person B paraphrases—puts person A's opinion in his own words. When person A agrees that person B has understood, then person B states his opinion.
4. Now person A has to paraphrase—restate in her own words what person B has said. When person B is satisfied that person A has understood him, person A can expand on her opinion.
5. This process is continued until both parties feel they have presented their case and that it has been understood. It is helpful to allow each person a few minutes to summarize, as best they can, the complete position of the other person.
6. During the process, both parties attempt to be objective in their summaries of the other person's viewpoint and to avoid sarcasm and ridicule of any points the other person makes.
7. It is also helpful to try to "read between the lines" and understand *why* the other person feels so strongly about his or her position.

SKILL

Listen with empathy to an opposing viewpoint.

Example

Person A:	I believe heroic medical interventions should not be made unless the doctors and nurses have the permission of the patient or the patient's family members.
Person B:	So you believe that extending life with technology should not be done unless a patient or his family wants his life extended?
Person A:	That's right.
Person B:	Well, it's my opinion that sometimes there isn't time for a discussion with the patient or the family members about the patient's

chances for survival. The medical experts
have to act or there is no decision to be
made because the patient is dead!

Person A: So you think that using technology is totally up to the doctors?

Person B: (clarifying) I didn't mean that. I mean, if
the patient is going to die if he's not hooked
up to the machines, then he needs to be
hooked up first and consulted later.

Person A: (trying to paraphrase more accurately) So
you think in an emergency the doctors
should be allowed to treat the patient in
any way that will save his life and talk to
him or his family members later.

Person B: That's right. You got it.

Person A: Well, I don't have a real problem with that.
But I believe that if the patient doesn't
want to be kept alive through technology,
and if he or his family members tell the
doctors that, then the doctors have to
abide by his wishes and "pull the plug."

Person B: So, basically, you believe the patient
should decide whether he will live or die—
or, if he can't decide, then his family
should decide for him.

Person A: (clarifying) That's not exactly it. He may
live or die whether he's hooked up to life-
supports or not. But it's his choice—or his
family's choice—whether he will be
hooked up.

Person B:: Okay, then it's the patient's choice, or secondly, his family's choice and not the doc-
tor's choice to continue him on life-
supports.

Person A: Exactly.

Person B: I believe it is part of a doctor's job to assess a patient's chances for survival; the
patient or the family can get too emo-

tional and decide to let someone die rather than be uncomfortable; and meanwhile, the doctor may know there's a good chance for recovery. Also, doctors are trained to save life at all costs. If we train them to take the patient's advice, then they could let him die just so they could take off early to play golf!

Person A: That's a lot for me to paraphrase. You believe, if I have it right, that doctors are more objective and less emotional than patients and family members, and they have more of an expert opinion about chances for recovery. And also you think it's dangerous to let patients or family members decide to pull the plug because then doctors don't have to worry about whether the patient could have lived a full life or not.

Person B: You said it better than I did!

Person A: Well, what I really think is that doctors should give their expert opinion to the patient and the family members. If they then decide, for whatever reason, not to prolong life with technology, then the doctors would have to abide by their decision.

Person B: So you think that the doctor should be an advisor or counselor and give them all the information he can, but the family should have the final power to decide what will be done.

Person A: That's exactly right.

Person B: Well, that sounds fair, but I just believe it's better to go for life, whenever possible. There are many cases of people recovering from comas or serious strokes thanks to life-support systems. If their families had pulled the plug to spare them pain or expense, they would have lost a loved one. Give life a chance.

Person A: You believe we should always choose to use life-supports in case the patient does, in some miraculous way, recover.

Person B: (clarifying) Not exactly. Recovery isn't always miraculous; sometimes the doctors can predict a good chance of recovery, and they should go for that chance.

Person A: So you would choose to use life-supports until someone is completely beyond hope of recovery?

Person B: Right.

Person A: Well, I have heard of many horror stories of people forced to stay on intravenous machines and respirators when they were completely paralyzed and had no desire to live. There are parents who don't want babies to be subjected to surgery and to spend time hooked up to equipment that hurts them.

Person B: So you believe the patient and his family should decide what the quality of life would be if the patient lived and use that as a basis for deciding whether to pull the plug?

Person A: Yes. Don't you think that's the only basis for a decision?

Person B: I guess I believe that giving it time is more important than rushing into a decision. I feel bad about the pain anyone may feel on life-support equipment. But, to me, going through the pain is worth it if there is a chance for a good life.

Person A: Who decides what a good life is?

Person B: I think you need to paraphrase my last statement first.

Person A: Okay. You believe in giving life a chance, even if it seems desperate. You think that, even if the patient wants to be off the life-support equipment, he needs time. And you believe the doctors are the ones who should decide what kind of time he needs.

Person B: Yes. And the patient may find that a life with limitations is better than no life.

Person A: So you don't think the patient should have the right to say no to life-supports?

Person B: I don't think he should have the exclusive right because I don't think he has all the information he needs to make the decision.

Person A: Well, my position is more simple. It's his body—or his parent's, wife's, or child's body. That gives him the right to decide what will or will not be done in a hospital. I agree it's important to get the doctor's opinion, but after that, his decision should be honored.

Person B: And I agree with you that it's his or her body, but I also think the doctors are more objective and knowledgeable, so they should be allowed to continue treatment if there's a chance for recovery. I can see why some of these cases have to be settled in court. That's not the ideal solution, but it's the best we've come up with so far.

Questions for Discussion

1. The participants in this dialogue did not end by agreeing with much of each other's positions. How, then, is this form of communication useful?

2. Where did you spot inaccurate paraphrases of the other's position? Why do you think these occurred?
3. Often, there is a strong emotional component to someone's position. Do you see hints of emotionalism in this dialogue? How does the paraphrasing minimize emotional outbursts or points of logical vulnerability? Under what circumstances should the emotional reactions of the participants also be brought to light?

EXERCISES

Purpose: To practice active listening.

1. In class, or at home, try using this listening technique when discussing an issue with someone who disagrees with you. Be sure to tell the other person the rules and get his or her commitment to abide by them (or you may be in for a good fight!). It may help to have a referee who is familiar with the technique and objective about the issue. Then report on your results by answering the following questions:
   a. Were you able to stay with the paraphrasing process? Why or why not?
   b. Did you and the other person attain greater understanding? If so, give some specific examples of what you learned about each other's positions.
   c. Was the relationship improved in any way?
2. Exchange a persuasive essay you have done (perhaps earlier in this course or in another class) with another student's essay; then do the following:
   a. Write a paraphrase of the other's ideas, clearly focusing on thesis statements and evidence used to support the thesis.
   b. Read the other student's paraphrase of your essay; comment on how well he or she understood and expressed your point of view. If there are misunderstandings in each other's viewpoints, try to discover why these occurred. If time permits, explain to the class any problems you encountered in trying to empathize with each other's ideas.

Precautions about Active Listening

Active listening was first suggested as a technique to be used by professional therapists. Over the years, various workshops have been set up for the purposes of training lay people to use active listening to improve their relationships. These workshops focus on the proper and improper use of the technique.

If you have never been formally trained in active listening, you may find it uncomfortable. However, practice and a basic knowledge of potential problems should enable you to use this very helpful communication tool successfully. Here is a summary of basic precautions in using active listening:

1. Avoid sarcasm and ridicule of the other person's statements; also, don't add negative connotations to what he or she says.

2. Don't "parrot" the position of the other person; just paraphrase (put into your own words) the ideas you hear.

3. If you find yourself getting upset, take some time out and assess what it is about this issue that makes it painful for you to be objective. There are some issues we feel so strongly about that there is no room for discussion. These strong feelings are usually connected with a personal experience. For example, if your cousin was killed by someone, you may believe that the death penalty is justified and any arguments against it make no impression when you consider the pain of your cousin and your close family.

   Your belief may be based on a value that you hold deeply; if you believe that abortion is the taking of innocent life, then statistics about the teenage pregnancy rate may seem somewhat insignificant.

It is helpful, as a critical thinker, to know the areas in which you hold solid convictions. You can then acknowledge points on an opposing side, but make it clear that those points are not strong enough for you to change your mind. The key is to understand both sides of an issue fully and to be open to new information; then you are responsible as a thinker when you, with good conscience, take a strong, even immovable, stand on an issue.

It is unrealistic to assume that you will have many opportunities for this kind of extended dialogue with someone who disagrees with you. The benefit of understanding the paraphrasing technique is that you can use it whenever it seems that something needs to be clarified in a discussion. Your use of this technique gives you credibility and the persuasive power that comes with calmness.

The person who stays cool and calm in a discussion seems secure in his position. The person who blows it by becoming overexcited and unfair to the opposition seems threatened, that is, logically vulnerable. Jumping up and down, name-calling, interrupting, and other forms of bullying serve only to make the person who uses these tactics seem foolish and unstable.

Your cool, clear mind—don't leave home without it!

Chapter Highlights

1. Our thinking can become less egocentric and more clear and fair when we recognize our defense mechanisms and our areas of logical vulnerability and when we develop specific skills for understanding the viewpoints of others.
2. Rationalization is a defense mechanism in which we try to justify or make sense out of things that are not sensible or justifiable.
3. Denial is a defense mechanism that involves repressing or refusing to recognize threatening information.
4. Points of logical vulnerability are topics about which we have trouble being rational.
5. Thinkers can manage points of logical vulnerability through the use of semantic devices.
6. Active listening, when used properly, can help us to clearly understand the viewpoints of others.

Articles for Discussion

It Happened

To Deny That the Holocaust Occurred Is
to Set the Preconditions for Another One.

**Guest editorial by Richard V. Pierard, professor of history
at Indiana State University**
from *Christianity Today,* March 9, 1992.

The emergence of David Duke as a political figure has again drawn public attention to the contention that no Jewish Holocaust occurred in World War II. The ex-Klansman has said that Hitler and the Nazis did not systematically and successfully destroy most of Europe's Jews.

For years, Holocaust denial has been a stock-in-trade of shadowy creatures on the extreme Right. In recent times, several pseudo-scholars have come forward to argue against the "extermination legend" and "myth of the six million." Through an elaborate process of distortions, half-truths, and falsification of data, these "revisionists" seek to convince the gullible that Hitler did not order the annihilation of the Jews, but instead had this "alien minority" placed in labor camps where they could not subvert the war effort.

Harsh war-time conditions caused the epidemic diseases and malnutrition in the crowded camps; crematories were necessary to dispose of the remains of the few thousand who died. Cyanide gas was used for delousing and fumigation in order to check the spread of typhus. There were so few Jews left in Europe because most had emigrated to North America or Israel. Pictures of gas chambers and emaciated inmates are fabrications. And so the story goes.

In fact, Holocaust denial is the ultimate Big Lie. The whole process of destruction is so well-attested through eye-witness accounts, official documents, and contemporary press reports that no one in his or her right mind could deny that it happened.

So why is such a monstrous falsehood perpetrated? The answer is twofold. One reason is anti-Semitism—the ongoing hatred of Jews that animates extreme rightist groups in North America, Britain, France, Germany, and elsewhere. The other is the intention to deny Jews the right to a land of their own, where they may live peacefully within secure borders.

Is Holocaust denial merely a Jewish problem? No, it is also an American Christian problem. We must never forget that anti-Semitism has its roots in the theology and practice of the Christian church, from the writings of the church fathers, through the Inquisition, even in the comments of Martin Luther. Moreover, the U.S. government and people did little to help Jews in the years 1933 through 1945. Opinion polls in our "Christian nation" in 1942 found that people disliked Jews more than the German and Japanese enemies, while officials in Washington pooh-poohed the accounts of extermination programs as "atrocity stories."

Evangelicals may try to evade the issue by arguing that the Holocaust was a product of theological liberalism. But we cannot let ourselves off the hook so easily. Robert Ross excellently shows in *So It Was True* (1980) that while our magazines reported the grim details of the Nazi policies, our modest attempts to persuade the U.S. authorities to do something lacked moral passion.

Likewise, conservative free church Christians in Germany supported the Hitler regime just as fervently as most in the official church did. In 1984, the German Baptists even issued a formal statement confessing that they had been taken in by the "ideological seduction" of the time. They had not stood up for truth and righteousness.

The bottom line is that to deny the Holocaust is to set the preconditions for yet another one. It behooves evangelicals to stand up and utter a forthright *no* to the "revisionists" and their fellow travelers. The very credibility of our faith is at stake.

Reprinted by permission of Richard V. Pierard.

Questions for Discussion

1. What would cause a person or group of persons to deny the painful history of another group of people? Does ethnocentrism or egocentrism play a role in this denial?
2. What should be the guidelines for any form of "revisionist history"?
3. Why does the author say that "to deny the Holocaust is to set the preconditions for yet another one"?
4. What other historical persecutions have been denied or minimized and for what reasons?

Ideas for Writing or Speaking

1. The United States' Declaration of Independence claims that "all men are created equal." How would a world in which all people were treated with equal respect and dignity work? Write or speak about what it would take to live in such a world and what that world would look like. If you don't believe that such a world could exist, write about the conditions that make it impossible.
2. Write or speak about another tragic event in human history. What lessons can we learn from this event? Are there actions that can be taken to prevent a reoccurrence of such an event?

Consider the following excerpt from *You Just Don't Understand* by linguistics professor Deborah Tannen, detailing differences between male and female conversational styles, which have been verified by research.

A woman I'll call Diana often begins statements with "Let's." She might say, "Let's go out for brunch today," or "Let's clean up now, before we start lunch." This makes Nathan angry. He feels she is ordering him around, telling him what to do. Diana can't understand why he takes it that way. It is obvious to her that she is making suggestions, not demands. If he doesn't feel like doing what she proposes, all he has to do is say so. She would not press her preference if she knew it wasn't what he wanted.

. . . Being on the lookout for threats to independence makes sense in the framework of an agonistic world, where life is a series of contests that test a man's skill and force him to struggle against others who are trying to bend his will to theirs. If a man experiences life as a fight for freedom, he is naturally inclined to resist attempts to control him and determine his behavior.

This world view has given rise to the concept of the hen-pecked husband: Many men resent any inkling that their wives want to get them to do things. Women's lives have historically been hemmed in at every turn by the demands of others—their families, their husbands—and yet, though individual women may complain of overbearing husbands, there is no parallel stereotype of a "rooster-pecked" wife." Why not? Seeing people as interdependent, women expect their actions to be influenced by others, and they expect to act in concert. Their struggle is to keep the ties strong, keep everyone in the community, and accommodate to others' needs while making what efforts they can at damage control with respect to their own needs and preferences. If a man struggles to be strong, a woman struggles to keep the community strong.

The misunderstanding between Diana and Nathan can be traced to habitual conversational styles typical of women and men—styles that take shape with the first words children learn to use at play. Diana's tendency to make proposals beginning with "Let's" is not just idiosyncratic. Researchers who study children at play have found that girls of all ages tend to speak in this way.

Psychologist Jacqueline Sachs and her colleagues, studying preschoolers between the ages of two and five, found that girls tended to make proposals for action by saying "Let's," whereas boys often gave each other commands. For example, in playing doctor, the little boys said things like:

"Lie down."
"Get the heart thing."
"Gimme your arm."
"Try to give me medicine."

When girls played doctor, they said things like "Let's sit down and use it."

Marjorie Harness Goodwin found exactly the same pattern in a completely different group—black children between the ages of six and fourteen, playing on the streets of a Philadelphia neighborhood. The boys, who were (agonistically) making slingshots in preparation for a fight, gave each other orders:

"Gimme the pliers!"
"Man, don't come *in* here where I *am.*"
"Give me that, man. After this, after you chop 'em, give 'em to me."
"Get off my steps."

The girls, who were making glass rings out of bottle necks, didn't issue commands. They made proposals beginning with "Let's":

"Let's go around Subs and Suds." (a corner bar/restaurant)

"Let's ask her, 'Do you have any bottles?' "

"Come on. Let's go find some."

"Come on. Let's turn back, y'all, so we can safe keep 'em."

"Let's move *these* out *first.*"

Other ways the girls proposed activities were with "We gonna" ("We gonna make a *whole* display of rings"), "We could" ("We *could* use a sewer (to sand down the glass surfaces of the rings"), "Maybe" ("Maybe we can slice them like that"), and "We gotta" ("We gotta find some more bottles"). All these are attempts to influence what the others do without telling them what to do. At the same time, they reinforce the identities of the girls as members of a community.

Children may be influenced by their parents' styles, just as adults are influenced by what they learned as children. Psycholinguist Jean Berko Gleason studied how parents talk to their young children, and found that fathers issue more commands to their children than mothers do, and they issue more commands to their sons than to their daughters. Sociolinguist Frances Smith observed a similar pattern in a public-speaking situation. Examining the practice sermons of male and female students at a Baptist seminary, she found that when referring to chapters and verses in their exegesis, the men frequently gave the audience orders, such as "Listen carefully as I read Luke, chapter seventeen." The women, on the other hand, rarely uttered imperatives but rather tended to invite the audience to participate, as in "Let's go back to verses fifteen and sixteen."

Given this pattern, Nathan is not far off the mark when he hears "Let's" as equivalent to a command. It *is* a way of getting others to do what someone wants. And yet Diana is also right when she says he should not feel coerced. The difference lies in the fundamentally different social structures of girls and boys, and women and men.

In the hierarchical order that boys and men find or feel themselves in, status is indeed gained by telling others what to do and resisting being told what to do. So once Nathan has deciphered Diana's "Let's" as her way of saying what she wants him to do, his next step is to resist her. But girls and women find or feel themselves in a community that is threatened by conflict, so they formulate requests as proposals rather than orders to make it easy for others to express other preferences without provoking a confrontation. Not accustomed to having others try to bend their will simply to solidify a dominant position, girls do not learn to resist others' demands on principle and don't expect others to resist theirs on principle either.

It is not that women do not want to get their way, but that they do not want to purchase it at the cost of conflict. The irony of interactions like those between Diana and Nathan is that the differences between men's and women's styles doom their efforts. The very moves that women make to avoid confrontation have the effect of sparking it in conversation with some men. Insofar as men perceive that someone is trying to get them to do something without coming right out and saying so, they feel manipulated and threatened by an enemy who is all the more sinister for refusing to come out in the open.[88]

Questions for Discussion

1. What does Deborah Tannen suggest are the reasons men and women perceive the word "Let's" differently when the word is used to make requests? Do you agree with her conclusion?
2. How do you make requests of others? Are there ways that people make requests of you that you find annoying? If so, is your reaction consistent with Tannen's conclusions?

88 Deborah Tannen, *You Just Don't Understand* (New York: Ballantine Books, Random House, Inc., 1990), pp. 151–155.

3. Several different sources of research are used to support Tannen's conclusions about the differences between how boys interact with boys and how girls interact with girls. Have you seen similar patterns of interaction in same-sex groups?
4. Do you believe, as Tannen states, that men generally seek independence and women seek community in their interactions with others? If so, what implications would these differences have in the workplace and in the family?

The following excerpt is from Gregory Williams' book *Life on the Color Line*. Williams lived his early years as a white child in Virginia in the 1950s, a time of enforced segregation between the races. When his parents separated and his father's business failed, Gregory and his father and brother moved to Muncie, Indiana, to stay with relatives. On the way to Muncie, Gregory discovered that he was really of mixed race; his father, a half-black man, had been passing as Italian-American. Gregory would be living with his black relatives in their segregated part of town.

Although Gregory's mother, aunts, and cousins lived only miles away from the black district, they did not acknowledge his existence. In junior high, Greg had black friends, but his white relatives and other white children rejected him both in and out of school. Being restricted to the black side of town also meant that Greg lived in poverty while the white side of his family was relatively comfortable.

This excerpt from his book details Gregory's first day of high school.

At lunch I entered the cafeteria and saw Ben Cook, a white cousin. In the joy of a new beginning, I gave him a friendly smile. His eyes widened in panic, and he quickly avoided my gaze. I realized he was going to be the same as at Wilson—no contact or recognition. I simultaneously felt rejected and relieved. He, with his slovenly attire and Shed Town buddies, was not someone with whom I cared to be connected in any way.

There were two cafeteria serving lines, the "a la carte" line, with a wide selection, and the cheap "A" lunch line. Ben made a dash for the "a la carte" side. I stood in the small "A" lunch line, thankful I had the necessary thirty-five cents. A pang of jealously overcame me as I watched Ben pile his tray high with sandwiches, chips, and desserts. I realized I did not have the four extra pennies for a second carton of milk. But Mrs. Reese, our neighbor, worked in the cafeteria. As she served the food, she winked, and she gave me very generous portions.

After lunch, some students gathered on the sidewalk in front of the building. Peeking out the glass doors, I saw many of the same white boys who had loafed at the diner across from Wilson Junior High School. Now they perched on the hoods of souped-up Chevys and Fords, smoking and flirting with many of the same girls. I climbed the marble steps to the auditorium. The smell of musty wood filled the air as I scanned the cavernous room. It rose almost three stories high and spanned over a hundred seats wide, starkly divided into three distinct sections, north, south, and a broad vacant middle. Black students huddled together on the south side. Whites filled the north. The middle section flowed between them like a deep unnavigable river. This was worse than Wilson, I thought. At least there I could hide in our corner of the recreation room. How could I maintain the anonymity I desperately wanted? Goose bumps popped out on my arms as I realized that, on the very first day, I had to make a fateful choice. If I sat with the white students on the north side of the auditorium, the blacks would believe I didn't want to associate with them. Yet, if I joined the black students, I would be an all-too-conspicuous "white" face in a sea of the multiple hues of brown.

I stood glued to the floor, turning my dilemma over and over in my mind. Finally, aware I had no real decision to make, I slowly moved down the aisle to join the black students. Another cousin, one of Aunt Bess's grandchildren, whom we playfully called "Jemima," sat in the middle of a chattering group of boys and girls. She was a beautiful, angular-faced, brown-skinned teenager, with long black braids. She hailed me immediately. Her mother,

Aunt Elizabeth, had fed Mike and me on countless Sundays when we trekked to her house in Whitely for chicken and dumplings and fresh-baked rolls. Giving her a relieved wave, I plodded down the aisle, unsure of exactly where to sit. There were so many new faces among the black students. I had an aching fear that even though I had made my choice, they might not accept me. Finally, I spied a vacant seat on the aisle. I took it, making my commitment, but remaining on the edge.

As I sat there self-consciously, feeling the burning stares of white students from far across the room, Jemima rose from her seat. Every muscle in my body relaxed as she sat beside me. Drawn by her bubbling presence, a group of students soon surrounded us. Some of the fellows were Bearcat football and basketball stars I had watched during summers at the Madison Street "Y." I reveled in the stamp of approval Jemima provided, but the lunchtime conversation took a turn that made me uncomfortable.

It all began when one boy speculated about what he might do if he had skin like mine. He claimed he would leave Muncie, pass for white, and get a good job. Another boy, who reckoned that lighter skin would bring him easy access to white girls, was quickly silenced with a chorus of hissing. Though I tried to feign disinterest, a third boy asked me point-blank why I didn't sit with the white students. I could only muster a weak "I don't want to." A senior basketball star, perhaps understanding my choice better than I did, spoke up.

"Greg is making his life less complicated. If he sat over there the white kids would find him out in a minute, and he'd be an outcast. He's over here with us, telling them, 'Here I am, deal with me!' Don't bother Greg. He's where he belongs."[89]

"Persistence," from *Life on the Color Line* by Gregory Williams. Copyright © 1995 by Gregory Williams. Used by permission of Dutton Signet, a division of Penguin Books USA Inc.

[89] Gregory Williams, *Life on the Color Line* (New York: Plume/Penguin Books USA Inc., 1996), 190–192.

Questions for Discussion

1. Our perception of reality is shaped to a large extent by our experiences. How do you think Gregory's viewpoint was affected by his poverty, his youth, and his experience as a mixed race person?
2. Students in the 1950s, in Indiana and elsewhere in the United States, socialized primarily with students of the same race, a practice that was reinforced by legal segregation. To what extent has this situation changed? What still needs to be done to promote racial reconciliation?

Breakfast and Cornrows

A Tale of Logical Vulnerability

by johndies, 1996
Used by permission of the author.

I sat staring at the back of her head for at least three hours. All right, maybe it was only twenty seconds, but it felt like three hours. What on earth is going on? In some places the braids were so tight that the hair stood out at right angles before drooping to the shoulders. It looked a little like the action of a horse's tail, just before doing his business. In other areas the braids were loosely started, halfway down the gathered lock of hair. My nearly twelve-year-old daughter had set a new standard for cornrows, but it was a standard that I did not understand. It was a disturbing beginning for the day, particularly before breakfast.

"I like it," she said.

"Yes, well, I can see that you would. All you can see is the front. The front is fine, nicely spaced, even braids. It's the back I'm talking about," I explained. As if I even cared about the neat front rows. I just didn't like it. I was being tested, and I didn't like that either. I rustled about the kitchen gathering the various items to pack for her and her brother's school lunches.

"I looked at the back when I was doing it. It looks fine. I saw it in the mirror," she replied.

Yeah, right. My daughter is a brilliant girl, kind, funny, but not very objective when it comes to her own opinions. The word stubborn comes to mind. She wasn't budging an inch and the two dozen cornrows were staying firmly on her head.

"Listen, you're really pushing the limits here. I mean, I understand that you don't mind being different, but it seems to me that you have an unhealthy desire to be "weird" or something. I really think you should think this over before going to school like that."

I felt I had some pretty strong ground here. I was giving due respect, appealing to her logic, sharing my judgment on the merits. And if that didn't work then I guess I expected for her to come around to my point simply on the basis that I, as her father, was disturbed.

"Okay, I thought about it and I think it's fine," she offered, and that was the end of the conversation.

Hmm, this was not going well. It was almost as if she sensed that my arguments were unsound and therefore unworthy of further attention. Was this true? What was the basis of my dislike?

A few days earlier I had found a box that sort of fell out of the pile stacked in the garage. A carton of icons, each one loaded with an entire database of memories. Not a lot of written words, no notebooks of young angst, no diaries of adventures. Mostly objects. A fender mirror from my first vehicle, a half-eaten high school diploma, a paper place-mat from a restaurant in West Yellowstone. Oddities with stories attached. My life in a box. And only one box at that. I could at least explain the half-eaten diploma. My dog ate it. He never touched my homework in three long years of high school, but as soon as I graduated, he ate my diploma.

Anyway, sorting through this collection I came upon an old photo of my ninth grade class. It was the typical photo where the entire class gathers on the front steps, and the photographer takes the shot hoping for a minimum of finger gestures, grimaces and general chaos. Somewhere on those steps was a younger and wiser version of myself. As I scanned those fresh faces I was surprised how familiar most of them were even after thirty-five years. Characters from the past, leaping fresh into my consciousness. It was a great time, a time of innocence, and years before any of these people made serious mistakes. It was, in some cases, the last year of the trouble free life of a child.

Laying my finger briefly on each face, I recalled what the future would bring. Here there was death in a traffic accident, speeding on a motorcycle, no helmet. Here there was madness, after a long series of drug addictions. And this fellow, a hopeless alcoholic. This young lady, drugs, welfare, four children before age twenty. More and more, drugs, jail, and death.

The whole class didn't fall into disaster. At least I don't think so. I'm not sure because I didn't know everybody. It just seemed that most of my friends had particularly hard lives. In fact, only two or three seemed to survive out of the two dozen that loosely hung together. I suppose I had thought about this before but this time I was struggling with the reasons. Was there something here, in this last innocent photo, that gave a hint?

Suddenly it came to me. None of us fit in. All of us were somehow on the edge, not quite a part of the whole. Different in thought, different in deed. Our stumbling identities only defined by our own association with each other. Bright in some cases, talented in others, but uniformly weird in all instances.

And now my daughter seems bent upon being weird in her own right. I had this mental flash of how many could I save, if I could just go back in time and warn them. Would they listen to a caring stranger? If they wouldn't listen, could I force them? I couldn't do it for them, but this was my daughter, and I was not giving her up to the bleak future of non-conformity. At least not without a fight.

All of this seemed to solidify in the few minutes it took to make her school lunch. As I made the cheese sandwich, I pondered her future. As I bagged her tortilla chips, I resolved to make a difference.

"Okay, that's it. No more cornrows. I tried to give you the freedom to make wise decisions and you refused, so now I'll step in and provide the rules. No more weirdness. You will not court weirdness nor seek to be different, or any of that stuff. You're too young and if you go on this way then what wild and crazy thing will you pull when you're eighteen? Later on, you can wear your hair however you want, but for right now, lose the braids."

Dead silence, shocked expressions. My son froze, his toast halfway to his mouth.

"Now?"

I could see in her eyes the deep hurt, even with the one word of acquiescence. She couldn't know what I was thinking, and didn't understand how I could react the way I was reacting. Her eyes just misted over and she prepared herself to walk whatever line I asked her to walk.

Now it was beginning to dawn on me that things hadn't gone quite the way I wanted. I knew I was struggling, but somehow the noose was just getting drawn tighter the more I twisted. I was almost swinging in the breeze due to my own efforts when my wife came in to the picture. Good, I'll explain what I did, she'll understand and together we will force, uh, together we will demand that, umm, together we will make it right.

"So, what do we do now?" I confided.

"Seems to me that *you* have done what you have pretty much on your own," she said quietly.

Whoops, definitely swinging in the breeze now, twisting slowly in the wind.

"Oh, sure. Now that's being supportive. I ask for help here and this is what I get," I said with some anger but more confusion.

"Its hard to be very supportive of someone who is wrong," she patiently explained.

Yeah, well, uh, huh. I knew it would come down to this. Skewered by the truth. It was the truth. My fear led me to over-control. My love led me to overreact. I can't stop my daughter from being different, I can't protect her from the unknown future. All I can do is love her and equip her with the tools of life. Part of those tools included discernment, confidence, faith in God, compassion, service, and discipline. And ultimately *I* needed to trust in God as well.

So, I called her over to apologize and to try to explain my actions. I thanked her for being obedient and I hoped that she understood that even parents make mistakes, and when that happens I believe the parent should make it right and apologize. She listened, and nodded, and seemed saddened about my loss of friends. I told her that her hair was her business and that I was just scared. I still didn't like the cornrows, though. She smiled and said, "That's okay."

She seemed at that moment much wiser than I.

Questions for Discussion

1. What was the "point of logical vulnerability," the subject about which this father had trouble being rational? Why was it a point of logical vulnerability for him?

2. When the author discovered how his emotions blinded his reasoning, how did he remediate his thinking and his behavior?

Ideas for Writing or Speaking

1. Do an exploratory essay or speech on a current problem. List several of the solutions given for this problem and explore the pros and cons of each solution. Some problems you might explore are health care, the creation of a balanced budget, shel-

ters for the homeless, teenage pregnancy, or illegal immigration. You might also want to choose a problem that has emerged on your campus.

Use this format in preparing your speech or essay:

a. Clearly define the problem.

b. Establish criteria for solutions. (For example, consider time and money limits.)

c. Come up with as many alternative solutions as possible. (If you are working in a group, brainstorm about possibilities.)

d. When possible alternatives are exhausted, evaluate each alternative against the criteria for solutions, showing an understanding of diverse viewpoints.

e. Choose the best alternative and explain why this alternative is the best.

2. Rent a copy of the classic film *Twelve Angry Men*. This film depicts the various viewpoints and prejudices of a group of jurors who have to determine the guilt or innocence of a man accused of killing his father. Before viewing the tape, consider the following excerpt.

The drive to help juries make the right decisions is drawing some ideas from human-behavior experts who have amassed a wealth of research on how jurors think. Decades ago, judges and lawyers assumed that jurors heard evidence piecemeal and began to analyze it in earnest only during deliberations. But extensive interviews of jurors in recent years have given rise to the theory that they construct evidence into mental "stories" that incorporate interpretations based on their personal experiences. "Jurors used to be viewed as passive objects," says Valerie Hans, a jury researcher at the University of Delaware. "Now we know they are very active in filling in missing evidence and making inferences." The studies are influencing some judges to give jurors more information about the cases they hear.[90]

After viewing the film, discuss the problems of ethnocentrism and egocentrism that influence the decisions of differ-

[90] Ted Gest with Constance Johnson, "The Justice System: Getting a Fair Trial," *U.S. News and World Report*, May 25, 1992, p. 38.

ent jurors and what arguments help them to be fair to the defendant.

3. Do an analysis of another film that deals with egocentrism or ethnocentrism, or with people's failures at understanding the perspectives of others. Some suggested titles include: *School Ties, To Kill a Mockingbird, The Great Santini, Philadelphia, The Dead Poet's Society, Schlindler's List, Pride and Prejudice, In the Heat of the Night, Guess Who's Coming to Dinner,* and *Gentleman's Agreement.* Explain how the problem of egocentrism, ethnocentrism, defensiveness, or lack of empathy is explored in the film. Then tell how the problem is resolved (or not resolved). Finally, state the applications of the film's theme for similar problems faced by people today.

4. Choose an issue about which you feel strongly and argue for the position that is opposite to your own real beliefs. Construct a persuasive speech or essay on this position, using one of the formats outlined in Chapter 10. Do thorough research on the stand you are defending, and be as convincing as you can.

   In the conclusion of your essay or speech, explain whether this exercise caused you to be more or less convinced about your original position on this issue. What changes, if any, did you make in your perspective concerning this issue?

5. Create a speech or essay on an issue about which you have no strong feelings. Research both sides of the issue and become acquainted with the benefits and shortcomings of each.

   In your discussion of this issue, articulate the conclusions of both sides and the reasons given for each conclusion. Note the strongest and weakest reasons for each side. Point out fallacious reasoning that is used to defend either position. In your conclusion, comment on whether you found either side to be more convincing and why.

CHAPTER TEN

Persuasive Speaking

What's Your Point?
How Do You Sharpen It?

*A critical thinker can organize ideas and
advocate for his or her beliefs.*

This chapter will cover:

◆ The three parts of a persuasive message
◆ Methods of organizing persuasive speeches
◆ Techniques for handling fear of public speaking

Most of this book has focused on evaluating the quality of arguments. As a critical thinker, you need to know what to look for when you read an article, watch a commentator or politician on television, or listen to a speech. Understanding good content in the arguments of others will help you as you make your own arguments, whether they be personal, social, or political. There are several other elements of public speaking that will help you to be more clear and persuasive, and they will be covered in this chapter.

When you present a formal argument, you are giving a persuasive speech with the goal of convincing your audience to accept certain viewpoints and take certain actions. Many of us have a picture of a person who is convincing as someone with *charisma*, an intangible quality that attracts others to them and to their ideas. Some people seem to have this personal power and often we can't explain why.

However, beginning with Aristotle, we have explanations, verified by research, about what makes a clear and convincing argument, and those ideas have formed the recommendations in this book. If you use what you know about the content and organization of a good argument and add some basic tips on public speaking, you can successfully present your ideas to both groups and individuals.

This chapter will explain how to use the principles of argumentation to create formal arguments.

Being an Advocate of Ideas: Communicating Publicly

The primary obstacle to effective public speaking is fear. Research indicates that fear of public speaking is the most common area of concern to Americans, ranking above the fear of spiders and death. When we stand in front of a group, we expose our ideas, our egos, and our bodies to a group of not necessarily sympathetic people. We may shake, quake, or decide to not show up when we are required to speak.

At one East Coast university, every graduate is required to take a basic public speaking class. When the administration discovered many students putting this class off until the last quarter of their senior year, or even not graduating because they refused to take the class, the speech department took action by initiating a special class for those who were terrified of public speaking. The class filled several sections every semester. So if you are experiencing anxiety about speaking and would rather skip this chapter and related assignments, take heart. You aren't alone in these feelings of fear.

It is possible to overcome public speaking fears to a great extent and most students who take a course in public speaking report improvement in their feelings of confidence by the end of a semester. In addition, those who are most afraid often prepare the best and therefore have well-researched and convincing arguments.

The Best Ways to Deal with Fear of Public Speaking

"All the great speakers were bad speakers at first."
Ralph Waldo Emerson, "Power," *The Conduct of Life* (1860)

What would you advise someone who has to give a speech and is feeling terrified? You probably have some techniques you would use, such as breathing deeply to calm yourself or memorizing your opening line to get you started. The basic recommendations of speech professionals are given in this section.

The first way to gain confidence is to choose a topic you believe in. When you really care about your topic (which is most often the case when you take a stand on an issue), you can more easily concentrate on convincing your audience and forget your self-consciousness. Secondly, you need to prepare well; then you can be confident that what you are saying has value to your audience, is solid, and includes relevant information. Preparing involves finding evidence to support your reasons and writing a clear outline of your ideas. You can evaluate evidence you find according to the principles discussed in Chapters 4 and 5, and this chapter will provide you with several organizational patterns for your ideas.

Finally, practice the speech so you know it well. Then, even if your mind goes blank temporarily, your mouth keeps on going. Use brief notes to help you with memory lapses; note cards function as mini security blankets. Number these cards (in case you drop them) and then refer to them only briefly as you speak. Also, get rest before you speak, do whatever relaxation techniques work for you, and concentrate on your audience rather than yourself. Look for friendly faces as you scan the room, and avoid people who look unhappy (unless everyone looks unhappy—then you might need to think about what you might have said to confuse or offend them).

Audience Analysis

One of the essential forms of preparation for a public speech is audience analysis. Knowing your audience gives you an added sense of preparation and familiarity, which reduces your fears of the speaking situation. In addition, you can make the most of your limited time when you know some important facts about your listeners. These include both *demographic* and *situational* factors.

Demographic factors include age, gender, racial and ethnic group, religious affiliations, economic status, occupation, and education. By considering these aspects of the audience, a speaker can plan better. For example, if the audience is made up of 16- to 18-year-old students, they may not be familiar with references to certain terms like "record albums" or to politicians and celebrities from the past. If most of the audience members are fine artists, they may not be as knowledgeable about applications of the Internet technology as would an audience whose business involves the daily use of the Internet. To be sensitive to the makeup of a particular audience, the speaker can research these factors with the person who asked him to speak. Or, a speaker may have an opportunity to interview or poll a sample of audience members.

STOP AND THINK

How could each demographic factor be an important consideration to a persuasive speaker?

Even more important to a persuasive speaker are the situational factors of a given speech: What is the group's interest in the speaker's topic and what is their disposition toward the topic? If a speaker is discussing U.S. involvement in another country's civil war and discovers that the audience knows very little about the situation, then she needs to give more background information. If, on the other hand, this particular audience knows a great deal about the situation, the speaker can use her time more efficiently to press the audience to accept her position about U.S. involvement.

When you consider an audience's disposition toward a persuasive topic, you can classify the audience as *believing, neutral,* or *hostile.* A believing audience agrees with your position on an issue; they don't need to be convinced about the correctness of the actions you propose. To use your time most efficiently with this kind of audience, you should concentrate on getting them to act on any proposals you make. You want to take them from being passive *believers* to active participants in moving policies forward.

A *neutral* audience is one that either does not know enough or does not care enough about your topic to have taken a stand on it. With a neutral audience, you need to provide the information they need to understand the topic and its importance. For example, if you are speaking against a tax reform that is currently under consideration, you can show your audience how the proposed new tax structure will really hurt them personally. Many people are moved primarily by realizing that an issue will directly affect their lives or the lives of their family and friends; show your neutral audience how the position you support will help them maintain or improve their own interests.

A *hostile* audience is one which is opposed to your ideas or policies. They may not shout or throw things at you, but you know that they think you are wrong in the positions you take. Your goals for this kind of an audience have to be much more modest than they would be for a believing audience. Often, the best thing you can do is present yourself and your positions in such a clear, calm, and reasonable way that the audience members can no longer negatively stereotype people who believe as you do. Focus your speech with a hostile audience on their reconsideration of some of their own ideas, rather than trying to move this kind of group to taking action on your ideas.

Hostile audiences often respond well to a persuasive speaking technique called *both-sides persuasion*. A speaker who uses both-sides persuasion will acknowledge the good points that cause his audience to believe as they do, but will then demonstrate how even these good points are overshadowed by the strengths of his side of the issue. For example, if you favor dress codes in local public schools and your audience is against them because they violate personal freedom, you might say the following:

> It seems to go against all of our ideas of freedom of expression and individuality to restrict students to only a few items of clothing. How can they experiment with unique styles that make personal statements when they are forced into one general look? I agree that individuality is an important value and that the solution of dress codes is far from perfect. But I believe that it is the best way we have found so far to safeguard another value, the value of life. Given the fact that teenagers are being killed because they are wearing what appears to be gang colors, and given the fact that several of our youth have been killed over expensive shoes and jackets that the criminals wanted to steal, I believe that any measures taken to guard their safety when they are in the setting of public schools are worth pursuing.

Both-sides persuasion lets your audience know that you have considered their viewpoints, that you agree with some of their principles, but that you have come to a different conclusion about the issue. Most people will be more open to your ideas if they know that you understand and respect their ideas.

When you know the disposition of the majority of your audience members, you can also structure your speech with greater thoughtfulness. Hostile audiences are most likely to be persuaded when you lead off with your strongest points. If you save your most convincing points for later in the speech, you may lose them completely as they argue in their minds with the weaker points they have heard. But if they hear a compelling reason to reconsider their position early on in your speech, then they may continue to listen with a more open mind. Believing audiences, on the other hand, respond well when you reserve your strongest points and end on a climactic note that creates unity and a desire to move forward to enact their beliefs. They like to be affirmed and inspired by an argument that builds from strong support to even stronger support in your final point.

The Three Elements of a Persuasive Argument: Ethos, Logos, and Pathos

Aristotle said that rhetoric (argumentation) involves using all the available means of persuasion, and he defined the means of persuasion as **ethos** (personal credibility), **logos** (logical organization and reasoning), and **pathos** (emotional appeal).

ETHOS: SPEAKER CREDIBILITY

Part of your ethos, your credibility or reputation as a speaker, will come through the same methods that help you to overcome speech fear. When you are well prepared to speak and have conviction about your topic, your audience will give you respect and attention. Speaker credibility can be achieved through specific effort and planning. Speakers are seen as credible when:

- They can be clearly heard by the audience.
- They show that they have done their homework on a topic by using well-cited research to support their key points.
- They are easy to understand because they are well-organized.
- They are easy to understand because they have rehearsed the speech before giving it.
- They show respect for the audience by using language and examples that can be understood (not too complex or too simplified) by the members of that particular audience.
- They reduce nervous, distracting mannerisms to a minimum (this can be done with practice).
- They dress appropriately for the speaking occasion.

When you enhance your credibility with these principles, believing audiences will be affirmed by your message, neutral audiences can be informed and even persuaded, and hostile audiences may be more open to your ideas.

LOGOS: LOGICAL ORGANIZATION AND CREDIBLE CONTENT

There are several traditional ways to support and organize formal speeches. In our time-conscious, media-saturated age, there are also variations to traditional methods of structuring speeches. Regardless of the format you choose, there are some essential ingredients to every organizational pattern that apply whether you have two minutes or twenty minutes to speak. To be a clearly organized speaker, use these principles, illustrated by Figure 10.1:

- Use an interesting introduction to capture the attention of the audience. Decide on your introduction after you structure the body of the speech, so that you know what it is you are introducing!

- Make your conclusion (thesis statement) clear early in the speech, immediately following the introduction.

- Tell the audience how you plan to support your position; list the key points immediately after you state your conclusion. This technique is called the *preview* of your speech.

- Announce/highlight each key point (reason). Figure 10.1 shows that each key point must be supported with evidence. The evidence must be cited (tell us where it comes from—the publication, author, and date). Use this structural outline to see which key points have enough verification and which need more supporting points. Note that each key point should also be strong enough to be a supporting pillar for the thesis statement.

- Use transitions between reasons for a smooth flow of ideas. Note that in Figure 10.1, the transitions flow between key points with a brief reference back to the thesis statement.

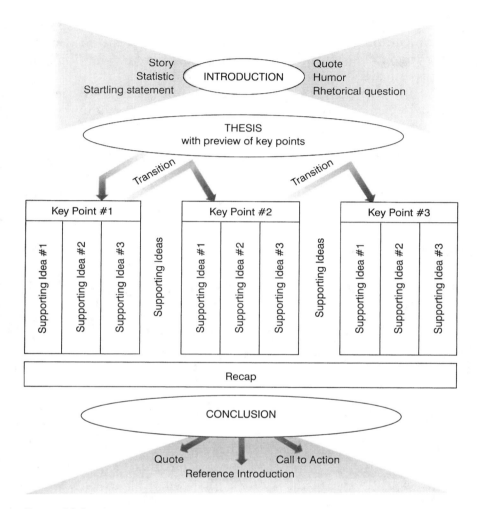

Figure 10.1

- Review your key ideas before making a concluding statement. The repetition of your ideas—first previewed in the introduction, then explained in the body, and finally summarized in the conclusion—helps to reinforce them in the mind of your audience.

As we have discussed, it is often effective to address and calmly refute the arguments for the opposing side of your speech.

Do this *both-sides persuasion* early on, in the body of the speech, if your audience is neutral or hostile to your position. On the other hand, if your audience is supportive of your position concentrate instead on moving them to action.

Several organizational structures are acceptable for the persuasive speech. Three of the most common will be highlighted in this chapter.

The first method is simply a statement of your conclusion followed by key points that are the reasons (support) for the conclusion. This speech is illustrated in Figure 10.1 and is structured as follows:

I. INTRODUCTION

In the introduction, you get the audience's attention and lead into your topic through the use of examples, quotations, statistics, or relevant anecdotes. In the last sentence of your introduction, you state your conclusion (sometimes called a thesis statement) and then preview (tell about) your key points.

II. BODY OF THE SPEECH

While the introduction serves to make a strong statement of your conclusion (thesis), the body of the speech answers the question "Why do you take this position?" The key points are all distinct reasons for drawing your conclusion. Cover each point, being sure to support each point (reason) with cited evidence.

III. CONCLUSION

The conclusion of your speech should include a review of the key points that support your opinion. End the speech with a call to belief or action.

The advantage of this method of presentation is that it is clear and simple; you are, in effect, saying "I believe (*conclusion*) because of these reasons, and you should too!"

Sample Speech Outline:

Mandatory AIDS/HIV Testing in Sports

by Saysana Saycocie

Introduction
Attention Step
I. A recent study reported in the *Washington Post* listed the top concerns of American citizens. An important concern of most Americans, second only to crime, is the AIDS/HIV crisis that we are facing.
   A. Twenty-six percent of American citizens are concerned about contracting this deadly virus, for which there is no known cure.
   These concerns are justified.
      1. *Current Health 2* magazine reported in February 1996, that there are 500,000 people in the United States with full-blown AIDS and that every 9 minutes another American discovers that he or she has AIDS.
      2. Every 15 minutes someone in the United States dies of AIDS.
   B. There is a myth in our culture that intravenous drug users and gay men are the persons primarily at risk for contracting the HIV virus. Contrary to this myth, many heterosexuals, among them prominent athletes, are increasingly contracting this disease.
      1. Former boxer Tommy Morrison recently announced that he has the HIV virus.
      2. Earvin "Magic" Johnson and Greg Louganis are also examples of athletes with the HIV virus.
   C. Because of the increasing frequency with which athletes are contracting this virus, there has been talk among various league executives and athletes about whether to have mandatory AIDS/HIV testing in some of the major contact sports. These sports include boxing, football, basketball, and wrestling.

Thesis Statement/Conclusion
I believe that there is a great need for mandatory testing for the HIV/AIDS virus in contact sports.

Preview
AIDS/HIV testing is needed for several reasons. Testing is needed to stop the spread and minimize the risk of contracting the virus from other athletes. Also, testing is needed to reduce fears and restore confidence among athletes. Finally, AIDS/HIV testing is needed to inform athletes of the status of their health, whether that status is good or bad.

Body:
I.   Mandatory HIV/AIDS testing is needed to stop the spread and minimize the risk of contracting this deadly virus.
   A. Medical experts often talk about "slim chances" or "minimal risk," but no expert has said that you cannot get HIV from participating in a sport from someone who has the HIV virus.
   B. Violence in contact sports make these sports risky, since the virus can be transmitted through blood.
      1. Boxing, for example, can be an extremely violent sport. The force of punches often exposes mucus membranes in the nose and eyes.
      2. Christine Gorman, writing for *Time* magazine in February 1996, discussed a recent case of two brothers, one of whom had advanced AIDS, who got into a violent argument. They repeatedly bashed heads and both bled profusely into each other's eyes and open wounds. After the fight, the previously uninfected brother tested positive for the virus.
   C. The Centers for Disease Control has found football to be another violent sport with potential exchanges of infected blood.
      1. A study was conducted on 11 teams in the National Football League. In 155 games among 538 players, the researchers counted 575 cases of bleeding injuries.
      2. In most of the cases, the players remained drenched in their blood along with the blood of other athletes.

Transition

I have discussed several reasons for acting on the concern about the spread of the HIV/AIDS virus in contact sports. Some people are concerned that privacy rights would be violated by mandatory testing of athletes. However, I believe that the right to health is more important than the right to privacy in this situation.

Athletes face great risk of harm due to the injuries they encounter as part of sports participation. It is not fair to also make them fearful of getting a fatal illness every time they enter a field, court, or ring.

II. Mandatory HIV/AIDS testing is needed to reduce fears and restore confidence for athletes.
   A. Fear of contracting a disease is too big a distraction for an athlete to ignore.
      1. Football, basketball, hockey, and other sports require intense concentration, and the slightest distraction can hinder the performance of an athlete.
      2. People can't perform at their peak if they are worried about getting a virus.
         a. Think about it: Would you go diving after a loose ball and possibly collide into someone who is infected?
   B. In weighing the risks of playing a sport, many good athletes might decide against it.
      1. When it comes to making decisions about my health, if there is a slim or minimal chance of excruciating death, I do not engage in the activity.
      2. Most people don't take unnecessary risks; for example, thoughtful people don't drink and drive.
      3. In the same way, thoughtful athletes will be less interested in engaging in a sport when dangers of fatal illness are increased.

Transition

Our athletes are more than performers paid to entertain audiences. They are also vulnerable human beings who are subject to illness. Uniforms and equipment have been developed to safeguard them from serious injury; in the same way, testing can safeguard them from deadly diseases. Testing would also add to their awareness of danger.

III. Finally, I contend that mandatory HIV/AIDS testing is necessary for athletes so that they can be aware of their own medical condition.
   A. Athletes may have a false sense of invulnerability.
      1. They may equate their physical fitness with a greater resistance to the HIV virus.
      2. Because of the attention showered on athletes, they may lead promiscuous lifestyles and be unaware of the dangers they face.
   B. Mandatory testing would lead to early treatment if a virus was discovered.
      1. Early diagnosis gives the best chance for treatment.
      2. Early diagnosis allows the athlete to better plan the remainder of his life and to decide whether to continue playing.

Conclusion

Today, I have discussed the need to safeguard the health and well-being of athletes through mandatory HIV/AIDS testing.

Review

I have argued that testing would reduce the risk of athletes contracting and spreading the disease, that it would decrease the fears and distractions of athletes as they participate in games, and that it would increase awareness and early detection of disease for members of the athletic community.

Closing Statement

For all of these reasons, mandatory HIV/AIDS testing is needed in contact sports. When athletes know whether they or their team members are positive for HIV or have full-blown AIDS, they can make more informed decisions about their own lives. Then we can address, to some extent, the pervasive fear of the spread of this virus.

BIBLIOGRAPHY

1. Christine Gorman, "Blood, Sweat and Fears," *Time* magazine, February 26, 1996, volume 147, No. 9, page 59.
2. "AIDS Crisis," *Current Health 2*, February, 1996.

3. Dylan Jones, "Magic's Return," *People Daily,* January 31, 1996.
4. Marsha F. Goldsmith, "Health and Human Rights Inseparable," *Journal of the American Medical Association,* August 4, 1993.
5. "What Americans are Concerned About," *Washington Post,* February 20, 1996.

Monroe's Motivated Sequence

A second organizational method is called **Monroe's Motivated Sequence.**[91] This method is very similar to the basic organizational format covered previously. Monroe's steps are especially effective when a speaker wants to motivate the audience to take action. Monroe's sequence involves the following five steps.

1. *Attention:* Get the audience's interest and attention; you can do this with provocative questions, statistics, or a relevant anecdote. End your attention step with your thesis statement (main idea) and a preview of your key ideas. This step is similar to the introduction step of the first method.
2. *Need:* The body of your speech begins with this step. Here you show your audience that a serious problem must be addressed. Discuss the extent and scope of the problem and how we are hurt by the problem.
3. *Satisfaction:* At this point, you present a solution to the problem that was introduced in the need step.
4. *Visualization:* This last part of the body of your speech is used to help listeners form a picture of what it would be like if your solution were in place. If there are aspects of the solution that would be of personal benefit to audience members, visualize those benefits in this step.
5. *Action:* This step is considered the conclusion of the speech. Here you summarize your ideas and request specific action of the audience members.

[91] Allan H. Monroe, *Principles and Types of Speech Communication,* 11th ed. (Glenview, IL: Scott, Foresman, 1990) pp. 180–203.

Problem-Solution Format

A third method of structuring persuasive speeches has been outlined in the *Northern California Forensics Association Handbook.*
This method also follows a problem-solution format.

1. *Introduction:* As in any speech, the introduction to a persuasive speech must put the audience at ease with the topic of the
   speech, must clearly state the purpose of the speech, and must
   give some direction about the course of the speech.

2. *Harms:* The harms section of the speech should answer the
   question, "How are we hurt by this problem?" Financial losses,
   personal injuries, and deaths caused by the problem are often
   detailed in the harms portion.

3. *Inherency:* The inherency section should answer the question,
   "Why does the problem exist?" The reasons for the existence
   of any problem can be categorized as either attitudinal inherency or structural inherency. Attitudinal inherency occurs
   when the sentiments of the public create a barrier to the solution of the issue or when those sentiments help to perpetuate the cause of difficulty. Structural inherency is a physical
   barrier that must be overcome in order to solve the problem.
   Such a barrier could be a law, the lack of trained personnel,
   or an inefficient system.

4. *Significance:* The notion of significance addresses the question,
   "What is the scope of the problem?" Significance is often described by details of the geographic range, quantitative preponderance, or qualitative weight of the problem. More often
   than not, the significance issue is handled within both the
   harms and inherency sections.

5. *Solvency:* This final section is arguably the most important part
   of the persuasive speech. It answers the question, "What can
   be done to remedy the problem?" It is important to address
   two issues within the solvency section. First, be sure to tell
   your audience how they can help specifically. Second, attempt
   to give an example of how your solution has worked in the
   past.

6. *Conclusion:* The conclusion of the persuasive speech should accomplish two goals. It should initially view how the advocated solution steps will affect the problem and it should secondly make one last appeal to the audience.[92]

Pathos: Emotional Appeal

Both positive and negative emotions can influence our thoughts and actions. As critical thinkers, we should be aware of a speaker who uses *only* emotional appeals as reasons for a conclusion. As speakers, we should appeal to our listener's emotions only when we believe it is appropriate and relevant to the issue we are discussing.

Most of the big issues we confront as a society, and many smaller ones, involve deep-seated feelings. Consider the reasons why people are for or against capital punishment, abortion, euthanasia, and a host of environmental issues. If a group is protesting the creation and sale of fur coats, the members of this group most likely feel deeply for the animals who are used to make the coats. On the other hand, those who have spent a lifetime learning to make the coats or who have a family depending on the sale of the coats feel equally strongly about their livelihood. Whatever your position on this issue, you can imagine the personal feelings that accompany advocacy on both sides.

Emotional appeal is important in making issues real for audience members. Hearing statistics about thousands of victims of drunk drivers does not move us as much as hearing the personal story of one victim and his family.

Responsible and effective speakers will use emotional appeal to show us the human impact of an attitude or a policy that needs to be changed. Let's say a speaker wants to persuade his or her audience that homeless individuals who are schizophrenic need to be hospitalized and given treatment. The speaker can and should use logos in the form of statistics, giving the estimated number of homeless who are schizophrenic and the medical

---

[92] Joe Corcoran, *Northern California Forensics Association Handbook* (Northern California Forensics Association, 1988).

needs that they have. However, the factor that will convince the audience to listen, the factor that will highlight the importance of this issue, is likely to come in the form of an emotional appeal. A few case histories of homeless schizophrenics and examples of the problems they face will do much to make an audience receptive to this problem and its possible solution.

Are emotional appeals ethical? Yes, if they are:

1. True and accurate

2. Used with solid reasoning

3. Based on healthy emotions

The third category, healthy emotions, needs to be considered by the speaker. Psychologist Abraham Maslow has suggested that all human beings have the same basic needs, which form the basis of human motivation.[93] When we as speakers or writers want to bring our audience to action, we can appeal to these needs.

The needs are listed in a hierarchy (see Figure 10.2). The lower level needs must be satisfied before people become concerned with higher level needs. We can ethically address *these* needs, using examples that stir the emotions of audience members:

1. *Physical needs:* These include the needs that guarantee our survival as people and as a species, such as food, air, water, rest, and the ability to reproduce.

   Example of use in a speech: Although you can discuss facts about scarcities of food and water in a speech, you also can use emotional appeals by asking your audience to imagine a world in which their children would not have enough food or water to survive. Since we all have the same needs, you can then ask the audience to empathize with people in other nations who are without adequate supplies of food or water.

2. *Safety needs:* These involve the need to be protected from harm to our persons and to have adequate levels of comfort, such as decent housing, safe products, and avoidance of sickness.

---

[93] A. H. Maslow, *Toward a Psychology of Being* (New York: Van Nostrand Reinhold, 1968).

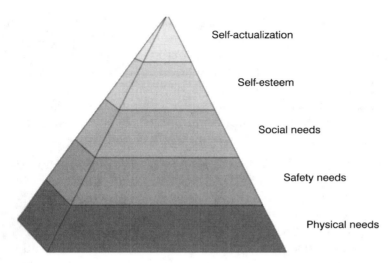

Figure 10.2

Examples of use in a speech: Speakers can legitimately use emotional appeals, such as graphic examples of accidents that have occurred at a dangerous intersection when they are advocating for a needed stoplight. They can tell about children who died or were disabled from faulty toys that should be recalled. They can describe the fear of those who live near "crack houses" to emphasize the need for more effective neighborhood law enforcement.

3. *Social needs:* These needs involve our desires to form alliances with others, to be included in group interactions, and to have close friends who love and respect us.

    Examples of use in a speech: Speakers can give examples of children with AIDS who have not been included in their peer groups as part of a speech on their need for acceptance in the community. Speakers promoting a social cause sometimes appeal to audience members' social needs by offering some form of group identification to them; for example, the Comic Relief fundraisers for the homeless offer T-shirts to contributing audience members.

4. *Self-esteem needs:* These needs concern our desire to feel like worthwhile, contributing members of society, whose lives have meaning and purpose.

Examples of use in a speech: Speakers can appeal to our altruism in helping others in need, which in turn gives us a feeling of making an important contribution. They also can help us to empathize with those whose professions are worthy of more respect than they are generally given, such as homemakers, preschool teachers, and mechanics. Seminar leaders often motivate audience members by promising to give them skills that will help them be more effective workers.

5. *Self-actualization needs:* When the basic needs are met, people are motivated to develop various potentials, to expand their horizons by trying new things or by becoming better at familiar skills. Included in the need for personal development is gaining a greater understanding of spiritual matters.

Examples of use in a speech: Speakers can appeal to audience members' desires to become more well-rounded by using examples of people who have taken on new professions or challenges late in life. They can describe the thrill of an outdoor adventure when encouraging audience members to buy a vacation package.

REMINDER
Use emotional appeals sparingly, as a means of getting your audience's attention and of highlighting important points.

EXERCISE

Purpose: To incorporate the knowledge of pathos into the writing of a speech.

Take each of Maslow's needs and write your own examples of how they could be incorporated into a speech as an emotional appeal.

EXERCISE

Purpose: To recognize the use of pathos in a speech.

Write or tell about a speech you heard that included an effective appeal to emotion. You might use the following format:

1. Explain the issue and the conclusion of the speaker.
2. Discuss the audience's predisposition to the speech and the speaker.
3. Explain how, specifically, the speaker used the appeal to emotion. Was it a story, an example, a personal testimony?
4. Talk about the placement of the appeal to emotion. Did it come in the introduction, body, or conclusion of the speech, or was it referred to throughout the speech?
5. Summarize your reasons for finding this appeal effective. Then comment on whether you felt the appeal was ethical.

Chapter Highlights

1. A critical thinker considers the best ways to organize and present ideas in order to be a strong advocate for an issue.
2. The best ways to deal with fear of public speaking are to choose an issue of interest to you, prepare thoroughly, and practice.
3. Good persuasive speakers analyze their audiences before preparing their speeches. Audiences may be believing, neutral, or hostile.
4. Ethos, the credibility of the speaker, is an important element of persuasion. Ethos is enhanced by the obvious preparation of the speaker and the manner in which he or she presents the speech.
5. Logos, the content and organization of the speech, is crucial to a persuasive message. Several organizational structures can be used to enhance the clarity and persuasiveness of a speech.
6. Pathos, emotional appeal, is powerful in its ability to persuade and should be used ethically.

Articles for Discussion

I am at the boiling point! If I do not find some day the use of my tongue . . . I shall die of an intellectual repression, a woman's rights convulsion.

Elizabeth Cady Stanton, in a letter to Susan B. Anthony

Speak for Yourself

by **Susan Faludi**
New York Times Magazine

"Oh, and then you'll be giving that speech at the Smithsonian Tuesday on the status of American women," my publisher's publicist reminded me as she rattled off the list of "appearances" for the week.

"What?" I choked out. "I thought that was at least another month away."

But the speech was distant only in my wishful consciousness, which pushed all such events into a mythical future when I would no longer lunge for smelling salts at the mention of public speaking.

For the author of what was widely termed an "angry" and "forceful" book, I exhibit a timorous verbal demeanor that belies my barracuda blurbs.

My fingers may belt out my views when I'm stationed before the computer, but stick a microphone in front of me and I'm a Victorian lady with the vapors.

Like many female writers with strong convictions but weak stomachs for direct confrontation, I write so forcefully precisely because I speak so tentatively.

One form of self-expression has overcompensated for the weakness of the other, as a blind person develops a hypersensitive ear.

"Isn't it wonderful that so many people want to hear what you have to say about women's rights?" the publicist prodded. I grimaced. "About as wonderful as walking down the street with no clothes on."

Yes, I wanted people to hear what I had to say. Yes, I wanted to warn women of the backlash to our modest gains. But couldn't they just read what I wrote? Couldn't I just speak softly and carry a big book?

It has taken me a while to realize that my publicist is right. It's not the same—for my audience or me.

Public speech can be a horror for the shy person, but it can also be the ultimate act of liberation. For me, it became the moment where the public and the personal truly met.

For many years, I believed the imbalance between my incensed writing and my atrophied vocal cords suited me just fine.

After a few abysmal auditions for school plays—my one role was Nana the dog in "Peter Pan," not a speaking role—I retired my acting aspirations and retreated to the school newspaper, a forum where I could bluster at injustices large and small without public embarrassment.

My friend Barbara and I co-edited the high school paper (titled, interestingly, *The Voice*), fearlessly castigating all scoundrels from our closet-size office. But we kept our eyes glued to the floor during class discussion.

Partly this was shyness, a genderless condition. But it was a condition reinforced by daily gendered reminders—we saw what happened to the girls who argued in class. The boys called them "bitches" and they sat home Saturday nights.

Popular girls raised their voices only at pep squad.

Whereas both sexes fear public speaking (pollsters tell us it's the public's greatest fear, rivaling even death), women—particularly women challenging the status quo—seem to be more afraid and with good reason.

We do have more at stake. Men risk loss of face, women a loss of femininity.

Men are chagrined if they blunder at the podium; women face humiliation either way. If we come across as commanding, our womanhood is called into question. If we reveal emotion, we are too hormonally driven to be taken seriously.

I had my own taste of this double standard while making the rounds of radio and television talk shows for a book tour. When I disputed a point with a man, male listeners would often phone in to say they found my behavior "offensive" or even "unattractive."

And then there were my own internalized "feminine" voices: Don't interrupt, be agreeable, keep the volume down.

"We're going to have to record that again," a weary radio producer said, rewinding the tape for the fifth time. "Your words are angry, but it's not coming through in your voice."

In replacing lacerating speech with a literary scalpel, I had adopted a well-worn female strategy, used most famously by Victorian female reformers protesting slavery and women's lowly status.

"I want to be doing something with the pen, since no other means of action in politics are in a woman's power," Harriet Martineau, the British journalist, wrote in 1832.

But although their literature makes compelling reading, the suffrage movement didn't get under way until women took a public stand from the platform of the Seneca Falls Women's Rights Convention.

And while Betty Friedan's 1963 *The Feminine Mystique* raised the consciousness of millions of women, the contemporary women's movement began to affect social policy only when Friedan and other feminists started addressing the public.

Public speech is a more powerful stimulus because it is more dangerous for the speaker. An almost physical act, it demands projecting one's voice, hurling it against the public ear.

Writing, on the other hand, occurs at one remove. The writer asserts herself from behind the veil of the printed page.

The dreaded evening of the Smithsonian speech finally arrived. I stood knock-kneed and green-gilled before 300 people. Was it too late to plead a severe case of laryngitis? I am Woman, hear me whisper.

I cleared my throat and, to my shock, a hush fell over the room. People were listening—with an intensity that strangely emboldened me.

It was as if their attentive silence allowed me to make contact with my own muffled self. I began to speak. A stinging point induced a ripple of agreement. I told a joke and they laughed.

My voice got surer, my delivery rising. A charge passed between me and the audience, uniting and igniting us both.

That internal "boiling point" that Elizabeth Cady Stanton described was no longer under "intellectual repression." And its heat, I discovered, could set many kettles to whistling.

Afterward it struck me that in some essential way I hadn't really proved myself a feminist until now.

Until you translate personal words on a page into public connections with other people, you aren't really part of a political movement.

I hadn't declared my independence until I was willing to declare it out loud. I knew public speaking was important to reform public life—but I hadn't realized the transformative effect it could have on the speaker herself.

Women need to be heard not just to change the world, but to change themselves.

I can't say that this epiphany has made me any less anxious when approaching the lectern. But it has made me more determined to speak in spite of the jitters—and more hopeful that other women will do the same.

Toward that end I'd like to make a modest proposal for the next stage of the women's movement. A new method of consciousness-raising: Feminist Toastmasters.

Questions for Discussion

1. Comment on the following statement by the author of this article: "Public speech can be a horror for the shy person, but it can also be the ultimate act of liberation." How can public speaking, even when we dread it, be liberating?
2. The author states, "Until you translate personal words on a page into public connections with other people, you aren't really part of a political movement." To what extent do you believe that speaking is essential for those involved with political, social, and religious movements?

Changing a Man's Mind

Anonymous, given as a conference handout at the Seventh Annual and Fifth International Conference on Critical Thinking and Educational Reform

Thomas Aquinas, who knew more about education and persuasion than almost anybody who ever lived, once said that when you want to convert someone to your view, you go over to where he is standing, take him by the hand (mentally speaking), and guide him to where you want him to go.

You don't stand across the room and shout at him. You don't call him a dummy. You don't order him to come over to where you are. You start where he is, and work from that position. That's the only way to get him to budge.

We have lost sight of this elementary psychological fact. The world is full of passionate advocates, screaming their own prejudices, and excoriating their opponents.

This does three things: (a) it makes the people who agree with you feel better, (b) it makes the people who disagree with you stiffen their resistance, and (c) it makes the people on the fence uneasy and skeptical that you are speaking the whole truth.

I have never known a single passionate and partisan argument to win over a person who disagreed with it, or even to persuade a person who was neutral on the subject. The chief reason being that all passionate and partisan arguments overstate their case and understate their opponents' case.

When you think that someone is wrong, and you disagree with him, the first task is to determine in what way he is right. This is not as paradoxical as it sounds: No view can be entirely wrong, and everybody has a little piece of truth by the tail. This is the piece we start with, we work from there, and concede as much as we honestly can.

Lord Acton said that we have no right to oppose a position until we can state that position in a way that fully satisfies those who hold it; until, indeed, we can make out a better case for it than the proponent himself can. (Most of us, of course, distort or lampoon the opposite position, and then proceed to demolish this straw man.)

And all this is much more than an academic exercise. The arts of argument and persuasion are so little known and practiced that disputants have no recourse to anything but violence. If people can't agree on how to disagree, there is no hope of reconciliation or compromise. And the art of argument is learning how to disagree productively.

We begin to fight when words fail us. And words fail us when we use the wrong ones to the wrong people for the wrong reasons.

It is far easier to be passionate in defense of what one believes than to comprehend why somebody believes something different. But, ultimately, only this comprehension (which is not agreement) can replace violence with dialog instead of the deafening monologues that lead to war.

Questions for Discussion

1. Comment on the following statement from this essay: "I have never known a single passionate and partisan argument to win over a person who disagreed with it, or even to persuade a person who was neutral on the subject. The chief reason being that all passionate and partisan arguments overstate their case and understate their opponent's case." Have you found that people who argue passionately overstate their own case and understate their opponent's case? Can you think of examples of this overstatement and understatement?

2. Can someone be persuasive and passionate and still be fair to the other side of the argument? If so, how? If not, why not?

3. Think of an issue that concerns you deeply. Can you see the "piece of truth" held by the other side? How could you use that

truth to persuade your opponent to consider the value of your position?

Dr. Martin Luther King used ethos, logos, and pathos in the following speech, which is considered a classic modern American address. He spoke at a time when segregation was still the law in many states. Although he was directly addressing the crowd gathered in Washington, D.C., he was also aware of the larger audience, much of which was hostile, that was being reached through print and electronic media. No one could have foretold the dramatic and historic effect that this speech would have for decades to come.

I Have a Dream

by Dr. Martin Luther King
Delivered at the People's March on Washington, 1963.

I am happy to join with you today in what will go down in history as the greatest demonstration for freedom in the history of our nation.

Five score years ago, a great American, in whose symbolic shadow we stand today, signed the Emancipation Proclamation. This momentous decree came as a great beacon light of hope to millions of Negro slaves, who had been seared in the flames of withering injustice. It came as a joyous daybreak to end the long night of their captivity.

But one hundred years later, the Negro is still not free. One hundred years later, the life of the Negro is still sadly crippled by the manacles of segregation and the chains of discrimination. One hundred years later, the Negro lives on a lonely island of poverty in the midst of a vast ocean of material prosperity. One hundred years later, the Negro is still languished in the corners of American society and finds himself an exile in his own land. So we have come here today to dramatize a shameful condition.

In a sense we've come to our nation's Capital to cash a check. When the architects of our republic wrote the magnificent words of the Constitution and the Declaration of Independence, they were signing a promissory note to which every American was to fall heir. This note was a promise that all men—yes, black men as well as white men—would be guaranteed the unalienable rights of life, liberty, and the pursuit of happiness.

It is obvious today that America has defaulted on this promissory note insofar as her citizens of color are concerned. Instead of honoring this sacred obligation, America has given the Negro people a bad check; a check which has come back marked "insufficient funds." But we refuse to believe that the bank of justice is bankrupt. We refuse to believe that there are insufficient funds in the great vaults of opportunity of this nation. So we've come to cash this check—a check that will give us upon demand the riches of freedom and the security of justice. We have also come to this hallowed spot to remind America of the fierce urgency of now. This is no time to engage in the luxury of cooling off or to take the tranquilizing drug of gradualism. Now is the time to make real the promises of Democracy. Now is the time to rise from the dark and desolate valley of segregation to the sunlight of racial justice. Now is the time to lift our nation from the quicksands of racial injustice to the solid rock of brotherhood. Now is the time to make justice a reality for all of God's children.

It would be fatal for the nation to overlook the urgency of the moment. This sweltering summer of the Negro's legitimate discontent will not pass until there is an invigorating autumn of freedom and equality. Nineteen sixty-three is not an end, but a beginning. Those who hope that the Negro needed to blow off steam and will not be content will have a rude awakening if the nation returns to business as usual. There will be neither rest nor tranquillity in America until the Negro is granted his citizenship rights. The whirlwinds of revolt will continue to shake the foundations of our nation until the bright day of justice emerges.

But there is something that I must say to my people who stand on the warm threshold which leads into the palace of justice. In the process of gaining our rightful place we must not be guilty of wrongful deeds. Let us not seek to satisfy our thirst for freedom by drinking from the cup of bitterness and hatred.

We must forever conduct our struggle on the high plane of dignity and discipline. We must not allow our creative protest to degenerate into physical violence. Again and again we must rise to the majestic heights of meeting physical force with soul force. The marvelous new militancy which has engulfed the Negro community must not lead us to distrust of all white people, for many of our white brothers, as evidenced by their presence here today, have come to realize that their destiny is tied up with our destiny. And they have come to realize that their freedom is inextricably bound to our freedom. We cannot walk alone.

And as we walk, we must make the pledge that we shall always march ahead. We cannot turn back. There are those who ask the devotees of civil rights, "When will you be satisfied?" We can never be satisfied as long as the Negro is the victim of the unspeakable horrors of police brutality. We can never be satisfied as long as our bodies, heavy with the fatigue of travel, cannot gain lodging in the motels of the highways and the hotels of the cities. We cannot be satisfied as long as the Negro's basic mobility is from a smaller ghetto to a larger one. We can never be satisfied as long as our children are stripped of their selfhood and robbed of their dignity by signs stating "For Whites Only." We cannot be satisfied as long as a Negro in Mississippi cannot vote and a Negro in New York believes he has nothing for which to vote. No, no, we are not satisfied, and we will not be satisfied until justice rolls down like waters and righteousness like a mighty stream.

I am not unmindful that some of you have come here out of great trials and tribulations. Some of you have come fresh from narrow jail cells. Some of you have come from areas where your quest for freedom left you battered by the storms of persecution and staggered by the winds of police brutality. You have been the veterans of creative suffering. Continue to work with the faith that unearned suffering is redemptive.

Go back to Mississippi, go back to Alabama, go back to South Carolina, go back to Georgia, go back to Louisiana, go back to the slums and ghettos of our northern cities knowing that somehow this situation can and will be changed. Let us not wallow in the valley of despair.

I say to you today, my friends, so even though we face the difficulties of today and tomorrow, I still have a dream. It is a dream deeply rooted in the American dream.

I have a dream that one day this nation will rise up and live out the true meaning of its creed: "We hold these truths to be self-evident; that all men are created equal."

I have a dream that one day on the red hills of Georgia the sons of former slaves and the sons of former slaveowners will be able to sit down together at the table of brotherhood.

I have a dream that one day even the state of Mississippi, a state sweltering with the heat of oppression, will be transformed into an oasis of freedom and justice.

That my four little children will one day live in a nation where they will not be judged by the color of their skin but by the content of their character; I have a dream today.

I have a dream that one day down in Alabama, with its vicious racists, with its governor having his lips dripping with the words of interposition and nullification, one day right there in Alabama little black boys and black girls will be able to join hands with little white boys and white girls as sisters and brothers; I have a dream today.

I have a dream that one day every valley shall be exalted, every hill and mountain shall be made low, and rough places will be made plane and crooked places will be made straight, and the glory of the Lord shall be revealed, and all flesh shall see it together.

This is our hope. This is the faith that I go back to the South with. With this faith we will be able to hew out of the mountain of despair a stone of hope. With this faith we will be able to transform the jangling discords of our nation into a beautiful symphony of brotherhood. With this faith we will be able to work together, to pray together, to struggle together, to go to jail together, to stand up for freedom together, knowing that we will be free one day.

This will be the day—this will be the day when all of God's children will be able to sing with new meaning "My country 'tis of thee, sweet land of liberty, of thee I sing. Land where my fathers died, land of the pilgrim's pride, from every mountainside, let freedom ring." And if America is to be a great nation, this must become true.

So let freedom ring from the prodigious hilltops of New Hampshire. Let freedom ring from the mighty mountains of New York. Let freedom ring from the heightening Alleghenies of Pennsylvania!

Let freedom ring from the snowcapped Rockies of Colorado!

Let freedom ring from the curvaceous slopes of California!

But not only that; let freedom ring from Stone Mountain of Georgia!

Let freedom ring from Lookout Mountain of Tennessee!

Let freedom ring from every hill and mole hill of Mississippi. From every mountainside let freedom ring.

And when this happens, when we allow freedom to ring—when we let it ring from every village and every hamlet, from every state and every city—we will be able to speed up that day when all of God's children, black men and white men, Jews and Gentiles, Protestants and Catholics, will be able to join hands and sing in the words of the old Negro spiritual, "Free at last! Free at last! Thank God almighty, we are free at last!"

Reprinted by arrangement with The Heirs to the Estate of Martin Luther King, Jr., c/o Writers House, Inc. as agent for the proprietor.

Copyright 1963 by Martin Luther King, Jr., copyright renewed 1991 by Coretta Scott King.

Questions for Discussion

1. How did Dr. King use the principles given in the essay "Changing a Man's Mind" to persuade his listeners?
2. How did Dr. King use ethos, logos, and pathos in this speech?
3. What aesthetic elements were used to create a unified, eloquent whole?

Ideas for Speaking or Writing

1. Speaking to an audience at Brown University, Dr. King's daughter Yolanda King stressed that our nation is still plagued by violence, racism, sexism, poverty, homelessness, hunger, drugs, and illiteracy. "We have not reached the promised land," King lamented. "That dream dreamed by my father is still a dream. We must continue to reach for solutions to remedy these ills." . . . Yolanda King's speech received the most response when she directed her message to Brown students in particular. "In every nook and cranny of university life, you can make a difference," she said.[94]

   Dr. King's speech seemed to set the criteria for reaching the "promised land." Write a speech or an essay about what needs to be done in order for us to build the kind of society that was modeled in the "I have a dream" speech.

2. Putting It All Together

   Create a persuasive speech using one of the three methods of organization. Consider methods of increasing personal credibility that are covered in the ethos section. Include emotional appeals and solid research. Use the following suggestions to guide your preparation. Do a structural outline, like the one illustrated in Figure 10.1, as you complete the following steps:

   • Choose an issue that concerns you. You can try to persuade your audience about a factual issue (Caffeine is/is not bad for your heart), an issue of value (It is/is not wrong for couples to live together before marriage), or a policy issue (Ruling by instant replay rather than by the calls of referees and umpires should/should not be mandatory in televised sporting events).

   • Take a stand (conclusion) on your issue and support your stand with at least three reasons.

---

[94] Linda Sharaby, "King Urges Realizing the Dream," *The Brown Daily Herald,* March 17, 1995.

- Give evidence to support your reasons; use evidence in the form of statistics, studies, authoritative testimony, and examples. You may also interview an expert about your issue. Be sure to give the source and the date when you cite evidence in the speech. Strive to keep your evidence current and turn in an outline and a bibliography on the day of your speech.

- Think about evidence that opponents to your position might offer. Within the body of your speech, discuss the opposing viewpoint and why it is not as sound as your own.

- Add emotional appeal through anecdotes, examples, or personal testimony.

- Begin the speech with a story, statistic, or quote that gets the audience's attention and explains the importance of your issue.

- Close by repeating the issue, your conclusion, and your reasons. End with a strong quote, a reference back to the introductory story, or other reminder to the audience of how they should believe or act now that they have this information.

- Begin planning your speech as soon as it is assigned to you so that you have time to find evidence, get organized, and practice before the due date. Rehearse the speech so that you feel comfortable looking up at the audience, and make your delivery conversational. Also, practice handling questions with friends or family members before you give the speech.

3 Find an issue of the journal *Vital Speeches* in your college or community library. Choose a speech that interests you and analyze it, using the following questions as a guide:

- What were the interests and concerns of the audience the speaker was addressing? Was the audience supportive, neutral, or hostile to the speaker's position? How well did the speaker adapt to his or her audience?

- What were the issue and conclusion of the speaker?

- How did the speaker use ethos, logos, and pathos to be persuasive? In what areas could the speaker have improved the speech?

- Were the reasons given to support the conclusion backed up by solid evidence? Were these the best reasons given?

- Did the speaker address opposing viewpoints in any way? Did the speaker refute the important points of the opposition in a fair and appropriate manner?

- Were there any fallacies in the reasoning of the speaker? Were the studies and experts cited clear and convincing?

- Were there aesthetic elements that helped the speech to be tightly woven and eloquent? Did the speaker use language elements, such as repetition or beautiful prose, to make his or her points? Did the speaker use the conclusion to refer back to attention-getting points made in the introduction?

- What is your overall impression of this speech?

4. Listen to a persuasive speech or sermon or watch one on television (if you get C-SPAN, you might be able to listen to a speech presented before Congress, the National Press Club, or another organization). Then analyze the speech, using the following suggestions:
   a. What were the speaker's issue, conclusion, and reasons?
   b. Was the audience for this speaker supportive of, neutral, or hostile to his or her ideas?
   c. To what extent did the speaker use ethos to establish credibility, logos to support his or her conclusion, and pathos to appeal to the audience's emotions?
   d. How did the speaker introduce and conclude the speech? Were there clear transitions throughout the speech? Give specific examples of these.
   e. Were you persuaded in any way by this speech? Explain why or why not.
   f. If you were hired as a consultant to this speaker, what advice would you give to improve his or her speaking?

Glossary

Active listening—Paraphrasing the thoughts of the speaker with the aim of empathic understanding of his or her viewpoint.

Ad hominem—A Latin term meaning "to the man" or attacking the person. Ad hominem occurs when a person is attacked on a personal quality that is irrelevant to the issue under discussion.

Ad populum fallacy—A fallacy that consists of a false appeal to the authority of "everyone." This fallacy is based on the assumption that a course of action should be taken or an idea should be supported because "everyone" is doing it or believes it.

Ambiguous—Having two or more possible meanings. Ambiguity in language occurs when the meaning of words is unclear or uncertain; such ambiguity can lead to confusion and misunderstanding.

Analogy—Explanation of one idea, object, process, or policy by comparing it to another, similar idea, object, process, or policy. Analogies are used to strengthen inductive arguments.

Appeal to tradition—A fallacy that occurs when a belief or action is supported on the grounds that it conforms to traditional ideas or practices.

Assumption—A belief, usually taken for granted, that is based on the experience, observations, or desires of an individual or group.

Audience analysis—A careful consideration of the demographic and situational factors of an audience in preparation for a speech to that audience.

Begging the question—A fallacy that occurs when a speaker or writer assumes what needs to be proven.

Biased—A sample that does not reflect a random, representative population. A biased sample does not provide adequate evidence to support a conclusion.

Causal generalizations—Generalizations based on causal factors, i.e. that state that a particular factor is responsible for a specific effect. These generalizations are used to strengthen inductive arguments.

Certainty—The certainty of the conclusion in a deductive argument is established when the argument contains true premises (reasons) which are stated in the correct form; when the argument has formal validity and true premises, it is impossible for the conclusion to be false.

Characteristic of interest—The specific question that a reseacher seeks to answer concerning a given population.

Claim—A statement or conclusion about an issue which is either true or false. The advocate for a claim will seek to prove the truth of the claim through evidence.

Cognitive dissonance—A theory that states that the need for congruence (consonance, harmony) is not only a human need but a drive, just as powerful as our drive for food and water. We are motivated by this drive and so we either try to understand or rationalize incongruence between beliefs and actions.

Conclusion—A position taken about an issue, also called a claim or an opinion.

Connotation—All the images—positive, negative, or neutral—that are associated with any given denotation by an individual or a group. The connotations of words include their emotional meanings. Both concrete and abstract words have connotations that are different for different individuals.

Control—The process of weeding out extraneous factors that could affect the outcome of a study between two groups of subjects in which one is exposed to a variable and the other is not.

Control group—A group of subjects from the sample who are not exposed to a variable created by the researcher.

Controlled studies—Research involving specific methods for comparing groups of subjects, in which one is exposed to a variable (or suspected causal factor) and the other is not. Controlled studies should be designed so that they can be duplicated (and verified or disproven) by other researchers.

Correlation—A relationship or connection between two objects or events. Noting a correlation is sometimes the first step in exploring causation.

Credibility—The *ethos* or believability of a speaker; the reliability of an expert or a study.

Critical thinker—Someone who uses specific criteria to evaluate reasoning and make decisions.

Data—The observations made and information collected by the researcher as he or she completes a study.

Deductive argument—An argument that follows formal patterns of reasoning and is aimed at establishing the certainty of a conclusion through presenting true premises in valid form.

Deductive certainty—*See* Certainty.

Defense mechanisms—Techniques aimed at self-protection through the avoidance of unpleasant realities.

Denial—A state of mind that blocks critical thinking by the repression of or refusal to recognize any negative or threatening information.

Denotation—The specific object or action that a word points to refers to, or indicates.

Double-blind study—A study in which neither the experimenter nor the subjects know which is the control group and which is the experimental group.

Doublespeak—Language used to lie or mislead while pretending to tell the truth. Doublespeak includes the use of *euphemism, jargon, gobbledegook,* and *weasel words.*

Egalitarianism—A belief system in which behavior is ethical when the same opportunities and consequences apply to all people.

Egocentrism—The individual version of ethnocentrism, which has been defined as a tendency to view everything else in relationship to oneself; one's desires, values, and beliefs seem to be self-evidently correct or superior to those of others.

Either-or fallacy—Polarizing a situation by presenting only two alternatives, at two extremes of the spectrum of possibilities; also called *False Dilemma.*

Empathy—The ability to understand another person's thoughts and emotions concerning an issue.

Enthymeme—A syllogism with a key part or parts implied rather than directly stated.

Ethics—Standards of conduct reflecting what we consider to be right or wrong behavior.

Ethnocentrism (sociocentrism)—The tendency to view one's own race or culture as central, based on the deep-seated belief that one's own group is superior to all others.

Ethos—One's credibility or reputation as a speaker; ethos is one of three persuasive elements of public speaking, along with *logos* and *pathos.*

Euphemism—The use of a less direct but softer or more acceptable term to describe an event, person, or object.

Expert—An individual who has education, significant experience, or both in a given area. The testimony of experts is used to support conclusions in arguments.

Experimental group—A group of subjects from the sample who are exposed to a variable created by the researcher.

Expert—An individual who has education, significant experience, or both in a given area.

Fairmindedness—A trait of a critical thinker involving respect for others, willingness to hear and understand different viewpoints on an issue, and an openness to change when new information or insight warrants that change.

Fairness Doctrine—A policy by which broadcasters must allow equal air time for all sides of an issue.

Fallacies—Errors in reasoning. Fallacies can be seen as (1) reasons that seem logical but don't necessarily support the conclusion, or (2) statements that distract listeners from the real issue.

False cause (also called **Post Hoc** or **Post Hoc Ergo Proctor Hoc**)—A fallacy that occurs when there is no real proof that one event caused another event; there is only evidence that one event came after another event.

False dilemma (either-or fallacy)—An error in reasoning that occurs when one polarizes a situation by presenting only two alternatives, at two extremes of the spectrum of possibilities.

Faulty analogies—Comparisons between one situation or idea to another which disregard significant differences that make this comparision invalid.

Framing—The deliberate or unconscious use of camera shots to influence audiences; also, the use of a number of techniques by journalists and broadcasters to create a particular impression of reality.

General semanticists—Individuals who study the effects of words on people.

Gestalt principle—A principle that states that our minds strive toward congruence and completion of information. If a message strikes us as incomplete, we will fill in the missing details ourselves.

Gobbledygook—Vague or inflated language used to confuse and overwhelm those who hear it.

Hasty conclusion—A fallacy in which a generalization is drawn from a small and thus inadequate sample of information.

Higher principles test—The test by which one determines if the principle on which you are basing an action is consistent with a higher or more general principle you accept.

Hypothesis—A speculation about what will be discovered from a research study.

Ideal value—A value considered to be right and good.

Indexing—A process by which one takes a general label (women, Catholics, Asians, Americans) and changes it to actual people. By indexing one effectively deletes the word *all* when it precedes a general category, since one can never know *all* about any given group.

Induction—The process of drawing generalizations from known facts or research to give strength and support to conclusions.

Issue—The question or subject under discussion.

Jargon—Specialized language sometimes used to exclude or impress people who don't understand the terminology.

Judeo-Christian Principles—Ethical behavior based on biblical principles found in the Ten Commandments and other prescriptions and on the desire to please and honor God.

Libertarianism—A system in which behavior is considered ethical when it both allows for one's individual freedom and does not restrict the freedom of others.

Logos—Logical organization and credible content in a speech; logos is one of three persuasive elements of public speaking, along with *ethos* and *pathos*.

Margin of error—A statistical range qualifying the limits of a survey's conclusion; the margin of error decreases as the random, representative sample of the population increases.

Method of agreement—A theory of causation postulating that the cause of an effect is found by noting that **x** is the only factor always present when **y** (the problem or the good effect) occurs; therefore, **x** causes **y.**

Method of difference—A theory of causation postulating that the cause of an effect is found by noting that the only difference between the event or effect (called **y**) happening or not happening is whether one element - **x** - is present.

Monroe's Motivated Sequence—A five-step method of organizing speeches; the steps include the introduction, harms, inherency, significance, and solvency.

Morals—Principles of conduct which distinguish right from wrong behavior; see also Ethics.

Multiple causes—A combination of causes which are presumed to lead to a specific effect.

Necessary condition—A condition (state of affairs, thing, process, etc.) that must be present if a particular effect is present. Equivalently, if the necessary condition is absent, then the effect cannot occcur.

New cases test—A test that asks you to consider whether your action is consistent with other actions in the same category.

Opinion leaders—People who are well informed, often through the media, about specific information and issues.

Pathos—The use of emotional appeal to support conclusions; pathos is one of three persuasive elements of public speaking, along with *ethos* and *logos*.

Placebo—A sugar pill or other benign treatment given to a control group when another group is given the treatment the researcher wishes to explore.

Points of logical vulnerability—Topics about which a person has difficulty being rational or objective.

Post hoc—*See* False cause.

Premise of contention—The premise of a deductive argument which is under dispute.

Projection—The process of assuming that what another person means is what we would mean if we had used the same words; this definition of the term is used by people who study communications and semantics and differs from the definition used in psychology.

Protocol—The design of a controlled research study.

Rationalization—A defense mechanism that underlies many others; it is our way of justifying or making sense of things that don't make sense and explaining things away that should be brought under examination.

Real value—A value considered to be right and good and that is acted upon in one's life.

Reality assumptions—Assumptions about what is true and factual.

Reasoning by analogy—Comparing one idea or plan to another for the purpose of supporting a conclusion. When we reason by analogy, we assume that since an idea, process, or event is similar in one way to another idea, process, or event that it is also similar in another significant way.

Reasons—Statements that provide support for conclusions.

Red herring fallacy—A fallacy in which reasons offered to support conclusions lead the listener away from the issue under consideration.

Reification—A process that occurs when words become more powerful and real than objective reality.

Role exchange test—A test which asks you to empathize with the people who will be affected by any action you take.

Romancing the product—A technique used by advertisers in which consumers are influenced to associate a product with something bigger, better, or more interesting.

Sample—Members of the target population who are studied by a researcher.

Self-fulfilling prophecy—A process whereby an expectation becomes a reality.

Semantic differential—A tool that allows semanticists to assess the cultural connotations of a word.

Semantic devices—Tools created by general semanticists which help people make their words more accurately reflective of reality.

Sensationalism—A method used to attract viewers by presenting more exciting stories over less exciting but perhaps more newsworthy ones; the most bizarre, visually interesting, or *sensational* elements of these stories are featured.

Slippery slope fallacy—A fallacy that occurs when serious consequences of a potential act are predicted and not substantiated by evidence.

Sound argument—A valid deductive argument whose premises are true.

Sound bite—An excerpt from a speech or report which is presented as summarizing, but which actually may distort the sentiments of the speaker or writer.

Statistical evidence—Data collected by specific methods that have been found to be reliable.

Statistical generalizations—Inferences drawn from statistical evidence that are used to give strength to an inductive argument.

Subjects—People or animals studied to get information about a target population.

Subliminal persuasion—Information meant to affect people on an unconscious level, some of which can be detected with training and some of which cannot be detected with the conscious mind, regardless of training. The existence and effectiveness of this latter form of subliminal persuasion remains under dispute.

Sufficient condition—A condition (state of affairs, thing, process, etc.) that automatically leads to the production of another event. If the condition is present, then the effect will definitely occur. The sufficient condition creates or causes the effect.

Suggestion—Presenting ideas or images in such a way as to reveal certain ideas or qualities and to conceal others.

Syllogism—A deductive argument consisting of two premises and a conclusion.

Target population—The group about which a researcher wishes to generalize.

Two-step flow—The phenomenon of consulting friends or acquaintences who have expertise in a given area before making decisions. The friends, called opinion leaders first (step 1) get their information from the media and then (step 2) pass this information on to others.

Vagueness—A problem that arises with the use of abstract words. A word or phrase is vague when its meaning is unclear.

Valid argument—An argument that is structured such that if its premises are true, then its conclusion cannot be false.

Value assumptions—Beliefs held by individuals which form the basis of their opinions on issues.

Value conflicts—Disagreements about the priority different values should hold in making decisions.

Values—Beliefs, ideas, persons, or things that are held in high regard.

Weasel word—A word used to evade or retreat from a direct or forthright statement or position.

Index

436   Index

6460127